LEGISLATIVE STRATEGY

Shaping
Public Policy

Edward V. Schneier
City College of The City University of New York

Bertram Gross
_The City University of New York, University of California at Berkeley,
and St. Mary's College of California_

St. Martin's Press   New York

Senior editor: Don Reisman
Managing editor: Patricia Mansfield-Phelan
Project editor: Erica Appel
Production supervisor: Alan Fischer
Art director: Sheree Goodman
Text design: Dorothy Bungert
Cover design: Circa 86, Inc.
Cover photo: Stacy Pick/Stock • Boston

Manufactured in the United States of America.
76543
fedcba

For information, write:
St. Martin's Press, Inc.
175 Fifth Avenue
New York, NY 10010

ISBN: 0-312-05192-1 (paperback)
      0-312-09698-4 (hardcover)

Library of Congress Cataloging-in-Publication Data applied for.

PREFACE

Almost every journalist or short-term observer of the Congress who writes a book about politics begins with a swipe at political science. "Forget what you read in the textbooks," they usually warn. "This is the way it really works."

Most of us who are political scientists (and who write those unrealistic textbooks) are equally contemptuous of the "Congresschlock" that these instant experts typically produce. Although we may secretly envy the breezy narrative style of the reporters and ghostwriters who produce the memoirs of legislative interns, pages, lobbyists, and cafeteria workers, we find it difficult to take most such works seriously.

In many cases, there is merit to both laments. Given the time that scholars have spent in interviewing members of the Congress, observing it firsthand and even working on Capitol Hill,[1] it is sometimes remarkable how little of the drama and force of the process is captured in our writings. The political scientist's approach to Congress, it can be argued, not only misses the excitement of the real world but slides over or ignores the factors of skill, happenstance, barter, and sleaze that often prove decisive on important issues. Additionally, in studying legislatures we are prone to slight their most important products— that is, laws and public policy.

Participant observers and journalists, for their part, are prone to portray deviant cases as typical and to take a pre-Copernican view of a system in which everything revolves around the office of whoever is telling the tale. Even the best-crafted case studies generally fail to locate key actors in their institutional contexts or to show how today's battle over one issue is often both prologue and preface to others.[2] Our goal in *Legislative Strategy* is to combine both approaches in what Bertram Gross once called "an action-theory marriage." In this scenario, "The aim is not to present final answers but to stimulate closer cooperation on these matters between men of action and social scientists and among social scientists themselves. Only then can a more mature body of . . . knowledge come into being."[3]

As in many case studies, our approach is structured around the calculations that go into the making, faking, and unmaking of national legislation. This is less a book about the national legislature than about national legislation. We are concerned in particular with the kinds of strategic and tactical choices that men and women of action confront in their attempts to approach and understand the Congress of the United States. Our focus in studying these questions is on the broader kinds of generalizations about such choices that are the stuff of both sound practical politics and a relevant political science.

The practitioner who wants to know how to approach a committee hearing will find no instant recipes here and few lists of dos and don'ts. The most successful strategies and tactics of legislating, we suggest, are rooted in understanding legislatures. The best formula for approaching congressional committees is to apply knowledge of how the committee system works and what happens after disgorgement from committee.

Where this book most differs from its academic counterparts on the one hand, and from case studies and how-to-do-it manuals on the other, is in its sustained consideration of strategic and tactical decision-making. Its most dramatic departures from conventional wisdom derive from the rather simple proposition that politicians think politically. Whereas most case studies and textbooks tend to treat participants, rules, and issues as independent variables, we view the struggles to define issues and change the rules as part of the process. Members of the House and Senate and most lobbyists are not "givens" in the process: in many ways they define themselves, and they do so for purposive reasons.

This book presumes that the reader has some general understanding of the U.S. political system. It is drawn, in part, from the second half of a larger textbook[4] that examines the electoral, political, and structural variables that form the context within which campaigns for and against legislative action take place. Policy advocates, like players in any game, must know the rules of play. It helps enormously to know the strengths and weaknesses of the other players. That little of this information is to be found in this book is not to minimize the importance of such knowledge. Like the sportscaster who assumes the audience knows the basic rules of play, we are talking largely to fans who know their balls and strikes well enough to consider the finer points of the game.

Like many sportscasters, we are also fans. We try not to root too hard for our favorites, but we make no bones of our general leaning toward more open debate over social justice, our general interests, and positions that are sometimes labeled progressive or liberal. Better the butcher's thumbs be openly displayed than hidden beneath the meat on the scale. The more serious possible charge is that we have written a book that is at base amoral. Because his advice to princes could be put to many uses, Machiavelli's name has become an adjective for tactics that, according to the *American College Dictionary*, "placed expediency above political morality, and countenanced the use of craft and deceit in order to maintain the authority and effect the purposes of the ruler."

There is no doubt that whatever gems of practical wisdom can be gleaned from this book could, like Machiavelli's nostrums for royalty, be used by conservatives and liberals, militarists and pacifists alike. Our excuse, if one is needed, is from the Greek proverb that "a wise enemy is better than a foolish friend." Better that laws be well crafted and understood by both supporters and opponents than sloppy, deceptive, or inadvertent.

Thomas Schelling, the most readable and probably the most brilliant contemporary student of bargaining and strategy, offers two explanations for the tendency of strategic studies "to be neutral, even cold-blooded, toward the parties in a situation. One is that the analysis is usually about the situation, not the individuals. . . . There is little about the abstract situation that tells the analyst which side he ought to be on."[5] Schelling's second reason is even more to our point. The key to strategic thinking, he argues, is the ability to see things from your adversary's position as well as your own: "It deals with situations in which one party has to think about how the others are going to reach their decisions."[6] In less formal terms, it means that folks have to take account of each other; and that, in a basic sense, is what democracy is all about.

Most of the important decisions that the Congress makes involve bargains and compromises and thus, in turn, strategies. It is not a system of policy-making for people who believe in revealed truths or in finding the "one best way" to solve any given problem. Representative democracy is founded in a skepticism about such simple solutions and a faith in the utility of making deals. "Conscience and divine sanction," as Schelling puts it, "may be scarce resources, and should not be wasted on rules of conduct that are easily enforced by other means."[7] Those other means of solving problems—politics, in a word—are the subject of this book.

By listing Schneier as the senior author of this book we defy the usual canons of scholarship. We do so, at Gross's insistence, to reflect the fact that most of the actual drafting was done by Professor Schneier. Those familiar with Professor Gross's 1953 opus, *The Legislative Struggle,* will see much of its texture and substance reflected here. Far less visible is the long process of collaboration, spanning more than twenty years, that undergirds almost every word of this work. That this is a far different book than *The Legislative Struggle* is as much a function of Gross's new insights and wisdom as it is of changing circumstances or the ideas of his coauthor.

Our acknowledgments for this book begin with our students whose contributions are greater than they or we can ever specify. Of no less importance are those members of the Capitol Hill community who provided much of the material for the text, frequent reality checks, and access to research materials. The commitment to this project—and to its longer cousin, *Congress Today*—of Don Reisman, our editor at St. Martin's Press, has been extraordinary. At various stages, this manuscript has probably been reviewed by more anonymous scholars and copy editors than have most acts of Congress. For their particularly useful comments on all or parts of the manuscript, special thanks are due to Tim Byrnes, Christopher Bosso, Jeff Fishel, and Larry Longley. As with the aforementioned, our wives, Norma Schneier and Kusem Singh, have nothing to do with errors of fact and interpretation and everything to do with whatever success it enjoys and, in particular, with keeping our collaborative efforts flowing smoothly.

Edward V. Schneier

Bertram Gross

BRIEF CONTENTS

CONTENTS

1

---- ✳ ----

CONSTRUCTING
A LEGISLATIVE
CAMPAIGN

F or those who want to see their policy preferences enacted into law, the
task is simple: win the votes of 218 representatives, 51 senators, and
one president. In the same sense, it is simple to build a house: take some boards
and nail them together.

As with homebuilding, something more is involved in lawmaking than
boards and nails. Architects of strategy and crafters of tactics are as essential to
the legislative process as they are to construction. Before those 218 representatives in the House can cast their votes, before the Senate assembles in its
chamber, and before the riding clerk delivers an enrolled bill to the White
House, an enormously complicated array of substantive and procedural steps
intervene. As with contractors, moreover, there are building codes to consult
and competitors whose bids must sometimes be met. Worse, from the perspective of the policy advocate, although the basic framework of previous statutes,
political coalitions, and procedural rules has already been built, they are always subject to revision and change. Just as a good working relationship is
established with a committee chair, he or she retires or loses the next election.
Just as you decide that the bill you are tracking can be fixed by a simple
amendment, the House Rules Committee sends the bill to the floor with a rule
that prohibits amendments.

Some people in the U.S. political system have a great deal of influence and
clout. Having the potential for political influence, however, is not the same as
getting one's way. The most powerful lobbyist, the most popular president can
be thwarted by a failure to understand procedural and political complexities.

1

Whatever a group or individual's capacity for influence may be, it is its strategies and tactics of advocacy that transform potentials for power into public policies.

———————— ✳ ————————

PREPARING FOR BATTLE

The word *strategy*, derived from the ancient Greek term for the art of generalship, tends, not surprisingly, to have strong military connotations. The images and language of military campaigns are found quite frequently in analyses of legislative strategy, and our argument is structured in much the same form as that of a military battle plan. From the outset, however, it is important to note that the perspectives of the military are not strictly analogous to those of politics. The strategies we describe are more those of games and game theory than of warfare. In legislation, as in most games, " 'winning' in a conflict does not have a strictly competitive meaning; it is not winning relative to one's adversary. It means gaining relative to one's own value system; and this may be done through bargaining, by mutual accommodation, and by the avoidance of mutually damaging behavior."[1]

Legislative strategists, unlike their military counterparts, are seldom interested in inflicting damage on their enemies. Especially in the loose party system of the U.S. Congress, alliances are fluid: your enemy on today's bill or resolution may be your ally tomorrow. Legislative campaigns, moreover, are more people-focused than contemporary wars: the military advantage conferred by superior arms has no close analogy in the legislative arena. Material resources are not trivial in politics, but "heroes, and influential figures behind the scenes, are usually recruited from those who specialize in the management of men rather than the management of things."[2]

Despite these distinctions, in its most fundamental outline the campaign for legislation follows the same essential contours as a military battle plan. A policy advocate seeking to make a law needs to make many of the same calculations as a general planning an invasion. Both must understand the strengths and weaknesses of their own forces and of their allies; be familiar with the legislative or military terrain and the rules of the game; and develop a knowledge of the enemy's forward and reserve capacities, and of how and when they are likely to be deployed.

Defining Objectives

"How to" books often begin by stressing the importance of establishing reasonable goals. When a person is dieting or beginning an exercise campaign, it probably makes sense to target a specific number of pounds to lose or miles to run. It's not so simple in politics, war, or games in which what you can and cannot do depends upon the actions of others. What you want, in such contexts, is tempered by considerations of what you can get.

To the frustration of many a general, lobbyist, and member of Congress (MC), the definition of basic objectives is frequently in the hands of others. To make it even more frustrating, those who give the marching orders often act as if they have read the books that stress the importance of defining objectives clearly. Politicians or kings, as a rule, give military strategists their basic orders. If a general is uneasy—as were some Americans in the Pacific theater in World War II—about demanding the enemy's unconditional surrender, it was not in their power to alter that part of the strategic context established by the president. A general who defies presidential directives, as General Douglas MacArthur did in Korea, is likely to be dismissed, as MacArthur was. Similarly, the power of both lobbyists and legislators is, as a rule, the power of agency. Their freedom to design appropriate legislative campaigns is to some extent constrained by the preferences of voters, or of the people who pay their salaries.

People in such fiduciary roles are often troubled by the "unrealistic" assumptions that outsiders often make about what can and cannot be done. What is less obvious but equally troubling is that those giving orders often do not really know what they want. As much as everyone agrees that it is essential to define one's goals, the question "What are your goals?" is embarrassingly difficult for most group leaders to answer. "One reason for the embarrassment is that human purposefulness is too complex and intimate to be fully understood or openly described."[3] Group goals are particularly elusive, since one individual or faction's interpretation may be quite different from another's. Goals, moreover, are easier to define the farther we are from achieving them. "It is easy enough to see plainly," Schelling says, "that there is too much inequality (or illiteracy, or ill health, or injustice). . . . But if it were up to me to decide *how much* inequality is not too much, or how much injustice, or how much disregard for the elderly or for future generations, I'd need much more than a sense of direction."[4]

If their ultimate objectives are clear (and that is problematic), their ability to provide meaningful guidelines for action seldom are. Often they are called upon to perform the kinds of miracles once described by former baseball pitcher Jim Brosnan. Faced with a particularly good batter at a decisive moment in the game, Brosnan was working on a strategy to get the final out. Just as he was about to make his pitch, the coach called time and trotted to the mound: "Keep it over the plate," he said, "but don't give him anything too good to hit."

Lobbyists and MCs are often asked to perform similar miracles. Their clients, even when they know what they want, often have unrealistic expectations about what can and cannot be done. Like Brosnan's pitching coach, they regard the question of how actually to do things as a minor detail. As much as the real worlds of both politics and baseball tend to blend questions of immediate problems and general goals, however, there are useful analytic distinctions between the two.

Strategy and Tactics

Military strategists have long emphasized these differences by distinguishing questions of *strategy* from those of *tactics*. If none have ever been able precisely to define the boundaries, the distinction remains analytically useful. Following Clausewitz, *strategies* are usually regarded as the general plans and allocations of resources designed to achieve broad policy objectives; *tactics,* as the specific maneuvers designed to achieve these and other immediate advantages.[5]

In a broad sense, the chapters of this book follow the contours of Clausewitz's classic distinction. As much as strategies and tactics blend in practice, a legislative campaign moves, as a rule, from the general to the particular, from evaluation and planning to direct contact and persuasion. The starting point in military, business, or political strategy is to analyze the framework for action. In Chapters 2 through 5 we consider these questions of context. We move in Chapters 6 through 9 to more specific persuasive maneuvers; and finally in Chapters 10 through 12 to the more strictly tactical choices that arise as actual decisions are made in congressional committees, on the House and Senate floors, and in implementing the laws.

Lawmakers, Bombthrowers, and the Faking of Public Policy

Throughout this analysis, we tend to assume that "those who initiate proposals . . . will tailor the policy content to have a chance to win."[6] Let us concede at the outset that this is not always the case. In describing *legislative* strategy we are not necessarily describing the strategies of all legislators, executive branch officials, or lobbyists. Participants in the legislative struggle often have other strategic agendas, such as reelection, that may or may not be connected with the passage of laws or the crafting of public policy. Indeed, many participants in the legislative process have little or no current interest in legislation. For them legislative outputs are means to other ends. At one level, this is commonplace: most of us are interested in doing our jobs, but we work, by and large, to pay the rent, raise a family, and keep busy. Lobbyists, similarly, are there to make a living, and being a representative or senator is also a job, the way in which 535 men and women earn their pay. In analyzing legislative strategy, we must be particularly careful, however, to disentangle the motives of those participants who, for one reason or another, are insincere in their pursuit of legislation.

Some policy advocates are uncomfortable with the give-and-take of legislative bargaining; others, thinking strategically, recognize that they are more likely to be successful operating in other arenas; still others are so accustomed to failing in the legislative arena that they would as soon see the process itself seriously weakened, if not destroyed. Many world parliaments, most notably that of Germany's ill-fated Weimar Republic, have included among their members substantial numbers of deputies, one of whose goals was the destruction of the parliamentary system. Although few MCs in the United States are manifestly antidemo-cratic, levels of commitment to the institution are variable. Some MCs, known colloquially to their colleagues as bombthrowers, actually look for opportuni-ties to embarrass the institution publicly. Representative Newt Gingrich's (R-GA) relentless insistence upon exposing the full extent of a 1992 scandal involv-ing the House bank, despite the fact that he himself turned out to be one of the more serious offenders, can only be explained in terms of a long-range strategy. He and other conservatives confronted with a House of Representatives that seems almost permanently Democratic and (from their perspective) liberal have little or no stake in the institution's prestige. On the contrary, when the White House was under Republican control their policy objectives were more likely to be met by shifting power to a conservative White House and Supreme Court.

Even for those who nominally control an institution, divided government, particularly when the administration is markedly more conservative than the congressional majority, may suggest strategies that have similar symbolic ends. During the Reagan and Bush administrations, Democratic majorities in the House and Senate frequently passed bills that they knew would not become laws. In 1991, for example, the House and Senate passed an amendment to the bill appropriating funds for the Departments of Labor and Health and Human Services. The purpose of the amendment was to overturn an administration rule that had banned the mention of abortion in federally funded family-planning clinics. President Bush had made it absolutely clear that he would veto any bill containing such an amendment. It was equally clear that neither the House nor the Senate could possibly muster the two-thirds majority needed in both houses to override the veto. Why then, did both houses persist in pushing bills that they knew would not become laws?

In this case, the Democrats were clearly trying to stake out a public posi-tion that would be helpful to the party's long-range electoral success. Rather than approaching the president quietly in hopes of working out some sort of compromise, the goal here is less the shaping of public policy than the staking out of distinct positions on a controversial issue. It is faking rather than making law. Lobbyists frequently employ similar strategies. In pushing bills they know will not pass, their immediate goal is not to make law but to take a stand. In their noblest guise, such hopeless battles are fought as part of a long-range strategy to put issues on the agenda for public discussion, to raise the conscious-ness of the legislature and perhaps the public. The more immediate motive may be simply that of saving the lobbyist's job by showing the flag for all to see.

Whatever the motives, the decision whether or not to pursue a legislative route is absolutely basic. The political process neither begins nor ends with legislation and lawmaking, and the timing and location of issue emergence is, to some degree, manipulable. It is always political. For policy advocates it is a fundamental and strategic question much like that facing a military leader planning an amphibious invasion. There are many shores to choose from, each with its particular advantages and disadvantages. In making their choices, military strategists must bear in mind the calculations of their enemies as well. Just as there were no abstract laws of military science to guide the Allied commanders to their choice of the Normandy beachhead in World War II, it would be idle to seek some neat formula by which one could automatically explain decisions on having or not having a bill.

———————— ✳ ————————

TO HAVE OR NOT TO HAVE A BILL

There are certain objectives that can be achieved only through the production of federal statutes, and others that can be achieved only through administrative or judicial decisions. There are some things that can be done only by the federal government, but the doctrines of federalism and the separation of powers are far less rigid than they once were. A broad and growing area of overlap makes it entirely possible for contesting groups to embark on two or more courses of action at the same time or to choose between them for their relative advantages and disadvantages. This is what Morton Grodzins, in his classic article on federalism, called "the 'multiple' crack attribute of American government." "Crack," said Grodzins, "has two meanings. It means not only fissures or access points; it also means, less statically, opportunities for wallops or smacks at government."[7]

The Area of Choice

The existence of choice can shift from one situation to another, and some groups have a great deal more crack than others. For many contestants the battleground is picked by opponents and competitors. For stronger groups the area of choice is theoretically broader, though force of habit or organizational structure may produce an equally restrictive inability to break with customary methods. Many law firms, for example, think almost exclusively in terms of private negotiations and litigation; some even consider lobbying "dirty." Generally, however, the ability to choose one's arena is itself a measure of power. "In politics as in everything else it makes a great deal of difference whose game we play. The rules of the game determine requirements for success."[8]

Overlap with the Administrative Process. In the course of the legislative struggle, the most common questions of choice relate to whether policy decisions shall be executive or legislative. The geographical distribution of federal funds can be left largely to executive officials, as in most procurement policies, or allocated in accordance with specific statutory formulae, as in the case of federal grants to the states for the construction of roads, hospitals, and schools. Congress has drafted some regulations in meticulous statutory detail while allowing agencies such as the Federal Trade Commission to decide the meaning of such deliberately vague terms as *unfair methods of competition.* Different divisions of the same agency may even have different degrees of discretion in making policy; consider the Agriculture Department, where "rigid" price support policies (i.e., legislatively mandated) have often applied to one commodity and "flexible" supports (i.e., determined by the Department) to another. Legislation can be used to overrule or erode administrative decisions, or to write them directly into law; and Congress may apply indirect sanctions—the threat of investigation or cuts in appropriations—to pressure bureaucrats into making decisions they would not otherwise make. In the course of the administrative process, in turn, many decisions are made that can be legitimately regarded as alternatives to legislative action. Indeed, compared with the 300 to 500 public laws typically enacted by each session of Congress, "the number of rules and regulations issued by agencies has reached, in recent years, as high as 7,000 annually."[9]

In many cases the overlap between the legislative and administrative processes is so complex as to virtually defy description. This has not prevented the subject from becoming the target of lively and seemingly endless debate concerning the propriety of one process being used on matters that are claimed as the exclusive province of the other. There have been few periods in American history when public life has not been marked by charges that executive officials have trespassed on the legislative domain, or, conversely, that congressional nitpicking—"micromanagement," to use the more fashionable jargon—undermines the administrative process and usurps executive power.

Objectively, such arguments about usurpations of legislative or administrative functions are somewhat strange, for the charge is essentially that some people should not have the power to do what they already have done. From this perspective it is hard to avoid the conclusion that charges of usurpation usually serve to disguise substantive objections to government actions. Their intent is to becloud, though actually they document, a line of broadly overlapping powers.

The area of choice is by no means limited to the overlap between the legislative and administrative processes. The social struggle is punctuated by numerous instances of groups being faced by a choice of using the legislative process or going to the courts, trying to obtain a constitutional amendment, seeking action by state or local governments, or carrying on their activities through nongovernmental channels.

Overlap with the Judicial Process.   In their policy-making role, the position of the courts in relation to the legislature is that of the inner of two concentric circles. There is nothing that can be done through a judicial decision that could not also be accomplished through legislation. It could be argued that a judicial decision deals with an individual case rather than a general rule. The fact is that legislation can provide or change the rule that governs the case. A long history of judicial decisions in a complex area of policy, such as antitrust law, is equivalent to a detailed series of amendments to the statute itself, except that the result of any one of these decisions could have been obtained or reversed by legislative action. The federal court system, moreover, is the creature of Congress: all federal courts below the Supreme Court are created, funded, and given their mandates by acts of Congress. Except for a few relatively trivial areas of "original" jurisdiction assigned to it in Article III, the basic jurisdiction of the Supreme Court—the cases it is allowed to hear on appeal—is that which Congress chooses to grant it.

The complicated and continuing controversy over the issue of school desegregation illustrates, over the span of thirty-five years, almost every possible facet of the overlap between the legislative and judicial processes.[10] The turning point in the modern struggle for racial equality was almost undoubtedly the Supreme Court's historic decision in *Brown v. Board of Education*. The *Brown* case was the effect of a deliberate "strategy of litigation" advanced by the National Association for the Advancement of Colored People (NAACP) in the hope that it "could achieve in the courts what seemed so completely unattainable in Congress . . . ."[11] The NAACP's victory in the *Brown* case, however, was but the opening skirmish in what has proven to be a long series of complicated interactions between the public and private sectors; state, local, and federal officials; and the legislative, executive, and judicial branches of all three levels of government.

It is important to remember, in analyzing the powers of the courts, that they are empowered only to decide real cases and controversies, legal actions in which someone can show that he or she has been hurt. Despite the ringing language of the *Brown* case, all the Court was really deciding is that the Browns had been hurt by the segregation policies of the Topeka, Kansas, School Board, and that their daughter had the right to attend a previously all-white school. The Court made it obvious that anyone else who brought the same kind of case would get the same decision, and in that sense *Brown v. Board of Education* became the "law of the land." The resistance of state and local governments to the decision could be overcome only if there was a true commitment of federal resources to the cause. For as long as the South engaged in the policy known as "massive resistance," schools could be desegregated only if someone in each and every community was willing and able to sue, or if the legislative and executive branches made a serious effort to implement the Court's decision. Not until 1964 was such a commitment made.

But as clearly as Title VI of the Civil Rights Act of 1964 seemed to prohibit the use of federal funds in support of segregated programs, "the general congressional readiness to accept local claims of bureaucratic abuse" made it almost impossible to draft effective guidelines to implementation.[12] Despite stronger and stronger rulings by the courts in ordering such unusual steps as busing and the redrawing of local district lines, the enforcement of court decisions depends ultimately upon the affirmative actions of other governmental bodies. And the more that desegregation has become synonymous with busing, the less likely such action has become. Not only did both the Nixon and Reagan administrations argue in court against a variety of desegregation plans, but Congress itself has become less and less sympathetic to the cause.

For our purposes, what is significant throughout this protracted struggle is the overlap and interchange between the legislative, administrative, and judicial processes. Throughout the controversy, charges of usurpation, excess, or dereliction of responsibility have been commonplace. In the *Brown* case and in subsequent rulings, the Court was accused of usurping legislative power: a "Southern Manifesto," signed by virtually every representative and senator from the South in 1954, accused the Court of a "clear abuse of judicial power" and called upon Congress and the states to redress the proper balance of power between governmental institutions. Supporters of school desegregation, for their part, accused President Nixon, in his message on busing, of precipitating "a potentially serious challenge to the authority of the Supreme Court."[13] When Congress failed to limit judicial authority significantly, Nixon in turn accused the Congress of a "manifest . . . retreat from an urgent call for responsibility."[14]

Cloaked in its prestigious robes, speaking its arcane jargon, wrapped in a mantle of constitutional legitimacy, armed with the power of judicial review, the Supreme Court holds awesome theoretical power. However, the Court's continuing authority rests very much on its sense of self-restraint, especially in using its power to rule acts of Congress unconstitutional. The area of overlap is extensive but always subject to legislative review. Direct legislative repeal of Court decisions is not uncommon;[15] at other times Congress may simply undercut the legal basis of a pending suit by changing the law in question.

Finally, with the concurrence of three-quarters of the states, the Congress can overrule the Court by amending the Constitution. Thus, the Supreme Court's 1896 ruling that a tax on income was unconstitutional was "overruled" by passage of the Sixteenth Amendment. A similar attempt to overrule the Court's 1916 decision ruling a federal anti–child labor law unconstitutional was, at first, less successful. Although a constitutional amendment banning child labor passed the Congress in 1924, its proponents were unable to get it ratified by enough states. Another attempt through legislation, a child labor provision in the National Industrial Recovery Act, was thwarted in 1935 when this act too was declared unconstitutional. Finally, in 1941 the Court withdrew from the contest and upheld the legality of the Fair Labor Standards Act of 1937, a bill that included a ban on child labor. Similar decisions in one field after another have overthrown judicial limitations on legislative action. In fact, the use of the legislative process coupled with a favorable decision by a Supreme Court majority is not only an alternative to the process of constitutional amendment; to all intents and purposes it constitutes the major way in which we go about amending our Constitution.

State or Local Action.   The nationalization of both the politics and the problems of modern society has changed both the extent and nature of the overlap between the national legislative process and the processes of state and local governments. In constitutional terms, the Supreme Court has come to accept virtually no limitations upon what can be accomplished through federal action.

In 1935 and 1936, when one Supreme Court decision after another torpedoed New Deal statutes, the issue of state powers was a live one. Particularly through a reinterpretation of the commerce clause, however, the Court in 1937 began a retreat that became a rout. Today one might go so far as to say that the commerce power has been interpreted so broadly and that interstate commerce now affects so many aspects of the economy that legislation dealing with economic matters will almost never be declared unconstitutional on these grounds. Even the most sacred reserved powers of the states, the so-called police powers regulating social and criminal conduct, have been seriously eroded by tying legislative strings to important federal grant-in-aid programs.

The states, for example, retain their historic right to regulate the sale of alcoholic beverages; but when Congress voted in 1985 to withhold highway funds from any state that did not change its minimum drinking age to twenty-one, every state fell in line. Clearly, the grant-in-aid device allows Congress to attach stipulations to the use of federal funds that might not be allowed through ordinary legislative devices.

Despite the constitutional reference in the Tenth Amendment to powers that are "reserved to the States," realistically there is no limit on what the federal government can do through legislation given sufficient political support. Such support, however, is not always available. For decades following the New Deal the issue of states' rights was one of the unifying forces that sustained Congress's conservative coalition in its fight against liberal programs. New force was added to this aging alliance with the efforts of the Reagan administration to dismantle many federal agencies and to decentralize the operations of others. When "categorical grants" (those specified by federal law for defined categories of recipients) were converted to "block grants" (in which blocks of money for broad programs are allocated to state and local officials), the power to allocate specific funds was supposedly moved out of Washington. In actuality, even the most narrowly defined categorical grant programs were never as centralized as they appeared. "Agencies live by congressional favor, and congressional power is a variable,"[16] a variable founded, moreover, in the local roots of legislative politics. Whatever the statutory constraints, budgetary control is often decentralized as a matter of political reality.

Private Action. With respect to a large proportion of private conflicts, there is little if any recourse to national legislation. This is true, in a narrow institutional sense, of breaches of contract between private parties, in which the obvious method of carrying conflict into public channels is the use of the courts. In a broader sense, the ability of private groups to keep their power private, to avoid legislative, executive, or judicial attention of any kind, is a test of power in a most basic sense. Despite numerous risks in shifting from private to public action, private combatants will often turn to government to redress an unfavorable balance or to secure added advantages. Even those who initially are most vociferous in their resistance to government action have sometimes become its strongest champions. Many government regulations of business illustrate this point. Responding to consumer complaints, the government intervened to create a wide range of new agencies, regulations, and controls on everything from airline schedules and fares to zoological research. "Gradually," Herbert Kaufman summarizes, "some observers began to suspect . . . that the regulated interests often benefited more from regulation than consumers did."[17] A wave of deregulatory sentiment that began to gather force in the late 1970s was in many cases most vigorously opposed by the very objects of the once-hated regulations. As Martha Derthick and Paul Quirk found in their case studies of the airline, trucking, and telecommunications industries, "The most active and powerful organized interests were opposed to the policy change. In none of the cases did the regulated industries decide that regulation was no longer in their interests."[18]

The uncertainties and risks that attend the shift between the public and private sectors do not run in one direction. Although the usual position of business is to resist the growth of the public sector, the deregulation cases show that the opposite can be true as well. As with the overlapping between the legislative process and processes of state and local governments, moreover, the general trend toward a larger federal role has been balanced by a contrary tendency on the part of Congress to delegate its legislative powers to private actors. Economist Murray Weidenbaum was among the first to point out that "increasingly, federal functions are being performed in the private sector and by state and local governments via the contract and grant mechanism."[19] One study estimates that as of 1982, "federal expenditures on contracting totaled almost one-fourth of the entire federal budget."[20] Under such conditions the line between public and private is difficult to draw.

Ballots or Bullets? Both the electoral process and its violent counterpart, revolution, are methods of effectuating change in the top leadership of government. As such they are not on the same plane as the legislative process, since they deal with the shift of power from group to group rather than with the use of power by any group. Nevertheless, there is a real area of overlap between these and the legislative process. In the course of the legislative struggle, choices are always arising as to whether it is best to work with the existing cast of characters or to emphasize change in the government. The women's movement continues to be divided between those who advocate a strategy based largely on the empowerment of more women and those who favor lobbying the existing power structure on behalf of feminist goals. The two goals are not mutually exclusive: the most effective lobbyists are often those who can demonstrate electoral power as well; but when major shifts in power and resources are sought, legislative action may be impossible until there has been an electoral change in the presidency or in the Congress. If an extremely radical shift is contemplated, resort to violence might even be needed as an adjunct of, or a substitute for, legislative action.

Less extreme than revolution are various forms of political protest. Mass demonstrations are sometimes used to influence the legislative process, sometimes to bypass it. "Protest groups may well be able to raise the saliency of issues on the civic agenda through utilization of communications media and successful appeals or threats to wider publics."[21] Protest activities may also be directed at other private groups, as in the case of strikes or boycotts. Although the targets may be private, they may invoke a legislative response. For example, in 1992 the president and Congress combined to force striking rail workers to abandon their picket lines and go back to work.

Advantages of the Legislative Process

Among the obvious considerations in the minds of those who ponder whether to travel the legislative highway are the smoothness of the road and the amount of assistance they are likely to obtain along the way. When it is believed that the chances of developing legislative support are great, there is far more reason to seek a proposal's embodiment in a bill than when the prospects for congressional help are slim. When the advocates of school integration confined their attention largely to the courts in the 1940s and 1950s, it was the unlikelihood of overcoming a Senate filibuster rather than a preference for litigation that forced the choice.

Such calculations aside, there are other important considerations that flow more directly from the character of the legislative process. Apart from the strategic location of friends and enemies, there are unquestioned advantages to be found in the legislative terrain. Some of these relate to the nature of the process, to the fact that a legislature is neither a bureaucracy nor a court, and that it therefore filters inputs differently. Some relate to the mere fact of having a bill, whether it blossoms into a statute or not. Some relate to the value of having a statute, even when the identical objective could be achieved through other processes.

By and large, the complexity of the process in Congress tends to enhance the power of those groups that would prefer to stop rather than promote new programs. Because a bill must successfully navigate many possible veto points—committees in both houses, floor votes in both houses, presidential vetoes, and so on—the legislative route is fraught with peril. But there are important norms, political incentives, and structural values that in some instances may lead policy advocates to choose the legislative process. First, the nonhierarchic character of Congress, the formal equality of all members, tends to give outside groups a fair crack at winning entrée, even for proposals out of favor at the time. Nor are vetoes quite as decisive. Although some MCs are more important than others, none are in a position to count votes as Lincoln reportedly did in a meeting with his Cabinet: "There are seven votes in favor, I vote no; the nays have it." Second, the norm of reciprocity that tends to prevail where purely local issues are involved enhances the strength of those proposing policies that relate to one part of the country. For political reasons too, local interests are more likely to receive favorable hearings in Congress than in the administrative or judicial processes.

A third important characteristic of Congress is its open acceptance of the legitimacy of lobbying techniques that would be considered breaches of judicial ethics or conflicts of interest for bureaucrats. Letter-writing campaigns, personal attacks on opponents, and campaign contributions can be used in ways that, to say the least, would raise eyebrows in other contexts. Finally, specialization in Congress, as reflected in the committee system, is somewhat different than administrative specialization. Bureaus seem far more likely than congressional committees to see themselves in conflict with other bureaus for scarce resources. Despite a growing tendency away from the distributive politics of previous eras, subcommittee recommendations usually receive favorable treatment in full committee, and committee-passed bills are likely to pass on the floor. In the administration, on the other hand, agency policies are carefully compared by bureau chiefs; departmental officials balance agency proposals against one another; the White House decides priorities between departments. To have access to the right subcommittee is usually a far better guarantee of victory than to be in favor with the relative agency. Generally, the legislative process is more hospitable to policy innovation.

The Importance of a Bill.   Introducing a bill in Congress is one of the time-honored methods through which a senator or representative can improve his or her position with constituents and interest groups. Even when their sponsors are not seriously interested in their own proposals, the process of introducing a bill requires so little commitment of energy that many MCs would agree with the representative who liked to introduce a series of bills designed to "illustrate, by and large, my ideas—legislative, economic, and social. I do like being able to say when I get cornered, 'yes, boys, I introduced a bill to try to do that in 1954.' To me it is the perfect answer."[22]

If no action is taken on a bill, it does minor damage to the sponsor; most bills die in committee. If it becomes a going proposition, so much the better. For junior members in particular, sponsorship provides a useful vehicle for learning one's way through the intricacies of the legislative process and interacting with senior colleagues. From the point of view of those interested in making their livings as lobbyists, bill introductions serve similar instrumental goals. For a professional lobbyist, activity—and getting a bill introduced is a visible action—"may make some clients and supporters feel that the Washington representative really is doing something, that he's on the ball, that there is a need to keep him there."[23] The ability to serve a member of Congress by providing a well-drafted statute is also the kind of activity that can score important access points.

One of the reasons why the introduction of a bill can serve as a real favor to an interest group or government agency is its unquestioned value as an educational and propaganda instrument. Even a poorly drafted measure puts its backers in the policy stream; it shows, when it comes to landing time, that you were there at take-off. A bill provides a concrete symbol to serve as a rallying point for a campaign. Its official format and trappings show that you have not just a problem but a viable solution to it. When a group's policies are vague and diffuse, a legislative proposal can provide a point around which an otherwise diverse coalition of groups can coalesce.

Because it is hard to fight something with nothing, a bill is an ideal instrument for warding off charges of negativism and demonstrating that you have a constructive position. Sometimes the principle that "you can't fight something with nothing" requires little more than a set of informal questions or arguments. Those fighting a proposed constitutional amendment banning abortion, for example, have asked whether such a ban would also include such birth control devices as the pill, which sometimes forces the ejection of fertilized embryos. Questions such as these have served to complicate what had previously seemed a straightforward but one-sided issue, and they have divided proponents of the proposed amendment into sponsoring competing bills. One of the biggest dangers to Social Security reform in 1982 was the existence of too many competing proposals.[24]

The attempt to divide and conquer by diversionary tactics may backfire. A famous instance was in 1965 when Democrats on the House Ways and Means

Committee accepted the Republicans' voluntary insurance substitute for Medicare as an addition to rather than substitute for the administration's plan. The result was an omnibus bill that went far beyond what either the administration or the Republicans had planned, and it put members of the GOP in the awkward position of having to oppose a bill that they had in large part drafted. Decades later, as the idea of extending national health insurance to all citizens began to gather force, Senator Russell Long (D-LA), chairman of the Senate Finance Committee, introduced several of his own proposals in the field. Never known as a particular champion of federal health programs, Long, it was said, "wanted to introduce this as a way to trot it out in case there was any bigger threat that was coming along. This was his way to take the steam out of a comprehensive plan whenever it looked like it might get serious."[25]

As an intellectual stimulus or expression, the introduction of a bill is one of the best ways of getting attention in the highly competitive marketplace of ideas. A bill can serve as an ideal trial balloon for executive officials who are wary of taking a course of action without first gauging public and congressional reactions. The availability of the legislative process for the launching of new ideas is one of the factors that helps protect the government against hardening of the arteries. Many a repressed bureaucrat has escaped tedium by taking his or her ideas in legislative form to a representative or senator, either directly or through the intermediary of a private organization. And of course the process can work the other way. Hugh Heclo interviewed one political executive who found that a subordinate had "gone to Congress and actually written the rider to the legislation that nullified the changes we wanted."[26]

Another advantage of the legislative route is manifest in the formative stages of a program. Efforts to coordinate the activities of executive agencies have often been ineffective; the only clearinghouse that operates regularly is the Office of Management and Budget (OMB). Under these circumstances sometimes the best way to get government agencies to work together is by having a draft bill circulated or introduced. If the bill itself doesn't force creation of an interagency task force, it is likely at least to require each agency to respond through OMB. In the private sector, too, a bill can serve a coordinating role. Weaker groups in particular may rely on those with better research abilities to provide focus. For example, "the National Turkey Federation, whose members are affected by many of the same regulations as the broiler industry . . . usually follows and endorses Broiler Council leads on legislative proposals. The National Cattlemen occupy the same leadership position for general meat industry issues."[27]

Apart from the need for coordinative machinery, many ideas can never be properly crystallized unless they are put into bill form. A memo or working paper can be vague as to questions of funding, methods of enforcement, and so on, and those who draft can often coast along on the knowledge that it will be subjected to the private criticism of no more than a limited number of officials. When ideas and inclinations are put into the form of a bill, the scope of conflict is changed; a wider public, wider both in numbers and in ranges of interests and concerns, is almost automatically involved. It can also change the strategic calculations of other key actors.

One of the great legislative battles of this century centered around President Roosevelt's highly controversial "court-packing" bill. The purpose of this measure was to change the character of the Supreme Court's decisions by adding more Roosevelt appointees to the bench. Roosevelt lost the legislative battle, but the consensus is that he won the war: in the famous "switch in time that saved nine," the threatened Court reversed its decisions on a number of New Deal programs.

Given the close ties between most administrative agencies and their congressional counterparts, a formal bill is often the last resort in the struggle for control over administrative practices. The mere threat of legislation can serve as a warning shot across the bow. The threat of legislation can also be used to encourage private action. The "self-regulation" of the tobacco industry in taking such "voluntary" steps as a ban on television advertising was a move clearly expedited by the fear that one of the more restrictive bills introduced in Congress might otherwise get more serious attention.

Bills can also serve electoral functions. At the 1960 Democratic National Convention, the party's nominee, John F. Kennedy, put the issue of medical care for the aged high on his campaign agenda. Returning to the Senate, Kennedy brought a Medicare bill to the floor despite the fact that a virtually identical bill had died earlier in the session. Although the bill was defeated, Kennedy used the largely partisan vote on the bill as a major issue in his campaign. It was similar calculations that led congressional Democrats in 1991 to push the abortion counseling bill mentioned earlier and a family leave bill in 1992 that they knew would be vetoed by President Bush.

The Importance of a Law.   If bills have a function, there is something far more compelling about those that become law. A law is a document that presumably has the force of the U.S. government behind it. As a pronouncement of a large number of elected officials, it has an aura of prestige and sanctity that is revealed with particular clarity in those legislative battles that have centered around objectives that could have been achieved through other routes.

In the 1960s, for example, Lyndon Johnson did not need the Gulf of Tonkin Resolution to justify U.S. military involvement in Vietnam. Passage of the resolution, however, gave him a public mandate for subsequent actions and allowed him to preempt potential opposition. Many of those who found it difficult to vote against the resolution under the pressure of the Tonkin emergency later came to feel that they had been trapped. Having voted the president the authority to take whatever steps he felt were justified, a senator could hardly turn around a few months later and criticize those very acts.

Perhaps the most curious uses of legislation to provide mandates for action have been recent efforts by Congress to mandate itself to cut budget deficits. Under the provisions of the Gramm-Rudman and Gramm-Rudman-Hollings acts of 1985 and subsequent years, Congress set targets for reducing the budget deficit that, if unmet, would result in automatic program cuts. Representative Barney Frank (D-MA) calls this a "reverse Houdini," after the magician Harry Houdini who was famous for his escapes from incredible predicaments.[28] Instead of freeing itself, Congress has in effect been tying itself in knots. At least it has been tying future Congresses: in the words of one senator, most of the "heavy lifting," the real mandates, are put off "beyond the next eighteen months so that all the senators who are running for election can get themselves elected" and be "on record in favor of balancing the budget."[29] Subsequent Congresses have proven remarkably adept at postponing and evading whatever real mandates Gramm-Rudman might contain, though that did not prevent them in 1990 and 1992 from attempting to write the unobtainable balanced budget into a constitutional amendment.

A law can also serve as a goad or guide to administration. In Richard Neustadt's words,

> Generally speaking, an administrator who wants to undertake a new program gains by prior Congressional sanction quite as much as Congress gains by demonstrating its authority. The more specific the sanction the better. It backs up the administrator. It lightens his load of counter pressures. The fight for Congressional approval enables him to test in advance the forces behind him and in his way. The terms on which approval is obtained give him a blueprint of the alignment of interests with which he will have to deal.[30]

Legislation, in effect, serves as a buffer against public displeasure and is particularly welcome to those who are in conflict with their environments. Think how much harder the bureaucrat's life would be if he or she could not say, "Sorry, but that's the law."

In a similar fashion, statutory backing is of more than passing importance as a weapon in the struggle to secure compliance from subordinates or in conflicts with other officials and groups. To almost any bureaucrat, statutory authority flowing directly from legislation is regarded far more highly than more transitory executive fiat. The elevation of President Johnson's Consumer Advisory Board into a statutory Consumer Protection Agency was resisted not just by business lobbyists but by other agencies who feared invasions of their turf. Interservice rivalries in the Department of Defense are often, in this same sense, most visible during the legislative struggle.

But as much as some agencies may seek the guidance and political protection of statutory control, conflicts also occur in which the aim of legislation is to give an agency power it doesn't want. Under President Reagan, for example, the Department of Education reversed established policy in the enforcement of anti-discrimination rules. In the *Grove City* case it won the backing of the Supreme Court for its interpretation of the law.[31] Congress reversed both the agency and the Court by passing a new law that spelled out in absolutely unambiguous terms the rules it wanted followed. This was, to be sure, an unusual case: in the normal order of things, legislation is the last stage of oversight, a sign that less formal means of communication have failed. When MCs feel that their directives are being ignored, their "initial preference," as Morris Ogul's interviews have showed, is for "informal discussion." The introduction of legislation is a stronger threat. And "the presence of formal hearings or of a formal investigation sometimes provides a clue to the breakdown of informal attempts to influence executive behavior."[32] To actually pass a bill mandating action is to tighten the screws still more.

A new legislative mandate can often be of value in enhancing the chances of executive agencies in obtaining increased appropriations. In every session bills are introduced authorizing this or that agency to undertake activities that it has always been empowered to undertake. The purpose is usually to mobilize additional support for increased appropriations. Authorizing legislation in setting a "ceiling" on expenditures does not mandate a comparable appropriation of funds, but political pressure at the appropriations stage grows stronger as the gap between appropriation and authorization widens. The effects of these gaps are enhanced by the institutional separations between appropriations, budgeting, and substantive committees in Congress. "Agencies stand to gain by exploiting these conflicts to their own advantage. They try to use an authorization as a club over the head of the appropriations committee by pointing to a substantive committee as a source of commitment to ask for funds."[33]

Jesse Jones, federal loan administrator under President Roosevelt, "had an expression, 'a shotgun in the corner,' which he often used in referring to powers not intended for use except as a club to bring recalcitrant borrowers or banks into line."[34] To make sure he had his shotgun in the corner, Jones was not loathe to ask Congress for statutory powers that he did not really need. The very existence of such powers made lesser sanctions more effective. An annual battle in Congress is to amend the foreign aid bill to deny aid to certain countries under certain conditions (until, for example, they stop violating human rights). Usually these amendments include an "escape clause" giving the president the authority to restore aid to the offending nation if he determines that such aid is in our national interest. Almost invariably these escape clauses have been invoked. Although every president since Truman has opposed such legislative interference in foreign policy, the amendments have often served useful purposes. Though they are seldom used, they stand as shotguns in the corner to keep recipient nations on their toes.

Disadvantages of the Legislative Process

The advantages discussed in the preceding section are relative rather than absolute. In any particular situation there are likely to be as many disadvantages in the use of the legislative process as there are advantages. Some of these relate to the hazards of the process itself, some to the futility of any statute that might get through the grind. The question of whether to have or not to have a bill necessitates a careful weighing of potential gains and losses. The downside of the equation is real.

The Uphill Grind.   The legislative highway is neither short nor easy. The road may be blocked entirely by small minorities of legislators in strategic positions—sometimes even by a single member. Efficiency has never been the strong suit of legislatures.

Another danger is the possibility that the very act of seeking legislation may stimulate legislative action of the opposite kind. In 1973, Senator Edward M. Kennedy (D-MA) became the prime sponsor of a bill revising the federal criminal code. So complicated did the process of refining this massive bill become that at one point Kennedy went to the Senate floor to speak against the very bill that listed him as its sponsor. Kennedy was not alone. During the ten years that this bill kept reappearing on the congressional agenda, it arrived in so many guises that supporters and opponents changed roles many times.

A more subtle boomerang evolved from the 1964 report of the Surgeon General's Advisory Committee on Smoking and Health. By demonstrating links between smoking and fatal disease, the report stimulated a ruling by the Federal Trade Commission (FTC) requiring (1) health warnings in cigarette commercials and (2) consideration by the Federal Communications Commission (FCC) of restrictions on advertising. It also revived antismoking bills that had been languishing in Congress for some time and, coincidentally, the tobacco lobby. What emerged was legislation requiring health warnings on cigarette packs *and* forbidding action by the FCC or FTC for a period of three years. The bill, as one observer put it, transformed "a congressional initiative to protect public health" into "an unashamed act to protect private industry from government regulation."[35]

It was with cases like these in mind that V. O. Key once observed that, "Except for the most important questions on which broad public discussions and understandings may be brought to bear, the administrative tendency is to limp along on the existing legal basis, no matter how unsatisfactory it may be."[36] Key's observation that it is often better "not to arouse sleeping dogs" needs further elaboration in the sense that the sleeping dogs may not be the hounds at issue. President Kennedy's preference for executive action in the field of civil rights was justified in large part by the argument that its introduction in Congress might both divert the attention of congressional leaders and so antagonize Southern Democrats that Kennedy would be unable to get their votes on other issues. Similar attitudes no doubt underlay the Reagan administration's decision to put such "social" issues as abortion, school prayer, and the death penalty on the back burner of its legislative agenda.

Beyond the fear of overloading the legislative agenda is the possibility that by seeking a bill one may close other routes. For a private group, decisions must be made as to how best to allocate resources: a focus on national legislation, for example, may necessitate diminished attention to the states or the bureaucracy. Finally, as many devious children have learned, mommy and daddy can't say no if they aren't asked. In cases in which there is a legal doubt concerning the power of the executive branch to achieve a given objective, the act of seeking clearcut legal authority tends to imply the inadequacy of existing laws and runs the risk of a negative answer.

Hollow Victories. "Legislative proposals," Harold Seidman has noted, "seldom are debated from the viewpoint of their administrative feasibility. Grubby details of planning, organizing, staffing, and developing the administrative system to translate laws into working programs are for someone else to worry about."[37] Whether or not this is a regular feature of the legislative process, it is worth noting that some statutes are by their very nature bound to provide surprises if not profound disappointment to many of their backers. General principles recede as they are hammered into statutory language and passed through the stages of the legislative struggle. They may be all but invisible as they are ultimately administered.

Some acts of Congress were never intended to be enforced. A federal law is only a piece of paper with a number, a great many words, and three names signed at the bottom. Whether there is any real compelling force behind it depends upon the precision with which it is drawn, the will and ability of those who are supposed to administer it, the willingness of Congress to appropriate needed funds, and the amount of organized political support it commands. As Arthur Bentley long ago pointed out, there is "a great deal of 'grandstand-play' law on the federal statute books," and with it "much dead-letter law, forgotten by the law officers of the government as well as by the people."[38] The complex structure of the legislative process sometimes produces such strange anomalies as the International Education Act of 1966. Signed into law by President Johnson and reauthorized for 1967 through 1971, the act created a new agency and a variety of programs designed to encourage international studies. But its sponsors were never able to get an appropriations bill through the House. So although there was, technically, an office and a program, it had no money and did nothing.

In some ways the International Education Act may have been a metaphor for its times. More than one of the ambitious programs of President Johnson's Great Society failed to achieve the potentials perceived by their partisans. A massive "outpouring of legislation that gave the appearance of a veritable revolution in American life" ran into a bureaucracy unprepared to absorb such change and a war in Vietnam that sapped the funds needed to put it into effect. The Great Society, as one of its architects now suggests, "was a victim of too much legislative action and too little executive action." He continues, "The stark reality was that life changed very little for the men and women at the bottom of the ladder—leaving many of them with the suspicion that they were victims of a razzle-dazzle con game."[39]

In a similar vein, the enactment of the Interstate Commerce Act has historically been marked as a major victory for farmers and shipping interests in a long battle against the railroads. It was not long before the hollowness of that victory became clear and the Interstate Commerce Commission (ICC) was seen to be more of a captive agency responsible to the very interests it was supposed to regulate. As the railroad lawyer Richard Olney told the railroads when the act was passed, the Commission could be used as "a sort of protective barrier between the railroad corporations and the people and a sort of protection against hasty and crude legislation hostile to railroad interests. . . . The part of wisdom is not to destroy the Commission but to use it."[40] The regulatory commissions provide the best, but by no means the sole, illustration of the ability, in the words of Justice Frankfurter, to "strangle a policy by administration."[41]

---- ✳ ----

CONCLUSION

The process of policy-making neither begins nor ends with Congress, and the legislative struggle neither begins nor ends with legislation. For policy advocates the area of choice is broad; different approaches offer differing probabilities of success. Even those who successfully pursue a legislative strategy may find their efforts under- or unrewarded in the longer run. Whether a program dies before it becomes law because of administrative sabotage or under-financing, it is dead nonetheless. But just as longevity in people is dependent, in part, on genetics and life-styles, so are some laws born stronger and made more resilient than others. Moreover, some interests are better positioned than others to triumph in the legislative, judicial, administrative, or private arenas. The area of choice is wide.

2

---✳---

CONTESTANTS
FOR POWER

T he trick of the successful traveling salesperson, according to the opening song in *The Music Man*, is that you've got to know the territory. In a military analogy, the ancient Chinese warrior-philosopher Zhang Yu argued that "victorious warriors win first and then go to war."[1] What is meant by this rather cryptic remark is that the strategic advantage goes to those who are best prepared, who have planned their victories before they fight.

Planning in both politics and war begins with careful assessment of the battle scenario, including realistic analyses of your own strengths and weaknesses; knowledge of other potential participants' game; and a thorough understanding of the rules. Unfortunately for both generals and policy advocates, there is a great deal of fluidity in these scenarios; but there is a relatively stable core of permanent residents on Capitol Hill. Their presence is important because of their potential for involvement. E. E. Schattschneider's classic observations on the ability of the crowd to control the outcome of a fight explains why it is so important for policy advocates to be aware of these groups: "conflicts are frequently won or lost by the success that the contestants have in getting the audience involved in the fight or excluding it."[2]

--- ✳ ---

THE LOBBYING COMMUNITY

Lawrence O'Brien, head of congressional liaison for presidents Kennedy and Johnson, described his image of the Washington community as one of

> two great armies facing one another across a vast field of battle. One army—our army—was led by the President and included in its ranks the

21

forces of organized labor, the urban political leaders, the emerging black political spokesmen, and many of the nation's intellectual luminaries.

Ours was a formidable force, and yet facing us was a no less powerful legislative army led by [the Republicans and] . . . backed by the vast resources of the American business community . . . as well as the medical profession, and important segments of rural and suburban America.[3]

Politics in the United States seldom configures in quite so neat a pattern. Rather than two armies along a clear line of battle, it is more like guerrilla warfare in which the front is everywhere and citizen-soldiers drift in and out of battle. O'Brien's main point, however, is well taken: policy groupings in Washington have long habits of association (alliance is too strong a word) that divide and bring them together in more or less predictable patterns.

The Major Private Groups

Every year, more than ten thousand groups and individuals are formally listed as Washington lobbyists.[4] Many others act like lobbyists but fail to comply with the rather loose registration requirements of the lobbying law.[5] Most of these groups, it should be noted, are not organized primarily for purposes of lobbying. The goal of most corporations, for example, is to make profits, not public policies. Even in their Washington offices, "the basic purpose of representation," one business lobbyist put it, "is commercial, and I think most of us have overriding commercial interests in Washington."[6] Even trade associations, although usually representing competing firms, often treat lobbying as a low priority activity: "most trade associations . . . exist primarily to provide services to member firms for which the latter are willing to pay."[7] Not surprisingly, the few studies that we have of business representatives in Washington show that most spend more time communicating with their own members than they do lobbying. Even for those groups whose explicit reason for being is legislative advocacy (e.g., environmental lobbies), substantial resources are devoted to recruiting new members and communicating with the old.

At the same time, lobbyists do lobby; and their presence on Capitol Hill is formidable. Numerically, at least, the largest single group is that representing corporations, many of which are, in effect, triply represented: (1) by their own lobbyists; (2) through so-called peak associations like the National Association of Manufacturers and the Chamber of Commerce; and (3) through trade associations representing a particular industry such as steel or airlines. One source estimates that between 1974 and 1979 alone, the number of corporate lobbyists in Washington almost doubled, from 8,000 to 15,000.[8] By the 1980s virtually every large corporation in the United States was represented on the Hill.

Although labor and management are not always in conflict, on the broad scale of conflict between "liberals" and "conservatives," business and labor are generally found at the cores of two opposing camps. As with business organizations, there are occasional signs of tension in the house of labor between the peak association (the American Federation of Labor and Congress of Industrial Organizations, or AFL-CIO) and more narrowly focused constituent unions.

Schisms in labor's ranks, however, are neither as numerous nor as deep as those that divide the business community. Much more troubling to organized labor has been its relationship with its putative friends in the Democratic party. Although labor has often served as a virtual coordinating group of the party's liberal wing,[9] Democrats have not always returned the favor. Yet by their close ties with liberal Democrats, they have more or less burned their bridges to many Republicans.

Any analysis of the liberal lobbying community must begin with organized labor, just as any analysis of the right begins with business. As with most groups, however, it cannot be overemphasized that lobbying is a relatively low priority of the labor movement. The AFL-CIO typically allocates only about 2.5 percent of its resources to its legislative department.[10] Organized labor, moreover, has been in a long-term period of political decline both in its numerical strength as a proportion of the work force and its ability to deliver the votes of its own membership. Increasingly, then, the key associational rival to business on Capitol Hill is found among so-called public interest lobbies.

To judge by their rhetoric, all lobbies are working in the public interest; still, there is a category of organizations, typified by Common Cause and the Nader organization, that are different in both focus and membership. Although the phrase *public interest lobby* is more commonly used, we have followed Andrew McFarland's suggestion of using the phrase *citizens' lobby* as a means of avoiding "the tangle of arguing about who *really* represents public interests."[11] Using this broader phrase, we include those groups comprised of members acting as citizens rather than as representatives of occupational, ethnic, or economic groups.

If business's presence as a major lobbying force in Washington grew most dramatically in the 1970s, the 1980s became the decade of citizens' groups. The fastest growing (both in numbers and influence) are those like the Sierra Club and National Wildlife Federation, which tend to combine the attributes of foundations, clubs, and pressure groups. The combined budgets of the leading consumer groups rose to more than $72 million in 1990 from $32 million in 1980, and environmental groups went from $70 million to $156 million in the same decade.[12]

Perhaps the most effective citizens' lobbies are those that focus on a single issue. A century ago, many followers of the Temperance Movement took an oath not to support any candidate for office who did not favor the prohibition of alcoholic beverages. A willingness to ignore party labels and all other issues made the Prohibitionists a potent voting bloc that few candidates could ignore. Similarly, the million-plus members of the National Rifle Association have, in more recent years, forced many candidates for office to "run scared" on the issue of gun control. Other citizens' lobbies, by way of contrast, are weak at the grass roots but strong in Washington. Given sufficient funding and talent, a handful of people with a typewriter and a photocopy machine can appear considerably more formidable than their numbers would warrant. Groups such as these can play an important role in raising new issues, as, for example, Ralph Nader did with automobile safety.

Most citizens' lobbies, and most other groups with substantial Washington offices—such as teachers' associations and professional societies—tend to stick fairly closely to their own agendas. Coalitions that make little *logical* sense, however, are not unusual. The American Medical Association, for example, long withheld a formal stand against cigarette smoking reportedly because of the political support on medical issues that it received from tobacco interests and tobacco-state MCs. The two major farm groups are found in opposite camps on agricultural and almost every other possible issue. The American Farm Bureau Federation has as consistently allied itself with business interests and the Republican party as the Farmer's Union has with labor and the Democrats.

Minority groups whose members tend to vote Democratic, blacks in particular—have tended toward the Democratic party and an alliance with organized labor, just as the Reagan and Bush administrations' positions on social issues pushed feminists in the same direction. But there seems as well to be greater fluidity now in the lobbying community than there was in the Kennedy-Johnson years. Such key groups as the fast-growing "grey lobby" of senior citizens, and even traditionally Democratic Jewish organizations, have been careful to keep their options open through long periods of divided government.

The Administration

Technically, government agencies are prohibited from using appropriated moneys to attempt to influence the Congress; if the law were ever to be enforced, the jails would bulge with bureaucrats. Virtually every department, bureau, and agency of the federal government includes an office of legislative liaison. Strictly speaking, its function is to serve as a source of information for MCs and their staffs. The line between providing information and advocating policies is elusive, however; in many of their operations on the Hill, government lobbyists are no different from their counterparts in the private sector.

As in the private sector, there is often tension in the government between the interests of the part and those of the whole. Frequently each agency "becomes a guardian of its own mission, standards, and skill; lines of organization become lines of loyalty and secrecy."[13] Particularly when it comes to the budget, agencies have vested interests in survival and growth. Denied funds by the president, they can, and sometimes do, end-run the White House by lobbying their friends on the Hill. In many ways, the history of legislative liaison in the executive branch is a history of the effort to stop such end-runs.

Centralizing Liaison. The first step in centralizing control was the Budget and Accounting Act of 1921. Until 1921, individual bureaus and agencies submitted budget proposals to the secretary of the treasury, who compiled them into a book of estimates sent directly to Congress. Presidents from time to time intervened to revise these budget estimates, but such interventions were rare.[14] Under Richard Nixon, half a century after the Budget Act, a change in the name of the Bureau of the Budget to the Office of Management and Budgeting symbolized a further extension of White House influence. At present, all legislative proposals from all bureaus must be cleared by OMB.

Similar trends are found in the history of formal liaison. For many years it was traditional to have the postmaster general serve as the president's semi-official lobbyist. Not until Eisenhower was there an official White House office of congressional relations. This meant that with few exceptions, individual bureaus generally assumed responsibility for the development and promotion of legislation. This practice, often encouraged by MCs, fostered a dispersion of executive energy, emphasized the special interests of administrative units rather than those of the departments, and catered to Congress's desire to keep a finger in the executive pie.[15] In the Kennedy and Johnson years, these activities too were centralized in the White House. Most formal agency and departmental liaison activities have continued to work closely with and through this expanded White House network. Whoever the president in power may be, it now appears that the administration's *formal* lobbying activities are more clearly centralized than those of any private group.

What you see is not always what you get. To be sure, budget and major legislative proposals are cleared by OMB, and virtually all formal agency contacts with the Hill go through White House liaison. Still, there is no way of preventing A (from an agency) talking with C (from the committee that deals with the agency's budget). Senior MCs and veteran staff aides on the Hill have long lists of bureaucratic informants.

Subgovernments. Career bureaucrats survive numerous administrations. Protected by civil service regulations, they develop a knowledge of the Washington community that few Cabinet officers, presidents, or White House aides can match. Through numerous interactions, both formal and informal, they are likely to be familiar, if not friendly, with the MCs and staffpersons who deal regularly with their programs and budgets, and with the major private sector lobbyists in their field. They are, in other words, key elements in the three-sided "subgovernments," or "iron triangles," that Douglass Cater, Ernest Griffith, and others have described as central to an understanding of the process.[16] Indeed, a case can be made that career bureaucrats are the central actors in these subsystems if only "because they have the most to gain by its continuance and the most to lose by its demise."[17] The power of well-placed bureaucrats is enhanced by their ability to deliver information or services to other subsystem actors. Lobbyists in the private sector can deliver votes or campaign contributions, but they are seldom able to intervene on behalf of an MC's aggrieved constituents.

Yet the limitations on bureaucratic lobbying are also formidable. Like it or not, they are part of a more or less hierarchical team. Central clearance devices impose formidable obstacles to dissent through channels; and to go outside channels, to become a "whistle blower," is a risky option at best.[18] There are more subtle forms of sabotage. A leak to a reporter, MC, or friendly lobbyist will often do the trick. A disgruntled bureaucrat can usually find some informal mechanism for leaking official secrets. The point remains, however, that government employees have considerably less freedom of action in lobbying than their counterparts in the private sector.

Other Governments

One by-product of the programs of the 1960s was a proliferation of Washington offices representing state and local governments. Although federal grant programs were not new, in purely quantitative terms the number of grant programs doubled between 1964 and 1968. Of equal importance was a qualitative change from grants that essentially supplemented existing state programs to those developed for new national objectives. State and local governments were "viewed as one among several instrumentalities assisting the federal government to achieve national objectives and goals rather than the reverse."[19] Given a far greater stake in federal legislation, state and local governing bodies felt a growing need for a presence in Washington not just to lobby for allocation formulae favoring their situations, but simply to get information about programs already on the books. The shift, begun under Nixon and accelerated under Reagan, toward so-called block grants (as opposed to categorical) has lessened these information needs, but the number of intergovernmental lobbyists continues to grow.

As in the private sector, there is a large variety of groups. In organizations like the Conference of Mayors and National Governors' Conference, there are the functional equivalents of peak associations. More specialized groups (e.g., those representing chiefs of police or urban public universities) correspond in a rough sense to trade associations; and individual agencies (e.g., the University of Southern Mississippi and the Port of Philadelphia) retain registered lobbyists. The conflicts between and among these groups are often severe, particularly when they are jockeying for the same pot of money. Organizations like the Governors' Conference are so torn by partisanship that they seldom take positions on controversial issues, and some states cannot even agree to maintain a common office. In 1980, the Illinois legislature, not trusting the governor's lobbyists, set up its own Washington office. New York has three: one each for the Democratic governor, the Democratic Assembly, and the Republican Senate. Sometimes they work together.

One final group that deserves brief mention under this heading is the representatives of foreign nations. There are few countries in the world that do not maintain both formal embassies in Washington and more specialized lobbying offices. A 1938 law that requires any "agent of a foreign principal" to register with the attorney general imposes rather onerous reporting requirements on such lobbyists, but it has not prevented some of Washington's most prestigious law firms and lobbyists from signing up. Once again, information gathering is a primary function of the lobbyist. Those familiar with U.S. politics are often far better equipped than those in the embassy to explain the meaning of a complex bill, predict the outcome of a vote, or understand who needs to be contacted about what. A major job of the "foreign agent" is the very routine work of filing reports. But the legislative interests of foreign governments, most obviously in the areas of foreign aid and trade, are quite substantial. Even a subtle shift in, say, product safety standards for a small country's major product can have dramatic economic repercussions. The embassy is perfectly capable of making its case for increased foreign aid; on more subtle, indirect issues it simply is not. Maybe, in a sense, that's what lobbying in general is all about.

———————— ✳ ————————

THE ORGANIZATION OF GROUP SUPPORT

Every active participant in the legislative struggle must decide what he or she is going to sacrifice in order to obtain the objectives that count the most. "Pursue one great decisive aim with force and determination," wrote the great military strategist Carl von Clausewitz.[20] Unless this is done, one's resources are too often dribbled away in pointless efforts.

When we survey the organized groups registered as Washington lobbyists, it is clear that no single group has a monopoly. Even on issues of direct concern, each can be shown to have lost significant battles; but the lobbying success of organized interests is not necessarily an index of power. Not all powerful interests are organized, and the argument that there are deeper and stronger currents cannot be ignored. Organization, at the same time, is important, and the resources expended on lobbying are not trivial.

Tangible Resources

The obvious starting point is with tangible resources such as money and members. Other things being equal, a large organization is more effective than a small one; a well-financed lobby more potent than a poor one. As much as it helps to begin with a large membership and treasury, other things are seldom equal, and much depends on an organization's capacity to use its resources effectively. Many of the largest groups in American society are essentially non-political; others are involved in the pressure system but enjoy only the partial support of their members. Some very small groups enjoy influence far out of proportion to their numbers. Numbers are important, even more so when they can be mobilized. "Labor," says one Capitol Hill observer, "has a lot of members—a lot of votes—in virtually every congressional district in the country. Nobody up here can ignore that."[21] Yet labor often loses, in part because numbers do not automatically transfer into votes or influence. Union members are less likely than, say, professionals to write their congressmen or talk to them personally. Their letters or statements, if made, are often less sophisticated. Numbers help but do not guarantee success, particularly if they are difficult to mobilize.

Status helps. In 1981, funeral directors scored a major victory when they persuaded Congress to overrule a set of Federal Trade Commission rules governing their conduct. On the merits, few MCs could have objected to the proposed FTC guidelines; but funeral directors, though not as numerous as union members, have clout. They not only write, but they often know their MCs personally and can provide valuable opportunities to press the flesh with important people in the district.[22] The funeral directors were able to win because they could insinuate themselves into the core constituencies of many MCs. Lawyers and certain other professionals are also advantaged in the group struggle by their social standing and specialized knowledge. "Most legislators," one California legislator said, "are awed by doctors" and other high status citizens.[23] Corporate chief executives are an increasing presence on the Hill as they attempt to cash in on the status factor. "Legislators reluctant to make time in their busy schedules to meet privately with an obscure lobbyist for the automobile industry will *make* time when the head of General Motors requests an appointment."[24]

Money helps. At a minimum, a group must be able to staff an office, communicate with its membership, and present its case; but just as a ranking of groups according to numbers of members is not a reliable guide to influence, neither is the amount of money spent. Indeed, large expenditures are often signs of desperation rather than strength. In constant dollars, the American Medical Association spent more money lobbying in the early 1960s against Medicare and Medicaid than it has before or since. It lost. The Maritime Unions hit the dollar top ten in the 1970s but failed to pass the Cargo Preference Bill. Some of the most powerful groups in the United States (e.g., investment bankers) seldom appear on the list of top spenders.

What money best buys is access and efficiency. Campaign contributions almost guarantee a line in congressional appointment books, and money can buy indirect influence. Good research costs money, and a slickly illustrated brochure may attract a wider readership than a smudgy mimeographed one. The better-financed lobbies often have access to computerized mailing systems that can alert their members to fast-breaking issues and perhaps even provide them with individualized letters or faxes that they need only sign and send to Washington in a seeming display of grassroots concern. Through its Biznet satellite communications system, the Chamber of Commerce can move even faster, making up-to-the-minute presentations of the business perspective on Washington events available to local TV news programs throughout the country, and sharply reducing the response time of its members on key issues. "A vote," one critic suggests, "will come up, business will generate a response, and by the time the average citizen reads about it in the paper it will be all over."[25] Whether or not this technological advantage is significant in practice, it is clearly an important resource available only to an organization that has substantial resources.

Bribery, although not unheard of in Washington, is not as common as many citizens suspect or as prevalent as in the past, but the boundaries between overt bribery and legitimate persuasion are not easily drawn. If a company offers to fly you home in a company plane, is that bribery? If an interest group or constituent offers you lunch, is it proper to accept? Lobbyists themselves are divided on the question of how effective "gray money" is. No one, of course, would admit to having offered an overt bribe. But the gray areas of campaign contributions, parties, luncheons, and free trips are occupied to the extent that one lobbyist of our acquaintance once had an expense account that exceeded his salary. Does it matter if you miss Congressman Smith's $100-a-plate cocktail party? Can you lobby more effectively over dinner than in a member's office? Do Superbowl tickets carry influence? We don't know; but it seems safe to venture that they don't hurt, and that those who can't afford them will never know. One lobbyist told us: "I can't think of an instance where my entertainment account has bought me influence on a particular issue. But in the long run there's nothing better than having a personal relationship with someone in a position to help. Sometimes I think I accomplish more in an afternoon on the golf course than I do in an entire day of office visits on the Hill."

Cohesion

Numbers help. Expensive gimmicks, such as the Chamber's Biznet, enable some organizations to communicate rapidly and effectively with their members. But no matter how well the Washington office is equipped, much of a lobbyist's clout is determined by the relationship he or she has with clients in the field. Group leaders are much like legislators in the sense that they represent constituencies whose interests are complex and difficult to discern.[26] Such ambiguities can be a source of power for the Washington office. Lacking a clear mandate on an issue of peripheral concern to members, the lobbyist is free to pursue his or her own issues or enter into long-standing coalitions that may or may not reflect the members' choices of allies. Needless to say, such "surplus profits," as Robert Salisbury calls the discretionary powers of lobbyists, must be "earned" by delivering the goods on core group issues.[27] In large part, moreover, ambiguous mandates are likely to limit rather than expand a lobbyist's effectiveness. "The problem of cohesion," David Truman put it, "is a crucial one for the political interest group. Other factors bear upon its capacity to assert its claims successfully . . . but the degree of unity in the group is probably most fundamental in determining the measure of success it will enjoy."[28]

Examples abound of interest groups whose lobbying activities have been compromised by splits in the membership. Truman cites the major farm groups and their historic support for restrictive taxes on margarine in favor of butter. As margarine came increasingly to be produced from domestic farm products, however, agriculture's peak groups "found it necessary to avoid the issue."[29] Umbrella organizations—such as the Farm Bureau, the AFL-CIO, and the Chamber of Commerce—are most likely to confront internal divisions of this kind, but even a relatively specialized trade association or large corporation can confront situations in which the interests of one division are not congruent with those of another. The need to present a united front is often used by group leaders as an excuse for centralized control, but internal democracy can cause real problems. For example, when it became known in 1982 that the Chamber of Commerce's Executive Committee was divided almost equally in its support and opposition to the president's emergency tax bill, the Chamber's lobbyists lost credibility. A divided organization not only loses effectiveness but may suffer internal injuries such as the loss of disgruntled members. "There is a definite feeling that it is better to have a strong association . . . than to weaken and debilitate [it] by inside rows. The main position is to keep the organization strong."[30]

The same rule applies, of course, in the executive branch. Nothing is more destructive of an administration's credibility than indecisiveness. In President Eisenhower's second term, as Richard Neustadt describes it,

> a technician from the Bureau of the Budget testified before a subcommittee of the House on the provisions of a pending bill within the field of his expertise. As he concluded, he remarked for emphasis that what he recommended was essential "to the program of the President." Whereupon everybody laughed. The hilarity was general and leaped party lines; to a man, committee members found this reference very funny.[31]

In Neustadt's account, the joke originated on the day President Eisenhower presented his budget message for 1958. Later that afternoon, his secretary of the treasury, George M. Humphrey, held a press conference in which he sharply challenged the premises of the administration plan. Immediately, the president lost the strategic advantage that his budget message usually provides: his ability to dominate the agenda for debate. Now the Congress was provided with two agendas. Disunity produced a crisis of credibility. "At the Capitol and in the press corps, and among spokesmen for the private groups most vitally concerned, reactions were as unsure as the situation was unusual; everybody looked to see what Eisenhower would do."

What he did was to compound the felony. Consistency is a corollary of unity, and teamwork has little meaning if the team leader is unclear as to his or her objectives. Thus, when Eisenhower attempted to defend his own budget, "there were few laughs in Congress or downtown, but many stricken faces, some delight, and considerable scorn."[32] In the months that followed, the president's indecision waxed as his credibility waned; a result was the hilarity that greeted the reference to "the President's program" cited earlier. The laughter reflected a fundamental erosion of the president's credibility that "cast increasing doubt not only on his skill but on his will." Both came to be discounted in the Washington community.[33]

Even a single incident can damage a president's credibility. This happened to Jimmy Carter early in his administration. As part of an economic stimulus plan proposed in January 1977, Carter's call for a $50-per-person tax rebate met a cold reception on the Hill. But Carter lobbied hard and managed to persuade the Democratic leadership to support the proposal. Under heavy leadership pressure, the rebate passed the House by a narrow, highly partisan majority; when the president convinced key Democrats on the Senate Finance Committee to support the proposal, it appeared as if it might slide through. Virtually on the eve of the vote, however, Carter—with no advance warning to his supporters—announced that he was withdrawing the proposal. As an exercise in inconsistency, it was a virtuoso performance that cast a long shadow on the effectiveness of the administration. Congressional Democrats felt as if they had been talked out on a limb only to look back and find the president sawing it off. For months to come, one White House lobbyist complained, "I heard that example used every time—'well, are you going to stick with us on this one?' "[34]

Problems of unity and consistency arise in different forms among private groups. Because they are relatively small, and because lower-level staff persons in the private sector are not protected by civil service, private groups seldom encounter problems of overt disloyalty in their Washington offices. Jeffrey Berry points out that in voluntary groups internal dissension is seldom visible because "most internal protest consists of the relatively passive act of failing to renew one's membership."[35] Some groups, particularly those with narrow, sharply focused issue concerns, enjoy a high degree of membership solidarity. For the larger organizations, however, attaining and sustaining consensus in the ranks is a recurring problem compounded by the fact that issues do not stand still. An organization that has achieved consensus on an issue may find that very consensus challenged by a subtle shift in the political winds.

The Washington lobbyist has two communication problems: one with the people he is trying to influence, and a second with the people he is supposedly representing. For many Washington representatives the latter is the more vexing problem. As one business lobbyist says, "It's easier for me to work the Hill than the home office. Part of the problem is that I don't carry much weight. They're in the business of producing—and making money. Politics is peripheral if not downright dirty. Getting them to take a stand on anything is like pulling teeth." Some lobbyists are more skilled than others at "farming the membership," and some groups give their Washington offices more latitude than others. Michael Hayes has suggested that groups that offer material benefits to their members are more likely than pure lobbying organizations to give their Washington offices a free hand.[36] At the same time, independence has a price: how credible are lobbyists who may not enjoy the support of their own members?

Like private groups, members of Congress are in a better position than members of the administration to control their staffs. Fierce loyalties are a hallmark of legislative staff, and it is seldom, even by accident, that a congressional office speaks with more than one voice.[37] Put two MCs together, however, and the situation changes. Coalitions on Capitol Hill are seldom stable.

It makes a difference. The unity displayed by the House Ways and Means Committee of Wilbur Mills (D-AR) was a major factor in its reputation for never losing on the floor. Education and Labor, conversely, has been equally notorious for its sharp internal divisions and a corresponding lack of success on the floor. Unity is important, because of what John Kingdon calls a "consensus mode of decision." If all perceived forces in the information environment point in one direction, there is no incentive to seek further information. Conflict induces search.[38] Thus, a key goal of any policy advocate is to minimize the amount of dissonance in the information environment. Internal unity is the first step.

Knowledge

Most MCs have neither time nor tolerance for ambiguity and vagueness. Policy advocates should be able to provide information fluidly and well; they increase their effectiveness as they increase their knowledge resources. The point seems so obvious as to need no elaboration, yet it is not so simple to actually define the point at which one knows something well enough. "Each of us has a point—some probability level—beyond which we will say that we know something. But all things fall short of absolute certainty: life itself might be a dream and logic a delusion. Still, because we act, we must decide, and how decisively we can act depends on how well we know the consequences."[39] Unfortunately for politicians, most of the issues they must decide involve situations in which consequences run toward the less predictable end of this continuum. If we knew with certainty how to end poverty, cure cancer, or lower the crime rate, we would probably do it: politics exists because we don't.

One way of dealing with this uncertainty is through a subtle shift of focus from the evaluation of outcomes to the weighing of preferences. Instead of asking who will be helped and hurt by a given decision, politicians have a tendency to redefine the question in terms of who *thinks* they will be helped and hurt. This shift of emphasis has a dual function. On the one hand, it transfers the burden of policy evaluation to those who presumably are the most capable of performing it, that is, the affected parties. At the same time, and more important, it transfers political responsibility: if a policy fails, the politician can claim to have done only what the group in question said it wanted. From the perspective of the policy advocate, this shift in focus puts an even greater premium on unity. To the extent that politicians deal in preferences, the more clearly such preferences are conveyed, the more credible the source. Only when there is conflict in the field are legislators likely to seek further information. The lack of internal democracy in most groups and the time devoted to internal communications have their roots in the problem of effectiveness.

A naive view of the legislative struggle looks upon the Congress as a passive target of pressures emanating primarily from myriad lobbyists swarming through the corridors of the Capitol. In some of the more extreme proponents of group theory (as, paradoxically, in elite theory and Marxian analyses of Congress), one finds a perspective that renders strategy and knowledge irrelevant. Professional lobbyists, class factors, and elite elements do play important roles in the legislative struggle, but a full-fledged legislative campaign involves both skill and rectitude. Many case studies have suggested that policy outcomes "reflect something more profound—a gradual supplementing, if not a complete supplanting, of the 'politics of interests' with a 'politics of ideas,' in which the power of a good idea or a symbolically appealing cause can be just as persuasive or forceful in the policy-making process as vested interest."[40]

Skill

Battles have been won and legislative contests lost because the groups involved have done their jobs well or poorly. But the skill factor in lobbying is important even before the emergence of a particular issue. There are certain people in the Washington community who, by virtue of their personalities, connections, or talents, are known as heavyweights—people who can get things done. Reputations can be overblown. Former members of the House and Senate, for example, are often presumed to be particularly valuable; indeed, they are likely, at a minimum, to know their way around the Hill. Yet there are liabilities, too. "The defeated member," one observer dryly observed, "is probably not strikingly capable."[41] Former MCs also make some people uncomfortable, perhaps reminding them of their own vulnerability or suggesting some sort of slightly illicit favor trading based upon past relationships.

The same generalization seems to apply to the so-called superlawyers, politically connected Washington law firms like Covington and Burling, or Arnold and Porter, who are known for their clout. One partner at Arnold and Porter, admitting they were sometimes "beneficiaries of some client's misconception that we . . . have inside power" or "were close to an administration," took pains to deny the real importance of such links: "proficiency is the thing that attracts clients—the notion that this firm can handle matters competently and effectively, regardless of the politics of the administration."[42]

Despite such disclaimers, some lobbyists do enjoy personal advantages. The first step in effective lobbying is access, the ability to get in the door. Money helps, as we have suggested. But there are certain individuals who have access, regardless of who they represent. Former MCs and most of Washington's superlawyers are advantaged by their personal friendships with key persons. Celebrities, such as movie actors and Nobel Prize winners, are likely to receive warmer-than-usual welcomes.

From the perspective of a group seeking representation on the Hill, professionalism is obviously important, but many groups regard it as a two-edged sword. To hire a professional lobbyist is to hire someone who knows his or her way around Washington but who is not really versed in the problems of the organization. And an experienced lobbyist "who has devoted many years to establishing credibility and good relations with their target government agencies may prefer to endanger their client relationships rather than their government relationships."[43] Conversely, the group member who is sent to Washington because of his or her ability to articulate group interests is unlikely to know the ways of the Hill. Political conflicts can also arise. One business lobbyist explained that

> most businesspeople don't like government, they don't like politicians, and they don't like Democrats. Unfortunately, those are exactly the people— Democratic politicians in government—that I have to get along with if I'm going to be effective. So there is a sense in which the more effective I become the less the folks in the home office trust me.

In 1959, Lester Milbrath asked a sample of 101 lobbyists and 38 persons in Congress what traits or skills make a lobbyist effective.

> The qualities most frequently mentioned by both lobbyists and congressmen were honesty and integrity. Many, especially in Congress, went so far as to say that if a lobbyist did not possess these qualities, he was completely ineffective. . . .
> Almost as essential to success is the requirement that the lobbyist be very capable and well-informed. . . . It is also desirable that the lobbyist be analytical, incisive and articulate.[44]

Other qualities that received frequent mention from Milbrath's respondents were agreeableness and persistence. It also helps if you like your job.[45]

Although Milbrath's 1959 data have never been systematically updated, his findings seem timeless: the personality traits described by his respondents are attributes that transcend issues and relate instead to what we might call a lobbying personality. Although they often compete with each other, there is in Washington a rather closely knit, identifiable community of fellow professionals who, if they don't share each others' goals, often respect each others' skills. Almost all would agree with Milbrath: honesty remains a paramount concern, as does subject-matter competence. MCs rely on lobbyists to provide accurate indicators of the attitudes and concerns of key components of their constituencies. They also seek guidance on technical policy issues and questions of legislative procedure. The lobbyist who lies, whether out of ignorance or calculation, loses influence.

Still, skillful lobbying is as much art as science. Different issues dictate different patterns of lobbying. And different lobbyists combine different skills. One lobbyist says:

> The individual has to . . . decide what his assets are and then use them to the maximum. [If] you can do research and develop tight information that is useful to congressmen and senators . . . you use that to the maximum. If your asset is sitting . . . in the Democratic Club, drinking cocktails and just hitting issues lightly but maximizing your contact with senators and congressmen, then you use that. . . . The tactics [also] have to vary with the kind of organization.[46]

Skilled lobbyists are not randomly distributed. Top people do not come cheap: the median compensation of Washington office directors was $128,600 in 1988, ranging up to a quarter of a million dollars.[47] A skilled lobbyist needs resources to be effective: expense accounts, political action committee (PAC) dollars, research assistants, and so forth. Some groups, moreover, are less able than others to retain lobbyists who are effective on the Hill. For example, a group whose members require constant courting needs a Washington office that is skilled in the art of grassroots politics, and effort expended on the folks is effort that cannot be expended on the Hill. Many organizations, moreover, are mistrustful of lobbying and regard their Washington representatives more as sources of information than as centers of political action. Party affiliation also has an impact, which is not entirely under the lobbyist's control. One corporate lobbyist, for example, described how his efforts to establish ties with a key House Democrat were nullified by the president of the corporation's decision to make a generous campaign contribution to the MC's opponent.

Where the battle lines on issues are so clearly drawn that the lobbyist has little room to maneuver, money, numbers, and other tangible group resources are almost meaningless. The skill factor comes into play primarily at the margins: in the areas of small amendments, "minor" revisions in the tax code, adjustments in language and emphasis. "On that type of lobbying, political or personal connections are premiums."[48]

The increasing complexity of many issues has made lobbyists in general more important and given a particularly important role to those who can explain technical issues to generalists. "As the issues increased in technicality," one study found, "no one congressman could be expected to know all the technical information about the issues. As a result, there is a greater reliance on staff by congressmen, and, in turn, the staffs rely on special interest groups for representation."[49]

Constituency Linkages

On the larger issues, and some smaller ones, the influence of Washington lobbyists can depend as much upon their association members as on their own efforts. To the extent that they are able to mobilize grassroots campaigns, lobbyists regard it as one of their more important tools. Indeed, for some groups grassroots lobbying has almost totally displaced direct contact.[50]

Grassroots lobbying takes three forms. In its most direct manifestation it simply involves the attempt to involve the group's members in the work of the Washington office. In its crudest form it resembles the phone conversation from a lobbyist to one of his members: "Hello, Johnny Bob? This is J. D. in Washington. Now this is who your congressman is. This is how you write him. You write this son-of-a-bitch and tell him how this is going to ruin you."[51] A more sophisticated variant of this technique is to locate influential friends of individual members. Said one business lobbyist,

> We have found that almost every congressman and senator has certain people in his district that he listens to. . . . Our local people, our local officers and plant managers in the area, should be alert to the problems here in Washington; and they could find out, if they didn't already know, whom a particular congressman listened to. Maybe they wouldn't even do the personal contacting, but they might talk to Joe Smith at the Rotary Club, who in turn had the ear of the congressman.[52]

Finally, the ultimate grassroots campaign involves large numbers of people in the process. For decades, banking interests have succeeded in blocking attempts to collect a withholding tax on the interest generated by savings accounts. One of their key weapons in the fight was a flyer enclosed in millions of bank statements urging depositors to write their congressmen in opposition to the tax. Similarly, Tuesday has been known in congressional mailrooms as "prayer day" in tribute to the many ministers who end the Sunday sermon by passing out pens for their parishioners to write Washington in favor of school prayer. MCs are generally skeptical of group-inspired letters. Says one member, "I have received letters starting off: 'Dear Congressman: Please write your congressman and senators and tell them so and so.' You can tell from the letters whether the people are really thinking, whether the issue is really important to them, or whether they are writing just because they have been told to do so. I pay little attention to the form letter."[53]

In general, three types of organizations are best able to mount grassroots campaigns. Groups with large numbers of potential supporters are clearly advantaged. The American Telephone and Telegraph Corporation, for example, before the courts broke it into regional divisions, was the largest private sector employer in the United States and had more stockholders than any corporation in the world. When its interests were threatened by a bill in 1982, Ma Bell elicited the help of her many owners and employees. In the spring of 1982, some MCs received more letters on the telephone bill than on all other issues combined. It did not pass.

The second condition determining a group's ability to mount a grassroots campaign is the willingness of its members to act. Medium-sized, single-issue groups, such as the National Rifle Association, are effective because their members are intensely committed and willing to express themselves. Similarly, groups whose members are highly politicized, like Common Cause, can often mount effective grassroots campaigns. Finally, some small organizations can be effective if their members enjoy high status. Professionals, acknowledged experts, and celebrities have better access to members of Congress than do most of us. A group's overall prestige or legitimacy is a more subtle factor, nicely encapsulated in Michael Hayes's comparison of senior citizens and welfare recipients:

> Senior citizens' groups possess extraordinary legitimacy, for example, partly because the serious problems they face . . . are widely regarded as not of their own making, and partly because eventually all of us must confront problems associated with aging . . . . By contrast, welfare recipients are readily characterized (rightly or wrongly) as failures living off the toil of others. . . . The contrast is striking, and it helps to explain why the aged were relatively insulated from major program cuts during President Reagan's term in office, while AFDC and Food Stamps were cut repeatedly.[54]

Resources and Influence

The power of a lobby is in part situational: Watergate was a boon to Common Cause; major assassinations have almost always been damaging to the gun lobby. Strategies and tactics can affect the political leverage accruing from particular events, but there are some lobbying groups that maintain long-range systemic advantages because they are in a position to provide members of Congress regularly with things that they need and want. In essence, these boil down to two: information and votes. From the perspective of the Hill, lobbies are service organizations. In the words of one member:

> A professional lobbyist becomes part of the woodwork here. He becomes a source of information. A lot of people talk about the "invidious special interests," but we shouldn't engage in legislation without knowing who's affected by it, and usually the people who are affected by it are the best sources of information. There are a few guys up here who vote a certain way because they're bought, but most of us don't like to deal with people who only have a short-range interest in us.[55]

Good lobbyists give MCs and staff persons ready access to expert (if biased) opinions on a wide range of technical questions, political intelligence on the attitudes of other members and important constituency groups, and a communications link with key subgroups of the population. Money can help buy such things. A large and easily mobilized membership can be translated into votes. And a skillful lobbyist can provide crucial political intelligence. "A lobbyist," says Bruce Wolpe, "is in the unique position of seeing the process unfold from a distance and can take effective advantage of that knowledge."[56] Access to these resources gives some groups an advantage, but "measures of lobbying resources," are not "measures of lobbying success."[57]

A few crude generalizations can be ventured. Interest groups, as a rule, are better positioned to block proposed actions than to nurture innovations. The more narrow and technical the issue and the lower its public visibility, the more important the role of the professional policy advocate becomes.[58] In other words, the influence of organized groups is in inverse proportion to the magnitude of the issues with which they are concerned. On large and controversial issues, MCs are in little need of information: they can find it in the media and in their mail, they can allocate staff resources to the problem, and they were probably briefed on the issue during their campaigns. On highly charged national issues, moreover, the theory of countervailing powers is likely to apply; there will be lobbies arrayed on both sides purporting to represent substantial blocs of votes. On issues such as these, MCs are likely to rely most on their own interpretations of public moods, on cues from colleagues, and on their own judgment.[59] This in no way suggests that lobbying is unimportant or that differences in group resources are not significant. We need only to look at the Internal Revenue Code, even after the 1985 reforms, to see how an accumulation of "minor" technical amendments can snowball into a major shift in public policy. Those resources that can be converted into things MCs want (information and votes) are important, and they are not evenly distributed. Indeed:

> to suppose that everyone participates in pressure-group activity and that all interests get themselves organized in the pressure system is to destroy the meaning of this form of politics. The pressure system makes sense only as the political instrument of a segment of the community. It gets results by being selective and biased; *if everybody got into the act the unique advantages of this form of organization would be destroyed.*[60]

———————— ✳ ————————

CONCLUSION: THE WASHINGTON COMMUNITY

In a real if not a legal sense, a lobbyist is anyone who wants to get something done in government. When one chooses to fight his or her battles on the legislative terrain of Washington's Capitol Hill, he or she becomes part of a large, highly diverse group of more or less well-organized policy advocates. Whether or not one actively seeks to form alliances with any of these existing groups, every policy advocate must be sensitive to their existence. Regardless of how remote your issue may seem from the concerns of any existing group, every lobbyist in Washington is a rival, if only for time.

Think of it simply as a question of numbers. There are, at a minimum, some 15,000 lobbyists in the Washington community. There are 535 members of the House and Senate, each of whom, in addition to talking with lobbyists, is serving half a million or more constituents, thinking about reelection, attending committee meetings, voting on issues, studying issues, and perhaps leaving some time for family and friends. Every minute that an MC or a staff aide spends with a lobbyist, moreover, is time that he or she is not spending doing what the lobbyist wants. The first job of any policy advocate is to get in the door. And that puts him or her in direct competition with every other lobbyist.

There is a more direct sense in which lobbyists must be aware of one another. "The outcome of every conflict," E. E. Schattschneider says, "is determined by the *extent* to which the audience becomes involved in it . . . [and] by the *scope* of its contagion."[61] Any one or all of the groups represented in Washington is a potential ally or foe; how many become that, and to what extent, is likely to be even more important to the success or failure of your efforts than anything you do yourself.

3

---- ✳ ----

THE LEGISLATIVE TERRAIN

T|he accepted norm of casual conversation on the Hill is not to ask "What do you do?" but rather "Who are you with?" The question underscores, better than academic prose, the representative quality of most jobs in this most political of American communities. Most folks you encounter on the Hill are "with" either an interest group, an executive agency, or a member of the Congress of the United States. It is this last group, the 435 members of the House and 100 senators, that are the center of attention.

---- ✳ ----

THE MEMBERS

Since it first convened in 1789, Congress has been an overwhelmingly male, white, middle-aged institution dominated by MCs who are considerably more affluent and better educated than the citizens they represent. The fact that MCs are drawn from a distinctive demographic elite is interesting, though not necessarily significant. For example, if holders of graduate degrees are overrepresented, there is no evidence that the more educated members of the Congress exhibit distinctive patterns of ideology, vote as a bloc, or follow any consistent pattern of educated behavior in making decisions. If the underrepresentation of blacks, women, and others has more important implications, one cannot automatically assume that electing more of them would produce changes in policy. Poor people who become MCs, for example, are no longer poor, and it is quite possible that some of their attitudes might shift with their incomes. Similarly, to demonstrate a causal connection between social origins and political behavior it is not sufficient to show simply that Catholic senators, women, or whatever behave differently. A correlation between social background and voting behavior "does not prove that the relationship is necessarily a causal one."[1]

Despite these caveats, important inferences can be made about the nature of the legislative struggle from the data on social origins. The very factors that lead to the choice of a political career are reinforced by the preferences of political elites and the electorate to produce a distinctive set of behavioral tendencies. These tendencies are important independent variables in understanding the legislative struggle. Without minimizing the importance of the legislative environment or of the rules and procedures of the Congress itself, we do not start with a blank slate. What F. Scott Fitzgerald said of the rich is true of MCs: they're different from us.

In part the difference *is* a question of social status. MCs are likely, by reason of background and upbringing, to be more comfortable socially with middle- and upper-class citizens. Even where there is a strong effort to represent a diverse constituency, subtle questions of attitude and demeanor sometimes emerge. In the 1991 Senate hearings on Justice Thomas's nomination to the Supreme Court, the all-male Senate Judiciary Committee was, in the eyes of many observers, markedly insensitive to the charges of sexual harassment brought by Professor Anita Hill.

Among those upper-status Americans who might fit the typical demographic model, the legislative elite tends to be drawn from a still more narrow slice. About two-thirds are drawn from brokerage occupations such as law, public relations, insurance, and real estate. It is a rare scientist or doctor who goes to Congress. Except for an occasional senator like Frank Lautenberg (D-NJ), corporate executives are even more scarce. Most important, perhaps, virtually all MCs have previously held office. The average rate of biennial turnover in both the House and Senate is around 15 percent. Even in 1992—when reapportionment, voluntary retirements, and an unhappy electorate produced the highest turnover rate in modern history—more than three-quarters had been there before. Of those who haven't, the vast majority have served previously in political offices at the local level.

Electoral Roots

The unrepresentative character of the Washington community is balanced, to some degree, by the electoral connection that keeps members in regular contact with the folks back home. Former Speaker "Tip" O'Neill's aphorism that "all politics is local" expresses a widely shared perspective on the job of being an MC. The Congress, as James Madison dryly observed, is "so constituted as to support in the members an habitual recollection of their dependence on the people."[2] But even to the extent that this dependence has a local focus, not all of the folks back home appear equally important. In almost every campaign the aspiring MC looks to a core of ten to twenty people for basic support. Beginning among friends and neighbors, this core expands according to the needs of the campaign but is likely to remain remarkably stable. As the people to whom the candidate "has entrusted his political career," they become the center of his or her effective constituency. "He knows them by name, as individuals. He thinks of them as his friends."[3]

If we imagine these personal friends as forming a small circle around the MC, the next ring is what Richard Fenno calls "the primary constituency: the strongest supporters."[4] These may not be on a first-name basis with the candidate, but they are the constituents who are there when it counts with campaign contributions or volunteer efforts. Frequently, this primary constituency has an ideological or partisan base. It might include fellow feminists, reform Democrats, or Vietnam veterans; perhaps blacks or small businessmen. Members of the primary constituency, to borrow a term from social psychology, become reference groups for MCs, those referred to as "my" people.

The third circle is more anonymous and less easily defined. Focusing on incumbents, Fenno calls it the "reelection constituency." We prefer John Kingdon's more inclusive phrase, the "supporting coalition."[5] Although not all politicians think in coalition terms, they do have some idea of where the votes come from. Almost always, the first reference is to party: Democrats or Republicans. Often geographic references arise: suburbanites, or the folks in Jefferson County. For nonincumbents, it is often the primary constituency, or a professional poll, that points the way for targeting the supporting coalition.

However defined, the supporting coalition is the foundation of a campaign. Smart politicians, as campaign consultant Matthew Reese advises, "pick cherries where the cherries are" by mobilizing their own voters before trying to convert others. Similarly, the supporting coalition is the likely starting point in shaping political loyalties: MCs "feel more accountable to some constituents than to others because the support of some constituents is more important than the support of others."[6] As one MC said of labor unions, "They've never supported me, and I never support them, so I'm not listening."[7]

In office, there is an initial tendency to reach for new groups; but unless redistricting or a population shift radically alters the district, the original coalition is likely to remain the MC's *effective constituency*, the people whose votes really matter when he or she looks homeward for political guidance. Fenno suggests that a reasonably secure incumbent is likely to show little interest in new supporters: "I don't have time to speak to constituents who are uncommitted," said one MC; "I'm so badgered by people to whom I'm obligated politically that I spend most of my time performing ceremonially before the people who agree with me."[8]

The largest circle of concern is the entire district, its voting citizens at least. Since the young and the poor are consistently and considerably less likely to vote in the United States than the elderly and the rich, there is bias here as well. Most candidates realize that they cannot please everyone; but all identify, in some respects, with their districts as geographical entities. Generally, incumbents extract the most mileage from this circle of potential support, particularly in performing the constituent services known as casework. If the district as a whole is not a direct political force, its impact may be significant in structuring the ways in which representatives and constituents perceive their relationship. If voters view their MCs in service rather than policy terms, the representative relationship is different. And if MCs think in terms of protecting geographic interests, policy is particularized and insulated from electoral control.[9] The MC who thinks in these terms, in the words of a disgruntled aide, "would be beholden no longer to philosophical, moral, or visionary definitions, or even the political and legislative issues the congressman voted on. Money for the congressional district in the form of specific federal spending projects would become our measure—a definition that all but guaranteed success."[10]

There are MCs—a growing number, we suspect—whose "inner circles" consist essentially of hired guns. For some gregarious members, the lines between circles blur in a sunburst of affability. And there are, as Fenno noted, significant changes over time. Once they have expanded their supporting constituencies to the point where they feel relatively secure of reelection, most members enter a more consolidative phase. Barring higher ambition or a dramatic change in the political environment, congressional "home styles" and the images of the district associated with them are remarkably stable. Having found a pattern that works, the tendency is to cultivate "the same supportive coalition election after election."[11]

The Expanded Constituency

No policy advocate is more effective than one who can deliver votes back home. Some organized interests are able to transcend district lines and become, in effect, adjuncts to an MC's constituency. Some MCs "adopt" constituents who live outside the geographic boundaries of their districts. If the first law of political survival demands staying in touch with district opinion, it is almost unavoidable that as MCs gain seniority they gain Washington "constituencies" that make the district increasingly less visible. Having reached Fenno's "protectionist" phase of relatively safe margins back home and a growing sense of the "competing tugs of a Washington career," they confront important turning points.[12] Even some of the second-term members interviewed by John Bibby found that "a lot of stuff with the constituents I delegate to a good staff," or that "I spend more of my time in committee and on legislative stuff than I did before."[13]

As the legislative career lengthens, the effective constituency expands. In the first campaign, a member of the House or Senate is likely to receive campaign contributions primarily from local sources, to get issue advice from local groups and friends, and to think largely in local terms. Once in Washington, he or she develops a constituency of lobbyists and colleagues who become increasingly important in both career and policy terms: local campaign workers are supplemented by staff from the Washington office and hired professionals, money will come increasingly from national groups. After three or four House terms, or during a second term in the Senate, the lure of power in Washington is likely to lead to a still greater "nationalization" of the effective constituency. The four circles of support—personal friends, the primary constituency, the supporting coalition, and the district as a whole—continue to exert an important pull, but they will increasingly be supplemented and displaced. Even the inner circles come to be perceived in a national context: a primary constituency rooted in local merchants becomes part of a network that includes the national Chamber of Commerce; ties with Democratic farmers back home resonate in contacts with the Farmer's Union in Washington; the concerns of blacks in your supporting coalition find sustenance in concerns of the congressional black caucus.

The Role of Money. Ideological, ethnic, and gender ties are links to expanded constituencies, but the item most likely to cross district lines is money. Campaign contributions flow freely and frequently across state and district lines; many MCs get more money from outside their districts than from within. In recent years, the political action committee (PAC) has become a major force in the system, accounting for more than one dollar of every three raised by winning candidates in the 1980s. As of 1990 a total of 4,172 political action committees were formally registered with the Federal Elections Commission.[14] They included PACs for almost every major labor union and large corporation, for trade associations, ethnic groups, and so on. Even *Time* magazine, which in 1982 wrote that "the power of PACs threatens to undermine America's system of representative democracy," had a PAC.[15]

Political money is not usually used to convert people. It is easier and safer to give to MCs whose positions you already know. This is one reason why incumbents receive more money than challengers. It is also a source of controversy in the literature. Popular articles and novels tend to depict all policy-oriented contributions as forms of bribery; politicians and many political scientists are more likely to view it as part of the system, albeit a part that can distort the process. There is general agreement that political money is seldom used openly, or even covertly, to buy votes: no experienced lobbyist is going to approach an MC and say, "Vote our way and we'll write you a check." At the same time, every candidate for Congress knows that potential contributions are related to issue positions. Lest they forget, there are occasional reminders, as in 1990 when the National Rifle Association pointedly gave Representative Jolene Unsoeld (D-WA) $4,950 the day after she introduced an amendment permitting domestic manufacture of assault guns. Whatever the effects of contributions on voting decisions may be, the one thing money does buy is access: the right to be heard. Access, as one lobbyist put it, "doesn't mean that we own them, of course. But the door is sure opened a little wider for us to get in and present our problems."[16] Through campaign contributions, a group or individual can move from the periphery to one of the inner circles of an MC's effective constituency, or at least avoid being forced to wait in the hall. PACs, according to one insider, "are basically responsive" to members and their campaign staffs who have fund-raising "down to a science."[17] Although cases of MCs retaliating politically against those groups that do not contribute appear to be "few and far between," about half of the changes in PAC contributions uncovered in one careful study were "defensive contributions to members they would rather not support."[18] Many PACs feel that they must contribute to key incumbents simply to maintain "a level playing field. We don't want the door shut in our face."[19]

Special Interests. The growing importance of PACs has been associated with a rise in the influence of special interests, corporate interests in particular. PACs certainly make such influence more visible, but it is less clear whether the thrust of influence is markedly changed from what it always was. "The hierarchical administrative structure of the corporation," as Alexander Heard's pioneering study dryly put it, "can be turned to many uses."[20] Corporate money was less visible but proportionately no less common in the days before PACs. What this suggests is that the rise of political action committees had a less dramatic impact on the sources of campaign contributions than published figures might have suggested. Until quite recently, indeed, the rise of the PAC presented, in Edward Epstein's felicitous phrase, "old wine in new bottles."[21] Heard's 1962 survey estimated that "well over 95 percent of the value of reported gifts of $500 and over made by officials of the nation's largest businesses were made on behalf of Republican candidates."[22] Other things being equal, about the same could probably be said about the contributions of corporate PACs in the 1990s. Other things, however, are not equal: PACs have always been far more likely to take account of strategic variables, incumbency in particular, than have individual contributors. Business PACs have been far more generous to incumbent Democrats, "particularly in the Democratically controlled House." Otherwise, it has usually been argued, "they support promising nonincumbent Republicans as part of a long-term strategy aimed at electing a more Republican, hence more ideologically congenial, Congress."[23] No longer. Even in open seats, it now seems that the bulk of PAC money leans less toward ideology than toward power.

There remains a tilt toward the Republican party in overall contributions that was particularly manifest in 1980 and 1984 when the party's presidential candidates seemed especially strong. The dominant tendency, however, is toward support of incumbents of the party in power. The most important change from the 1970s to the 1990s has been for PACs to support not only the majority's incumbents but their challengers as well. Even in open seats, when Democrats have a House or Senate majority, they are able to "out-PAC" Republicans.

Despite their increasing ability to attract corporate campaign funds, Democratic MCs are considerably less likely than Republicans to take a generally probusiness position on major issues. The fact that so much business money now flows into the campaign coffers of "antibusiness" candidates is a source of major frustration to Republican party leaders. At the same time, many Democrats are concerned about the cumulative erosion in the party's record on issues associated with these funding patterns. "Democrats," R. Kenneth Godwin argues, "will not support business interests when they are pitted against an organized group that can provide an alternative source of electoral support in line with traditional Democratic ideology." Problems arise when "business interests are opposed by unorganized interests such as the poor" or in cases of low-visibility issues of concern only to very small numbers of special interest representatives.[24]

For example, two resolutions passed by the House in 1982 exempted professionals from Federal Trade Commission regulations and overruled a set of FTC regulations on used car dealers. Studying the House votes on these issues, Kirk Brown found a marked tendency for Democrats in particular to respond to political action committee contributions regardless of ideology. "In short, despite their party's pledge to support consumer protection, Democrats rather than Republicans were more likely to respond to PAC money."[25] While issues such as these do not dramatically shift the overall orientations of the two parties, the accumulation of many special interest policies can have the same ultimate effect.

Perhaps the clearest impact of political action committees has been to reinforce the already substantial advantages of incumbents seeking reelection. Whether PACs significantly distort the process in other ways is a source of continuing controversy. On marginal issues of particular concern to rather narrow interests, such as the FTC rules on used cars, it is possible to show a strong relationship, transcending ideology, between PAC contributions and specific issues. The suggestion that PACs underlie the rise of special interest politics and bias the system in their favor overstates the case. PACs are useful adjuncts to interest group activities; if campaign contributions from Washington-based organizations were prohibited, most patterns of access and influence would remain untouched.

None of this belies the importance of political money. Talking with politicians, as one businessman puts it, "is a fine thing but with a little money they hear you better."[26] If it seldom buys an election, it has been known to rent a campaign or two. And the area of campaign finance is one in which the upper-class bias of the U.S. electoral system is most nakedly revealed. Poor people, as a rule, are less likely to run for office, to participate in candidate recruitment, to be active in campaigns, or even to vote; but they can, and sometimes do, engage in all these activities. Campaign finance is the one path of influence that the poor, and most of the middle class, are by definition denied. Insofar as money provides a system of representation, the system is one that overwhelmingly favors the business community. Corporate and trade association PACs provide a majority of PAC dollars, but "most business money does not even arrive through the PAC mechanism."[27] Individual donors remain the single largest source of campaign finances and wealthy businesspeople the largest source of individual contributions.

✳

STAFF

A lot of people work on Capitol Hill. If we count only those directly employed by the House and Senate, there were more than twenty-three thousand in 1989.[28] That's less than the State Department, but more than the departments of Education, Energy, or Labor. A private-sector employer the size of the Congress would rank among the largest one hundred in the United States.

Sources of Staff

Although there is a hard core of long-termers on the Hill, particularly on committee staffs, short tenure is the rule. The Obey Commission found that more than half of committee personnel and almost three-fifths of member office staff had been employed for less than two years. Recognizing that Capitol Hill is a good place to be *from* more than 40 percent are still in their twenties.[29] Given long hours and dubious compensations, professional levels are remarkably high. Committee aides are more likely to have technical backgrounds and to be drawn from the Washington community than are the more locally recruited, "liberally educated generalists" of member staffs;[30] but in both ranks the number appointed only because of political contacts is small and shrinking.[31]

The staff allowance for House members allows an average of about seventeen personal staff persons per office; senators, depending on their state's population, may have as many as a hundred. Typically (though many variations make it difficult to generalize) the highest paid aide is the administrative assistant (AA), sometimes called the chief of staff or executive secretary. At a salary of between $40,000 and $90,000, the AA is the top staff person in seven of every ten offices.[32] In about fifty House offices, the district office director or the press secretary is the top aide. In only about thirty is the legislative assistant (LA) the highest paid.[33] The AA is usually the MC's closest confidant, the staff person most likely to be from the district and to have been part of the member's original core constituency. Legislative aides (again recognizing that generalization is difficult) are likely to be "Hill rats,"[34] hired more for their knowledge of the Washington world than for their connections with the member. Few representatives or senators assign more than a third of their staff lines to legislative affairs: district services and press relations take priority.

In the Senate, it is not uncommon for the top LA to get as few as three or four hours a week of the senator's time. Because of his or her closeness to the member, it is sometimes better for a policy advocate to have access to the AA than the LA. In the case of more senior members, the preferred route of access is often through an MC's committee or subcommittee staffers. Here, too, they are likely to find considerably more subject-matter expertise, though it is the rare hill rat who is professionally trained. Most staffpersons, at all levels, are lawyers or liberal arts–trained generalists.

Under the 1946 reorganization, committee staff members were to be elected by majority vote "without regard to political affiliations." In practice, appointments fell largely into the hands of committee chairs and ranking minority members. Two patterns emerged. By one, a clear division is made between staff members assigned to the majority and minority. By the other, staff members are allocated to the various subjects covered by the committee. Although this latter system is described as "nonpartisan" or "task-oriented," it has often served as a thinly veiled device for denying staff to the minority. Dispersion of powers to subcommittees has helped spread the availability of staff assistants among committee members, and most committees—especially in the House—

currently allow the minority party to fill about a third of professional slots. To this day, however, there are committees and subcommittees that are staffed effectively by the majority party, and many more in which staff members are essentially responsible to the chair or ranking minority member. The Obey Commission heard numerous complaints from junior members of both parties about staff help.[35]

In the most common pattern, majority and minority have distinctive offices and roles. On these committees, "Majority staff often view themselves as the major 'legislation writers,' with minority staff included in decision making primarily when votes are needed or for reasons of legislative strategy."[36] The minority staff also serves as a point of access for lobbyists whose positions have been rejected across the hall. Patterns are similar on subcommittees, but loyalty to the chair or ranking minority member is the norm.[37]

Staff Power

Studies of bureaucracy are full of examples of middle-level administrators using technical knowledge to defy nominal superiors. Capitol Hill would seem susceptible to the establishment of such independent operations, particularly those in which professional staffs, through long relationships with counterpart executive agencies, could develop independent working agreements. Arthur Maass offers as an example a case in which "abnormally close relations" between the Environmental Protection Agency and a Senate subcommittee "tended to exclude from decision making on environmental policy not only the White House but also the full Congress." Under the direction of the subcommittee chairman, Senator Edmund Muskie (D-ME), the committee staff drafted statutory language so complex that even the top agency people had trouble comprehending what the bill did. "On at least one occasion, the staff drafted language that may have been intended to mislead the Congress."[38]

The author is quick to point out that this situation arose in the Watergate period of a weakened president, and it is unlikely that the staff could have gotten very far without the tacit support of Senator Muskie. Usually, too, there are countervailing forces: minority staff, other agencies, private groups. From the staff perspective, nonetheless, policy is the name of the game. Many come to the Hill out of loyalty, an interest in seeing things from the inside, or a desire for experience; but especially for the overworked and underpaid, such motives wear thin. What keeps the juices flowing is the sense of having an impact, of knowing that your idea is embodied in law.

Staffs generate ideas and work: "once a staff person gets a certain area of expertise, he is forever handing you a bunch of memos and saying you ought to get into this and you ought to get into that."[39] In extremes, "members find themselves serving staff."[40] This seeming autonomy, however, is largely a function of an ability to anticipate member preferences, much "as any attorney would for a client in a parallel situation outside Congress."[41] Although this does not preclude policy entrepreneurship, it puts it in a member-focused context. The concept of loyalty, important throughout the Hill, is most clearly manifested at the individual staff level. "The guiding principle . . . is to place the member's interest above all else."[42]

The growth of staff, Michael Malbin concluded, has given MCs more but not necessarily better information, since there are now even more assumptions and contradictions to question.[43] Although added staff resources have given individual MCs and committees more tools for screening information and outside influences, they have also given lobbyists and other policy advocates more points of access. One of the main consequences of staff growth, paradoxically, may have been to increase the legislature's need for help. It is perhaps tacit recognition of this fact, as much as media attacks on congressional perks, that have stalled the growth of the legislative bureaucracy. The total number of Capitol Hill employees is about the same now as it was in 1975.

A relatively small proportion of staffers, moreover, have policy roles. Whether or not an MC physically distinguishes the two functions by placing many of his aides in the district office, most assign at least half of their aides to constituency-oriented and clerical chores. A crowded office is not necessarily busier on legislative issues than one with fewer hands on deck, as a growing number of representatives and senators put their local people to work back at home. The tricky part, from the perspective of an outsider, lies in trying to figure out who in the legislative shop is worth seeing. When the MC is busy, are you being given quality time by someone who will then brief the member, or are you being diverted away to a staff person with no clout? This is a particularly sensitive question in the Senate, where staff aides themselves often have trouble getting on the senator's personal calendar.

---------------- ✳ ----------------

ORGANIZATION

For many years, conventional wisdom had it that legislatures were dominated either by strong committees or by strong parties. The British-style cabinet, it was said, could not tolerate the rivalry of a viable committee system. World (and even British) parliamentary realities are far more complex. The British Parliament has been and remains one of the world's most highly centralized legislatures; the U.S. Congress one of the least. As in most organizations, however, the dynamic of power is constantly changing.

Specialization and the Congressional Division of Labor

The committee system in Congress closely resembles a classic bureaucratic division of labor in which fields of specialization are closely related to the functional needs of the organization. Each subunit is generally responsible to the less-specialized unit above (subcommittees report to full committees, and full committees to the general membership of each house). There is a relatively high degree of professionalization: members of the Agriculture Committee, for example, are usually familiar with farm policy problems and specialize in them during their careers in Congress. As in most bureaus there are both "line" units (such as Agriculture, Armed Services, and Interior) that process the main "products" of the organization, and "staff" units (such as Appropriations, Budget, and Rules) that provide support for these main line activities.[44] The congressional division of labor closely resembles that of the executive branch. Logic, of course, would suggest such symmetry. The same reasoning that would lead the House and Senate to create a Department of Energy would, one would think, lead to the creation of Energy Committees to oversee it.

The "imperious authority of the standing committees," to use Woodrow Wilson's classic phrase, represents more than a convenient division of labor. Committee and subcommittee autonomy decentralizes legislative power and helps maintain the autonomy of the U.S. Congress. It follows that access to key committees is an important source of power. Just as interest groups have fought to have their programs represented as close to the top of the bureaucracy as possible, preferably at the Cabinet level, so have countless groups agitated to create or maintain their own subcommittees and, better yet, full committees.

Structuring the Committee System. Since the birth of the standing committee system, there has never been a period that has not been enlivened by jurisdictional conflict. Decentralization, manifested in the rising powers of subcommittees, has added to the seeming confusion. In part this is due to subject-matter complexity: the problems of legislative policy are so interrelated that it would be impossible ever to eliminate overlapping areas. Even if this miracle could be achieved, new subjects would arise (as with energy issues in the 1970s) that were not foreseen in the original pattern.

Jurisdictional conflicts are also due to the efforts of pressure groups and executive agencies to have legislation they want referred to friendly committees and legislation they oppose to hostile ones. In addition, they arise from the interest of individual members, particularly committee and subcommittee chairs, in expanding their personal power and prestige. If nothing scares a bureaucrat more than the prospect of reorganization, nothing more nakedly reveals concerns for legislative turf than periodic battles to formally restructure the committee system. Explaining the failure of the Bolling Committee reforms in 1975, two close observers suggest that its proposed "jurisdictional package threatened too many careers and jurisdictional patterns to gain passage."[45] Not only were MCs and committee staff highly sensitive to perceived losses of control, but many important interest groups preferred "to preserve and protect established relationships, even at the risk of forging new ones that might ultimately prove more fruitful for them."[46] Many observers are predicting a similar fate for the proposals of the reform committee created in 1992.

Careful draftsmanship can help to steer a bill toward one or another committee. The proper choice of sponsors and a friendly attitude on the part of the presiding officer will also contribute. In the Senate, the traditional respect for the prerogatives of the individual senator has meant that considerable attention is paid to the sponsor's wishes concerning the committee to which his or her bill should be referred: indeed, Vice President John Nance Garner often boasted that he *always* honored the sponsors' wishes for referral. Tightened rules have made Garner's successors less generous, and committee shopping has always been difficult in the House. Indeed, committee chairs, particularly in the House, are likely to have a good deal more clout than bill sponsors in cases of dispute. Sometimes an open jurisdictional struggle on the floor of the House or Senate occurs, as in 1977 when a reluctant Senate Commerce Committee reported a bill deregulating the trucking industry in part to forestall a Judiciary Committee "raid" on its jurisdiction.[47] House leaders have resorted increasingly to multiple referrals as a means of avoiding such disputes, a tactic that makes the job of policy advocates infinitely more complex.

In committee operations, possession is often nine points of the law, and possession can often be determined not by what bills are referred to a committee but by what comes out. The only formal limitations on what may be reported relate to appropriations. Committees other than the Appropriations committees are not allowed to actually appropriate funds. Likewise, the rules forbid Appropriations committees from including legislative provisions in their appropriations measures. Substantive committees have learned to evade these restrictions by sheltering funds from the appropriations process by devising various "obligational" formulae. Even the strict House rule against legislating in appropriation bills has been so frequently bypassed under suspension of the rules or general consensus that it is almost a dead letter.

Subcommittee Rules and Roles. The committee reforms of the 1970s required all House committees to create a minimum number of subcommittees with clearly defined jurisdictions. As with attempts to define full committee jurisdictions, however, changes in the formal rules have not substantially altered the underlying political forces. The fate of a particular bill is sometimes decided before it is formally introduced when committee and subcommittee jurisdictions and memberships are decided. The fate of a 1983 automobile airbag bill, for example, "was sealed at the beginning of the Ninety-seventh Congress, when Congressman John D. Dingell, as chairman of the Committee on Energy and Commerce, eliminated the subcommittee to have been headed up by New York Congressman James Scheuer, who favored such legislation."[48]

Although the long-range trend since the reorganization of 1946 has been toward subcommittee government and the dispersion of legislative power, a graph of these tendencies does not follow a straight line. As subcommittees are created, so are they destroyed. The numerical proliferation of subcommittees, moreover, does not necessarily point to a corresponding increase of role. Indeed, figures compiled by Steven Smith and Christopher Deering show a surprisingly mixed pattern with differences between the House and Senate being particularly striking. The House, as expected, has been substantially decentralized:

> a majority of the meetings at which substantive policy decisions are made . . . now are held in subcommittee. . . .
>
> In contrast, the aggregate Senate pattern has remained unchanged. Most referred and reported legislation is not sent to subcommittee. The Senate is far more full committee-oriented, and senators can participate more fully in shaping major legislation there than in the House.[49]

Do these changes, particularly in the House, make a difference in terms of the nature and outcome of the legislative struggle? A transfer of power to smaller units seems almost certain to have policy and oversight implications. It "gives members even more opportunities to develop strong political ties to special interests and agency officials in an environment where more neutral or critical members and outside interests are absent."[50] The triangles of interest developed in the narrowly focused subgovernments that result were, paradoxically, a target of many reformers in the 1970s. The tendency is particularly deplored by "those who take a negative stance toward interest-group politics," but it is "highly functional" for those, like Heinz Eulau, who see it as "enhancing the access of interested publics to the legislative struggle."[51]

Whether the devolution of activity to the subcommittee level in the House has given special interests a greater lock on policy or served simply to enhance the access of a broader spectrum of groups depends in part on the committee in question. Different committees, as Fenno shows, have different decision rules, structures, and norms.[52] Smith and Deering found even greater variety in the decision-making patterns of Senate committees. Writing of the House Foreign Affairs Committee in 1973, Fenno said that "The crucial fact about these subcommittees is simply that very little happens there. With the exception of the subcommittee handling State Department regulations, they report out almost no legislation. Their function is one of information gathering, to which end they hold hearings and consume information. Members . . . describe them as 'really minor things dealing with picayune matters.' "[53] This would appear to be the present reality on most Senate and some House committees. Even where subcommittees go beyond information gathering and "picayune matters," the overall decision-making patterns and norms of the full committee may vitiate their power roles. Even after a series of reforms that apparently unleashed the subcommittees of the House Foreign Affairs and Banking Committees, the real locus of power was not much changed: "the reforms of the 1970s have not decentralized decision making as much as they have broadened participation."[54]

Despite such variations, the general trend has been toward the decentralization of real power. Particularly in the so-called constituency committees, those dealing with largely distributive issues, the model of autonomous subcommittees is more the norm. "The Committee," as one member of House Interior put it, is "a rubber-stamp of subcommittee decisions. . . . We often do not even have a quorum in the full committee when we pass on subcommittee bills."[55]

Party Organizations

In a parliamentary system, the leader of the majority party becomes, in effect, the chief of state. The members of the majority party go on to elect his or her Cabinet, and the minority party (or parties) elects a "would be" leadership of its own. Separation of powers in the United States produces a different system of party leadership that brings a rather different sort of leadership to the fore.

The roles of both party and committee leaders in the United States are considerably more ambiguous than those of their counterparts in most other democracies. Even when their party controls the government, the speaker and Senate majority leader are at once the president's most important allies and most significant rivals. They are, in European terms, part of the government even as they are part of its opposition. Because the electoral constituencies and election terms of senators, representatives, and presidents are not coterminous, they look to different constituencies.

The constituents of the leaders of the congressional parties are their fellow members. Elected by the party caucus, they serve at its pleasure, so much so that Roger Davidson is not far off in his whimsical suggestion that the very words "congressional leadership" may be "a contradiction in terms."[56] This is true, fundamentally, of all leaders: generals, coaches, bureau chiefs, and presidents are in a sense agents, too. There is a fairly strong consensus among students of Congress, however, that party leaders, more than most, are highly dependent upon the expectations of their followers. The process of choosing party leaders, moreover, is very much an inside game. Interest groups can and sometimes do have an impact on the structure and staffing of subcommittees and full committees; seldom are they a factor in party leadership contests.

Although the Senate is formally presided over by the vice president and led by the president pro tempore,[57] the real leaders of both houses are elected by the party caucuses. In the Senate the key positions are those of minority and majority leaders. Their deputies and various leadership committees may or may not play important roles or even meet. Not until Howard Baker (R-TN) became minority leader in 1976 did Senate Republicans have anything that could be described as a formal whip organization. When Democratic Majority Leader George Mitchell (D-ME) began convening regular meetings of the Policy Committee in 1989, it was the first time in twelve years that this seemingly important body had met.[58]

Although the personal preferences of House leaders also affect the uses made of other party leaders and committees, House party structures are less flexible. Party organizations in the House are also far more visible in the functioning of the institution than they are in the Senate. The largest and most visible leadership organization in the Congress is the majority party whip organization of the House. Including nearly a third of the members of the Democratic caucus, the primary functions of the whip organization are communication and monitoring. It is an interesting commentary on the nature of the Congress that its most elaborate central guidance organization is essentially an intelligence agency.

In a broad sense, the role of the leadership is analogous to that of a central bank. Unlike the standing committees (who, to stretch the analogy, are like business firms), the leadership produces nothing; but it processes most big transactions, serves as a central clearing house through which all major deals must clear, keeps records of who owes what to whom, and—like a bank—extracts interest and fees in exchange for its services.

Centralizing Committees

Although party leaders are the most visible instruments of central guidance in the Congress—as standing committees are the most viable agents of decentralization—there are committees, five in particular, that often play centralizing roles. These are the House Rules Committee, and the Budget and Appropriations Committees of both houses.

Since the speaker regained control over majority party membership of the Rules Committee, it has tended to function as an arm of the leadership. Its performance, in this respect, has tended to be protective of committee majorities as well. To further complicate its role, the Committee is beholden in the broadest sense to the House majority. When the Rules Committee becomes too subservient to the speaker, as it did in the early 1970s, it will be unable to get its decisions ratified on the floor. In balancing demands from its three "constituencies," House Rules occupies a unique position in the legislative system. It has no Senate counterpart, and its role as an instrument of central control, as an adjunct of committee government, and sometimes as an independent policy force has shifted from one year to the next. We classify the Rules Committee as a centralizing force because it has tended, in most sessions, to act as a brake on allocation. Under the most recent speakers—Jim Wright and Tom Foley—the Rules Committee has become a major force in shaping the strategic contexts within which legislation is considered on the floor.

The traditional distinction is between open and closed rules, the latter being one that, in essence, does not allow a bill to be amended on the House floor. Since the 1970s, however, the Rules Committee has become increasingly creative in devising variations. Rules are becoming increasingly specific as to precisely what kinds of amendments will be allowed, who can offer them, and when. On most controversial bills, "prospective amendment sponsors normally have to prepare their amendments well in advance, appear before the Rules Committee to explain the importance of their amendments and why they should be included in the rule, and perhaps appeal to the Democratic leadership for assistance in getting the amendments to the floor."[59]

Taken together, the combination of "closed" and "complex"[60] rules increased from 12 percent in the 94th Congress (1975–76) to almost 22 percent in the 99th (1985–86). Other kinds of restrictions have reduced the number of truly open rules, in which all kinds of amendments are allowed, to just over half of the bills reported (down to 55 percent in 1985–86 from almost 85 percent in 1975–76), and to fewer than 15 percent on major issues.[61] This does not count the growing number of bills bypassing the Rules Committee entirely under suspension and other fast-tracking procedures.

The leadership's increasing resort to restrictive rules has been enormously frustrating to Republicans, who, overwhelmed in committee, are denied the satisfaction of even forcing the majority Democrats to cast embarrassing votes on the floor. Even within the majority party, the Rules Committee is caught on the horns of a dilemma pitting central control and its associated values against dispersed powers. At the same time, the size of the House combines with the complexity of many issues to necessitate if not a Rules committee, something very much like it.

If a program involves money, it must also involve the Appropriations committees. In Fenno's classic study, House Appropriations was depicted as a cohesive body whose budget-cutting norm produced frequent conflicts with the more generous authorizing committees. There were some areas, such as public works, where the norm was not as strong; others, such as defense (not covered by Fenno), where it may have been inoperative.[62] By the late 1960s, moreover, the appropriations process proved itself less immune to the programmatic fragmentation that characterizes the committee system, and other committees had become increasingly adept at putting their programs in budget categories that were beyond the reach of the appropriations process. A growing sense that subcommittee government and the politics of allocation had put the process out of control was an important factor in the 1974 creation of the House and Senate Budget Committees.

As instruments of central control, it would be difficult to match the effectiveness of the Budget Committees in constraining the options available to the other committees in 1981. However, that session's reconciliation battle marked a high watermark. Budget's ability to cap other committee spending plans has steadily eroded with the committee's basic functions having been fundamentally undermined by the so-called budget summit of 1990. Here, the agreements reached in a series of meetings between President Bush and the House and Senate party leaders in effect performed the committee's work for the next three years. Working through the Appropriations Committee, moreover, MCs have become increasingly adept at avoiding caps and limits by sneaking over-the-limit new expenditures through the back door of so-called supplemental appropriations.

Whether working as arms of the leadership, as quasi-independent forces, or under the umbrella of leader agreements that limit their options, the five centralizing committees briefly analyzed here have tended to act as brakes on allocation. Just as party leaders are weaker in the Senate, so are its centralizing committees. This makes it somewhat easier for policy advocates to get what they want from the Senate as opposed to the House. But there is one more force of restraint to consider.

Procedural "Hierarchy"

One way of resolving conflicts is to discourage innovation. If policy advocates believe it is pointless to try, there will be few proposals for change; if proposals for change are rare, conflicts are unlikely to be serious. When an organization delegates power to district offices, specialized agencies, or outsiders, it can often postpone or delay conflict. If resources are scarce, however, such allocational strategies ultimately bring the chickens home to roost: priorities must be set. Centralizing committees and party leaders have sometimes played the role of villain, telling the patrons that there is no free lunch. And they have, with perhaps greater frequency, delegated that role to the president. From its early days, however, Congress has reinforced its nay-saying ability with a uniquely complex set of procedures. Although these patterns are often associated with hierarchical forms, it is conceivable to organize the pattern of decision-making in such ways as to encourage innovation and teamwork. Similarly, collegial bodies may or may not employ serial patterns of decision-making. Unlike the Congress, for example, where a negative decision by X (a standing committee) virtually precludes action by Y (the House or Senate as a whole), most state legislatures require their committees to report all bills back to the floor with either a positive or negative recommendation. In most parliamentary systems there are only two effective points of decision-making, the cabinet and the general assembly.

The Congress of the United States in this respect is the most procedurally hierarchic of world legislatures. Nowhere is there a more complex pattern of serial decision-making. Nowhere is the veto more emphasized. The Congressional system, as Robert Bendiner colorfully describes it, recalls

> those beloved but nerve-wracking board games of childhood in which a series of perils had to be survived before one's counter could be brought safely home. According to a throw of the dice or a number spun on a dial, a player would advance his counter along a winding and colorfully pictured path until it landed on a space bearing some legend as "Fall in Pigsty, Back Ten Spaces." . . . The obstacles were numerous and frustrating, and just as one approached the end of the journey, he was sure to confront the greatest danger of all, a space just short of the goal bearing some such inscription as "Caught in Bear Trap, Start Over."[63]

As in these board games, the serial process of decision-making in Congress introduces numerous opportunities for the delay or defeat of legislative proposals. There are, or can be, close to fifty separate pigsties and bear traps at which "a single negative action may be sufficient to defeat the bill." To put it another way, "Agreements reached must be cumulative."[64] To become law, a bill must go through a separate process in both the House and Senate and survive the threat of a presidential veto. If it involves the expenditure of funds, the number of obstacles is doubled. Defeat at any stage—in committee, on a procedural motion, in the Senate or House, in one of the appropriations committees— almost invariably means starting all over again.

This complex and cumbersome system is designed to protect MCs from their own greed. Serial decision-making serves as the functional equivalent of central control in the allocation of resources. As might be expected, it is most rigorously applied to situations involving the expenditure of money, and lightly applied to situations that do not. Legislation requiring federal funds, for example, is triple-filtered through the system: it can or must be part of the overall targets set by budget resolutions; it must pass all obstacles as *authorizing* legislation and be signed into law; then it must clear a similar obstacle course for the *appropriation* of money, the amount of which cannot exceed (and is usually less than) the amount authorized. At the other extreme, there is almost no institutional control over costless or nearly costless credit-claiming activities: individual members are virtually unrestricted in their ability to send out newsletters, do constituent casework, introduce bills, insert material in the *Congressional Record*, and so on.

CONCLUSION: THINKING ABOUT ACCESS

In a broad sense, there are two systems of formal power in each house: the elected party leaders and their appointed deputies in the party system, and the seniority-based committee and subcommittee leaders of the committee system. They are, in general terms, rivals for power; the former represent the forces of centralization, the latter decentralization and the division of labor. Roles and powers, to be sure, are seldom fixed. To understand how power is divided among committees or enforced by the leadership, it would be futile to chart the power wielders and list the office holders for any given year. A few years later both list and chart would be out of date.

Congress is not simply a formal organization, it is a social institution in which informal norms of behavior supplement and supersede the formal rules. No matter how good our theories of organization or how thorough our understanding of a particular organization may be, most important decisions are ultimately made through "The Fateful Process of Mr. A Talking to Mr. B."[65] Who talks to whom and with what effect? We all know intuitively that people communicate differently in different settings. A lawyer talking to another lawyer says things differently than in talking to his or her spouse, child, or dog. Formal organization, nonetheless, is important.

The structure of the U.S. Congress facilitates lobbying. Because committees and, in some arenas, subcommittees play so important a role in shaping the details of legislation, most lobbyists can focus their attentions on a few key members. High reelection rates mean that the key faces don't change very often, so that access gained is likely to last. The committee or personal offices of these MCs, moreover, usually include one or more staff persons who are sufficiently close to the member to speak authoritatively on his or her behalf. In this sense, it would be difficult to conceive of a legislature better designed to facilitate special interest lobbying.

On the other side of the coin, there are two serious impediments to policy advocacy of this kind. First, the main outlines of most decisions are beyond the immediate control of most policy advocates. For good reason, politicians are wedded to the core constituencies and electoral coalitions that put them there the last time. PAC money can help insinuate a new group into an MC's supporting coalition, but it takes time. The general outlines of the votes on most major issues are set. The second problem for those outside the system is the series of checkpoints on committee government that have been built into the decision-making system. Subsystem majorities can be sufficient on relatively trivial and uncontested details of legislation, but your opponents—if you have any—have many cracks at undoing what committees do. It is much easier to block action in the Congress than to get it.

4

※

ESTABLISHING
INFLUENCE

I n a body as large and diverse as the Congress of the United States, it should
come as no surprise that some members are more important than others.
Short-range tactics relating to specific bills will be discussed in subsequent chapters. In surveying the terrain, however, a policy advocate must be sensitive both
to the questions of structure and formal role described in Chapter 3, and to the
informal norms and codes of behavior that make some legislators more important than others. Our focus here is on the strategies an individual MC might use
to increase his or her personal standing in the House or Senate—how a member,
or by extension, any policy advocate, becomes effective.

※

THE "INNER CLUB"

If there is an "Inner Club" or "Establishment" in the House or Senate, most
observers would agree that it is more difficult to locate than it was in the
1950s. In both houses, the Senate especially, formal rules have been tightened
to take up the slack created by the attenuation of collegiality. The rise of
subcommittee government in the House has "raised a large fraction of the
House membership from the relative obscurity that previously accompanied
service in the House."[1] For both the House and Senate, there are more "incentives, and rewards for nondeliberative behavior, specifically for the kind of self
promotion that serves a legislator's electoral ambitions but does not contribute
to serious reasoning about public policy."[2]

These changes have made people in Washington increasingly reluctant to
identify an Inner Club than they were three or four decades ago, but there

remains considerable consensus about which members are effective and which are not. "I haven't seen anything that can be construed as a club," one Senate staffer has said, "but you could find widespread agreement about a group of Senators—crossing ideological lines, because ideology has very little to do with prestige and power and respect around here—who are considered to be, one way or another, the movers, the heavyweights of the Senate."[3]

Ross Baker makes the same basic point about the norms, or informal codes of behavior—such as apprenticeship, specialization, and reciprocity—that were the keys to entry in the old Inner Club.

> Norms, or at least understandings which govern interpersonal behavior, persist in the Senate, but where they reside, for whom they are relevant, and by whose hands they are enforced must be reappraised. . . .
>
> What appears to have taken up the slack created by enfeebled general norms and folkways (which now seem little more than folklore) is a structure of private understandings among individual senators—not mandated from above and not eternal—which serve as the bonding agents which allow the institution to endure.[4]

Fewer MCs than in the heyday of the old Inner Club think it important to observe what seem like outdated norms. The oral tradition of party and committee leaders lecturing freshmen on how to get along, of senior members snubbing a junior colleague who dares to speak up, are relics. More issues and more subcommittees have combined to water down both the formal barriers and informal norms of specialization.

Yet even as "private understandings" seem to have displaced the more visibly sustained norms, they are not substantially different from the old folkways. In classifying colleagues, in identifying the movers and heavyweights, MCs use just about the same kinds of criteria they always have. Senior MCs are, arguably, less overbearing in their behavior. "Before the reforms in the committee system," one member says, "we were always expected to laugh at the jokes of the chairmen. After the reforms, it was amazing how funny *our* jokes became."[5] Despite such changes in the atmosphere surrounding the pathway to power on Capitol Hill, those pathways run along the same essential routes that they always have. Seniority still matters.

The Movers and Shakers

The first place to look in seeking to identify the Inner Club is at formal titles. When former Senate Majority Leader Robert Byrd described his occupation as "slave," there was irony as well as insight in his observation. As much as effective leadership is based on followership, it is also a fountain of real power. The party leaders are important; so are committee chairs.

The rise of what is called subcommittee government has combined with other reforms to expand the circle of formal leadership and, it is frequently suggested, to erode its base of formal powers. According to Norman Ornstein,

Conventional wisdom would suggest that the reforms of the 1970s that gave power to rank-and-file members and to subcommittee chairmen came at the expense of committee chairmen and other senior leaders. In addition, the series of changes that opened up congressional deliberations, through more roll-call votes on significant floor and committee decisions, and through open committee meetings and markups, took away the leaders' ability to influence their colleagues behind the scenes.[6]

This perspective both ignores important aspects of the postreform period and romanticizes the past. "It is often overlooked," Ornstein says, "that the rules changes, especially in the House, also explicitly added substantial formal powers to party leaders."[7] Even more frequently overlooked is the degree to which the power of the now-discredited Inner Club was based on personal powers of influence and persuasion. The standard for measuring the declining power of Senate leaders, for example, has always been Lyndon Baines Johnson, the prototype of the powerful majority leader.

If leadership power has declined since Johnson, it is generally overlooked how much it had increased under him. Indeed, LBJ's immediate predecessors in office—the cantankerous William F. Knowland (R-CA), the affable but ineffective Scott Lucas (D-IL), and the invisible Ernest McFarland (D-AZ)—are more footnotes to the history of the Congress than *any* of Johnson's supposedly weakened successors. In a similar vein, evidence of the "declining" power of committee chairs is often teased from extraordinary cases. Those who cite the towering presence of, say, Wilbur Mills (D-AR)—who dominated the House Ways and Means Committee in the 1960s—can of course find evidence for the declining power of committee chairs by comparing Mills with most of his successors. If, however, they were to compare the forgotten nonentities who chaired House Commerce in the 1950s with John Dingell (D-MI) of the 1980s, or the Senate wimps of the "preform" Finance Committee with Russell Long (D-LA), quite a different picture would emerge.

Whether there is or ever has been a congressional Inner Club, whether formal leadership powers have been strengthened or weakened, our point here is simply that leadership roles are crafted and won, not conferred. Formal roles are important, but now—as always—the extent of influence they provide is as broad or narrow as their holders make them: "Influence does not simply come into existence. It is the result of interactions among human beings, of their individual interests, values, and concepts of what moral rules, if any, ought to be controlling, and of their different perceptions of the situations in which they are operating."[8] In a world of perfect information and Machiavellian morals, such calculations might be simple. Influence would accrue to those who most shrewdly play to the constituency concerns of others. David Mayhew has shown that such an assumption can be used successfully to explain many facets of the legislative struggle,[9] but he would be among the first to concede that other variables are involved. MCs do not have perfect control over what it takes to win elections; they have their own opinions and peculiarities, and the group life of the legislature is also an important variable. In short, the legislative struggle for influence is multidimensional, there are no sure roads to power, and influence will derive from a blend of strategies.

Increasing Personal Regard

"Some people," Walter Murphy notes, "are blessed with a warmth and sincerity that immediately attracts other human beings."[10] Others have to work at it. Having weathered the test of campaigning for office, MCs are likely as a group to score higher on personal charm than, say, judges. But there is little doubt that some are more charming than others, and that interpersonal relations can play an important role in the group life of the legislature. "Sociability in the institutional context," Ross Baker argues in his study of the Senate, "can be very useful to a Senator."[11] Lyndon Johnson was a master of such gestures. Part of it was his extraordinary capacity for detail, for learning about what made the Senate tick. "It seemed that he got there aware of the backgrounds of most of the members, and he took the trouble to learn about the ones he didn't know about. He was like a novelist, a psychiatrist. He didn't stop until he knew how to appeal to every single senator and how to win him over."[12]

In the larger House, it may be somewhat more difficult to know all of one's colleagues. At the same time, there are more opportunities for direct personal contact. The House floor is a particularly good place to learn through observation and to meet colleagues. Since seats are not assigned, as they are in the Senate, there is more movement and interaction. Personal relationships, even those that cross party lines, are relatively common.

Strong personal friendships are relatively rare in the Senate, and even in the House, caveats apply. In the words of the late Clem Miller (D-CA):

> This intense, clubby, personal relationship constantly smacks with great force directly into the cold, cruel hardness of the vote. The close friend you were grimacing with not two minutes before votes with the other people. You may be able to shrug this off by rationalizing that "he's voting his district," but frequently it hurts. . . .
>
> This alteration between the role of buddy and executioner, in greater or lesser degree, creates great strains that often become almost intolerable.[13]

Although Baker suggests that "this incompatibility between knocking and forming friendships can be exaggerated," he goes on to note that deep friendships are rare. What are more common, he argues, are "special purpose friendships," friendships that involve only one facet of peoples' relations with each other. Friendliness, in other words, is part of the job, and the "benefits to be reaped from a social relationship clearly flow from the intramural rather than extramural variety."[14]

One of the benefits derived from sociability is insight. "It helps senators avoid dealing with each other as abstractions or bearers of political labels,"[15] and it has important effects on the struggle for power.

> While congressmen are quite ordinary in general outline, their practice of the political art has made them knowledgeable in assessing one another.

Their instincts, sharpened by this conflict of the personal and the impersonal, enable them to characterize each other to the finest hair. . . . Power . . . is the respect which accrues and adheres to those individuals who are best able to stand this daily etching process.[16]

Part of this process is purely social, which is common to most institutions. A social gesture, a speech or thank you note commending a fellow member for his or her handling of a bill, even something so simple as a warm greeting to a fellow member taking a group of constituents on a tour of the Capitol, all become part of the judging process. And there are occasions when charm alone may suffice. Miller offers an example in describing a member from Florida whose

> appearances on the Floor are always heralded with high good humor. The somber aspect of the Chamber takes on a lighter hue. Members stream in from the cloakroom. "——— is on," is the word. "Did you hear what he told them?" After one of his speeches, everyone feels better and usually the Member from Florida feels best of all. This congressman rarely speaks without a purpose, larded as it is with friendliness and cheer. . . .
>   And this man can charm the birds out of the trees. Partisan lines soften, and political gunboats cease cannonading, and the hard-bitten . . . vie with one another for the nicest things to say.

In the instance described by Miller, the Floridian was seeking to expedite a project for his district opposed by the powerful chairman of the Appropriations Committee. So deftly did he handle himself that "The committee Chairman threw up his hands and sat down. The amendment was agreed to by voice vote. Everyone was happy."[17]

Charm may carry the day on a relatively minor, local issue, and it may help in other ways as well, but the most important personality traits are those that relate more specifically to the legislative task. Baker identifies the four most important of these as empathy, integrity, diligence, and restraint.[18] Let us deal with each in turn.

Empathy, the ability to appreciate another person's position and feelings, is basic. Without some mutual understandings between people, bargaining is impossible. Just as "lack of rapport can severely limit opportunities for influencing the Court's work,"[19] insensitivity to ones' colleagues can be a source of legislative impotence. At a minimum, one expects a colleague to be able to disagree without being disagreeable, and to understand that conflict over one issue does not preclude cooperation on another. Members expect each other to play to the folks back home by sometimes attacking a colleague of different opinions, and to fight for what they believe; but they also expect a decent respect for the rights of others. Alan Simpson (R-WY) once tried to convey this distinction to his colleague Jesse Helms (R-NC) in a blistering speech on the Senate floor. Helms had launched a filibuster that, though doomed to defeat, threatened the Christmas vacations of ninety-nine other senators. "Seldom," Simpson exploded, "have I seen in my legislative experience . . . a more obdurate and obnoxious performance. I guess it's called hardball. In my neck of the woods we call it stickball. Children play it."[20] Knowing the difference between hardball and stickball is critical.

In a broader sense, empathy is at the base of a leader's ability to develop a sense of the House or Senate. Former Senate Democratic Leader Robert Byrd of West Virginia, not known for his personal warmth, is a master of counting votes. "I understand," he once said, "that I am not very well liked around here anyhow. I did not get elected to be liked here. I got elected because I thought I could do a job."[21] Like most party leaders, he has a sense of who to talk with about what. As Randall Ripley puts it, "The leaders are aware of the mix of personalities, beliefs, and district characteristics represented by their members. . . . They have an idea of the general political views that may sway his behavior."[22]

Integrity also ranks high on the list of character traits associated with personal influence. One former member commented:

> The most important thing in the Senate is credibility. . . . When someone gets up to say that something is so, and if you can have absolute reliance that he is right, *that* is credibility. And that is power. If you've done your homework and you know what you're talking about, that is power. It takes time to build up. Over the years that is one thing that has not changed in the Senate.[23]

Credibility, of course, implies integrity. Being caught in a lie is a cardinal sin: "Your personal integrity in the House is absolutely vital. We are all politicians and we all share the same code of honesty. Break it and you might as well not be here."[24] Rarely is an MC caught in an overt lie, suggesting, for example, that a bill will do X when it is really Y; but ultimate respect goes to those who take integrity a step further, who not only avoid untruth but willingly divulge the whole truth. Here, for example, is one liberal Democrat's tribute to the more conservative Russell Long (D-LA): "Long was very candid. You would ask him a question and he'd probably say, 'You don't want to vote for this,' because he'd already evaluated my ideological thinking which is different from his in many instances. Now he didn't need to gratuitously tell me that, but he'll tell me and give me the answer."[25]

Diligence and hard work also command respect and combine with integrity to enhance credibility. Despite growing reliance on staff and the increasing individualism of many members, the House and Senate remain collegial bodies. Members rely on each other for information and advice. "You *can't* be knowledgeable about every bill that comes up. But *somebody* knows *something* about the bill. . . . You've got to trust people who know more about a thing because you just don't have enough hours, enough years in your life to learn all you should."[26] It helps if diligence is accompanied by intelligence, but intelligence unaccompanied by hard work will not suffice. For those in formal positions of authority, attention to detail is vital. Ted Kennedy lost his Senate leadership position to Robert Byrd in large part because many Democrats considered Kennedy lazy.

Finally, there is the criterion of restraint, the personality trait that encourages MCs to "mutually recognize the primary natural law of political survival."[27] Like empathy, restraint implies a feeling for the political concerns of others. Some members have gone so far as to refuse to campaign against an incumbent member of either party. At a more mundane level, it involves more trivial matters of simple courtesy: not carrying on a loud conversation while other members are engaged in debate, avoiding gratuitous insults and "cheap shots," and so on. The more powerful MCs are frequently capable not just of restraining themselves but of cooling conflicts between others. Former speaker "Tip" O'Neill, though capable of intense partisanship and combativeness, had a sense of humor and timing that frequently served to defuse tense situations. He could fight hard without damaging his opponent's self-respect. Gerald Ford frequently tangled with O'Neill, first as minority leader and later as president, but he often went out of his way to describe him as a close personal friend.

The Use of Sanctions

In one of the more famous chapters of *The Prince,* Machiavelli poses the question of whether it is better to be feared or loved. The wise prince, he concluded, would be both a lion and a fox: "a fox to recognize traps, and a lion to frighten wolves."[28] An MC lacks the autonomy of a prince, but there are lions as well as foxes on Capitol Hill, and some combine elements of both. What sanctions are available to those who would act like lions? Clearly there are fewer than in the recent past. Committee chairs, compelled to run for reelection, must be far more deferential than the czars of the 1960s. The party leaders, though strengthened in some respects, are generally viewed as less capable of inflicting punishment. In the Senate, it is possible for an individual to delay proceedings substantially and for a relatively small and determined group to frustrate action for quite some time. Under normal conditions, however, the only sanctions readily at hand for the individual MC are his or her vote and ability, through debate or other means, to challenge the views of other members. Since a single vote is seldom decisive in either the House or Senate, only those with numerous allies can be expected to use this sanction with any consistency. Debate is not likely to be perceived as particularly threatening. The effectiveness of sanctions depends, as a rule, on the aspirations and attitudes of those being acted against. Those who choose to play a "bombthrowing" or "outsider" role, for example, are less likely to care about being denied such institutional goodies as committee assignments, leadership positions, or bill passage. Those from safe seats are less vulnerable to the kinds of sanctions that might diminish their reputations than those who face difficult reelection fights.

The most important kinds of sanctions applied in Congress are those that are applied collectively. The most extreme, a vote of expulsion, has been used only in extreme cases. Far more common is the withholding of various rewards such as desired committee assignments. Persistent norm violators are seldom seated on prestigious committees. Since reform of the seniority system, subcommittee chairmanships have similarly been denied to those who have in some way or another offended their colleagues, though even here the threat is more common than the actual denial. Unpopular members are also likely to encounter legislative difficulties, such as having problems in getting their bills or amendments passed, not being asked to cosponsor popular measures, or finding few cosponsors for their own bills.

Party leaders often play an important role in orchestrating these collective sanctions. Edmund Muskie (D-ME) was generally well respected by his Senate colleagues, yet it was not until late in his Senate career that he was able to win assignment to a prestigious committee, a failure that Muskie attributed to a meeting early in his Senate career with then Majority Leader Lyndon Johnson. Before Muskie took his seat, it seems, he had a meeting with Johnson in which the majority leader explained how difficult it could often be to make decisions. "Many times, Ed," Muskie recalls Johnson saying, "you won't know how you're going to vote until the clerk calling the roll gets to the M's." Johnson went on to discuss some of the issues likely to come up in the next session, giving particular emphasis to a compromise Johnson was trying to reach on an attempt to modify the Senate's cloture rule. Despite the majority leader's increasingly forceful pleas, Muskie remained silent until Johnson said, "Well, Ed, you don't seem to have much to say." "The clerk," Muskie replied, "hasn't gotten to the M's yet." And that single phrase, according to Muskie, changed the direction of his Senate career.[29]

Johnson's successors, it appears, are more likely to behave like foxes than lions, to favor the carrot over the stick. The use of leadership sanctions is by no means unknown. The speaker can and does use his power of recognition as both sanction and reward. Party leaders can reward or punish through scheduling decisions. But mostly the powers of party leaders derive from more subtle sources of persuasion and favor trading; withholding favors rather than applying sanctions is their most effective tool. "I don't even think," said one MC, "about the leadership in terms of a threat."[30] Most party leaders would concur: even Johnson, Doris Kearns says, "reassured himself that open coercion was not a practical possibility. . . . [H]is instrument would be the power of persuasion." In reality, Kearns goes on to point out, "the line between persuasion and pressure" is thin and ambiguously drawn; the receipt of "regular rewards from a benefactor who will also be the source of future benefits can create a dependency close to coercive power, because the ability to bestow also implies the authority to discontinue or refuse as a sign of disapproval or as a punishment."[31]

Since seniority no longer assures committee chairs of tenure, they too must think more in terms of persuasion than overt coercion. They are further constrained by the need to anticipate the reactions of the parent body: it is a Pyrrhic victory to block action in committee only to be beaten by an end-run on the floor. Within their bailiwicks, however, committee chairs often have more sanctions available to them than do party leaders. Although committee business is technically conducted by majority vote, the reality (especially in matters like scheduling) is often quite different. One Senator told Randall Ripley:

If a member were to bring up a bill which the chairman didn't want on the agenda that week, the chairman would usually be supported by a majority. Some chairmen simply say, "I am not going to bring it up," and that involves an appeal from the decision of the chair, which is rarely taken and would be more rarely successful. Also, the chairman has the sole right in the committees on which I serve, in the setting of hearings on any given legislation. So he has the power to call up bills, the power to designate the hearing dates, the power to call an executive session for the purpose of reporting the bill out. There are technical defenses against this power, but, in my experience, they don't work.[32]

For those who do not occupy formal leadership positions, the range of available sanctions is small. Even in the Senate, except for the threat of an end-of-session filibuster, the use of procedural sanctions against a determined majority is at best a short-run tactic of delay, likely to produce a backlash effect and diminish a member's standing with his or her colleagues. The use of such personalized sanctions is common in political fiction: the plot of Alan Drury's *Advise and Consent*, for example, turns upon a threat to expose one senator's homosexual past. But it seems to be rare in practice. As Baker puts it,

> Pushing personal animus to the point of open warfare simply makes little sense in a body as compact as the Senate. There are few places to hide there, and the satisfaction of habitually baiting a personal adversary can have negative political repercussions. The principal political support for a senator is external, and his downfall can usually be assured only through rejection by his constituents, not by anything a fellow member can do by way of attempting to reduce his effectiveness.[33]

The ultimate sanction, of course, is to hit where it hurts with the folks back home. To endorse and campaign for someone's opponent may or may not be an effective ploy. Party leaders have often helped direct campaign contributions to needy members, and other MCs have gotten into the game. Henry Waxman (D-CA), as a relatively junior member, was a pioneer in using his fundraising ability to help raise campaign contributions for less affluent colleagues; Senator Jesse Helms's (R-NC) financial network has been widely credited with the election of other conservative Republicans, some in primary contests against other Republicans. A national figure, like the speaker or a Kennedy, can help a candidate raise money, draw a crowd, and attract media attention; but American politics is still, at base, local politics, and the effectiveness of outside intervention is open to question. It can also cause friction with colleagues, particularly in intraparty contests. As Baker puts it, "A ringing endorsement by a senator of a colleague's primary opponent is difficult to excuse by invoking partisan loyalty and comes much closer to a personal rebuff."[34] Friction between Senator Helms and some of his Republican colleagues in the Senate is attributable in part to the senator's involvement in such intraparty fights.

There are more indirect ways of affecting a colleague's chances of re-election. In the 1950s, Senator Joseph R. McCarthy was able to inspire both fear and loathing on the campaign trail by implying that a fellow senator might be "soft on communism." Similarly, Senator Estes Kefauver's hearings on the links between organized crime and labor unearthed connections with the Democratic party that were an important factor in the defeat of Majority Leader Scott Lucas (D-IL). The modern variant on these themes is ethics. In 1987, Newt Gingrich (R-GA) gave one of his staff aides virtually a full-time job developing an ethics case against (then) Speaker Jim Wright (D-TX).[35] In the 1970s, Representative Andrew Maguire (D-NJ) had demonstrated the effectiveness of such charges when he introduced a resolution condemning fellow Democrat Bob Sikes (D-FL) for alleged conflicts of interest. The resolution failed to pass the House, but Sikes's opponent used it in his campaign and Sikes lost. Although Wright's ultimate downfall and Sikes's defeat can both be traced to the actions of their colleagues, the problem with such sanctions is that they may produce a backlash. McCarthy was ultimately censured by his Senate colleagues. Kefauver, despite claims of seniority and his status as the Democratic party's candidate for vice president in 1956, was passed over in his 1957 bid for a seat on the Foreign Relations Committee. Maguire was denied nomination for a Senate seat that he was favored to win by the spoiler campaign of an MC's daughter whose campaign was essentially financed on the Hill.

With rare exceptions, then, the carrot is more effective than the stick. The individual member of the House simply cannot, under ordinary circumstances, effectively punish another member without risks. The most effective sanctions are those that are collectively applied. And that necessitates coalitions.

Bloc Formation

Short- and long-term alliances are important sources of power in both war and politics. Statistically it can be shown that a bloc of ten senators always voting together would win more than 95 of every 100 votes taken, if other votes were randomly distributed. Such conditions are unlikely to obtain where voting behavior is not random and blocs are difficult to maintain, but the logic of bloc formation is compelling and the existence of numerous formal and informal groups has long been a fact of legislative life.

Aside from parties, which receive separate attention, the most common legislative alliance is an affinity group, a bloc based on an inherent likeness or set of shared experiences. These include organized caucuses such as those uniting blacks, women, Northeasterners, or those from steel-producing districts; state delegations; classes of MCs elected in the same year; ideological coalitions such as the Conservative Opportunity Society; issue-specific alliances, which are loosely organized to push a single issue or bill; and informal factions of like-minded colleagues. Less important, though not entirely without significance, are alliances that arise through personal interactions: those who play tennis or use the gym together, alliances based on personal friendships, shared apartments, and so on.

Maintaining cohesion is the major problem of all such groups. It is a problem with two major components. The first is that of defining the boundaries of the group's concerns. For the Black Caucus, for example, unity is likely to be achieved with little difficulty on the issue of U.S. policy toward South Africa or making Martin Luther King Day a national holiday. But is there a black position on the dairy program? Even where there is consensus on goals, the second challenge to group unity is over tactics: when, if ever, is it better to accept half a loaf rather than none? From the perspective of the individual legislator, these questions can seriously affect the value of joining an alliance. As much as bloc formation can enhance bargaining power, it can restrict freedom of action; there may even be coalitions that hurt.

Let us look first at the positive side of the equation. In the waning weeks of the 1983 session, two relatively small blocs of House members were able to exert disproportionate influence by virtue of coalition. A group of freshman Democrats, who had campaigned in 1982 against the Reagan budget deficits, failed in an attempt to gain consideration of a package of tax increases and budget cuts designed to redeem their campaign promises. Frustrated by their own party leadership, they joined a group of conservative Republicans in blocking a debt-limit bill that also included a package of key Democratic programs. The leadership refused to move, and the freshman eventually capitulated; but to the press and to their constituents they had made their point. Even more successful was the Black Caucus in its effort to ban economic dealings with South Africa. The vehicle they chose was an already controversial administration bill increasing the U.S. contribution to the International Monetary Fund. Because the vote was expected to be close, the leadership needed the Caucus vote and agreed to the South Africa amendment. This jeopardized the bill's chances in the more conservative Senate, where the bill had passed without the South African amendment. Although a majority of both the House and Senate conferees were opposed to the amendment, the closeness of the House vote made it apparent that it could not pass over the opposition of the Caucus. If the conferees (and the administration) wanted a bill, they had to deal with the Black Caucus; the Caucus, for its part, had to accept moderating amendments or risk defeat in the Senate, a course of action that could have (but did not) split the Black Caucus. By bargaining as a bloc, the Caucus did not get the total ban it wanted, but it did extract far more from the Senate and administration than anyone had predicted.

The general effectiveness of a bloc depends on four variables: its size; the bargaining situation; its cohesiveness, or ability to do what it says it will do; and its general position in the House or Senate. Size is so important a variable that it needs little discussion except as it relates to the bargaining context. Quite obviously, the closer the likely outcome of the expected vote, the more important even a small bloc becomes. But frequently there are bargaining situations in which antibloc strategies can be effective, particularly when the blocs are large. One possibility is for an opponent to press arguments on which bloc members are known to disagree.[36] In the 1950s, for example, congressional Democrats appeared to have reached a consensus in favor of federal aid to education. However, the majority coalition was never able to work its will because its opponents succeeded in raising issues, such as aid to parochial or segregated schools, that made it impossible for some members of the bloc to vote for final passage.

The education bloc was, in a sense, too large to hang together. But smaller blocs can also have problems of cohesion. For example, state delegations vary enormously in effectiveness. In the late 1960s, when the Cook County (Chicago) delegation threatened to vote against all administration programs unless the Office of Education withdrew its proposed economic sanctions against the city's segregated schools, the threat was credible and the administration backed down. A similar threat from New York or Los Angeles, cities without powerful party machines, would have been far less credible.

Bloc effectiveness is also a function of the group's position in the House or Senate. In many circumstances, power depends on an ability to confound prediction. One secret of Sam Rayburn's success as speaker was his ability to bank on the votes of his normally conservative colleagues in the Texas delegation. Similarly, in the first two years of the Reagan administration, two groups, conservative Democrats known as "boll weevils" and moderate Republicans known as "gypsy moths," were often pivotal to both the administration and the Democratic leadership.

Whatever their effectiveness, blocs are an important feature of the Washington community to the extent that it is generally "in the interest of each legislator to belong to at least one weakly formed coalition."[37] The autonomy the individual loses by joining an organized group is balanced by enhanced numbers, formal identity, and the system of communications that organization can bring. At a minimum, bloc membership provides the individual MC with a means of escape from outside pressures: "I'd like to help you, but the caucus hasn't taken its position" is always a good excuse. And who can be hurt in his or her campaign if it can be shown that every other member of the state delegation, every other black, woman, or whatever, voted the same way? At best, a cohesive and strategically large enough coalition can have power far out of proportion to its purely numerical strength.[38]

Knowledge and Ability

The influence of a bloc derives in part from its mathematical ability to effect the outcomes of directly relevant and indirectly negotiable votes. But the strength of a bloc in the long run, like the strength of an individual, depends as well on less tangible factors. A winning reputation helps, as do intelligence, credibility, and formal position. Unreliability does not. It is just as damning to be known as "one of *those* idiots" as "*that* idiot," and the latter reputation is something you can at least do something about.

For any decision-maker, good information is a treasured resource. While it is true that subjective factors such as personal likes and dislikes play an important role in the legislative struggle, the desire to make good public policy is a significant variable. How does an individual member enhance his or her credibility as a source of information? His or her first step, of course, is to become informed. Ability helps, as does the background a person brings to the job.

Whether the norms of specialization and hard work are as rigidly enforced as in the past, expertise sufficient to be of use to one's colleagues cannot be achieved without both. John Manley's description of former Ways and Means chairman Wilbur Mills (D-AR) could be extended to apply to effective members in general. Mills, Manley says,

> earned the approval of the Committee members on his hard work and his mastery of the subjects coming before the Committee. Moreover, by becoming an expert Mills has reduced the cost of Committee membership to others. Members who are unsure of the answers to complex questions can rely on his judgment and expertise, and those members who do not care to immerse themselves in technical complexities are confident that he knows what he is doing. By acquiring some degree of expertise the Chairman has allowed other members "to perform rewarding activity with less effort, less anxiety, or in less time—in general, at lower cost." And by lowering costs to others Mills has raised his own influence.[39]

Other forms of expertise are also important. Those who know the rules, or who can anticipate the "moods" of the House or Senate, acquire strategic advantage. And there is a point at which knowledge merges (or fails to merge) with personal regard to define effectiveness. An able and informed member who lacks credibility is as ineffective as an affable dope. There is a merging too of bloc strength or formal position and knowledge. When Mills was its chair, Ways and Means seldom lost a vote on the floor in part because of his personal standing and knowledge, in part because he usually brought a united committee to the floor. Other committees—the perennially divided House Education and Labor Committee comes first to mind—lose more than they win. Where the members of Ways and Means had a reputation of doing their homework and working things out among themselves, the members of Education and Labor have not.

Ideology is also a factor. In seeking expert advice, MCs tend to look to those who generally share their point of view. Mistrust of the Education and Labor Committee, for example, is most frequently expressed by conservatives whose views seldom prevail in that committee. When a committee or individual develops too sharply defined an ideological image, it may damage his, her, or its, credibility, particularly among those who do not share the ideology. One opponent of military spending, for example, argues against the view that "just because someone got a committee assignment that he's an expert. He'll learn something through absorption, just by sitting there, but he learns biases too, and you end up getting prejudiced information. I don't think Armed Services Committee members are especially experts, and they're certainly biased."[40]

Ability and knowledge are important in another, less direct sense. Those members who have carved out areas of specialization sometimes emerge as spokespersons for particular points of view. One thinks of Senator Sam Nunn (D-GA) on national defense issues or the late Claude Pepper (D-FL) on senior citizens as MCs who have been widely quoted and respected for their identities with certain causes. To vote with such a person on "his" issues is a way of immunizing yourself against attack by potential opponents. How can you be accused of being against senior citizens if you voted with Pepper? This brings us to our final pathway to legislative power.

———————— ✳ ————————

THE OUTSIDER STRATEGY

Most of the strategies of influence we have discussed here, and most of generalizations about norms, revolve around intramural relations among MCs. For all their importance to some MCs, the outsider role has been an accepted and increasingly popular orientation. Certain "outside" strategies, moreover, are compatible with an insider's role orientation. Members of the House and Senate frequently enter long- and short-term alliances with interest groups and agents of the executive branch whose influence can in turn be used with other MCs. Few if any lobbyists, for example, were initially interested in the internal rules changes pushed by congressional reformers in the 1970s. A number of groups did become active and influential in the fight as the result of an intensive effort on the part of the Democratic Study Group to show the lobbyists how the proposed reforms would affect them.

Use of the press involves more sensitive considerations. You can say what you want to the folks back home, but national media are different.

> Competition for national publicity is disruptive to intra-Senate harmony. One way to make national news is to play a significant part in the making of important legislation. This is not a role that can be played by all senators simultaneously and . . . is most often and easily played by those senators with the least need for publicity. The ordinary senator can usually make national news only through such frowned upon practices as "grandstanding"—making sensational speeches, engaging in "personalities," excessive partisanship, and other forms of behavior calculated to get his name in the headlines without legislative accomplishment.[41]

Even when national publicity is directly related to legislative work, it may alienate colleagues. The crafting of legislation is a collective endeavor; the press is more often interested in personalities. An MC who puts months of hard work into a bill is unlikely to enjoy the sight of a colleague taking credit for it on the nightly news.

The outsider strategy has generally been most effective in the early stages, what is sometimes called the "agenda setting" stage of the process. The stage at which it is probably least effective is during the deliberative process of revision, bargaining and amendment. Tactically it may sometimes be possible to blow apart a legislative logjam by going public. But because the bargaining process includes diverse interests, the individual who goes public risks incurring resentment. In the latter stages of the 1983 fight over increased appropriations for the International Monetary Fund (IMF), President Reagan needed a substantial bloc of Democratic votes to get the bill through. Even after the Senate had reluctantly accepted the Black Caucus amendment on South Africa, the revised bill almost lost the House after the Republican Congressional Campaign Committee sent out a fund-raising letter that cited the IMF vote as evidence that the Democrats were soft on communism. The letter, of course, neglected to mention the president's strong support of the bill. Only after hard bargaining and a public apology from the president did the bill pass.

CONCLUSION: INFLUENCE IN THE POSTREFORM CONGRESS

The 1970s was a decade of unusual instability in Congress, yet there were and are significant continuities as well. The most visible change was an increase in the incidence and acceptance of outside-oriented advocacy styles. As one House member put it:

> What is happening, I think, is that the collegial system is disintegrating. . . . Let me suggest to you that the two most effective Republicans in recent years . . . have been Henry Hyde (Republican, Illinois) and Jack Kemp (Republican, New York). In very real ways they have achieved power in the House and in the country that very few other Republicans in the House have. . . . And they have both done it by being mavericks, by being very stubborn, by getting outside their zones. Kemp is not on Ways and Means, yet he is the dominant tax figure in our party. . . .
>
> And they do it by using the new forms of power, to the point where Henry Hyde—who is aggressively pushing a nasty issue (anti-abortion proposals) that nobody wants to vote on—comes within three votes of beating the classic insider Republican for the conference championship.[42]

Before joining President Bush's Cabinet, Kemp typified this new force in Congress. Yet he remains the exception that both tests and confirms the rule. Part of his rise to power was based on old-fashioned congressional virtues such as charm, integrity, and credibility: he played both lion and fox. Yet his rise to insiderdom was based also in the peculiar status of a party that has been out of power for so long that not one of its present members has helped elect a speaker or held a committee chairmanship. Many House Republicans, the younger and more conservative ones in particular, are resentful of their status as semipermanent outsiders and have manifested that resentment in challenges to existing folkways. They are not yet numerous enough in the party to elect a minority leader, but they do constitute a large enough bloc to command and receive positions of leadership. One of those positions went to Kemp, and even more surprisingly in 1989 to the even more acerbic Newt Gingrich.

How this bloc would react if the Republicans took control of the House is difficult to say, but the 1981–86 experience of Senate Republicans in that regard is instructive. There were some rough moments in the first year when Democrats were not consulted on questions of scheduling, or when committee chairs refused to schedule witnesses for the minority. But such instances were rare, and most observers report a softening of hard-line attitudes. In the words of one veteran staff person in 1983, "Obstruction is one thing when you're on the outside looking in, and quite another when you're running the store. Now it's *our* leadership that gets blamed if we can't put together a budget, *our* government that doesn't run if the money isn't appropriated." Even Jesse Helms (R-NC), probably the most outspoken of the New Right Republican mavericks, seems to have softened.

> When Helms entered the Senate in 1973, the chamber was dominated by liberals. . . . Being an outsider freed him to operate within the Senate much as he chose.
>
> In 1981, however, Helms became part of the Senate's majority and had to show more respect for the positions taken by his party and president, even when he disagreed with them. Though his ability to raise money was not affected directly, his freedom to fight for his causes was curtailed.[43]

What a striking parallel there is between this observation and Michael Foley's general propositions about the liberal Democratic mavericks of the 1960s. As they began to win, as they became more the majority faction, "the liberals gradually developed a new appreciation of compromise, legislative diligence, specialization, and institutional loyalty."[44]

To be sure, there have been significant changes in both the Senate and House. In both bodies, the close nexus between the "Establishment" and political conservatism has been broken. Power is more dispersed. Norms are less visibly enforced. MCs simply aren't as nice to each other as they used to be, and work on the Hill just isn't as much fun. It is more like an arena and less like a club; yet some MCs, regardless of seniority, ideology, or party, continue to have more inside power than others. If the outsider role is more frequently played, the instructions to an ambitious freshman would be pretty much what they were three decades ago: spend your first few years learning your way around. Develop an area of specialization. Do your homework. Learn the issues, the institution, and its rules. Do not demagogue thy colleagues or embarrass the institution. Cultivate colleagues both on a personal basis and, when possible, by empathizing with their needs and "going along." Maintain your principles but show a willingness to compromise. Vote party when you can. Never deceive a fellow member. Don't waste his or her time. Secure allies by joining coalitions and becoming a credible source of information and advice.

None of this will guarantee a position as majority leader or chair of an important committee. By doing the right things in Washington, one may very well be doing the wrong things back home; and no matter how well respected one is on Capitol Hill, reelection is the bottom line. Certain natural graces are also important. Chance can also be a factor: sudden turnovers due to deaths and electoral upsets can catapult some members to committee chairs rapidly while the longevity of colleagues makes perennial bridesmaids of others. And formal power is important. But the policy advocate needs to look beyond titles to identify those whose adherence to the norms, whose personal charms, and whose talents make them stand out.

5

LEGISLATIVE
INTELLIGENCE

L egislators, more than most of us, confront incessant streams of data, piles of unreadable reports, lines of claimants. Like us, they must learn to be selective: to decide how much they need to know before casting a vote and who must be heard. To trace the path of legislative intelligence is, in a sense, to trace the path of power. There are other important sources of influence, but to know who listens to whom is to know a great deal about who gets what. Because it is typical that "only a small portion of the information available is ever recorded by the organization, the processes by which the initial screening takes place have extraordinary importance in determining the final decision."[1]

THE NEEDS AND CAPABILITIES
OF INDIVIDUAL MEMBERS

Most people probably take it for granted that MCs know what they are doing. The idea that one might "cold turkey" a speech prepared by an aide, or vote on a bill never read, is disquieting. Yet we could hardly have it any other way. Most legislative decisions are made by men and women who have little direct knowledge of the problem at issue. "The best I can do," said a typical MC, "is to devote my time to the major pieces of legislation which come before the House, and rely on others for advice in connection with less major legislation."[2]

This dependence upon others need not be a serious obstacle to sound public policy. In legislatures, as in life, informed decisions can be made by uninformed human beings. Indeed they usually are, or at least they are made by

73

persons who lack direct, personal knowledge of the relevant facts. If the sign reads "Detour, bridge out ahead," we are usually better off relying on the instructions of those who make such signs than personally testing bridges. In a complex world it is rational and essential for each individual to remain ignorant of the details of most of the components of most of the choices he or she must make.

Because no individual MC can fully understand even a fraction of the decisions Congress must make, the solution to the intelligence problem, if there is one, must be institutional. It must be a system of information processing that at once satisfies the needs of individual members and, because it is a representative body, allows constituents to be heard. One would hope that it also results in sound public policy.

The Environment of Choice

Most decision-makers continue "to invest resources in procuring data until the marginal return from information equals its marginal cost."[3] They don't look for more information than they need. MCs are less able than most of us to act "rationally" in postponing or avoiding decisions. As members of a collegial body, they must often cast votes at times chosen by others on issues others have framed. MCs are not as able as many decision-makers to beg off entirely and decide that an issue is too trivial or peripheral to their department to bother with. MCs are also less free to choose their sources. As in all organizations, there are certain people it is best not to ignore: a junior MC will listen to a committee chair, whether the information is useful or not, just as a junior executive will listen to a corporate vice president. MCs, however, must also give audience to a wide variety of outsiders, less because they can learn from them than because they cannot afford to offend.

> For a man of active intellect the most severe condition of politics is to abstain from the full and constant use of his powers. He must be willing to submit to boredom and make the effort to conceal it . . . sitting through long meetings where the business transacted and the ceremonies performed are almost identical with what took place at the meeting the evening before, which was dull the first time.[4]

And the listening, oh, the listening. A constituent proffers a ten-minute harangue on the evils of dog-owners who fail to clean up after their pets. Your temptation is to point out that you're a senator, not a dog-catcher. The neighborhood nut calls collect to complain that the local druggist was surly. You listen. A person who knows nothing about economics offers a program for ending unemployment. It's crazy, but you don't hurry to say so. Other occupations, such as bartenders and outside salespeople working on commissions, have similar problems, but politicians spend more time than almost any other group listening to people who have nothing to offer from an informational point of view.

Looking at bureaucracies, Anthony Downs argues that most information, "is used as a means to some decisionmaking end."[5] Unfortunately, it is not simple to assign a single motive or end to congressional decision-making. In the Congress, information is often acquired for reasons having little relationship to decision-making. Even among participants there is confusion as to how much information is needed for such ends as reelection, constituent service, and institutional advancement. There are members of Congress whose major goal and ambition is to serve the people of their districts; others seek to be movers and shakers on Capitol Hill. The similarities, however, are greater than the differences. Whatever a member's orientation to the job may be, there are certain decisions that must be made. Recorded votes on the floor, votes in committee, answers to constituent mail, queries from the press, all demand some sort of decision. Few of these decisions can be made on the basis of complete information, postponed, or delegated to others.

Political Intelligence

Most MCs are political incrementalists. They tend to believe that the groups and issues that won election last time are basic to victory in the future. Their goal in office is generally to consolidate existing support and expand incrementally to similar blocs. On some issues, certainly on those of major concern to his or her district or state, the MC has no difficulty knowing the attitudes of core constituencies. If in doubt, guidance is usually at hand from close advisors and friends, and from the supporting coalition. If there are no conflicts in what John Kingdon calls the "field of forces . . . then the congressman votes with that field."[6] Acquiring political intelligence becomes important when there is conflict in that field, or when the normal field provides no cues.

This kind of situation, in which the supporting coalition provides no real guidance, is quite common when we confine the concept of the "field of forces" to the district. It is less common when we expand the concept, as Kingdon does, to include the Washington community. When a city MC votes on a farm issue the field of forces may be different, but the tendency to go along with one's field remains. Lacking a reason to do otherwise, most MCs will vote with their party, committee, or whatever uncontested cue is available. On many routine decisions, it makes sense to "get along" by "going along." Only when members get mixed signals, when party and constituency leaders disagree or when key components of the supporting coalition are at odds, is there a search for more information.

Because there is no alternative to relying on others, a top priority is to find reliable sources of advice and information. Because the problems are both political and factual, the ideal sources are those that combine insight into the factual aspects of policy proposals (what does it do?) with a shrewd awareness of their political implications (who does it affect?) and prospects (what are its chances?). Outside areas in which he or she has special competence, the MC needs information that combines evaluation of a program's significance, meaning, popularity, and relationship to other issues. The most economic form in which such information can be packaged, paradoxically, is the one that contains the least data.

The best intelligence a legislator can get is a reliable directive to vote yes or no.

The joker in this deck is the word *reliable*. The more information is evaluated and processed, the greater its utility but the less its reliability. One is faced with a dilemma: the best information a legislator can have is least likely to be free of distortion, unless the source is totally reliable. Because time is limited, the individual legislator must plug into an intelligence network that can provide a maximum of trustworthy guidance while requiring a minimum of effort to discover its meaning. His or her primary intelligence problem, and the primary intelligence problem of the institution as a whole, is to develop a reliable network of information processors. In other words, when MCs complain about their information problems it is not because there is too little available; what they usually have in mind is a scarcity of "intelligence"— processed information—rather than data. Their problem, in a nutshell, is to locate reliable processors and evaluators.

Legislators and Information: How Much Is Enough?

MCs "engage in an extended search for information only rarely."[7] Many issues are simply too peripheral to a member's constituency or committee concerns to require serious research. Learning on many other issues has already taken place: incumbents find that the same issues arise year after year; junior members find they are voting on issues that arose in their campaigns. Changes take place at the margins.

> No one was born yesterday; past experience with these programs is so great that total reconsideration would be superfluous unless there is a special demand in regard to a specific activity on the part of one or more strategically placed Congressmen, a new Administration, interest groups, or the agency itself. Programs are reconsidered but not all together and generally in regard to small changes.[8]

In a world of decisional complexity, working on the margins is a blueprint for survival; Charles Lindblom's method of "successive limited comparisons" dramatically reduces both the number and complexity of alternatives.[9] Because problems recur in slightly altered form, there are few issues on which an individual MC must undertake more comprehensive analysis. Existing policy is taken as a given, even as a rule, by its previous opponents. No matter how bitter the annual battles over the budget may be, there is no fight at all over 95 percent of it. Only when the context changes does it make sense for a rational legislator to seek new information. Nor are they likely to get it. The more closely an MC becomes identified with a particular point of view, the less likely he or she is to hear from those who disagree. Lobbyists, too, work at the margins.

Preferred Suppliers

One way to find out where MCs get their information is to ask them. In 1977, the Obey Commission did just that with a questionnaire sent to every member of the House; David Kozak did the same with a selected sample. Neither got a random response, and the questions were different, but together they provide a rough quantitative answer to the question of where congressmen get their voting cues.[10] The first generalization that can be made from both of these studies is that generalization is difficult. MCs turn to different sources in different contexts. The Obey Commission found, for example, that 38 percent of those responding relied heavily on other members when it came to legislation not from his or her committee, but that only 11 percent mentioned colleagues as information sources for committee work. Kozak emphasizes "issue contexts" and shows, for example, that the more complex the issue, the more members are likely to turn to their personal staffs. One staff assistant with experience in both the House and Senate adds another important distinction:

> If you wanted to find out about some piece of legislation on the House side there was always a Congressman who knew all about it. You could get him aside and he would go down the list of political as well as practical matters. Here in the Senate the Senators are not experts. You have to go to the staff. First, I call the office and find out as much as possible. They usually refer me to a committee staff person. Committee staff many times know the practical but not the political issues. You have to know both to make a decision on a bill.[11]

Another difference between House and Senate is the far greater importance in the House of internal groups, the party whip systems in particular. The frequent meetings of the party caucus, and expanded reliance on the whips, especially during Jim Wright's tenure as speaker, became a key source of intelligence to House Democrats. Informal groups such as the Democratic Study Group, the Republican Wednesday Group, and various state delegations have long played important roles in the House intelligence system.

There appear to be marked variations between MCs in the relative weight given to staff and colleagues. "I myself," one claimed, "don't have to go anywhere beyond my own staff. My LAs [legislative assistants] know how I think. I'm heavily reliant on them."[12] Another claimed not to "have a staff like that. I'm the only expert in this office."[13] Aside from Kingdon's finding that junior MCs were more dependent on staff than those with more experience,[14] if there is an explanation for these variations, it has not been systematically researched. We strongly suspect, however, that the variations in trust MCs accord to staff on the one hand and colleagues on the other is most closely related to their orientations toward the legislative process. Outsiders, we hypothesize, are most likely to rely on their own offices, while those most attuned to such norms as reciprocity and specialization take their cues from fellow members. Whatever the differences may be, a general reliance on inhouse suppliers of information should not be surprising. Proximity is a key factor, of course. When you rush out of a meeting with constituents or a committee hearing to cast a vote on an amendment to an obscure bill, who else is there to consult? In the case of personal staff, that's what they're paid for. Staff members presumably understand the member's political needs and inclinations as well as the issues, and if their loyalty is in question, the MC is in big trouble. Indeed, as Kingdon says,

> It might be more fruitful to conceive of staff not as an influence *on* a member, but rather as an extension *of* a member. Because of the highly personalized hiring and firing practices, the strong tendency of staff and member to hold similar orientations and ideologies and even to have been closely associated prior to the aide's employment, and the close working relationship between staffer and boss, it may have been more appropriate to think of staff and member as parts of a single decision-making unit than as separate agencies.[15]

Colleagues possess particularly useful attributes. Readily available at the time of decision, they are able to furnish concise, evaluative information that takes account of politics as well as substance. They are also known quantities, part

> of an ongoing social subsystem, one that will continue after the issue of the day is forgotten. The member who wishes to remain in good standing in that subsystem is accountable for his advice. Few issues are important enough to risk practicing deception on colleagues, and the potential cue taker is secure in that knowledge when he selects another member as his source of evaluation.[16]

Time constraints enhance the importance of cue-giving. Former MC Charles Vanik (D-OH) explains:

> Sometimes you stagger into the room, you don't even know what they're voting on. . . . The deliberative time is such time as is required to see how someone else voted. You sort of have to match that up with other people from your area. . . .
>
> Now I'd say about two-thirds of the average member's votes are follow-the-leader votes. Two-thirds. I don't condemn the system. . . . Deliberation does not always demand independent judgment. Consistently knowing who to follow—that's a very important thing.[17]

There are negative cue-givers as well as positive, and some peoples' guidance counts for more than others. As Vanik's remarks suggest, state and regional blocs tend to be fairly important. A fellow partisan from the same state makes a particularly useful resource since he or she has probably studied the issue from a political perspective similar to your own. "Cue-givers," moreover, "need not be individuals. When overwhelming majorities of groups that the member respects and trusts—the whole House, the members of his party or state delegation, for example—vote the same way, the member is likely to accept their collective judgment as his own."[18] Particularly when there are strategic or procedural issues involved, party leaders serve as important cue-givers. Indeed, party whip notices and the liberal Democratic Study Group's bill summaries ranked ahead of committee members and reports in Kozak's survey.

The relative weakness of constituents, lobbyists, and administrators in these surveys is deceptive. If we trace the flow of information back to where the staff and colleagues got their information, a very different picture emerges. The more we trace decisions back from final passage, to committee rooms, markup sessions, and drafting conferences, the less contained the information network becomes.

———————— ✳ ————————

THE FLOW OF LEGISLATIVE INTELLIGENCE

No doubt there has always been a two-step flow of communications to Congress.[19] Informal gatekeepers, different ones for different subject-matter specialties, were probably as important in the information structure of the First Congress as in the most recent. But the basic pattern of information flow in early Congresses was different, and the evolution of the system is instructive.

The Changing Path of Legislative Intelligence

In *The Federalist*, James Madison argued that the Congress could provide itself with most of the information needed to legislate. Assuming that each MC would "be acquainted with the interests and circumstances of his constituents . . . it will be found," Madison wrote, "that there will be no peculiar local interests that will not be within the knowledge of some representative."[20] State laws would provide models for federal statutes and they in turn for each other: "Past transactions of the government will be a ready and accurate source of information."[21]

The flow of information in early sessions was relatively simple. Informed by past acts of the Congress and other legislative bodies, each individual member served as a communications link between his or her constituency and colleagues. In this network, each individual MC was a gatekeeper of information regarding his or her state or district. With the exceptions of the state legislatures and executive officials, no organizations inside or outside the Congress processed information.

Specializing the Flow. Gradually a considerably more complex pattern evolved. The initial change was internal: "A few of the members," as Madison had predicted, "by frequent reelections [became] thorough masters of the public business . . . not unwilling to avail themselves of those advantages."[22] Congress developed an institutional memory, a division of labor, and a data system to structure and enhance the disparate perspectives of individual members. Probably because of its larger size and faster turnover, the House was first to alter and institutionalize the gatekeeper function. By the end of the nineteenth century, the standing committees of both houses had become gatekeepers in more senses than one. The committees as institutions and their members as individuals became primary sources of factual information for other MCs and acquired the power to choke the information flow altogether by burying a bill. As a result, much of the important selective process of deciding which issues are worth the time to become informed about is done in committee, a process that most other legislatures assign to the executive.

Further enhancing the significance of intramural communications patterns in Congress was the professionalization of the institution. As the proportion of incumbents increased from fewer than half to slightly better than 90 percent, the information system changed, too. The more of Madison's "masters of the public business" the House and Senate contained, the greater became the possibilities for specialization, and the more patterns of mutual trust enabled MCs to look to their colleagues rather than to outside sources for information. In essence, what Congress did by becoming a careerist institution and dividing its work among specialized units was to filter a large part of the incoming information through mediating agencies. Similar trends, though manifested at a later date, may be found in most state legislatures; but few states and even fewer foreign legislatures have either specialized their information systems or so thoroughly freed them from executive control.

The nineteenth-century establishment of an independent committee system dramatically changed the nature of its information system. The revolt against Speaker Cannon further enhanced the power of standing committees to control the flow of information to the floor, and the Legislative Reorganization Act of 1946 wrote this power into the rules. By "clarifying" committee jurisdictions, the Reorganization Act all but took away from the speaker and majority leader discretionary authority over the assignment of bills. This in turn gave the committees and their chairs the power to regulate the flow of information by deciding which bills would go to the floor. More recent reforms have even further dispersed the locus of legislative intelligence by enhancing the staff resources of subcommittees and full committees. The price of such specialization has been the fragmentation of gatekeeping power. From the perspective of the individual MC, the greater the dispersion of expertise, the more he or she must accommodate to fragmentation. "We may come here," as one member said years ago, "with deep interests in subjects unrelated to our committee, but we are so busy there that we never get around to thinking through or drafting legislation covering other matters. . . . So we begin to concentrate on the committee on which we serve even though our interest may not lie there."[23] As much as members of the postreform Congress have shown an increased tendency to challenge the standing committees on the floor, they do so largely as novices.

Changes in the Information Environment. Both anticipating and following these internal changes have been similar trends in the information environment. Perhaps the most important of these is the increasing immersion of the Congress in a world of outside specialists. In both public and private sectors, specialized groups are playing an increasingly important role in structuring the flow of legislative intelligence.

There was, no doubt, pressure activity in the First Congress, but it was not until relatively recent times that interest groups became a major source of information to legislators. At a national level, indeed, relatively few organized groups even existed until quite recently, and the role of administrative agencies as sources of information and initiative was relatively small.

Thus, there has been added to the legislative information system a set of exogenous gatekeepers. These outside groups influence the legislative information system in a variety of ways. They filter and process both information and policy preferences, provide facts and points of view, sometimes even affect the strategic context. Equally significant is their role in initiating proposals and setting the legislative agenda. Whether or not they have the political clout to pass a bill, many large groups do have enough influence to assure its consideration and thereby to assure its clientele that information on the subject will be presented. Finally, these groups have an impact on the internal structure of Congress itself. The interaction between structural changes in the executive and legislative branches has often been noted; the same reciprocal process may take place less obviously between private groups and public bodies. When the federal government began to play an important role in funding higher education beginning in the mid-1960s, it was not long before numerous colleges and universities opened offices in Washington. In the more venerable cases of the Agricultural Extension Service and the Farm Bureau, or the National Rivers and Harbors Congress and the congressional committees on public works, the patterns of structural parallelism may be clearly traced.[24] As Mark Peterson points out, "the number and range of interest representatives increased at precisely the same time that the structural reforms in Congress created more points of access to be exploited."[25]

Invisible Colleges of People and Knowledge. Such structural parallelism tends to isolate policy subsystems from one another. How completely the policy-making process has been fragmented into policy subsystems is not really at issue here. Whether or not one accepts the general image of iron triangles as an accurate depiction of the way in which power is distributed, it is a reasonably good approximation of how the information system works. *In the market for policy information there are few significant general suppliers or consumers.* The recipients of information have, so to speak, gone to bed with the suppliers. The inter- and extralegislative gatekeepers bring similar perspectives to bear on most problems; their political needs and inclinations run along parallel lines; and they are, through long-nurtured habits of interaction, highly sensitive to each others' needs. MCs seek and are given committee assignments that relate to the interests of their constituents, and the committees are staffed by those who are either recruited directly from, or who develop close ties with, those same interests. They become members of the same "invisible colleges," a term used by scientists to describe those working on the cutting edge of the same research field who share research ideas long before they reach the general public. As with such scientific networks, those on Capitol Hill are each others' major sources of information, and they rather frequently exchange jobs. Bills are drafted and negotiated in sessions involving MCs, lobbyists, and executive officials from the same "college." Once agreement has been reached at this level, there is "considerable reluctance to do anything that would either upset that delicate balance or start a chain reaction of amendments."[26] Indeed, once agreements have been reached in a policy subsystem, those who have participated in the negotiations may have a vested interest in withholding information from other potential participants, even when they initially disagreed. These conditions, one former MC argued, have "corrupted [the] deliberative process from one of gathering as much information as possible and spreading it out on the record for the rest of Congress . . . to one of squirreling away what information the senior members of the committee have acquired . . . so that the committee's decision . . . becomes the decision the full Congress adopts."[27]

In the postreform Congress, the dispersion of power to subcommittees has in one sense added another, more specialized gatekeeping barrier to the flow of legislative intelligence. In another way, it has made the system more complex and, if you will, pluralistic. Not only is it no longer possible to push an issue by contacting a few powerful committee chairs, but there is also a greater possibility of jurisdictional overlap and challenge on the floor. The growing staff resources of individual members have introduced further potential points of challenge and dissent, and conflict at the subsystem level has a tendency to elevate power to higher levels. Party leaders, moreover, have moved aggressively, through devices such as multiple referral, to (1) foster conflicts between subsystems, and (2) recentralize some sources of intelligence by upgrading the research facilities of the whip organizations, policy committees, and so on.

Changing the scope of conflict (to use Schattschneider's term) is an important tool of central leaders; but if we pose the problem strictly in terms of information, the more MCs are overwhelmed by conflicting messages, the more likely they are to turn to those that are most familiar and issue-specific. The more general the source of information, the less it can be counted upon as a source of expert advice, and the more likely it is to be hampered by other demands on its time. According to Harold Wilensky, "It is likely that staff experts communicate most freely with colleagues in the same specialty, second with colleagues in the same unit of the workplace, then to subordinates, and last—with greatest blockage and distortion—to superiors and rival agencies."[28]

On any given policy proposal, any given legislator is likely to receive his or her information indirectly, in the neatly packaged form of the committee bill and in the accompanying statements of support and opposition together with the proposed amendments of committee members.[29] Other sources of information are available: MCs may check directly with the relevant executive agencies and outside groups, attempt to determine the attitudes of their constituents, read their whip notices, or consult with various subject-matter experts, trusted advisors, or horoscopes. However, limitations on time, the limits of his or her ability, and the demands of the job sharply limit the practical extent to which this can be done. In many instances they may find that these supplementary sources are themselves depending on the very invisible colleges that informed the committee.

Paradoxically, a highly fragmented information system can give added leverage to centralizing institutions. For presidents as for party leaders, "the very number of pressures permits them latitude in decision-making by giving no single interest a monopoly on access."[30] In the executive branch, the White House (in particular its Office of Management and Budgeting) is an important source of legislative intelligence. On the Hill, one cannot discount the importance of party leaders and the budget and appropriations committees. Even in the private sector, some peak associations such as the AFL-CIO and Chamber of Commerce proffer information on issues that range far beyond the confines of the subgovernmental policy triangles in which they most frequently act. The ability of such central institutions to effectively counter the invisible colleges in the intelligence system is often in evidence when less central sources are in conflict.

Such central sources of information can also cancel each other out. By providing alternative sets of economic assumptions to those of the president, the Congressional Budget Office has given a new weapon of information and propaganda to policy advocates. Because the mass media tends to confine its focus to the larger stories emerging from these larger organizations, questions of general priorities and levels of issue visibility are often answered at this level. They tend, however, to confine themselves to a relatively small set of issues, late in the process, and are thus unlikely to add anything new to the system.

Intake Systems

Nothing in Washington better illuminates the nature of legislative intelligence than that much-maligned institution, the congressional hearing. However tedious these hearings appear, however much scholars may be repelled by their ritualistic redundancies, a case can be made that few mechanisms could be better designed to meet the information needs of American MCs. Their manifest function "of transmitting information, both technical and political," has typically been described as "the most familiar function, but probably the least important."[31] From the perspective of the scholar this is plausible: hearings seem designed to show only that legislators are men and women with near infinite capacities for boredom.

From a legislative perspective, however, it is not difficult to understand why a typical day will find as many as fifteen to twenty House and Senate committees and subcommittees taking testimony. Here we see the legislative division of labor in action. A relatively small percentage of the membership, largely self-selected for its interest in the subject matter and usually with long experience in the field, is given the job of interfacing with outside experts. They do so in a context that forces the confrontation of opposing viewpoints without doing violence to collegial relations. Through clever questioning of a witness a legislator can challenge a colleague's perspectives without challenging the person. Meanwhile, he or she can learn what he needs to know through interpersonal communications, a type of interchange particularly congenial to the personality type of the politician.

The importance of the face-to-face aspect of hearings is enhanced by its adversary nature. Because so many legislators have been trained as lawyers or in other brokerage occupations, most of them are well prepared to arrive at some kind of judgment on the basis of a comparison of cases. Finally, as incumbent politicians, legislators tend to develop an acute sensitivity to the political nuances of presentations. Year-to-year variations, changes in the positions of key client groups, the gradual erosion of hardline positions into negotiable attitudes—these are the subtle aspects of organizational and agency presentations that astute politicians often find. Through the hearings on a bill, areas of possible compromise may also emerge. Many anthropologists now believe that the reactions of the audiences to many rituals are more important than the rituals themselves. MCs have long understood this point.

> It is often said that hearings develop the facts of the case. It might just as properly be said that hearings develop the prejudices of the sitting members, and through them the relative party stances which will be displayed later. Committee staff members follow the hearings with care. Their ears are carefully attuned, not necessarily to witnesses, but to the reactions of committee members. These revealing comments will furnish an index of opinion vital to an estimate of the concessions necessary to pass a bill.[32]

Hearings are by no means the most important sources of information on the Hill. One study found that House members average only half an hour a day in hearings.[33] But as almost every case study of an act of Congress shows, the political dynamics of formal hearings frequently have substantive impact. The kinds of transactions that take place in the hearing room—verbal, adversarial, political—are manifestations of similar off-camera dialogues in every corner of the Capitol complex. Word travels fast on the Hill, and a slight shift in the position of the administration or of a key interest group, elicited in such environments, quickly becomes known to the subsystem actors. The printed record of a hearing provides legislative assistants and speechwriters with ready access to its advocates' best arguments for and against a bill. Given four or five hours to write a speech on a subject they know nothing about, Hill staffers often resort to the art of "creative plagiarism," paraphrasing from committee hearings the major arguments, quoting key experts, and lifting important facts. A shrewd witness lards his or her testimony with dramatic examples, startling juxtapositions of facts and figures, and other tidbits of soundbite material in the hopes that they will receive extended life and exposure through these efforts.

---------------- ✳ ----------------

SOURCES OF INFORMATION
AND MISINFORMATION

Different kinds of decisions involve different information systems. On trivial matters and in subject-matter areas that lack competitive constituencies, committee control is virtually complete. On big, national issues and those that spill into other disputes, alternative sources of information are often sought, particularly with respect to district opinion. Indeed, on issues such as these the information system may come to closely resemble the Madisonian model described earlier. Most of the time, however, on most issues there is a two-step flow of information. More often than not it is a three- or four-step flow.

A growing reliance on personal staff and a concomitant decline in collegiality has not changed the basic pattern. Legislative assistants turn to just about the same sources as the MCs themselves, though to committee staff instead of committee members, to party organizations rather than leaders. Many of these sources rely in turn on others: for example, party leaders or organizations look to the relevant committees for guidance; the Democratic Study Group touches base not just with the Committee but with relevant interest groups as well.

The complexity of this process has confused some students of the legislative process, particularly those who rely on superficial participant observations or interviews with members. Interviews show us clearly, for example, that lobbyists score few conversions, pressure almost no one, are seldom mentioned as sources of information on issues, and are far more likely to interact with those who already share their attitudes than with those who need to be persuaded. But to show all this is not to show that lobbyists do not play decisive roles in the legislative process. If there is a two-step flow in the legislature, it takes only one strategically placed MC to insert a special-interest amendment in the tax code, one small clique to insure a protective tariff for glass, one cotton subcommittee to mark up a cotton subsidy program and push it through. The MCs who serve as gatekeepers in these instances are unlikely to feel as if they were under pressure, and a completed interview schedule might show that beyond the sponsors, not a single MC had altered his or her behavior at the behest of an outside force.

Much the same argument can be made with regard to the influence of executive agencies. As with interest groups, the fact that most MCs are not pressured by executive officials on most bills does not mean that the bills themselves are not the product of executive lobbying. Because there is a two-step flow of communications within the legislature, agency access to the relevant committee or subcommittee is all that is required to exert influence. The normal information flow of a legislature is such that subsystem communications obviate the need for system-wide pressure. The degree to which the White House controls, or is captive of, these channels is another question.[34]

Supplementing the Normal Flow

There are times when the normal channels of information do not work. The legislative process is analogous under some of these conditions to a system of legal appeals. Like lower court decisions, the decisions of the standing committees are seldom appealed but usually involve questions of considerable significance when they are. As with the courts, the appeals mechanism is usually invoked when the issues to be raised with the higher authority are somewhat broader in scope than those raised at the original trial. If, for example, important interests other than a committee's policy clientele are affected by a decision of that committee, they are likely to appeal that decision to the floor or to press the leadership for referral to more than one committee. The budget committees are likely to invoke fiscal considerations in times of general cutbacks or anticipated program expansions. Or, at a later stage, still other interests and political forces may appeal through appropriations.

When such appeals are made (or, in Schattschneider's words, when the scope of conflict is changed), the normal flow of information is supplemented. More MCs seek information about the issue in question. The basic pattern of consultation with colleagues on the relevant committee is still likely to have primacy; but if the appeal is to be viable there must be competing communications from constituents, from the White House, from party leaders, and from others. The broader the issue, the more the sources an MC is likely to consult.

Nonetheless, these supplementary sources of information are likely to become serious suppliers on relatively few issues. Even when they are consulted or considered, they are likely to be given less weight *as sources of information* than other sources. The White House can sometimes alter the political context of the legislative struggle. Under certain political conditions, the budget committees can make the information resources of policy committees superfluous. And the power of the White House, working directly on individual representatives and senators through party leaders or the mass media (a forum almost uniquely accessible to the president), cannot be ignored. White House power does not derive from its informing ability. Nor does that of most central sources. It is only through extraordinary efforts on their part that presidents, party leaders, or broadly focused policy coalitions can break the normal flow of legislative intelligence and force MCs to consider new or different data sets.

The quality of legislative intelligence is a function of its sources and flow. If the information system fails, it fails either because exogenous gatekeepers, interest groups, and executive agencies in particular are blocking or failing to provide full information; or because internal gatekeepers are impeding, misinterpreting, or failing to understand important sources of information. Many of the reforms of the 1970s were aimed at this latter problem. The opening of committee markup sessions was designed to force the airing rather than the obfuscation of possible areas of disagreement within policy subsystems. Although the dispersion of powers to subcommittees narrowed the number of MCs serving as initial gatekeepers, procedural reforms within the committees, particularly in the House, dispersed authority away from the handful of seniority leaders to a wider spectrum of members. On many committees, moreover, deliberate attempts were made to assign members to them who were not in sympathy with the interests that had previously dominated.

Increases in the personal staff allowances of members have also provided a means of checking up on the committees: instead of simply relying on the committee's interpretation of a group or agency position, an MC can use his or her staff to go directly to the source. A sharply rising number of floor amendments in the House is one reflection of this growing tendency to bypass, or at least supplement, the normal system of gatekeeping. By creating the Office of

Technology Assessment and upgrading the Reference Service of the Library of Congress, moreover, the postreform Congress also gave its internal specialists access to presumably unbiased sources of outside information. In part because they lack bias, because they are better able to provide information than intelligence, such research shops have seldom been major forces in the system. By their very existence, however, they help keep other players honest, and their studies sometimes do filter back in an influential manner. Like the budget committees, they can balance the propaganda edge that the administration often has in information wars. Nonetheless, the basic flow of legislative intelligence is through the channels described here: the first and most fundamental problem of a policy advocate is to get his or her message into the system.

The Continuing Struggle for Access

Nothing is more crucial to successful lobbying than the identification of the gatekeepers whose words carry weight. "What I offer," says one successful lawyer/lobbyist, "is the knowledge of who to talk with about what." Ideally, one hopes to become a "preferred supplier" to key gatekeepers, the person or group they regularly turn to when they need information about a particular problem. In the long run, one strives for a closed loop, an iron triangle of information that unites the key bureaucratic, legislative, and private sector actors in a given policy arena. One hopes to convert controversial issues into routines, situations in which policy-makers inherit adjustments among conflicting interests, mandates that define the boundaries of acceptable disagreement.

That such stable policy networks can exist over relatively long periods has been shown time and again. They can also crumble with surprising speed, as happened in the area of energy when the Arab oil embargo occurred in 1973. In the words of Charles O. Jones,

> The *cozy little triangles* which had come to characterize the development of energy policies had become *sloppy large hexagons*. Demands by environmentalists and public interest groups to participate in decision making, involvement by leadership at the highest levels in response to crisis, and the international aspects of recent energy problems have all dramatically expanded the energy policy population . . . up, out, and over—*up* in public and private institutional hierarchies (e.g., the involvement of presidents of companies and countries, rather than just low-level bureaucrats, and of congressional party leaders rather than just subcommittees); *out* to groups that declared an interest in energy policies . . . and *over* to decision-making processes in other nations or groups of nations.[35]

As the routine became controversial, the usual sources of energy intelligence, oil companies in particular, lost their positions as preferred suppliers and their control over energy policies as well.

There is little that a lobbyist can do to control the impact of an event as dramatic as the Arab oil embargo. But damage control and access are sides of the same coin: a primary goal of any policy advocate is to secure a position as preferred supplier and to keep his or her clients from feeling a need to look up, out, or over for further information. For most lobbyists most of the time, the pattern of information flow in the legislature makes this a manageable job. In its simplest form, the job of the policy advocate is to identify the key gatekeepers in both houses, secure their confidence, and provide them with sufficient intelligence to persuade other members of the House and Senate that there is no need for them to conduct further searches for information.

Certain groups bring inherent strengths and weaknesses to the job of lobbying. Professionals, for example, bring prestige and credentials; single-issue groups have a focus that more diversified groups cannot match. Some groups (e.g., corporations and church groups) are advantaged by being institutionalized: they already have their meeting halls and typewriters. For corporations, much of the research work of the lobbying office has already been done as a tax deductible cost of doing business. In filing an environmental impact statement, for example, a company has done the work that might be needed to defend a project politically; an environmental group on the other side would have to start from scratch.

Many of the larger groups, moreover, have long-established relations on the Hill that virtually guarantee access to some MCs as they all but preclude it to others. Different kinds of issues call forth different strategies, and the same tactics that work in one context may fail in another. Even the "normal" flow of legislative intelligence described here can lose its meaning when a major disruptive force, like the Arab oil embargo or the strong intervention of a popular president, alters the political context.

As with legislators, however, the key problem of all policy advocates— regardless of size, shape, or ethnic origin—is the problem of time: their time and the time of those they are trying to see. There are few junctures in the legislative process at which the perspectives of political scientists and practitioners diverge more dramatically than in the perceptions of the conflicts among lobbyists for access to key members. Whether they are defending or attacking pluralist theory, debunking or redefining the concept of polyarchy, the tendency among students of politics is to look for instances of real or sham patterns of competition among competing interests: labor versus management, small farmers versus large, and so on. This is an important and useful way to look at the political process. It makes far less sense to a professional lobbyist who sees the competition for access in more global terms. His or her primary rival for access is not a competing group but *all* groups, not a rival interest but *all* interests that might distract attention. "Your hope," says one lobbyist, "is to be known as 'good ol' Joe.' Just plain 'Joe' will do. 'Some guy from ———' isn't real good. And your worst fear is that when you shake hands for the twenty-third time he's still meeting you for the first time."

The first step in effective lobbying is to become part of the member's field of forces (to use Kingdon's term), someone whom he or she is not meeting for the first time. There are gimmicks one can use to stand out, but most have already been tried. Basically, access derives from the ability to provide the MC with something he or she wants. In a most fundamental sense, that boils down to one of two things: information or political help. Properly done, there is nothing more useful to members than providing them with good information. By successfully providing it, the policy advocate can gain a form of access (that of preferred supplier, if you will) that no other form of lobbying activity can buy—access so subtly potent that the lobbyee no longer sees the lobbyer for what he or she really is. "How do I know when I'm doing my job? When they call me." Although such contacts never show up in the interview protocols of those tracing patterns of influence on Capitol Hill, these may well be the most important information transfers of all. When the LA to a senator calls upon Lobby X to draft a bill or speech; when a subcommittee staff director calls Lobby Y for figures on the projected impact of a proposal; when the representative of Z is invited to sit down with staff aides trying to hammer out acceptable language for a key paragraph—that's access. And access breeds access.

Not to be overlooked is the political intelligence a good lobbyist can provide the legislator. This too is a cumulative resource that feeds on itself: the more MCs you have access to, the more helpful you can be in telling others what's going on. The more knowledgeable lobbyists and agency liaison agents can be particularly helpful to junior members because of their experience in parliamentary procedure, bill drafting, and some of the more arcane but interesting questions that one might hesitate to ask another member: What is the chairman really like? Who allies with which coalition on the Appropriations Committee? Which of many claimants really has final say on energy matters? Is she serious in offering this amendment?

Even the more senior members (and their staff people, especially) frequently turn to lobbyists for political intelligence. Major strategic decisions are often worked out between MCs, staff aides, and lobbyists: Who should we deal with about what? Who do we approach first on the Rules Committee? Will Senator X withhold her amendment if we do Y? Some of these deals are best arranged member-to-member, some at the staff level; but logrolling works best when the log is kept low in the water, when the deals are hidden from public view and perhaps from the logrollers themselves. MCs, as we shall show in greater detail in later chapters, seldom engage in explicit vote trades; but the restraints are off when dealing with lobbyists who sometimes wind up having "to spend a great deal of time working on issues that are of little concern to their employer, but are of interest to the Congressional Big Man who has power over their employers' interests." In many ways, "lobbyists are by no means just outsiders trying to influence the system of legislative processes. Rather, they are the internal conduits by which the process operates—the communications links among the members of Congress. . . . [W]ithout them, the practice of politics would grind to a halt."[36]

The Special Problems of White House and Agency Liaison

Political climates, like the weather, can be unpredictable. A president, even one as popular in his first years as George Bush, can spend political capital quickly; as much as visibility can be a source of strength to a popular president, it can be a liability to one whose star is on the wane.[37] Thus, although presidents have the capacity to involve a larger public in most issues, they generally choose not to make such appeals. Nor, as a rule, do presidents do as much congressional arm-twisting as many outsiders think: hard evidence and rational arguments play a larger part in presidential-congressional conversation than the outsider, obsessed with talk of power and "deals," often realizes. As Ralph K. Huitt, political scientist turned executive branch lobbyist, once said, "The most effective tool is so simple it sounds naive, and it is hard to credit. It is knowledge, expertise, and a command of the business at hand."[38] That kind of information is most likely to be found in the outer circle of executive power in the more specialized bureaus and agencies. Far more knowledgeable but far less visible than the president and his immediate advisors, they are also advantaged by having more frequent and regular contact with their counterparts on Capitol Hill. Frequently the two groups work together. For example, Eric Davis interviewed a member of President Carter's White House staff who indicated that it was White House policy to have departmental lobbyists "do almost all the errand running." Problems demanding special knowledge were farmed out to the department and agency lobbyists most likely to have the knowledge. "In addition," the staffer continued, "they can help us . . . on bills with members they have special relations with. Jack Stempler (at Defense) may not care very much about (election day) voter registration, but if he calls up Congressman 'Bombs Away' and tells him he thinks voter registration is a good thing, that Congressman's going to be very likely to vote for it. After all, this is Stempler from the Pentagon calling."[39]

Such coordination and cooperation is obviously useful to the White House and may, from time to time, yield results. Yet particularly as one moves to the lower levels of the bureaucracy, the likelihood of its being effective decreases dramatically if it is displaced from its knowledge base. How sincere is "Stempler from the Pentagon" likely to be when he makes his call? Does he say, "Listen, Bombs old buddy, this voter registration stuff is important. Let me fill you in . . . ," or, "Bombs? Listen, I'm getting a lot of flak from the White House on this voter registration stuff (whatever that is), and I promised I'd call you. Consider yourself called. Now, while I've got you on the line, let's talk about some really important stuff . . . "

Even when the lobbying bureaucrat is sincere, it is not clear that he or she is likely to be effective outside the sphere of his or her known area of knowledge. Bombs Away has learned to trust the technical advice of certain people in the Department of Defense. That relationship of trust may even develop into a more general pattern of understanding and friendship; but unlike a congressional colleague, the bureaucrat cannot offer political empathy or reciprocity and is assumed to have a particular ax to grind. Outside experts who go to the well too often on matters they know little about may soon wear out their welcome on matters they do.

Every president has sought, and some have succeeded, to coordinate the manifold lobbying activities of the executive branch. Standing between the White House and the agencies are the middle levels of administrative authority and information—department heads and their immediate staffs, and the Office of Management and Budget. As sources of legislative intelligence, they have neither the president's access to publicity and political clout nor their subordinates' expertise and close contacts on the Hill. Both their power and intelligence are derivative and therefore suspect. The director of OMB or the Cabinet official is useful as a source of political intelligence largely to the degree that he or she is reflecting the White House point of view or exposing areas of division in the administration. As director of OMB in 1981, David Stockman was successful in pushing a program of budget cuts in large part because he was perceived as having the full backing of a highly popular president. He failed to trim Social Security later that year in part because many MCs believed (correctly, as it turned out) that the president's position on Social Security was "soft."[40] When a Cabinet official testifies before a congressional committee, the factual information he or she provides is of trivial interest: most committee members know more. But the political content of his or her message serves as an indicator of the unity, flexibility, and commitment of the administration and is anything but trivial, particularly if the Cabinet member is close to the president.

Congress expects Cabinet members to spend a good deal of their time on the Hill, despite the fact that interviewed congressmen almost never mention high-ranking administrators as sources of information, pressure, or voting cues. The explanation for this seeming irrationality lies in the system of political intelligence in which departmental secretaries play at least four important roles.

First, the Cabinet member is a key source of political cues. Inhabiting an unusually sensitive political domain, "Cabinet members function in a twilight region of executive-legislative responsibility with all of the dilemmas of role conflict which that produces."[41] How he or she functions in this zone of ambiguity is a key indicator of the balance of political forces that obtain in the environment. "If he appears as the President's man, he may aid his superior and may or may not (probably not) improve his own departmental position. If he operates independently of the President, he may aid his own future and may or may not (probably not) help the President."[42] Wherever he or she chooses to operate on the continuum between these extremes, it will be noted on the Hill. Cabinet members deal not with Congress, but with specialized parts of it—committees and subcommittees—that are acutely sensitive to the political dynamics of subsystem politics. If Congress itself fails to pick up the nuances of a secretary's performance, there are those whose job it is to strike the message home: lobbyists and the specialty press.

This leads to the second important role of administration leaders in the system of legislative intelligence; their ability to alter the visibility of an issue. When the secretary of X testifies before a congressional committee, it may or may not make the evening news; but it will be reported somewhere, usually in a medium likely to reach the interests most directly affected. The secretary of commerce's statements on steel imports may not be featured on NBC News, but they will get thorough coverage in the journal *Iron Age*. Through such media, a third impact of Cabinet member activity is likely to emerge through the reshaping of the lobbying activities of private groups and—more especially—of lower level bureaucrats. Finally, administrative lobbying at all levels plays an important defensive function. Regular contact on the Hill can help build personal bonds, sensitize the administration to particular congressmen, and generally provide what former Secretary of State Acheson once called "stopping rat holes."[43]

———————— ✳ ————————

CONCLUSION: TIMING THE MESSAGE

The "normal legislative process," according to one student of lobbying, is one in which negotiations are "restricted to private meetings among privileged insiders. In this way, potential points of conflict are less likely to be revealed to those who might be less effectively organized."[44] Terms such as *iron triangles* or *subgovernments* have often been used to describe these relatively closed systems of information and influence. They may convey an image of greater stability and control than actually exists in most policy areas. Thus, terms such as Heclo's *issue networks* are gaining acceptance. Issue networks are less tightly structured and involve more participants than the subgovernments that are usually bounded by the jurisdictions of a single subcommittee, government agency, and interest coalition. As with the old iron triangles, however, "An issue network is a shared knowledge group" whose participants are united by their expertise.[45] Such "knowledge groups," or "invisible colleges," as we have called them, vary in size and composition. On some issues, they closely resemble the classic iron triangles. On others, the boundaries of knowledge and involvement disappear into a shapeless fringe of part-time players and generalists. Even on a single issue, as was powerfully shown in Bosso's study of pesticides, the number and range of involved players can change dramatically from one year to another.[46] Whether a policy subsystem is open or closed, large or small, is seldom a matter of chance. Changes in the scope of conflict usually come about because someone wanted them to. If we are to understand the politics of legislation, "We must understand how competitors seek to broaden or narrow the scope of conflict."[47]

The growth of the lobbying community has combined with the rise of subcommittees to reduce the predictability of policy domains. "Although more points of lobbying access are open," William Browne argues, "each policy domain is subject to frequent political change, risk to long-standing policies, uncertainty as to which values count most in deliberations over any issue, and great anxiety among those interests that have long had their way."[48] Established groups have obvious interests in walling off their issue domains and posting the land, so to speak, with "no hunting" signs for all others. This interest exceeds the desire to simply maintain control. Issue niches (to continue Browne's analysis) provide "a recognizable political identity" that "helps structure the organization both internally and externally."[49] In terms of our analysis, the stability of issue niches is also an important timesaving device. Like MCs, outside policy advocates have numerous demands on their time. They operate most efficiently and are less likely to waste the time of others when they focus on the issues they know best. Whatever the dynamic of power may be, the dynamic of the information system is toward compartmentalization. A popular president who carefully chooses a limited set of issues, a clash of interests between established subgovernments, shrinking resources, even a well-developed argument or idea can bring about an abrupt shift. Such challenges to subgovernments are part and parcel of the legislative struggle but are "probably more volatile and erratic than subgovernment politics. It often possesses a 'flash-in-the-pan' character with no lasting, major changes in outcomes."[50] Power gravitates to the informed.

6

---　✳︎　---

LEGISLATIVE
PARENTHOOD

I t is a few seconds after the noon hour. The presiding officer raps the gavel, and the chaplain invokes the blessings of God on the U. S. Senate. As the prayer ends, there is a confused bustle. A motion is made to approve the journal without reading. The majority leader confirms the schedule agreed to the previous day and receives mumbled consents to a three-minute limit on statements during the morning hour. Three senators await recognition to reprint articles, editorials, and other miscellaneous items in the *Congressional Record*.

As these events transpire, a senator snaps his or her fingers. A page jumps from the dais and a moment later lays a typewritten document in a tray beside the bill clerk, who sits on the lowest tier of the three-level rostrum. The bill clerk writes a number on the first page, notes with approval the suggestion for committee referral, and sets the document down in a tray from which it will be taken for overnight printing. A bill has been born!

On the other side of the Capitol building, MCs drop their proposals in a special "hopper" where an agent of the speaker collects them for numbering, committee referral, and routing to the Government Printing Office. About the only significant difference in the thousands of bills introduced in each house every year is that the numbers on those originating on the south side of the Capitol begin with the letters "HR" and those from the north begin with the letter "S."

———— ❋ ————

CONCEPTION, PARENTHOOD, AND SPONSORSHIP

Every bill, in a formal sense, has a sponsor. Since his or her name is publicly inscribed on the first page, it is a polite tradition to refer to the sponsor as the author or drafter of the bill. The press follows this tradition largely because it is easier to label a bill by a sponsor's name than by using its formal title. Although some MCs take pride in crafting their own bills, most have complex origins and are drafted by skilled draftsmen on the Hill, in executive agencies, or in the offices of private associations. Occasionally, the sponsor knows little or nothing about the bill that bears his or her name. "In 1890 a bill was passed," wrote an old-time senator in his autobiography, "that was called the Sherman Act for no other reason that I can think of except that Mr. Sherman had nothing to do with framing it whatever."[1] While this may have been a slight exaggeration, there are countless other cases that readily fit the description. In analyzing the birth of a bill, one must consider sponsorship and authorship separately. Both are essential to the birth of a bill, but just as with a child's father and mother, each has a different function.

The Sponsors

In countries operating under the Cabinet system, the administrative arm of the government can introduce legislative proposals by its own action. Anyone in the United States may draft a bill; but under our system of separated powers only a senator or representative may introduce it in Congress. Beyond the rules excluding outsiders, House and Senate rules on sponsorship are loose. Any MC—except by custom the Speaker of the House—may introduce a bill at any time that the Congress is in session as long as it is personally signed by its sponsors.[2] Any number of senators or representatives may be listed as cosponsors, but since bills cannot be copyrighted there is nothing to prevent a member from photocopying a colleague's bill and introducing it in his or her own name. Except for certain requirements as to format, there are no constitutional or ethical restrictions on what a member may choose to sponsor as a bill or resolution.

The Goals of Sponsorship. Usually, MCs sponsor bills because they would like to see them become laws. They allow themselves to be listed as cosponsors for the same reason. Bills, however, can serve important functions even when they have little chance of becoming law. Bills can serve as devices for gaining public recognition, staking out campaign positions, achieving publicity, and so on. Even when the sponsors are not seriously interested in their own proposals, the process of introducing a bill is so simple as to be almost a reflex action in many offices.

The use of sponsorship as a means of satisfying the demands of outside groups is sometimes revealed when the words "on request" appear after the sponsor's name. This device is most frequently used when an MC wishes to indicate general sympathies with the goals of an interest group or government agency without committing to the legislation's specific approach. Somewhat different in intent was Senator John McClellan's "on request" sponsorship of the Johnson administration's 1967 Crime Control Bill. Using the administration bill as a starting point, McClellan cashed in on the prestige of White House endorsement as leverage "to convene his subcommittee and hold hearings on the state of crime in general and his own favorite solutions to the problem in particular."[3] By the time the final bill emerged, it was all but unrecognizable to those who had originally put it together. Somewhat analogously, Majority Leader Richard Gephardt (D-MO) introduced the administration's 1992 budget proposals on request (though he jokingly suggested substituting the words *by default*) after President Bush failed to find a single member of his own party willing to sign on. As Gephardt planned, the president's bill was soundly defeated.

In the early days of the century, exposés of state legislatures pointed to the introduction of many "strike" bills, bills that could injure a given interest and were introduced for the purpose of obtaining protection money. While strike bills have become uncommon at the state level and are rare in Congress,[4] the principles behind them live on. Sponsorship brings discretionary power, including—in some cases—the power to negotiate a bill's demise. Although it would be difficult to substantiate a charge that someone had sponsored a bill in order to kill it, the logic of the situation is clear. No one can be more effective in counseling against precipitate action or accepting crippling amendments, particularly if he or she should happen to be the chair of the committee to which the bill is referred.

Personal Responsibility. Sponsorship sometimes carries with it responsibility as well as celebrity. Beyond its function of registering a point of view, it often involves a host of supplementary activities—answering correspondence on the bill, defending it before colleagues, seeking clearance from the appropriate administrative agencies, and discussing it with proponents and opponents. "When things go well, sponsorship can provide a member with long-range advantages difficult . . . to achieve in other ways. His discussions of the proposal within the committee, and perhaps later in the House, permit his colleagues to appraise him in circumstances highly favorable to him. . . . The experience may hasten the development of the member into an effective legislator."[5]

When we get down to actual cases, relatively few MCs acquire such experience. Except in the case of committee and floor amendments, junior members and those in the minority party seldom have the opportunity to sponsor important legislation. A notable exception was former Speaker of the House Sam Rayburn's successful sponsorship of a railroad securities bill during his first term in 1913; but even though junior members are considerably better positioned in the postmodern Congress, success in passing a major bill is still worth writing about.[6] Since there is no rule against the introduction of identical

measures by more than one MC, "many members with little seniority introduce bills which they regard as representing important contributions to existing law and eagerly anticipate the personal benefits to be reaped from passage,
only to discover that identical or nearly identical bills are introduced later by
the chairman. The latter bills are the ones considered by the committee."[7]

Virtually all viable pieces of legislation carry the names of high-ranking,
majority party members of the committees that processed the bills. As one
minority party senator was told by a colleague who had "stolen" all his local-
interest bills: "I can get them passed. As long as your name is on those bills, I
can see that they don't pass. If you want the bills passed you have to surrender
them to me."[8]

Even when a minority member is given credit for his or her work, the glory
may be short-lived. In 1988, for example, Democrats allowed a veterinary drug
bill, sponsored by the well-liked Iowa Republican Tom Tauke, to pass the
House; but the bill that came back from the Senate, though virtually un-
changed in substance, had a Senate bill number and, of course, a Democratic
committee chairman listed as its sponsor. In the waning days of the 100th
Congress, Tauke lost his bid for glory to the realities of party and seniority.

This kind of bill theft is not entirely political. Sponsorship frequently en-
tails leadership skill as well as the clout of party or committee leadership. By
serving as prime sponsor, a representative or senator becomes the focal point of
a campaign. Experts continue to play a part in devising strategies, in phrasing
amendments, in producing new drafts. It is the congressional sponsor, however, who is counted on to be there at the right time to defend the bill in
committee, protect it on the floor, handle relationships with the president, and
conduct (but not necessarily devise) parliamentary maneuvers.

Given the growth of staff in the bureaucratized, postreform Congress,
there is no doubt that some of the most important facets of the process of bill
development take place at the staff level. One interesting side effect of this
trend has been the enhancement of the responsibilities of those sponsoring bills
and amendments. For almost invariably it is their staff persons to whom questions of detail are delegated. The choice of sponsors, therefore, is one of the
primary problems facing anyone who seeks legislative action. An obvious consideration is whether an MC will regard his or her sponsorship lightly or
actually assume leadership, a question less of motive than of time. "I don't
believe," one Representative said, that anyone "in the House . . . can do a
really effective legislative job on any more than two bills in a year. . . . This
implies that you know reasonably well the position of each of the other members on the bill and the important amendments that may be proposed, and that
is an incredibly time-consuming job."[9]

Choosing a Sponsor. From the perspective of a policy advocate, the ideal
sponsor is a respected, well-liked majority party MC who chairs the relevant
committee and doesn't have much else to do. Since that kind of person is hard
to find, policy proponents must often settle for a less-than-ideal combination.
Though it is not as crucial in the Senate, membership in the majority party is
very likely to be a part of that combination. One staff member of a House

committee told us that he judges how seriously an interest group wants a bill by who they get to sponsor it. "If it's a Republican, I know that they're just showing the flag. It's not a bill anyone has to worry about."

Almost as important is committee membership. A lack of proper committee connections may mean that a member's bill will not even appear on the agenda. As former Senate Finance Committee Chairman Russell Long (D-LA) once said of an ill-fated health insurance bill sponsored by Ted Kennedy (D-MA), "Kennedy gets all the press, but the Finance Committee gets all the jurisdiction."[10] The growth of legislative clearance in the Office of Management and Budget makes such connections more important. Even when the presidency is in the hands of the other party, committees seldom act in the absence of departmental reports and some kind of clearance from OMB.

These departmental reports are not normally provided to individual members except on the request of the committee chair. For an MC who knows his or her way around Washington or who has close ties with the administration, it is possible to get an informal opinion on what the departmental position might be. With White House connections it is possible, sometimes, to predict the position of OMB. But neither a department nor OMB "would be inclined to give you an actual report of what their position would be on the legislation until it was requested by committee."[11] In divided government, when the administration is slow to respond or appears to be stonewalling a bill, the committee may go ahead on its own; but the process of securing clearance has become an accepted norm.

Provided that one can find a sponsor with appropriate party and committee affiliations, a series of more subtle judgments must be made. Politics is a competitive sport, and for most politicians winning is the name of the game. Victory, however, means different things to different people. To some members, getting a bill through Congress can become an end in itself. In Earl Latham's study of one very complicated bill, for example, the sponsor seemed "less concerned with making and sticking to a single comprehensive position on the legislation he had favored than he was in getting it passed."[12] Such "unprincipled opportunism"—as those with vital stakes in the legislation probably called it—is a frequent source of conflict between MCs and those on the outside. Most of the time it is probably better to have some kind of bill than no bill at all, but the outsiders, in the end, are Monday morning quarterbacks. When the rush is on, when amendments are blitzing from all directions, it is generally the sponsor who must decide when to settle for less, when to hold out, when to scramble, and when to eat the ball. It helps if he or she is on your team.

It also helps to have a sponsor who brings some sort of personal prestige to bear. The reputations of some members on some issues are so impeccable that their names as sponsors are worth their weight in votes. It is also nice to be liked. Congressman Barney Frank (D-MA), for example, attempted to defeat a 1984 bill that would continue to subsidize public power in several western states. The sponsor of the bill was Congressman Morris Udall (D-AZ), chairman of House Interior and one of the body's most personally popular members. As Frank recalled:

> Mo's a public power guy, a westerner, and it was his committee handling the bill. The environmentalists were with us; the old system was wasting water. It was bad economics. I talked to some guys on the floor. I said, 'Look, on the merits of the bill you should be with us.' And they said, 'But how can we vote against Mo?' It was a fairly close vote but we lost. We were opposing Mo Udall, and we love Mo. We lost because of Mo—a good example of personality affecting politics.[13]

What this case suggests is that bill sponsorship has symbolic as well as positional and substantive significance. Moreover, the symbolic effects of the sponsorship game are significantly expanded by rules that allow for the listing of more than one name on a bill.

Multiple Sponsorship. Although sponsorship by one member is technically all that is required, the practice of obtaining multiple sponsorship has developed as a means of spreading the action. Many a bill is introduced simultaneously by a pair of strategically placed senators and representatives by whose names it becomes colloquially known. A senator's name may not technically appear on a House bill (or vice versa). A bill such as the Simpson-Mazzoli Immigration Revision Act (named for Senator Alan Simpson, R-WY, and Representative Romano Mazzoli, D-KY) was, in this narrow sense, an individually sponsored bill in each chamber; but its title more accurately reflects the very real cooperative efforts that went into its planning, development, and eventual passage. In other cases, multiple sponsorship is a valuable symbol of bipartisan support, as in the original Gramm-Latta budget resolution that gave President Reagan one of his first major victories on the Hill.

The House for many years did not permit more than twenty-five names on a bill. This provision was consistently evaded by introduction of identical bills, and it was finally abandoned in 1979. Many representatives and senators actively seek to include as many cosponsors as possible on a bill. This is particularly important for those who face opposition from the relevant committee leaders. In the House, the aggressive pursuit of numerous cosponsors sometimes serves as the functional equivalent of a discharge petition, just as it can be used in the Senate to indicate the futility of a filibuster.

The morning mail in most offices usually contains at least one "Dear Colleague" letter requesting the member to enlist as a cosponsor on some new proposal. Usually these requests are from colleagues. From time to time, however, outside groups serve as agents of coalition-building at this stage.[14] On rare occasions the party whips become involved: for example, in 1987 the House Democrats, in a matter of minutes, rounded up 177 cosponsors in a show of force on a key trade bill.[15] Typically, "Dear Colleague" letters are sent indiscriminately to all senators or representatives; however, selective searches of cosponsors are not unheard of, and it is often the follow-up contact by phone or in person that makes the difference. Few members dismiss these requests out of hand, although there are some who refuse on principle to cosponsor bills.

In part, this reluctance stems from a desire to preserve the fiction that the sponsor of a measure is, or ought to be, its author. There are practical reasons, too—for example, the fear of becoming closely associated with a proposal that one has not fully researched. This lesson was learned by former Senator Birch Bayh (D-IN) early in his career. One of Bayh's major goals was the creation of an Indiana dunes national park that combined parkland with a deepwater port. Senator Paul Douglas (D-IL) had introduced legislation on the same subject that differed in significant respects from the Bayh proposal. To court his senior colleague in hopes that an agreement could be reached, Bayh signed onto a number of Douglas's bills, including one designed to exonerate an old friend of Douglas's from charges that he had marketed a phony cure for cancer. As the Food and Drug Administration's case against the drug became public, Bayh's position became increasingly embarrassing: ties of friendship could explain Douglas's role, but what was the junior senator from Indiana doing on the bill? Fortunately, the session ended before Bayh's cosponsorship was publicly noticed.

If the goal is legislation, majority party and committee dominance cannot be ignored. The more controversial the bill, however, the more important it becomes to supplement these necessary support systems with strategies of sponsorship that symbolically coopt potential opponents within the party and without. Attempts to touch all key bases are common, as in the 1992 Senate bill to regulate cable television. Here the three main sponsors included a liberal Democrat, a Southerner, and a Republican, each of whom occupied a key leadership position: Inouye (D-HI) was chair of the subcommittee that reported the bill; Danforth (R-MO) was its ranking minority member; and Hollings (D-SC) was chairman of the full Committee on Commerce.

The Authors

The authorship of a bill is generally harder to trace. The question, "Who drafted this bill?" is most often asked by those seeking a culprit. And it is often avoided for just that reason. In reality, moreover, it must be noted that the specific language of legislation is seldom the product of a single hand. The ideas and phrases found in most bills have complex histories. Experience counts: political experiences in previous legislative wars, the experiences of those who have administered or been subjected to existing statutes, and the experiences of those who have worked in state and local governments or in problem-solving private agencies. In The Federalist, Madison predicted that the problems of drafting new laws would "become both easier and fewer. Past transactions will be a ready and accurate source of information to new members."[16]

Madison was both right and wrong. Improvements in existing laws have become neither easier nor fewer (indeed, statutes seem to breed even more statutes), but the process of drafting such improvements has become increasingly founded in "past transactions." In a broad sense, almost all new laws are incremental, based on a series of "successive limited comparisons" with existing statutes.[17] Most new laws, in effect, are amendments—by elimination, substitution, or addition—to existing laws. One classic essay uses the phrase *common law of legislation* to describe this building process. In the states, says Frank Horack,

> Statutory precedent grows as case-precedent grows. . . . Legal science calls this the doctrine of stare decisis. The legislative process is similar. For example . . . Connecticut adopted a statute relieving the operator [of a motor vehicle] from liability to a guest, except for "willful or wanton conduct." Twenty-three states followed that lead. Described in juristic language, the legislatures have followed the rules of precedent. In popular language, the statute has been copied. The result is the same.[18]

At the congressional level, statutes are sometimes borrowed from the states or foreign governments: the federal prison furlough program, for example, was modeled on a very successful program in Mississippi. But MCs can find statutory ideas even closer at hand by simply borrowing, receiving, or stealing them from other members of their own house, or from the other body. At each new session, members borrow routinely from their own previous efforts. It is almost a ritual in each House and Senate office to go through the files at the beginning of a new Congress and dust off the failed bills for reintroduction. New members quite frequently reintroduce those of their predecessors, particularly those that pertain to local issues. And there are some bills that borrow conceptually or by analogy. The 1988 bill mandating a health warning on alcoholic beverages was patterned on older legislation requiring a similar label on cigarettes.

Often, too, there is a clever crafting together of issues. In the early 1990s, for example, the state of Montana faced a series of potential crises in the aging of old earthen dams. It became clear that neither of the normal channels for such projects—the Army Corps of Engineers and the Bureau of Reclamation—had any available funds. However, the state's lobbying office dredged up a statute designed to protect Indian lands (which were downriver from some of the decaying dams), which became the hook for legislation seeking federal help.

Once the process of drafting has begun, it is a continuous one. On major legislation it is a conglomerate enterprise with broad participation by many authors, borrowing from here and there, with amendments and substitutes offered from all directions. Even when the language is his or her own, a skillful bill drafter consults widely before putting words to paper. The Elementary and Secondary Education Act of 1965 is an excellent example of what might be called an agency-drafted bill. Almost without modification, the draft prepared by the Office of Education was the bill that became the law; indeed, a key strategy of the bill's congressional sponsors was a policy of resisting all amendments. What appears to have been an agency-drafted bill, however, was actually the product of a wide diversity of sources. During his 1964 campaign, President Johnson reinforced his commitment to steering a federal aid bill through Congress by appointing John Gardner the head of a blue ribbon task force on education. The task force report, though technically sound, was greeted on the Hill as politically impractical. But the prestige of the Gardner committee forced groups interested in the issue to reevaluate their traditional positions and gave the White House an opening to negotiate a viable bill. A series of meetings that brought together interest group spokespersons, representatives from the Office of Education, and key members of the House and Senate developed a series of understandings, especially on key church-state issues.

Working on the basis of these understandings, the bill itself was drafted in the general counsel's office of the Department of Health, Education, and Welfare. It wove into a working bill these agreements and a variety of new and pre-existing proposals. Title I, for example, was a slightly modified version of the popular Impacted Areas Bill of 1950; the idea of patterning the aid formula on the approach used in poverty legislation came from Senator Wayne Morse (D-OR) and his subcommittee staff director. Altogether at least twenty people in the Office of Education, on the Gardner task force, and from the White House, major interest groups, and both houses of Congress could claim some significant share of authorship.[19]

Unlike the Elementary and Secondary Education Act, the 1970 bill creating a National Health Service Corps appears to have been drafted on the Hill, and in purely technical terms it was. Here too, however, the real origins of the bill were considerably more complex. Faced with budgetary pressures from the White House and OMB, the Health Services and Mental Health Administration was in no position to publicly back new program initiatives. This did not prevent the agency from "conspiring with Congress" by sending some of its more able bill drafters to provide the Senate subcommittee staff with "technical assistance."[20] Though they were later pressured into withdrawing (to the extent that one staff aide suspected deliberate sabotage), the "dance of legislation" that had actors from the House, Senate, the relevant agency, and private groups waltzing through the various stages of the drafting process is quite typical.[21]

Whether major bills are prepared on the Hill, in the offices of executive agencies, or by outside interests, they are more often than not products of joint endeavors. Sometimes "congressional preparation" of a bill involves nothing more than a careful checking, somewhere in Congress, of a draft prepared elsewhere. Agency bills may actually grow out of the interests, queries, and concerns of members of Congress. The actual locus of decision-making, which is hard enough to follow in any event, is complicated by the fact that many authors, like ghost writers, cover their tracks. Those who advertise their roles in preparing a bill for a senator or representative run the risk of undercutting the status of the MC and of placing themselves in very delicate working relationships.[22]

At the other extreme, there are those whose modesty knows no bounds, particularly after they have gone on to other jobs. Perhaps it is only natural that people associated with one phase of a complex and conglomerate operation should regard themselves as occupying the center of the universe and not realize how many other authors are involved. In the development of the Federal

Reserve Act, Woodrow Wilson's close adviser, Colonel House, certainly regarded himself as a major force behind the scenes. Yet to Senator Carter Glass (D-VA), Colonel House's version of the authorship of the bill was so scandalous a lie that Glass wrote an entire book to set the record straight and prove his own pivotal role.[23] His was not the last such book to be written.

Taboos. The problem of finding the "real" authors of legislation is further compounded by numerous taboos concerning who should and should not draft legislative proposals. Authorship by the Chamber of Commerce, the AFL-CIO, or any other interested party is often regarded as tainted, at least by the bill's opponents. Protests of this type, however, have rather a ritualistic tone: they are based—and everyone knows they are based—not so much upon theoretical principles concerning who should draft a bill as upon its substance. Where there is broad agreement on substance, these taboos tend to be forgotten. The participation of interest groups in the Elementary and Secondary Education Act was not merely admitted in debate, it was stressed. The argument was made in both houses that the bill should be approved in the form in which it was introduced *because* the key groups—Catholics and non-Catholics, wealthy districts and poor—had all participated in drafting the proposed formulae. Still, in 1970 when the ship-building lobby put together a similar coalition, uniting labor and management from both coastal and Great Lakes regions, publicity was not welcomed. "Some day," one Congressman mused at the House hearings, "you will have to tell us of all the back-room discussion that went on before this was evolved." "I think it may be better," replied Commerce Secretary Maurice Stans, "if that is just left to history. The result is the important thing."[24]

Although it is true that many of the taboos formerly associated with authorship, strictures against interest group involvement, and executive agency participation in particular have eroded with time, the preparation of a bill remains an essentially strategic phase of the legislative struggle. What may appear to be a simple act of legal writing, or a technical recording of general principles is often a problem of substantial political importance. One lawyer's experience in drafting a relatively simple state law for a group that seemed to know what it wanted is instructive. To the lawyer,

> it was perfectly clear at the first conference that the committee's "agreement in principle" amounted simply to a unanimous opinion of the committee's members that the problem before them was an important one and that there ought to be a law to do something constructive about it. . . .
>
> Our drafting conference proceeded smoothly so long as the discussion centered on the broad objectives to be accomplished by the new legislation. But, as always, there were subordinate policy issues of which the committee had not thought until the draftsman raised them and requested the committee's instructions. Which of two administrative bodies should be entrusted with enforcement of the statute, or should an entirely new authority be created to carry the policy into execution? How severe should the sanctions be, and what procedural rights would be guaranteed to persons affected by the statute without interfering too much with its administration?[25]

Because of questions such as these, "it is a long and rocky road from a layman's bright idea to a matured and workable statutory provision."[26]

These problems in maintaining a consensus when dealing with specifics frequently enter into the strategic calculations of policy advocates. Not infrequently they impinge upon the decision of whether to pursue a legislative route at all. Clearly there are times when ambiguity is the key to consensus: there was a point during House consideration of Social Security refinancing, for example, when "neither the full nor the subcommittee had a formal bill to work on." One staff member told Paul Light, "We need a working document, but we can't have any bills floating around. They'll just become targets. It's better to write a committee bill after we've made the agreements."[27]

At the same time, it is often the case that coming in with the first draft of a bill is like beating other gunslingers to the draw. The burden of criticism, amendment, and change is with the other guy; the times and terms of debate have already been fixed. Opponents of the 1965 school bill had to impeach the administration's formulae before they could introduce their own; to become advocates, they had to be critics first, and few MCs have time to be both. "Whoever gets to do the drafting," one Senate aide has argued, "whoever puts it down on paper first is setting the tone, even if it gets edited."[28]

To be sure, not all drafting decisions are politically loaded. Those in the Senate and House offices of the legislative counsel, and some staff members and bureaucrats, are extraordinarily adept at molding inchoate mumblings into effective bills. Simply to search the existing corpus of law and find suitable language to convey the full intent of a new law's sponsors is no mean task. But for important policy proposals, most MCs prefer non-neutral sources: "When I want to put together a bill," one Congressman said in a recent interview, "I want to work with someone who shares my prejudices and concerns. The Legislative Counsel is fine for little stuff, but on important bills I turn to my friends." In the case of this particular MC, a subcommittee chair, his "friends" were usually members of his subcommittee staff or—when fellow Democrats were in control—members of the relevant administrative agency. But it is not uncommon to find MCs turning to friendly interest groups, or even college professors with legislative experience, for help.

Executive Drafting. Charges that executive agencies are usurping legislative powers in drafting bills were once commonplace. Since the days of Franklin Roosevelt, however, attitudes have changed. "Don't expect us to start from scratch on what you want," one committee chairman told an Eisenhower administration witness in 1953. "That's not the way we do things here—you draft the bills and we work them over."[29] Not only is the administration expected to provide such initiatives, but the absence of administration drafts is generally regarded as tacit indication on the part of the president that he or she does not seriously want the legislation at all.

Prior to the Kennedy-Johnson years, when the use of special policy task forces centralized important aspects of legislative parenthood, executive initiative was centered in individual departments and agencies. Major items, particularly those with significant budgetary impacts, were submitted to the Bureau of the Budget to determine whether or not they were "in accord with the program of the president" (the highest recommendation), "consistent with the program of the president" (merely not objectionable), or "not in accord with the president's program." Bills in the last category were not sent to Congress. In addition to those bills cleared through the Bureau, each department was expected to call upon its bureaus and agencies to produce an annual wish list of new programs for possible inclusion in the president's annual State of the Union and budget messages.

This process has been steadily centralized to the point at which, as one MC puts it, "it sometimes seems as if every piece of paper that circulates in this town must be cleared by OMB." Since the 1970s, the Office of Management and Budget now has responsibility for the clearance—in both fiscal and policy senses—of all proposed drafts of legislation. What this means in reality, however, is not clear. Certainly the formal process is in place: Heclo tells how even as President Nixon was drafting his resignation speech, "a top White House bureaucrat . . . continued to receive telephone calls from congressional staff asking whether or not pieces of relatively minor legislation were 'in accord with the President's program.' "[30] It would be naive, however, to assume that central clearance can ever be fully effective at the drafting stage. Almost by definition, the more "central" the actor, the less he or she is likely to have grasped the technical issues involved. A case in point is the Reagan administration's attempt in 1985 to put its imprimatur on agriculture policy. As William Browne describes it,

> the Reagan administration's interest in early farm bill deliberations took the form of rhetoric, challenging growing costs of farm programs and calling for the elimination of most price supports. Conflict between White House advisers, the Office of Management and Budget, and the [Department of Agriculture] led to a very late submission of a farm bill. When it arrived in Congress, USDA officials were left to defend a proposal that in the wake of the farm crisis struck most members as what one called "at best a joke and at worst a philosophical tract."[31]

Browne goes on to note that the administration's unworkable draft left "interest representatives greater latitude in promoting their own initiatives" and left "USDA experts" without "much leadership in the farm bill process."[32] One suspects, however, that in some dark corner of the Capitol or USDA, departmental experts were as active as ever helping to provide "technical" support.

————————— ✳ —————————

TIMING THE OFFSPRING

The choice of time is a vital element in all phases of the legislative struggle. The entire fate of a bill may hinge upon when its supporters launch a campaign on its behalf. Timing has become an increasingly crucial factor as workloads increase. The option of staying in Washington for a week or two to clean up loose ends is not viable when Congress is already in year-round sessions. One former senator has suggested that "We have now reached the bottom of time. There is no more left. I have been here when the Senate was in session on New Year's Eve . . . with the work of the Senate uncompleted. The prospect of reaching the end of a calendar year with important work which cannot then be completed before the year is over is frightening."[33]

Timing in the Narrow Sense

In a narrow sense, the choice of time involves selecting which part of a presidential or congressional term would be best, and whether action should be initiated in one house of Congress before the other. It may also involve considerations of when a controversial measure should take effect.

The "Normal" Flow.   A bill defeated or not acted upon before adjournment is history. If the next Congress is to consider the proposal, it must be introduced again. Usually, then, there is a flood of legislative proposals in the early days of a term of Congress—including many repeaters from the previous session—a flood that tapers slowly, becomes a steady stream, and then narrows to a trickle toward the end of the two-year term. The pace of enactment flows in the opposite direction. It begins with a trickle in the early months as congressional activity is focused primarily on hearings and committee markups. The pace of enactment expands steadily throughout the session and reaches a flood tide in the final weeks, particularly in the final weeks of the second session, which tends to be more productive than the first.[34] The productivity of a legislature cannot be measured simply by counting the number of bills passed, but in purely quantitative terms virtually all legislatures peak at the finish line. The logjam in the closing days of most state legislatures is notorious; although it is frequently deplored, it is not at all uncommon for a state to adopt literally hundreds of statutes a day as the clock runs down. In part this bunching is explained by institutional variables: it takes time to steer a bill through the many pitfalls of the legislative terrain. Also, as all college students know, there is a natural human tendency to work harder under the pressure of finals. But the strategic element in the flow of legislative business is not insignificant.

Just as seeds that are slow to germinate should be planted early in the spring, so, as a rule, should important bills be introduced at the first opportunity. On certain questions, early introduction is imperative. This is particularly true of any measures likely to be combated by delaying tactics in committee or on the floor. At the end of the session, when competing demands on congressional time are high, it is much more difficult to deal with dilatory tactics. When the Senate is in the equivalent of football's "two-minute drill," filibusters almost invariably succeed. At this late stage, moreover, with most bills reaching the Senate floor by unanimous consent, "holds" take on greater meaning. Used to accommodate individual senators with scheduling problems, a "hold" placed on a bill in the final drill can become, in effect, a veto.[35]

Complex pieces of legislation, such as those involving tariff and tax policies, also tend to require prompt action because the process of amendment eats time at all stages. When the issue is amendments to the rules, only the opening session will suffice.

However, there are certain advantages to waiting, if not for introducing a bill at least for having it brought to the floor. With up to a third of some state legislatures' business being conducted in a last-minute orgy of business, it is often the case that some real sleepers slip through. Although such logjams tend to be less severe at the federal level, the tactic of slipping bills through in a crowd is not unheard of. Recent administrations have discouraged legislative initiatives by encouraging delays in appropriations bills. The required "continuing resolutions" keep existing programs alive but are usually passed under such tight time constraints that significant changes are discouraged. The end of session period in recent sessions of the House has also witnessed a flood of bills passed under suspension of the rules, which, by prohibiting amendments, forces the House to consider needed policies on a "take it or leave it" basis. Popular bills, such as those that lower taxes, can also slide through at this stage with less line-by-line scrutiny than they might otherwise attract. It was probably with this in mind that Russell Long (D-LA), former chairman of the Senate Finance Committee, "often endeavored to have 'the last train out of the station,' a practice that shows his keen understanding of the importance of timing in the legislative process."[36]

The Electoral Cycle. An ever-present consideration in timing is the problem of forthcoming elections. A presidential election year is widely regarded as providing a particularly unpropitious occasion for proposing action unpalatable to large groups of voters, such as a tax increase. Most MCs can cite specific instances of bills that, in their opinions, were passed over because of election-year jitters.[37] Despite this widespread assumption, the general case is difficult to prove. In a survey of seven Congresses, Charles Jones found, contrary to expectations, "that many measures are held over from the first to the second session before final action is taken." Analysis of these bills "simply does not support the proposition that controversial legislation is avoided in election years."[38]

Indeed, there are frequent instances in which controversial bills have been pushed in election years in order to establish or reinforce campaign themes. In 1988, for example, Democrats persisted in tying plant closing legislation to a foreign trade bill despite (or perhaps because of) the virtual certainty of a presidential veto. Despite such cases, and although Jones's data show no clear pattern of election year phobias, it is widely believed on the Hill and in most state legislatures that controversial bills are less likely to succeed in even-numbered years. And presidents, it seems, are less likely in general to take positions on legislative issues in election years.[39]

The more important effect of electoral cycles is retrospective. "Mandates" from the voters are usually perceived as having short lives. "I keep hitting hard," Lyndon Johnson said of his early days in office, "because I know this honeymoon won't last. Every day I lose a little more political capital. That's why we have to keep at it, never letting up. One day soon, I don't know when, the critics and the snipers will move in and we will be at stalemate. We have to get all we can now, before the roof comes down."[40]

The Reagan administration's attempt "to hit the ground running" in 1981 was based on similar calculations. Although students of the presidency disagree as to its origins and significance, analyses of public opinion polls have shown almost every administration following a "cycle of decreasing influence."[41] From the time of Franklin Roosevelt's first hundred days—which put in place the legislative foundations of the New Deal—most presidents appear to have scored their major legislative victories in the first year of their first terms.[42]

Which House First? Another important tactical decision—one that usually comes more at the reporting than the drafting stage—is the choice of which house in the bicameral Congress to try first. Introduction can be limited to one house or the other, though this usually indicates that the bill is of minor importance.[43] The constitutional requirement that all revenue bills begin in the House has usually been honored; but the fact that this rule was ignored, with hardly a whimper of protest, in the Senate-initiated tax bill of 1982 shows that the decision is basically political. How the bill is scheduled often involves complicated negotiations involving sponsor egos as well as tactical factors. Sometimes it is best to start in the most friendly body in hopes that a big victory will have a bandwagon effect. Some observers have cited Republican control of the Senate as a key feature of the political context accounting for the early successes of the Reagan legislative agenda.[44] Sometimes the attitudes of members of the relevant committees are the key variables: whichever committee holds its hearings first is likely to get the most publicity and perhaps set the tone for subsequent debate.

The diverse rules of the houses are also a consideration: the ability of the House, through closed rules or suspensions, to keep a bill clean of amendments sometimes suggests a strategy of going to the Senate first in order to limit lobbyists for revision to one crack at the bill. The Senate's looser rules on amendments also make it possible to avoid hostile Senate committees by initiating action in the House. Thus, civil rights advocates in the 1950s and early 1960s avoided Senator Eastland's conservative Judiciary Committee by bringing House-passed bills directly to the Senate floor as amendments to otherwise trivial bills. This tactic was used in reverse in 1982 when the House, by amending a Senate-passed tax bill on the floor (instead of one originating in its own Ways and Means Committee), was able to go directly to conference, where the Senate's "proclivity to accept 'helpful' amendments" opened the bill to special interests.[45]

There are instances in which legislative strategists like to initiate action in the more hostile body. This is particularly true when the main issues involve amendments and procedures rather than general principles. Even though amendment is theoretically easier in the Senate, those who want a law are increasingly constrained as the session winds down to take what they can get. This was what proponents of federal aid to education had in mind in 1965 when they brought the House-passed bill to the Senate with a "no-amendment" strategy. Senate managers rejected even the most trivial technical amendment to avoid having to go to conference and jeopardize the delicate balance of political forces that had passed the bill in the House.[46]

Divided government adds still another dimension to the "who goes first" dilemma. Although everybody knew in the early 1980s that something had to be done to refinance the Social Security system, no one wanted to bite the bullet first. According to Paul Light, "The White House worried that the Speaker could pass a bill, while the Speaker worried that he could not." In such an atmosphere of "mutual fear and uncertainty" a national commission was created—essentially "as a front for secret bargains"—that took away the political onus of going first and paved the way for eventual compromise.[47]

The Budget Cycle. Budget reform has added another set of strategic options to the process, though not to the extent once hoped. By requiring Congress to set target figures early in the session, the idea was to force comparisons between programs and slow the process of incremental increases. Established ceilings would force special interests and their subcommittee friends to operate within limits devised by the House and Senate as a whole, and new spending programs would have to be justified early in the session, to an audience of the entire Congress. Instead, there developed a "recurrent pattern of highly publicized, controversial, 'tight' budget resolutions in advance of the fiscal year, followed by quiet revisions to allow more spending once the fiscal year is under way." Second and third budget resolutions accommodating new subgovernment initiatives by raising the supposedly "binding" figures of earlier resolutions became common. "Clearly," Dennis Ippolito argued in 1981, "the budget-cutting sentiments that shape spring budget resolutions wilt when actual program cuts are considered."[48]

In some sessions of Congress since Ippolito's study, the Reagan administration showed that a determined administration working cooperatively with legislative leaders could substantially alter these dynamics. According to one close student, "Priority decisions have increasingly dominated budgetary politics as Congress and the president struggle to control broad revenue and spending aggregates over multi-year periods. While program and operation decisions—budgeting at the micro level—remain critical, they have increasingly been subject to top-down constraints."[49]

Nothing could illustrate such top-down constraints more dramatically than the binding multi-year limits on spending agreed to in the 1990 White House–Congress summit. What such top-down constraints mean strategically is that the locus and timing of legislative advocacy have been changed. Policy advocates must strike earlier or on a broader front than in previous years; it has become difficult if not impossible to slip a major initiative into the policy stream late in the game.

The Flow of Tides

Long-Range Cycles. The history of U.S. law reveals cyclical trends at least as sharp as the rise and fall of business activity and employment. The first years of the New Freedom of Woodrow Wilson, the New Deal of Franklin Roosevelt, and the Great Society of Lyndon Johnson together account for perhaps 80 percent of the major acts of social reform introduced in this century. Wars, recessions, and social crises have major impacts on the Hill, as can dramatic events. Washington insiders frequently talk of the "mood" of a given session of Congress, what social psychologists might call the "frame of reference."

Washingtonians consume a lot of time trying to read these tea leaves, to decide if the public is ready to be led, if leaders are ready to lead, or if anyone cares one way or the other. They consult polls, newspapers, the mail, and most frequently, each other. For years afterward they write books and articles explaining why they were right and others were wrong in their judgment of the mood. Could Ronald Reagan have pushed his social agenda and dealt with issues such as abortion and school prayer without jeopardizing his economic program? Whether the time was right for such a sweeping program of change in 1981 we may never know. What we probably can predict is that books and articles arguing both sides will be appearing for quite some time to come.

Some legislative proposals, of course, have little relation to the economic or political climate. Year in and year out the departments and pressure groups bring in bills designed to expand a bureau, change the status of reserve officers in the Navy, or provide for another attack on the water hyacinth problem in the Mississippi delta. Yet whenever an idea for legislation calls for drastic changes in the status quo, there is a natural disposition in favor of waiting until the time is ripe. Despite a strong campaign pledge to present a major civil rights act at the opening of the 87th Congress, John F. Kennedy waited for nearly three years—until public reactions to the beatings of civil rights demonstrators forced his hand—before taking a bill to the Hill. According to most of his biographers, delay was forced by considerations of timing rather than principle: "There was no indifference to campaign pledges," wrote Theodore Sorensen. "But success required selectivity. . . . He would take on civil rights at the right time on the right issue."[50] Whether Kennedy could have used his power, rhetoric, and prestige to hasten that process, we will never really know, but there is no doubt that the problem of timing for Kennedy was not simply one of deciding how hard and how fast to push on civil rights. "He had a wide range of presidential responsibilities; and a fight for civil rights would alienate southern support he needed for other purposes."[51]

Polluting the Stream. If only because Southerners occupied so many key positions in Congress, the ramifications of civil rights policies were among the most important variables in the legislative struggle for Kennedy and for most presidents of that period. One departmental liaison official argued that these effects could sometimes be felt even on bills having no direct relationship to the issue itself. "It was inappropriate," he argued at one point, to push his department's program in the House of Representatives, "because the Attorney General's trip into the South had so irritated the southern contingent in the House that they were refusing to cooperate."[52]

In the last two years of the Johnson administration, liberal opposition to the war in Vietnam tended to have a similar polluting effect on other aspects of the administration's program, particularly in the area of foreign policy. Because liberals joined with traditional opponents of foreign aid, the program was cut to record lows. A wide range of legislative efforts to trim defense budgets and limit presidential powers may also be traced at least indirectly to the war. And of course there are few better examples of presidential disability than that of Nixon and Watergate. After the so-called Saturday night massacre when Nixon fired the Watergate prosecutor, "All over town officials shook themselves free of the White House, released by suspicion from deference, distancing their programs from his person."[53]

It is important not to mystify this process and treat the mood on Capitol Hill as if it were the mood of an individual person. To the day he left the White House, Richard Nixon had strong supporters on Capitol Hill, and bills supported by the president were passing by comfortable margins. But the flow of executive influence was changed; the frame of reference for anything coming from the White House was tinged with Watergate.

The astute policy advocate understands and accommodates to the moods and capacities of the legislative system. Lyndon Johnson, arguably the shrewdest student of legislative timing ever to occupy the White House, once likened his legislative agenda to "a plate. It had to be kept full, but never piled too high. A serving of this and a serving of that, but never let the food spill off the table."[54] This sense of the system's capacity extends to its subsystems as well: Congress as a whole might be able to handle six or seven major bills simultaneously, but the Ways and Means Committee or Banking, Finance, and Urban Affairs cannot. A lobbyist pushing a tax proposal is not going to succeed when the Finance and Ways and Means committees are in the middle of Social Security. A president who pollutes his own legislative stream by clogging it with undifferentiated bits and pieces will likewise fail. Jimmy Carter, Light notes, did not present a particularly long list of legislative proposals to Congress, but his failure to establish priorities led to a situation in which "the Carter agenda was perceived as massive by Congress." In the words of one congressional aide,

> Most of the committees felt that Carter's attitude was both arrogant and inept. They expect the President to contribute to the legislative agenda, but not by asking for everything. If hospital cost containment can wait, the President should say so. If welfare reform has to come tomorrow, the President is welcome to give the signal. Instead, Carter sat up on his high horse and said, "Take all or nothing." Congress decided to take very little.[55]

Catching the Flood Tide.   The ability to appraise legislative cycles accurately is of particular importance to the congressional leadership and to the president, both of whose prestige may suffer from untimely actions. The late Speaker of the House, Sam Rayburn, derived his power and influence in large part from "a grasp of the House's many moods perhaps unmatched in modern times."[56]

If there has ever been a time in the affairs of American politics when the time was ripe for legislative action, none could match the beginning of the Roosevelt administration in 1933. Bill after bill was transmitted from the White House and promptly brought back for presidential signature. Soon, however, the honeymoon of the magic "one hundred days" came to an end and the relationship between the White House and Congress returned to a more normal cycle of ups and downs. Similar cycles of legislative productivity came into being with the impressive electoral victories of Lyndon Johnson in 1964 and Ronald Reagan in 1980. No massive crisis comparable in scope to the Great Depression can be used to account for the remarkable success of either. Rather, they appear to have flowed from the confluence of different streams, not the least of which involved the tactical skills of Presidents Johnson and Reagan.

In 1964, Johnson was clearly aided by the legacy of the Kennedy mystique, an image of an aborted vision of an American Camelot that Johnson skillfully exploited in leading Congress to the enactment of programs that had eluded Kennedy himself. Second (and perhaps most important to Johnson) was the outcome of the 1964 election, which gave the president both the mandate of overwhelming victory and, more important, a decisive edge in both houses of Congress. Finally, it can be argued that many of the achievements of Johnson's hundred days were programs that had been in the pipeline, nurtured and developed through years of careful planning in the Kennedy years.

If the list of Reagan accomplishments is not quite as long, it is no less impressive in light of obstacles that did not exist in 1964. Unlike Johnson, whose party enjoyed margins of better than two-to-one in both houses, Reagan had to work with a barely Republican Senate and an overwhelmingly Democratic House. His program, moreover, was not particularly popular in the polls. To use Anthony King's phrases, he was neither a "superman" overcoming great odds nor a "surfboarder" coasting on a great wave of popular sentiment.[57] The tide that Reagan followed was that which flowed into the hole created by the apparent collapse of traditional Democratic economic policies; it was Reagan's astute political sense to follow this tide by concentrating his early attention almost exclusively on those kinds of issues. Fred Greenstein's suggestion that no president since Johnson had confronted a Congress so predisposed ideologically to accept his policies is true (1) only in this negative sense, and (2) only as applied to budgetary issues.[58] When he later attempted to move to social issues, foreign policy, and so on, "many in his administration were very soon looking back on his achievements in 1981 with something approaching nostalgia."[59] It was timing that made the difference. "The Reagan White House," as Jeff Fishel astutely observes, "developed a sophisticated strategy for overcoming the political costs of reversal and deferral, particularly deferral. Reagan permitted some of his more controversial proposals, the social issues, for example, to slide on and off the agenda, without seeming to alter the rhetoric of his conservative principles in supporting them."[60]

The wise strategist knows that legislative tides do not run on schedule; yet there is an almost palpable rhythm to the process, cycles of surge and decline that, like the tides, must be navigated.

Swimming against the Tide.   The classic case of successfully swimming against the tide is perhaps that of George Norris (R-NE) in the fight for what became the Tennessee Valley Authority. There was certainly no more unfavorable climate for public power proposals than that existing in the 1920s when

Norris decided to begin building a record for his ambitious program. For many years, every effort he made to obtain a bill met with defeat until finally, in 1933, the combination of widespread unemployment and the Roosevelt administration's search for programmatic help tipped the scales. For the Roosevelt administration, Norris's years of spadework provided a ready-made program that had been tested in the legislative arena along with a golden opportunity to cement a growing alliance with the progressive wing of the Republican party.

The same approach was taken by Representative John Blatnick (D-MN) in 1959 when he decided, despite the near certainty of a presidential veto, to press vigorously for enactment of a far-reaching program of water pollution control.

> There were two chief incentives for pressing vigorously. . . . A presidential veto would clearly cast the Republicans as villains and the Democrats as heroes in the cause, and would establish an appealing campaign issue for 1960.
>
> A second incentive was that a prospective veto would bring considerable publicity to the program. Proponents believed that grass roots support was vital to expanded legislation and especially to action on state and local levels. Blatnick . . . and his colleagues felt that they were laying the groundwork for later action—presumably in 1961 with a Democratic President to accompany a Democratic Congress.[61]

Blatnick, like Norris, was swimming against the tide in full public view: his thrashing was calculated to be seen. John Kennedy, in the view of his defenders, swam against the tide less publicly but no less effectively. Eschewing the hopeless battle on Capitol Hill, Kennedy carefully prepared the legislative terrain for the day when the tide would turn. By working to strengthen party leaders in the House and Senate and the liaison capacities of the administration, he increased the system's ability to respond. By researching the proposals for action, he had a clearly defined agenda in hand for Johnson to push through in 1965 when the tide finally did turn.

However it is done, an advantage of swimming against the tide is that it provides a period of maturation and growth. When it is done publicly, as with Norris and Blatnick, it puts all parties to the legislative struggle on notice and gets people accustomed to new ideas. In this public phase details are not terribly important, as Wilbur Cohen discovered when he brought a draft of a national health insurance bill to Robert Wagner (D-NY) in 1943. To Cohen's surprise, the senator went ahead and introduced it without even looking at it.

> I was shocked, you know, and when I asked him why he did that, he said, "Well, it probably won't become law until twenty-five years from now, so why should I worry about whether one detail or another is correct in the bill?" And he turned out to be right. He had the ability of a great legislator to introduce an idea when it was still foreign to the electorate and the media, and he accepted that as part of the role of leadership in the Congress.[62]

Testing the Water. One final strategy of legislative parenthood, which combines skills of both timing and draftsmanship, is that of initiating new programs without arousing general suspicion. The politics of public works frequently involves years of incremental development from feasibility studies to massive projects. Having spent this much money, the argument goes, why not finish the job? A classic case was the Tennessee-Tombigbee Barge Canal. It was finished over the strenuous objections of President Carter, not so much on the merits (Carter was right in judging it a massive boondoggle) and not just for its powerful legislative allies (although it didn't hurt to have the Senate minority leader and president pro tempore as Senate sponsors), but because it had already cost $1.5 billion and would cost almost as much to fill in as it would to finish.

Commenting on a seemingly inconsequential juvenile delinquency control bill that Senate liberals tried to slip through in 1959, one of its sponsors suggested that "if we could get half a loaf, if we could get a foot in the door, if we could get the Federal government committed, by making a small start in the way of studies of juvenile delinquency, that would be the wise thing to do."[63] Whether because of or despite the senator's candor, this bill lost.

Passage of even a minimal bill is valuable in a number of ways. First, it tends to deflate arguments in principle that might subsequently be raised: in the case of juvenile delinquency, for example, passage would have established in law the responsibility of the federal government for activity in the field. Second, actual passage can bring in its wake a new administrative agency that takes on the advocacy of expansion. Finally, establishment of a new program tends to alter the frame of reference viewed from questions of "why" to problems of "how and how much."

Timing in the Short Run

Once a bill has been placed on the Senate calendar or cleared by the House Rules Committee, the problems of timing fall mainly on the shoulders of the majority leader and speaker. The leadership almost always works in consultation with the bill's sponsor, committee or subcommittee chairs, and the opposition leadership in setting firm dates. Despite such constraints, leadership control over timing is one of its most important sources of power. To varying degrees, control of the clock is a significant factor in explaining the powers of committee and subcommittee chairs.

Bringing in the Absentees. On closely divided issues, the outcome may be decided less by *how* those present vote than by *who* is present. The legislative strategist must know in advance not only who his or her supporters are, but whether they will be present at key points in the process. "Rarely," says Randall Ripley, "can more than two or three members be persuaded to miss a final roll call deliberately," though it does happen. On the federal pay raise bill in 1964, for example, "an entire committee, made up largely of opponents, was convinced by the Democratic leaders to take a field trip the day of the vote."[64] Subcommittees, where frequently as few as four or five members constitute a quorum, are particularly sensitive to maneuvers based on attendance, though the norm of reciprocity discourages abuse of this maneuver.

From time to time one finds in the Senate pages of the *Congressional*

Record a series of curious dialogues at the conclusion of roll call votes in which senators repeatedly ask, in incredibly verbose ways, if they are recorded on the vote. What is happening here is not a display of mass amnesia, but a deliberate stall to allow absent members to return from the barbershop or dining room to the floor.

Electronic voting in the House allows less latitude once the vote is under way. Even when the fifteen-minute clock ticks down to zero, however, the vote is not officially over until the presiding officer announces the result, and his or her right to extend that period is clear. A very different problem for party and committee leaders is that of filling an elusive quorum. Abe Lincoln, it is said, once jumped out of the window of the Illinois General Assembly to avoid being counted as present; the rush to the doors in committee meetings sometimes approaches stampede proportions. This is one aspect of strategy that is largely a minority tool. Except when the House is meeting in the Committee of the Whole, a legislative quorum typically is half the membership: 50 senators, for example, or 8 members of a 15-member committee. If it appears as if those present have, say, 42 senators planning to vote yea and 12 nay, the minority can win by going home. This tactic works best at the end of the session when normal absentee rates are high. To counter it, the leadership has taken steps such as chartering planes to bring supporters back to Washington, locking the doors of the Chamber (unlike the State House in Illinois, the House Chamber has no windows for a latter-day Lincoln), and even, in one case in 1988, ordering the arrest of absent senators.

Controlling the Flow of Business. Lyndon Johnson, as Senate majority leader, was a careful student of policy rhythms. Rowland Evans and Robert Novack argue that at least two aspects of what they call "the Johnson Procedure" dramatically changed the Senate. The first was to discard the "civilized twelve noon to five o'clock" cycle of business that had characterized the upper house's work habits.

> Johnson . . . drove the Senate into night sessions—beyond nine o'clock, to eleven, to midnight. Late hours, he shrewdly calculated, dulled the desire for debate. With senatorial brains addled by fatigue and generous libations poured in anterooms, combativeness diminished. The Senator who was ready to fight Johnson at three o'clock until the snows came was only too ready at midnight to accept a unanimous consent agreement—*any* unanimous consent agreement—if only he could go home to bed.

"Stop and go," Evans and Novack argue, "was the twin sister of the night session." Johnson brought legislation to the floor in bursts—three of four major bills one week, then nothing of consequence for the next two or three.

> Exhausted by the numbing consideration of one bill after another in a short span of time, the Senate was infinitely more pliable and at the mercy of Johnson's debate-limiting unanimous consent agreements.[65]

By scheduling legislation in bunches, Johnson was also able to enhance the possibility of spillover effects from one bill to another. Thus, under certain conditions, he was able to keep the coalition formed around one issue alive during consideration of the next, a tactic frequently employed by policy advocates. Party leaders have always tried to bring certain kinds of bills to the floor when feelings of partisanship run high—for example, as is particularly likely after veto override votes or issues involving congressional patronage. Nobody wants his or her bill on the agenda in the wake of a vote on a divisive, emotional issue like abortion. Sometimes a policy advocate will attempt to coattail his or her proposal on the emotional loading of a related issue, as Representative Ford (D-MI) unsuccessfully attempted in 1985 by introducing a resolution memorializing Armenian victims of Turkish "genocide" just hours before the House was scheduled to debate an anti-apartheid bill.

The leadership's ability to "pull" a bill from the floor is usually an attempt to save rather than kill it. The bill creating the Department of Education, for example, never came to a vote in 1978 because the opposition of the National Education Association (NEA) made passage unlikely. Not until the administration sat down with the NEA did a revised version pass in 1979. Similarly, Speaker Rayburn in 1963 kept postponing action on the Agriculture Committee's cotton bill. At issue was the totally unrelated Area Redevelopment Program, a favorite of Northern Democrats, which had gone down to a conservative coalition of Republicans and Southern Democrats that included Agriculture Committee Chairman Harold Cooley (D-NC). The bill sat on the House calendar throughout most of the session, and even with strong leadership and administration support it passed in November by only a narrow margin.[66] A year later, Rayburn used a more abrupt maneuver to deal with the same basic rupture in the party. An agreement by which Southern Democrats would support the food stamp program in exchange for Northern votes on a major farm bill was unraveling amidst rumors that one side or the other would not honor its commitments. Rayburn abruptly recessed the House for the second time in the same day for the avowed purpose of paying respects to the body of General MacArthur, which was lying in state in the rotunda. Rayburn's real desire, of course, was not to attend a second viewing but to keep his coalition from coming unstuck.[67]

---- ✳ ----

CONCLUSION: THE POLITICS OF BILL DEVELOPMENT

The arts of sponsorship and parenthood represent attempts to put policy proposals in favorable frames of reference, to provide positive cues to as many legislators as are needed to secure passage. An act of Congress is something more than a referendum on policy preferences. The contest between advocates of alternatives A and B, of spending X dollars or Y, is the most visible part of the legislative struggle, the part focused upon by the press. Of equal importance is the struggle to position issues and define alternatives. Every bill is related to every other bill if only in the sense that it competes for legislative time and attention. More than that, "A legislative enactment is seldom a clean decision of important issues. It is normally a verbal formula which the majority of congressmen find adequate as the basis for their continuing policy struggle."[68] This is by no means to denigrate the importance of verbal formulae. Language is important. And each bill, as much as it can be viewed as part of an ongoing struggle, is also a potential law affecting people's lives.

7

---- ✳ ----

THE ART OF
DRAFTING

Legislative drafting is an art that can be learned but not formalized. Beyond certain technical conventions, the authors of a bill are continuously faced with important programmatic and political choices. A bill is not just a proposal for action; it is itself a form of action that involves setting objectives and defining strategies of bargaining. It is a proposal for change in the distribution of who gets what, when, and how; it is a marker on the trail of social conflict.

---- ✳ ----

THE SUBSTANCE OF A BILL

The Asking Price

When a person thinks of selling a car, three figures usually come to mind: the price one would like; the price one expects; and, finally, the asking price. If sellers ask too much, they run the risk of frightening off would-be purchasers. If they ask too little, there is no room for bargaining. Framers of a bill face the same problem. In the case of appropriation bills or bills to authorize future appropriations, the considerations are identical. Like those selling cars, "Agencies do not usually request all the money they feel they could profitably use." At the same time, it is important not to ask too little. If you don't do some "padding" or leave room for bargaining, you find, in the colorful words of one official, that "you get cut and you'll soon find that you are up to your ass in alligators."[1] Even with policies that cannot be measured in quantitative terms, the problem is similar. In both cases the primary problem is to find language that strikes a mean between what one really wants and what one could ultimately agree to take.

Figure Flexibility. The process of preparing most appropriation requests fits this pattern. Since it is usually taken for granted that the Office of Management and Budget makes substantial reductions in the amounts requested by most agencies, it is easier to justify any agency request that has made it through to the president's final Budget Message. At the same time, OMB itself often leaves room for the legislature to make further cuts in certain programs, particularly those of high visibility like defense and foreign aid. The word *pad,* as Aaron Wildavsky writes,

> may be too crass to describe what goes on; administrators realize that in predicting needs there is a reasonable range within which a decision can fall and they just follow ordinary prudence in coming out with an estimate near the top. . . . Another way of looking at it is to say that in many cases "padding" consists of programs the agency wants badly but can do without, a matter of priorities.[2]

Some of these priorities have acquired an almost ritualistic nature. Because MCs like to be able to tell constituents that they voted to cut foreign aid, the executive budget in this area is invariably padded. Presidents tend, conversely, to "low-ball" requests for public works, knowing that Congress will raise the ante. Moreover, every bureaucrat knows that neither Congress nor a corporate board of directors is going to balk at finding the money needed to finish an almost complete capital structure. It is thus an almost invariable rule of budgeting—both public or private—that there will be a strong tendency to overestimate operating costs and to underestimate capital cost projections. There is, generally, a certain amount of game-playing here: in their heart of hearts, most MCs are sympathetic to the long-range importance of foreign aid, but they see it as a tough vote to sell back home. Similarly, although most presidents may publicly rail against congressional waste, they are not as hostile to local development projects as their budgets might suggest. Everyone, in a sense, has an interest in kidding themselves as to how much a capital project will actually cost.

Ideological Flexibility. The drafting of the Full Employment Bill presents an example in qualitative rather than quantitative terms. The original draft set forth an unqualified responsibility to "assure" continuing full employment. To have asked for a full commitment to actually providing the jobs would have transcended the realm of practical consideration. To have asked for less would have been to draft a bill that both lacked inspirational quality and left little room for bargaining. In a similar vein, four decades later and from a radically different ideological perspective, the Reagan administration's preference for the elimination of numerous government programs came to the Hill in the form of relatively moderate budget cuts, reorganization proposals, and minor modifications of language. As one administration official put it, "Look, we're not in the business of committing political suicide. There are swamps everywhere and one of our jobs is to keep the president out of as many as possible. Sometimes he listens, sometimes he doesn't . . . . He has well-honed antennae himself; he knows when to push and when to pull back, when to drive hard and when to wait it out."[3]

Evasion or Postponement.   The problem of the asking price can be evaded, disguised, or postponed. Government, in Felix Frankfurter's words, "sometimes solves problems by shelving them temporarily."[4] Such evasions sometimes arise from difficulties in framing a consensus: "A legislature eagerly ducks a tough question if answering that question threatens the passage of a bill for which a consensus has developed."[5] It can also be wise policy, as Justice White pointed out in a 1972 Supreme Court case: "When Congress created the Federal Trade Commission in 1914 . . . it explicitly considered, and rejected, the notion that it reduce the ambiguity of the phrase 'unfair methods of competition' by tying the concept of unfairness to a common law or statutory standard or by enumerating the particular practices to which it was intended to apply." White went on to quote a House Conference Report that had suggested that "It is impossible to frame definitions which embrace all unfair practices. There is no limit to human inventiveness in this field. Even if all known unfair practices were specifically defined and prohibited, it would be at once necessary to begin all over again."[6]

For Whom and from Whom?   Inseparably linked with the problem of how much to ask for are questions of for whom and from whom. The greater the number of groups for which one asks benefits, the broader the potential base of support, although this must be balanced by the fact that the more numerous the portions cut from the pie, the smaller each portion becomes. Nor is it a matter of indifference to decide who shall cut the pie: whether the statute itself shall define final allocations or give the knife to one agency as opposed to another is essential not only to the process of preparing a bill but also to the organization of support.

Most MCs are adept at discerning how the pie is cut. For many bills, the distribution of costs and rewards is obvious. When an army truck runs over a cow and a private member bill is used to reimburse the owner, the question of "for whom?" is relatively straightforward (although the farmer's lawyer will probably take a cut). It is equally clear that taxpayers will be footing the bill. On bills of a public character, distribution patterns become more complex. In the preparation of legislation dealing with federal aid to education, for example, a perennial issue has been whether all of the pie goes to public schools or some to religiously sponsored institutions. There is also the question in this and most other grant programs of how the funds should be distributed geographically, what kinds of special student needs (if any) should be taken into account, and how much of their own resources the recipients should be expected to provide.[7]

On the other side of the ledger, the government is continuously faced with the problem of raising cash. No matter how much government incomes are disguised under such euphemistic terms as *revenue enhancement* or *user fees,* most individuals and organizations believe that a tax is a tax and that the burden should be shifted to others. A typical attitude, expressed in a favorite saying of former Senator Russell Long (D-LA), is "Don't tax me, don't tax he, tax that man behind the tree."

A similar problem of "from whom?" is faced in the development of nationwide regulatory measures. Indeed, government regulations are often perceived by their targets as imposing costs of action no less onerous than direct taxes. To relieve the problem of acid rain in the Northeast by regulating the emissions of midwestern industries is, from a midwestern perspective, to put a tax on midwestern industries. If Ohio's public utilities, for example, are required to install expensive scrubbing devices or switch to more expensive fuels, the cost of electricity will go up. How much should Ohio's utility customers be expected to pay for whatever cleaning effects these regulations might produce in Vermont?

By Whom? In the case of most legislative proposals, the choice of which officials are to have power or funds is no less important than more substantive issues. In fact, the decisions on who does what are often the answers to the problem of who gets what.

The first problem in deciding "by whom" within the structure of the government involves determining which officials should get the new or increased powers or funds. Should they be given to an existing bureau or agency, to one newly created, or to a so-called independent board or commission? Should the programs be undertaken directly by the federal government? If not, to what extent should funds be channeled to state governments as contrasted with local agencies? In either case, how much control should federal officials be expected to exercise? Within the federal bureaucracy, there are choices as to the degree of independence each agency has from presidential control, and whether—or to what degree—future spending levels will be subject to budgetary controls. Congressional mistrust of the Nixon White House helped fuel what Allen Schick called the "Seven Years Budget War,"[8] which raged from 1967 through 1974 and re-emerged in the Reagan years. Battles between appropriation, authorizing and budget committees on the Hill, and between the Congress and the White House resulted in a dramatic increase in the number of mandated expenditures that congressmen like to call "entitlement" and presidents refer to as "uncontrollable spending." By mandating instead of authorizing the payment of various kinds of benefits to all who can demonstrate eligibility, Congress placed strong limits on both bureaucratic discretion and presidential control.[9]

The drafting of legislation may also involve questions about relationships with the private sector. As in the War on Poverty's ringing yet recondite call for the "maximum participation of the poor," an administrative agency can be required or authorized to consult with those who are affected by its activities.[10] More specifically, advisory committees may be established in the bill itself. If so, who and how are the members to be appointed? Are they to be limited to advisory functions or given powers and funds of their own?

Then there is the problem of legislative provisions with respect to the courts and the Congress. A bill may subject administrative decisions to a thorough review by the courts. Or it may limit the function of the courts to overthrowing an administrative decision only on the grounds that it is "arbitrary and capricious." A bill may or may not include a "severability" clause, meaning that if one part of the statute is ruled invalid, the rest may stand. By defining government benefits as "privileges" it is possible, as in the case of veterans' benefits, to virtually exempt them from judicial review.[11]

A long-standing method of review is the requirement that reports be submitted to Congress. Literally hundreds of programs are required to file reports ranging from once a year to every thirty days. In many cases, proposed executive actions are subject to congressional veto, although the constitutionality of such vetoes is questionable.

Specificity versus Discretion

There is also the vital problem of how much substance should be contained in the bill itself and how much discretion should be left to executive officials, private actors, local governments, and the courts. The ideal of avoiding too much detail on the one hand or providing insufficient clarity on the other is rarely approximated. When those who support a bill doubt that executive officials will do what is desired, there is a strong inclination to spell out the duties of the administration in minute detail. Democratic Congresses in the Reagan and Bush years were particularly inclined to mandate specific administrative actions. At the same time, it is difficult ever to predict all the circumstances and cases that may subsequently arise. Nor is it always desirable.

Sometimes a statute that for strategic or parliamentary reasons has been vaguely drafted achieves specificity through the back door, as it were, in the form of a contrived legislative history. In negotiating the 1970 amendments to the Economic Stabilization Act, for example, House and Senate conferees were barred by the rules from inserting new material. But in the conference report and in subsequent House debate, a carefully cooked legislative history was produced that made perfectly clear a legislative intent that can be found nowhere in the language of the bill itself.[12]

Justice Scalia, before he was appointed to the Supreme Court, was particularly vocal in expressing doubts about the usefulness of committee reports as a guide to legislative intent: "routine deference to the detail of committee reports," he wrote in one widely cited opinion, "and the predictable expansion in that detail which routine deference has produced, are converting a system of judicial construction into a system of committee-staff prescription."[13]

At the other extreme, an elaborate facade of detail can be constructed to conceal what in substance is a blank check. One World War II bill, the Contract Settlement Act of 1944, included a detailed list of items that could and could not be included in the calculation of compensation to war contractors; yet the section ended with a provision stating that whenever it was appropriate, "the contracting agencies may establish alternative methods and standards." In other words, the guides for administrative action had no force; they were written into the bill as window dressing to give some MCs an illusory feeling of control. Likewise, the annual bills authorizing foreign aid programs regularly name various foreign governments whose aid will be terminated unless the president determines that it is in the interest of national security to do otherwise. Since everyone knows that the president will make such a determination, the purpose of these provisions is to give MCs the opportunity to vent their feelings without actually changing government policy.[14]

At a purely technical level, attempts to achieve linguistic precision may be overly specific to the point that they actually confuse real purposes. One law school text on legislation cites the case of a bill that prohibited the encouragement of immigration to the United States. Because the bill specifically exempted only actors, lecturers, and singers from the prohibition, the courts were left with the question of deciding whether *any* other groups—ministers or nonsinging musicians, for example—could be considered exempt. "By trying to be comprehensive, the drafter produced a statute that could yield unjust results and might not prove flexible enough to deal with new occupational groups."[15]

Policy Declarations

Declarations of general policy often seem useless. They are sneered at by those who think a statute should simply authorize, direct, or prohibit. "A well drafted act," says one guide to bill drafting, "requires no extraneous statement within itself of what it seeks to accomplish nor the reasons prompting its enactment."[16] As with legislative histories, however, preambles and descriptive phrases can have an impact on subsequent acts of enforcement and adjudication. During consideration of the Securities Act of 1934 and the Public Utility Holding Company Act of 1935,

> representatives of the exchanges and the utilities . . . spent no little effort in an attempt to change some of the language of what professedly is nonoperative phraseology. The years have proven that from their standpoint they were right; for both the trend in meaning given the operative provisions of the legislation and the character of subsequent administration was determined, in large measure, by the form and content of the recitals.[17]

———————— ✳ ————————

THE FORM OF A BILL

Questions of form—how much ground to cover in a single measure, how various items should be ordered and presented—are not unrelated to questions of the asking price. The choice between various forms of resolutions, between appropriation bills as contrasted with other legislative bills, between ordinary laws and constitutional amendments, is one that invokes the simultaneous consideration of what one can get as well as what one wants.

The Type of a Measure

Most statutes begin their legislative careers as bills headed in the House as "H.R." and in the Senate as "S." They may be public or private; private bills are usually reserved for laws designed to benefit only a specified person or group.[18] However, many acts of Congress are in the form of resolutions rather than bills.

Resolutions. There are three forms of resolutions: a simple resolution prepared for action in one house of Congress only; a concurrent resolution; and a joint resolution. A Senate or House resolution is the method whereby each house handles its own rules of operating procedures and instructs its committees. Rules proposed by the House Rules Committee to govern the conduct of House business come to the floor as House Resolutions. A Senate or House resolution is often used to call upon the president or an executive agency to submit a report on a given subject. Although such a resolution does not have the force of law, it is usually complied with unless it touches on sensitive political matters. Representative Lee Hamilton's (D-IN) H. Res. 171, which in 1985 called upon the president to provide the House with information and documents relating to the covert training of "certain counter-terrorist units" (i.e., the Nicaraguan Contras), was, for example, ignored by the Reagan administration.

A concurrent resolution (H. or S. Con. Res.) is approved by both houses but not sent to the president. Except when they deal with the internal business of Congress, concurrent resolutions lack the force of law and merely express the intent of the two branches of Congress. There are, at the same time, two uses of simple and concurrent resolutions that have considerable substantive significance. The most controversial is in the legally dubious exercise of so-called legislative vetoes. As defined by one of its closest students, this "is an effort by Congress, by one house of Congress, or even by a single committee or chairman to retain control over the execution of laws *after* enactment."[19] Typically, Congress passes a law delegating certain rule-making powers to the executive branch under the condition that the proposed rules be submitted to Congress (or one of its committees) before going into effect. The Congress is then given a fixed period of time—usually thirty, sixty, or ninety days—to "veto" the rule or, by failing to act, allow it to become law.

Because resolutions, unlike ordinary statutes, are not subject to presidential action, the Supreme Court in the *Chadha* case ruled the legislative veto an unconstitutional breach of the separation of powers. Yet despite the Court's seemingly unambiguous statement that delegated powers can only be vetoed by "bicameral passage followed by presentment to the President"[20] (i.e., by ordinary law), legislative vetoes are still exercised. Indeed, the ink on the *Chadha* decision was barely dry before Congress passed and President Reagan signed still another law containing a legislative veto provision.[21] Technically and legally, executive branch officials may now avoid the veto process; practically, they do not. As one Commerce Department official explained a post-*Chadha* decision to submit a reprogramming request to the House and Senate Appropriations Committees, "whatever the particulars of the legalities might be, one ignores appropriations subcommittees at one's own peril."[22]

The second significant use of simple and concurrent resolutions occurs in the budget process in which the annual budget resolutions set overall guidelines for the House and Senate. These concurrent resolutions set spending guidelines, known as "302(a) allocations," that are supposed to guide individual committees in their spending decisions. Unless there is a bill to require compliance (such as the Reconciliation Act passed by Congress in 1981), individual committees may or may not comply. The rules allow points of order to be raised against the consideration of legislation that violates 302(a) allocations. This has been a fairly effective device in the Senate, where it requires a three-fifths vote rather than a simple majority to waive such points of order.[23]

A joint resolution is for all intents and purposes the same as a bill. Except when used as the vehicle for a constitutional amendment, it is signed by the president and has the full force of law. As noted in the official manual of House precedents, most joint resolutions are

> used for what may be called incidental legislation, such as extending the national thanks to individuals, welcoming dignitaries, notice to a foreign government of the abrogation of a treaty, declarations of military policy, and correction of errors in existing law. In the modern practice, joint resolutions have been used for major legislation of a general nature only where it is desired to use a preamble.[24]

The most controversial joint resolution in modern history was H. J. Res. 1145, the so-called Tonkin Gulf Resolution, which passed the House and Senate by nearly unanimous votes in 1964. Ignoring the warning of Oregon Democrat Wayne Morse that Congress was "in effect giving the President . . . warmaking powers in the absence of a declaration of war," Congress whooped the resolution through with little debate and few dissenting votes. David Halberstam argues that Morse "was right, of course. By using a joint resolution rather than a more serious bill or a declaration of war, Johnson had it both ways; the Congress signed on without really declaring war."[25]

Seldom do resolutions—simple, joint, or concurrent—achieve the political or historic importance of Tonkin Gulf. Constitutional amendments aside, most important acts of Congress make their way through the legislative struggle as bills.

Appropriations and Authorizations. Theoretically, there is a clear distinction between an appropriation bill and all other bills. The former is supposed to be confined to the provision of funds authorized by other legislation. Even an appropriation bill that allocates more than the authorized amount of funding for a program is considered "legislation" and subject to a point of order. If the point of order is sustained, the offending item is stricken. Legislative bills, conversely, are not supposed to provide funds but merely to authorize maximum limits for future appropriations. Evasions of these guidelines are commonplace. The most straightforward evasions are through the increasingly common bills that reach the floor under rules that specifically waive points of order. Even without such direct evasion, there is a broad borderline area in which either type of measure can be used. An appropriation of zero dollars has the same effect as a bill that abolishes a program; or, if an appropriation act embodies certain prohibitions on the use of funds, it can be just as effective as substantive legislation. Legislative policy can also be snuck through the back door of supplemental appropriations. Although Congress in theory appropriates funds through separate appropriation bills each year, missed deadlines often necessitate the passage of "continuing resolutions" that allow agencies to keep functioning. And emergencies or miscalculations can necessitate passage of last-minute "supplementals." These emergency bills can also become "Christmas trees," decorated by the Appropriations committees with all manner of legislative ornaments. The 1985 Fiscal Year Supplemental, for example, included such goodies as a boll weevil eradication program, $171 million in new water projects, and a study of "cigarettes with reduced propensity to ignite upholstered furniture."[26]

The advantages to be gained by sneaking legislation into appropriation bills, particularly at the end of the session, derive from the importance of these bills for the functioning of the government. An appropriation bill invariably gets passed by Congress in one form or another. And presidential vetoes are rare. Moreover, the appropriation process is an ideal avenue for those who are afraid of public attention and who want to avoid a full airing of the issues involved.

At the same time, there are both organizational and strategic reasons for preferring to legislate in a more traditional manner. Organizationally, those who are not members of the Appropriations committees can logically be expected to prefer "regular" bills. Moreover, a cleverly constructed regular bill can be used to both authorize a program and fund it. As much as 70 percent of the federal budget is estimated to be in such "off-budget" items. Most common are the so-called entitlement programs in which spending levels are determined by the numbers of persons entitled to grants. For example, Congress defines by statute the kinds of college students who are entitled to Pell grants: the amount spent on Pell grants in a given year is determined not by appropriations but by the number of applicants who meet the eligibility requirements. In effect, levels of spending on higher education grants are processed by substantive committees and never go through Appropriations.

Advice and Consent. In the field of international relations, the president can sometimes avoid the Senate's right to advice and consent by signing executive agreements rather than treaties. The use of executive agreements has grown as a method of attaining an international agreement without having to run the gauntlet of the two-thirds requirement in the Senate. Congressional sensitivity on this issue has helped produce a variety of devices that bring Congress into the process while still avoiding the two-thirds requirement of a treaty vote.

One of the more interesting and unusual of such evasions was practiced with regard to arms limitations agreements with the former Soviet Union. The basic framework of agreement was a series of weapons restrictions established under the so-called SALT I agreement, which expired in 1977. A new agreement, SALT II, was negotiated by the Carter administration but was never submitted to the Senate. Instead, both the Carter and Reagan administrations publicly agreed to adhere to the agreement's limits for as long as the Soviet Union showed equal restraint. Although opponents of the treaty argued that this represented an unconstitutional avoidance of the Senate's advice and consent powers,[27] Congress in effect went along by not appropriating funds for weapons systems that would have violated the agreements and, in 1982, prohibiting the expenditure of funds for any weapon whose procurement would exceed SALT levels.

Although many observers have noted a resurgence of congressional assertiveness in the foreign policy arena, a more subtle shift in the locus of congressional power has also taken place. The growing tendency of presidents to avoid Senate advice and consent procedures that motivated the reforms of the 1970s has not really been curbed. Instead, the treaty process has been increasingly displaced by joint resolutions signed by the president, a device that "permits both chambers of Congress a voice in the agreement procedure, but eliminates the severe constraint of the approval of two thirds of the Senate that is basic to the treaty."[28] Whether such a shift in the locus of foreign policy power is constitutional is academic, as there is little likelihood, *Chadha* notwithstanding, that the Court will abandon its traditional stance that such issues "belong in the domain of political power not subject to judicial intrusion or inquiry."[29]

The Scope

The drafter of a 1991 bill to establish a national military park in Corinth, Mississippi, had no concern with the problem of scope. There was only one park to be created, and no related subjects logically could have been dealt with in the same measure. Those who drafted the Tax Reform Act of 1985 faced an entirely different situation. They were dealing with a broad and complex field in which there were dozens of points that might properly be dealt with in one bill and dozens of others that might be reserved for separate handling.

Omnibus Measures. The drafters of the 1985 tax bill were quick to see the advantages of an *omnibus bill,* a term used to describe a bill composed of many parts, each of which might also stand on its own two feet. Drawing upon (1) a 1982 proposal introduced by Senator Bill Bradley (D-NJ) and Richard Gephardt (D-MO), (2) a 1984 Republican plan introduced by Jack Kemp (R-NY) in the House and Bob Kasten (R-WI) in the Senate, and (3) a Reagan administration plan developed by the Treasury Department in 1985, the House Ways and Means Committee held extensive hearings on these and other proposals in the summer of 1985. Reflecting the complexity of the proposals, more than four hundred organized interests came to plead their causes. Virtually every MC, Republican and Democrat, "owed one" to at least one of these special interests. Although many groups were accommodated on the road to final passage, the monumental scope of the bill (the final draft ran to more than nine hundred pages) helped the bill's proponents beat off numerous attacks. Through a process of mass psychology that continues to defy conventional wisdom about the nature of the legislative struggle, a sort of "reverse Christmas tree" consensus gradually emerged. Individual members gradually came to recognize that for every special exemption they could get through, the general principle of reform would be diluted by sixty more. It was a rare moment.

In a similar vein, the key to Social Security reform in 1984 was the principle of shared sacrifice. "Given interest group pressures, no package could have succeeded by concentrating on just one segment of society. And no one segment could have provided enough money on its own to cover the deficits. By taking a little from everyone, Congress and the President could cancel out some of the opposition."[30] Far more common in the drafting of omnibus bills is the spreading of benefits, a process that is particularly common in the area of public works and other subsidy programs. The late Senator Wayne Morse (D-OR) used to call impact aid the "trading stamps" of federal aid to education. Because subsidies to "federally impacted" school districts (those where there were large concentrations of federal employees, as in areas surrounding military bases) went to more than half of the congressional districts and states, the inclusion of impact aid in a general education bill was an important factor in final passage.

Also common in omnibus legislation is the compensation of pleasure with pain, as in a classic sweet-and-sour sauce. The attempt in 1989 to link a congressional pay raise with stringent restrictions on outside income is a nice case in point, even though it failed in the Senate. The omnibus approach also provides the opportunity to execute a hidden ball play. The broader the scope of a measure, the more the chance of carrying along to enactment provisions that would otherwise stand no chance. Even when such provisions are stricken, the omnibus bill provides bargaining room to its backers. In the case of tax reform, for example, both the administration draft and that of the Ways and Means majority staff included provisions that each knew were unacceptable to the other side. These provisions served as *hairy hands*, a term from the advertising industry that seems particularly apt to an appreciation of legislative strategy.

Let's say you are filming a commercial for a particularly critical representative of a beverage company. Knowing that the sponsor will object to *something* in the picture, thus requiring an expensive second run, you film one take with a particularly ugly, hairy hand grasping the sponsor's product. The hope is that the sponsor will be so concerned with deleting the hairy hand that he or she will ignore whatever other flaws the film might contain. A journalist once telephoned a member of President Reagan's congressional liaison staff to inquire about "some funny proposals in their farm bill for peanut farmers and sugar. I asked if these were to buy votes and he started laughing. These are probably put in because that's what they wanted to do, but . . . they were expendable parts of the proposal. . . . They could use them as bargaining chips. A lot of times it is that crass [or hairy]."[31] The broader the scope of a bill, the more it can hold extra provisions that, like a balloon's ballast, become most useful when they are thrown over the side.

A particularly important purpose of omnibus bills is to confound veto strategies. The more important an appropriation bill is to the president, and the more urgent the deadline, the more likely it is to come to the White House burdened with extraneous materials that the president would never otherwise accept. "In the lame-duck December session before President Reagan was inaugurated, no fewer than 148 Senate amendments were added to H. J. Res. 637, the Continuing Appropriations Resolution necessary to keep the government running when Congress adjourned."[32] Almost every conceivable means of avoiding restrictions on legislation in appropriations bills were used by senators secure in the knowledge that President Carter was faced with the choice of signing the bill or presiding over a government that could not meet its payroll or debts.

Narrow Measures. In many situations a narrowly drafted bill is more appropriate than an omnibus measure. Many years ago, bills to exempt railroads, newspapers, insurance companies, and major league sports from the antitrust laws were handled separately. Had they been combined into one measure, the amount of public attention they would have attracted would have been a great impediment. As it was, the backers of each separate bill made their case for one particular type of exemption. None of them had to assume the onerous burden of defending a measure that would have been attacked as wrecking the antitrust tradition. By limiting the scope of a bill, moreover, one limits the list of potential groups whose opposition might be aroused.

> A later tactical amendment to narrow the coverage of a bill will not help the bill's passage as much as conservative drafting in the first place. What the sponsors seek is peace on one flank. . . . To let some groups off the hook is no compromise to those left on the hook. Furthermore, lobbyists threatened by a bill may agree at an early date to stick together even if some of their clients are amended out of the bill's coverage.[33]

Another consideration is that the greater the number of bills, the greater the opportunity for MCs to claim credit as sponsors. Although bills designating special days (e.g., Public Law 98-54, which created National Atomic Veterans Day; and Public Law 98-97, National Sewing Month) are usually passed with no dissent, the idea of combining them in a single omnibus resolution would violate their basic raison d'être.

A narrowly conceived bill can often slip through the crevices of congressional or executive opposition at a time when a broad measure is stalled in its tracks. Senator Pete Domenici's 1977 waterway bill was attached, for strategic reasons, to a public works authorization proposal; but when it became apparent that the public works bill would encounter an almost certain presidential veto, Domenici realized that he could save his own proposal only by downsizing it. In a sense, he may have lucked into the best of both worlds: he achieved the visibility in the House that only the omnibus bill could generate, and—in the end—the bargaining flexibility with the White House that could be gained only with the simpler bill.[34]

As acorns have the capacity to become oaks, small bills sometimes serve as the seeds for far more ambitious programs. The food stamps program originated in 1961 as a small pilot program to dispose of surplus agricultural goods. It was made permanent in 1964 and nearly doubled in 1969 after Senate hearings revealed the existence of substantial malnutrition among America's poor. Between 1969 and 1977, when the program was again expanded by legislation, participation grew from three million to more than eighteen million monthly participants. Although it is doubtful that its original sponsors had anything like this scale in mind, one suspects that they were thinking about something more than a simple pilot program.

Many MCs are aware of these tendencies and have heard the story of the nomad who allowed his camel to warm its nose in the tent. (The camel, of course, was soon occupying the whole tent.) "Faced by a small bill with large potential, a legislator is hard put to determine his appropriate course of action."[35] Can we warm the camel's nose without giving up the tent?

> A variation of this problem occurs when a bill has precedent-setting potentials. One of the great federal legislative battles of 1972 concerned a guarantee of loans to Lockheed corporation. By congressional standards the money involved was modest, yet the implications of the bill as a precedent in the area of business-government relationships gave it a significance far beyond its own dimensions.[36]

Finally, the smaller the scope of a bill, the easier it is to prepare. A new bill can be drafted with less strain and more speed.

Design for Combat

It is sometimes noted by legislators that most of their real battles take place at the margins. Between 90 and 95 percent of the issues considered are routine. To be sure, much that goes uncontested in the present was the object of violent contention in a past day; and much of the seeming harmony in the legislative struggle is the product of "out of court" settlements that reflect hard bargains skillfully negotiated out of the jury's sight. However, if we could separate the truly "important" measures from those that really are routine, it would be found that each important bill is a fighting document that reflects a combat design as clearly as a military maneuver reflects a battle plan.

For better or worse, the statutory style of most common-law countries is derived from the work of Sir Henry Thring, who became counsel to the British Parliament in 1869. It is not enough, Sir Henry insisted, for a law to reflect "a degree of precision which a person reading in good faith can understand; but it is necessary to attain, if possible, a degree of precision which a person reading in bad faith cannot misunderstand."[37] Despite the best efforts of Sir Henry's heirs, such levels of precision continue to prove as elusive as the basic conventions of form and format remain the same.

Titles. Beneath the number, which is assigned by a clerk, every bill or resolution must have a title. Because the regular title is usually too long for ready reference, increasing use is made of special sections providing for what is called a short title. The 1946 bill "To establish a national policy and program to assure continuing full employment in a free competitive economy, through the concerted efforts of industry, agriculture, labor, State and local governments, and the Federal Government" contained a phrase in Section 1 that said simply, "This Act may be cited as the 'Full Employment Act of 1945.' " The short title was invaluable in publicizing the measure, and the bill was seldom referred to by any other name. If it gave the false impression that enactment of the legislation would automatically provide full employment, a more subdued or honest title would have weakened the bill's chance of passage, and truth-in-

labeling bills do not apply to legislation. Many titles, indeed, "are designed to conceal rather than explain their contents." For example, one congressional bill that was labeled as "A Bill for an Act to Reduce Taxation," proved on examination to "increase the rate of taxation on every item in it."[38]

Legislative advocates have been known to frame titles in ways that they hope will affect committee referrals. The classic case was the Civil Rights Act of 1964. It was framed in the House as a bill to amend the criminal code so it could go to the liberal Judiciary Committee, and it was framed in the Senate as a bill regulating interstate commerce to avoid Senator Eastland's (D-MS) Southern-dominated Senate Judiciary Committee in favor of the more liberal Commerce Committee. Multiple referral has made this option less viable, though it never was terribly common. "Committees guard their jurisdictional turfs closely, and the parliamentarians know and follow the precedents."[39] But it is always worth a try, as Senator Domenici (R-NM) discovered when his bill to impose an "inland waterways charge" was successfully steered to the Public Works Committee instead of to Finance, where such bills had usually been referred and defeated.[40]

Statement of Purpose. Another labeling device involves prefacing a bill with a statement of purposes. Legally, such a statement is neither conclusive nor controlling; it can be useful in setting forth the need for legislation, in serving as a handbook of arguments on behalf of a measure, and in guiding interpretations of intent, but seldom is it given great weight. As Francis McCaffrey warns, "The fact that a bill passed both Houses of the Legislature does not establish that the legislators who voted for its adoption were in accord with the legislative declaration accompanying it."[41]

Subdivision. The section is the basic unit of a bill. Each section may be divided into subsections, each subsection into paragraphs, subparagraphs, and lines. The various sections can be assembled into titles or even into separately lettered parts of titles, which, if bills become laws, have a tendency to become part of the political vernacular. Insiders like to show that they are insiders by talking about "Title I funds," "subparagraph 9 exemptions," "section 7(f) rules," and so on.

It is common to emphasize the strong points in a bill by putting them at the beginning. More controversial points can be buried later in brief and unobtrusive language, or described in such technical terms as to induce sleep in all but the most dedicated reader. Detachability is also a major consideration. "If its several parts are too tightly dovetailed together, if it is so constructed that a modification of one part necessarily involves modification of other parts, an amendment made in the course of debate may throw it hopelessly out of gear."[42] The careful draftsperson, therefore, often erects his or her structure along lines of a large, rambling, one-story building rather than that of a skyscraper. Although this structure sometimes makes legislation seem impossibly repetitious, the format ensures that almost any part can be removed or revised without irreparable injury to the other parts. This has the added advantage of allowing more room for the addition of new provisions. At the same time, one way of warding off amendments is to draft a bill whose parts are so technically or politically interrelated that removal of a single piece will turn the whole structure into a house of cards.

Relation to Existing Legislation.   With respect to the language of a bill itself, a primary fact to be reckoned with is the prior existence of a tremendous body of related language in statutes, administrative regulations, and judicial decisions. Thring's suggestion that an intelligent reader should not have to look beyond the statute itself in order to comprehend it is laudable in theory but of dubious practicality.[43] A good example is the Interstate Commerce Act, which was first passed in 1887 and has since been directly amended by almost a hundred separate statutes and indirectly affected by many other acts of Congress. The Act as amended now encompasses hundreds of pages of definitions, regulations, categorizations, and rules of procedure that loom large over the heads of all who would attempt to draft new measures dealing with the regulation or deregulation of transportation. It makes it virtually impossible to formulate a transportation bill that can be fully comprehensible in its own terms. Similar situations exist with regard to the tax code and other long-tilled fields of public policy.

Because of these complexities, one of the first decisions that must be made for legislation in these fields is whether a bill should be drafted in the form of amendments to existing law or as a new measure. In the House, there is a subtle difference in the rules of germaneness that apply in the two cases: by amending an existing act, one is somewhat more likely to open the whole area of legislation to revision. A 1967 bill amending two sections of the Food Stamps Act of 1964, for example, was ruled sufficiently broad to open other sections of the 1964 bill to amendment. Only rarely, however, does a new bill open the previous act to unrelated amendments.[44]

In some settings, the use of the amendment approach is adopted for its propagandistic value. In one classic case, the Taft-Hartley Act—generally considered an anti-union measure—was offered as an amendment to the prolabor Wagner Act. "Why," asked one observer, "call it an 'amendment' when it is a radically different law? The answer is that it was politically wise to do so, because the sponsors knew that large masses of workers would bitterly resent a repeal of the Wagner Act, hence the misleading designation of 'amendment' to the Wagner Act, implying that the Wagner Act essentially was retained."[45]

Intelligibility.   It is sometimes thought that the test of good drafting is to determine whether the product is intelligible to a lay reader. At the other extreme is Lord Thring's previously cited standard of precision, a standard that, in some cases, can make legislation all but unintelligible to anyone who has not studied law, Latin, lexicology, and linguistics. To attempt simplicity in many legislative areas is profitless. Despite our sympathies with one old-time Congressman's delightful attack on "gobbledygook,"[46] there are numerous areas of legislative concern in which the use of jargon is virtually inescapable, and in which the only way to state a thing in clear-cut terms is through highly technical words.

To whom should a statute be comprehensible? Although "chicken thieves . . . do not steal from ignorance of the larceny statutes," there is a need

for understanding among many persons besides those members of the legal community who have tended to monopolize the drafting process.[47] "When a draftsman labors over a nascent bill, it is a judge who is nearly always in his mind. Treatises and casebooks are filled with examples of how judges construed ill-fated laws in the past. These are the precedents which guide draftsmen in conceiving the ill-fated laws of the future."[48] Ironically, judges seem increasingly disinclined to engage in mechanical applications of statutory language. Instead, they look to debates, committee reports, and the words of legislators themselves to find out not what some slick draftsperson meant, but what the legislature meant when it voted on the bill. Thus, while bills are drafted on the assumption that "the obscure official version will be applied by the judges . . . modern judges show a great inclination to disregard the official language and apply the version that Congress consciously agreed to."[49] That MCs are aware of this tendency is attested to in the words of Congressman Jack Brooks (D-TX): "I'll let you write the statute if you let me write the committee report."[50]

The Use of Deception

The bargaining process often requires a certain amount of deception. Perhaps the most common tricks of draftsmanship have been achieved through rather simple abuses of language. Most bills providing special tax concessions, for example, are drafted in such general terms as to make it difficult to identify the true beneficiaries. One of the 174 so-called transition rules granted by the Senate Finance Committee in the 1986 Tax Reform Act applied only to General Motors, which was identified in the bill as "an automobile manufacturer that was incorporated in Delaware on October 13, 1916"—and that was one of the more obvious euphemisms.[51] One of Robert Moses's favorite tricks in drafting bills for the New York State Legislature was to incorporate language from arcane statutes into contemporary bills: language, not incidentally, that was quite at odds with everyday usage.

The United States Housing Act of 1937 stands as a classic example of a case in which its sponsors used mathematical rather than linguistic trickery to mislead potential opponents. The bill called for subsidized loans to the developers of low-income housing in which government payments of 3.5 percent would be largely reimbursed by 3 percent annual interest payments from the developers. To the laymen and to Congress this appeared to provide a total subsidy over sixty years of $(3.5\% - 3.0\%) \times 60$, or 30 percent—not a bad deal. After the bill was passed, however, some members of the real estate lobby consulted amortization tables and discovered that the real federal subsidy was more like 100 percent. If the full implications of this formula had been clear before enactment of the statute, the probability is that the amount of subsidy would have been reduced considerably. At the same time, the revelation a few years later of the real meaning of the Act's provisions unquestionably added fuel to the high flames that were lit by opponents of any type of public housing. In 1939, when President Roosevelt asked for additional funds for the program, one speaker after another on the floor of the House denounced the subsidy provisions of the 1937 Act, and the proposal was overwhelmingly rejected.

Such acts of overt deception are rare; because there are so many more sophisticated staff people and full-time lobbyists on the Hill, they are becoming rarer. The most frequent forms of deception practiced today are designed more to deceive the general public than insiders. Certain subtle forms of legislative sleights of hand nonetheless remain available. The most widely practiced is that of cooking the legislative history of a bill without changing its wording. Indeed, on some occasions the actual specifics of legislation have been contained not in the bill at all (where they could be amended or changed on the floor) but in the committee report. In 1967, for example, the Senate Appropriations Committee decided to require certain public housing developers to contribute 5 percent to the costs of new projects. Since this would quite obviously have been ruled out of order as legislation in an appropriation bill, the Committee put its instructions in the report accompanying the bill rather than in the bill itself. The Committee pointedly reminded the administration, in debate on the floor, that failure to follow the "recommendation" might endanger this and future housing appropriations as well.[52]

---- ✳ ----

THE ARSENAL OF AMENDMENTS

It is a rare bill that is regarded even by its staunchest backers as a finished document to be voted on in the form in which it is introduced. Sometimes the sponsors of a bill will amend their own measure even before it obtains consideration by a committee. If the committee-consideration stage is reached, proposals for amendments fly thick and fast. In committee markup sessions and on the floor, the key maneuvers and major votes usually relate to amendments rather than to the bill as a whole.

There are many differences between an amendment and a bill. A bill can be vetoed by the president. An amendment cannot, since the president (unlike the governors of many states) has never been given the power of a line-item veto, which would allow him to reject a portion of a bill. Amendments get less public attention than bills. Since they usually deal with what seem to be minor details, they are hard for the press and many outside observers to understand. Sometimes they pile up one on top of the other in a manner that defies comprehension by anyone except a small handful of MCs, experts, and lobbyists. So complex are the rules for considering amendments that more than one-sixth of the current parliamentary precedents of the House are devoted directly to the practices governing their consideration.[53]

Amendments for the Offensive

The traditional method of opposing a strongly backed measure is to propose crippling amendments. This was the highly effective strategy devised by Senator Henry Cabot Lodge and his small group of irreconcilables in their fight against the League of Nations. Rather than make a frontal attack upon the Versailles Treaty itself, they proposed one reservation after another. They thereby drew public attention away from the major issue, split and confused the Senate supporters of the treaty, and by the time the final vote came, had developed a measure that was no longer acceptable to President Wilson.[54]

The same strategy was used by Southern MCs in hopes of scuttling the Civil Rights Act of 1964. Knowing that such key House leaders as Majority Whip Hale Boggs (D-LA) were unable—for their own political reasons—to provide vigorous leadership, and being aware of the tendency for Northern liberals to be lax in their attention to the details of action on the House floor, the Southerners offered more than one hundred separate amendments to the bill. Thanks to the work of the Democratic Study Group (which, in effect, took over the functions of the party whip system), only "a few amendments were adopted, [and] there was not a single occasion on which one opposed by managers of the bill got through."[55] President Carter's Panama Canal Treaty also survived this kind of attack in the Senate in 1978, but only after thirty-eight days of debate and an extraordinary lobbying job by the administration.

A striking variant of this approach occurs when MCs deliberately attempt to "make the bill as bad as possible so it would be easier to vote against it."[56] The difficulty with this strategy is that it depends on members' ability to engage in strategic voting: to cast votes, in other words, for proposals they don't really favor (and that might hurt them politically with the folks back home). Far preferable is the strategy of "perfecting" a bill to death. This was the net effect (though not always the intent) of various "Powell amendments" in the late 1950s. Originally proposed by Harlem Democrat Adam Clayton Powell, the amendment provided that no funds in whatever program was under consideration could go to segregated facilities. When these amendments were offered to liberal programs such as ones involving aid to education, they often gained the backing of conservative Republicans not normally known for their support for civil rights. Some simple math explains why.

There were, roughly, 160 Northern Democrats in the House, almost all of whom would support both federal aid and the Powell amendment. They were balanced by a similar number of Republicans, most of whom typically would oppose both the bill and the amendment. Passage of the bill depended on the votes of moderate Southerners who could not support the Powell amendment or any program to which it was attached. With sincere voting, the lineup would have been something like this:

	Northern Democrats Yea-Nay	Southern Democrats Yea-Nay	Republicans Yea-Nay
For the bill (unamended)	150-10	65-50	20-140
For the amendment	150-10	0-115	60-100
For the amended bill	150-10	0-115	20-140

In other words, the bill could only pass—and then by the relatively narrow margin of about 235-200—without the Powell amendment. With it, it would lose by 170-265. What happened, of course, is that conservative Republicans became the Powell amendment's most enthusiastic backers. After a variety of programs were defeated by these numbers, Representative Powell himself began voting against Powell-type amendments: "The amendment," he explained on one 1960 vote, "is being used to kill the housing bill."[57]

This strategy of perfecting a bill to death is particularly effective in a committee that is not representative of the House or Senate. Because House Judiciary is, by and large, a liberal committee, the National Rifle Association (NRA) once instructed its supporters in the Committee not to oppose strengthening amendments to a gun control measure. "The way we look at it," said one NRA lobbyist, "the stronger the bill that comes out of committee, the less chance it has of passing on the floor."[58]

One of the most effective types of crippling amendments deals with matters of administration and enforcement. When a new function for a department is proposed, a favorite device is to offer an amendment switching the administration to another agency that is either unfriendly to the program or incapable of administering it. Since agency jurisdictions have their parallels on the Hill, the effectiveness of these devices is reinforced by legislative concerns for turf. Senate Agriculture Chairman Herman Talmadge (D-GA) surprised and angered some of his friends in the farm bloc when he voluntarily "re-referred" a 1972 pesticide control bill to the Commerce Committee. According to one account, Talmadge's gesture had less to do with pesticides than with a proposed amendment to a totally unrelated Commerce Committee bill that would have transferred the Department of Agriculture's meat and egg inspections to a new agency. "Agriculture," Christopher Bosso writes, "was caught this time between its traditional prerogatives on pesticides on the one side and by an assault on equally fundamental interests on the other."[59] Talmadge chose to punt.

There is also a category of amendments that can seriously weaken a program's effectiveness without seeming to. A proposal providing extensive powers of judicial review can tie up the administrators in endless litigation while appearing to be quite innocent of hostile intent. In the battle for civil rights, a favorite tactic in the Eisenhower years was to require jury trials for those found guilty of various discriminatory practices. In the 1950s, Southern juries were almost always all white and unlikely to be particularly sensitive to the civil rights of colored people; but who could vote against the American tradition of the right to a trial by a jury?

Finally, there are hostile amendments offered to make a point. Although it was clear, early in 1981, that a modified version of the Reagan budget (the Gramm-Latta compromise, as it was known) was going to pass, a group of liberal Democrats in the Senate insisted on a series of amendments restoring cuts in such popular programs as aid to education, food stamps, and so on. "The point," one senator put it, "was to make a point."

Defensive Amendments

From time to time the process of bargaining is nakedly exposed on the House or Senate floor through the amending process. A revealing case occurred on the Senate floor in 1977 when the Foreign Relations Committee reported a bill endorsing President Carter's proposal for a gradual withdrawal of U.S. troops from South Korea. When the minority leader announced his intention to oppose the measure, it quickly became clear that the bill was deeply mired. Trying to avoid an embarrassing defeat for the new president, Majority Leader Byrd offered no less than seven amendments, each slightly more damaging than the one before, weakening the committee bill. Finally, a minimal declaration— "that U.S. policy toward Korea should be arrived at by joint decision of the president and the Congress"—was approved. It didn't constitute a victory for the president, but at least it wasn't a defeat.[60]

On many occasions supporters of a bill will offer amendments of their own. If hearings in the other body, for example, or a newspaper article reveals defects not taken into account at the committee stage, a perfecting amendment will be prepared. These are known generally as committee amendments, and they are usually afforded privileged status. In the House, the Rules Committee sometimes grants "modified" closed rules in which only committee amendments are allowed, and in both the House and Senate, committee amendments take precedence over most others.

There are interesting ethical dilemmas that arise when the opponents of a bill discover a fatal flaw such as a provision that for legal or other reasons will make the law unworkable, unconstitutional, or both. "The dilemma is whether to alert sponsors of the bill to the defect, so the bill may be turned into a technically sound legislative product, or instead to leave the defect in the bill, where it may prove fatal to the sponsor's objective. Working conscientiously on an objectionable proposal is referred to as 'building a bridge over the River Kwai.' "[61]

Somewhat more complicated is the dilemma of the legislator who finds "a proposal objectionable in general, but abhorrent in some detail." If he or she amends the bill to strike its worst provisions, the result may be to make final passage easier. Worse, by working to improve the bill, one may create false impressions that raise issues of sportsmanship. "There is," Davies notes, "a general attitude that if a legislator or lobbyist gets his amendment, the bill should get his vote or endorsement. If he is not going to support the bill after winning his amendment, it is important that he tell sponsors in advance that he intends to stay negative even though the amendment is added."[62] Those who fail to take such precautions risk being deemed irresponsible by opponents and stupid by their friends. It is testimony to the desire of many MCs to make good public policy that amendments of this kind are not uncommon.

Riders

In 1918, when the agriculture bill was before Congress, the "drys" succeeded in attaching to it an amendment providing for wartime prohibition of intoxicating liquors. In 1980, a bill setting nutritional standards for baby formulas was amended to increase federal penalties for selling marijuana. These widely separated amendments were both classic examples of *riders,* a term that "generally refers to a provision tacked onto a bill that is not germane, or pertinent, to the bill's purpose."[63]

Riders are most common on appropriation bills, where they can effectively sidestep regular committee consideration and evade presidential vetoes. In its most common form, a rider to an appropriation bill restricts the uses to which funds may be put. The notorious Hyde amendment, for example, prohibits the use of funds appropriated to the Department of Health and Human Services to be used for funding abortions. Although this is not the same as a law outlawing abortion (which would probably have been ruled unconstitutional), the effect is to outlaw Medicare-funded abortions.

Unlike riders such as this one, which limit the uses to which federal funds can be put, riders that change existing law are likely to be ruled nongermane, particularly in the House. It has become increasingly common, however, for both the House and Senate to waive their own germaneness rules and allow such riders as the marijuana amendment previously mentioned. So common have riders of both types become that the line between authorization and appropriation bills has become murky at best. In one 1980 case,

> Of the two days of House debate devoted . . . to the Treasury and Postal Service appropriations bill . . . scarcely an hour was given to discussion of money matters. The rest revolved around a string of controversial riders that did such things as prohibit the government purchase of typewriters from communist countries, restrain the IRS from taking tax-exempt status from private "white flight" schools and stop consideration of a withholding tax on interest income. Of the 19 amendments adopted, only one altered the funds appropriated in the bill.[64]

Any bill that seems destined to achieve final passage tends to attract those who want a "free ride." Author Mark Twain found this out during the course of his labors on behalf of copyright legislation to protect authors against the unauthorized publication of their writings. "See here, Uncle Joe," he complained to Speaker Cannon, "does every fellow who comes here get hitched up to a train he does not want to pull?"[65]

The answer is murky at best. Although House Rule XVI, section 7, seems clear enough—"no motion or proposition on a subject different from that under consideration shall be admitted under color of amendment"—there is, even here, a large "twilight zone" whose scope is difficult to predict. It begins with "how generally the Chair will see particular bill's subject."[66] That determination, in turn, can be shaped to some degree by the way in which the bill reported by the committee is drafted, or more directly, by the way in which it comes to the floor. Following a rule that suspends points of order is the most obvious way of negating the germaneness rule, but a "clean bill" reported by a committee can sometimes accomplish the same objective by so broadening the subject as to make a wide variety of measures technically germane. If the bill is so broad as to impinge on the jurisdiction of another committee, it is subject to a point of order that amounts to a germaneness test unless the bill has already been referred to that committee. The Energy Emergency Act of 1973 was drafted in very comprehensive and wide-ranging terms: "Faced with a very broad bill, the Chair took a very broad view of the bill's subject for germaneness purposes."[67]

The House's germaneness rule limits the scope of the amending process. How strong these limits are, however, is a question answered less by formal rule and precedent than by strategic context. Quite the opposite is true in the Senate, where the formal rules place almost no restrictions on the substance of proposed amendments. In Ross Baker's comparison of the House and Senate, "The absence of a general germaneness rule in the Senate was pointed to by most of the senators interviewed as the procedural difference between the House and Senate that most enhanced the power of senators.[68] He offers the example of the Gramm-Rudman-Hollings Act of 1986. According to one of its authors, the Act had to be introduced in the Senate because House rules were too restrictive. Only when he got to the Senate could he offer

> the Gramm-Rudman-Hollings law as an amendment to the debt ceiling extension, a bill that has to be passed on a timely basis for the government to continue to function.
>
> Now I just could not have done that in the House. Because they would have ruled my amendment nongermane.[69]

CONCLUSION: THE LANGUAGE OF COMPROMISE

Perhaps the most delicate test of the bill drafter's art is his or her ability to devise linguistic formulae that allow different sides in a conflict to reach agreement. The process of what is sometimes known as "massaging" a bill can take place at the staff level behind closed doors, sometimes in full sight on the House or Senate floor. Frequently bill drafting involves the delicate juggling of grand concepts or the bargaining of one principle for another. It can also come down to a single word, as in what Stephen Bailey described as the "battle of the thesauruses" during conference committee consideration of the Employment Act of 1946.[70]

The important point is that the art of drafting, for all its technical components, is inseparable from the art of legislative compromise. Law is language: the making of law is a fight about words, and it is a fight without discernable beginning or end. Each draft of a bill represents, in an important sense, a verbal summary of the balance of political forces at a particular stage of the legislative struggle. Even after final passage and signing by the president, a law remains a verbal formulation defining the parameters of further conflict.

8

✳

ORGANIZING SUPPORT

A naive, "black box" view of the legislative struggle looks upon the Congress as a passive target of pressures emanating primarily from private interests. Professional lobbyists, class factors, and elite elements do play important roles in the legislative struggle, but a full-fledged legislative campaign involves a shifting cast of characters whose roles are as transient as they may be invisible. Since every bill produces its own unique pattern of bargaining and coalition formation, no case study can ever convey the "true" nature of the legislative struggle. Yet certain patterns do seem to recur, and a successful legislative campaign requires both an understanding of these patterns and skill in putting them to use. It is these understandings and skills that translate wealth, people, and strategic situations into power; that extend such power through the organization of support; and that put it to effective use.

✳

CONTEXTS OF BARGAINING

Only recently have students of Congress become as sensitive as most participants to what David Kozak calls the "contexts of congressional decision behavior," the realization that different patterns of politics obtain according to the nature of the issue under consideration.[1] "There is," as Amitai Etzioni puts it, "no one effective strategy of decision-making in the abstract, apart from the societal context in which it is introduced and from the control capacities of the activists introducing it."[2]

What makes this problem even more complex is that issue contexts change. A highly volatile, broadly public issue becomes accepted policy, argued only among specialists who tinker on the margins of minor change. The same conservatives who in the 1970s insisted that antipollution laws would destroy U.S.

140

industry now sound like yesteryear's wild-eyed environmentalists. Liberals who, in the Carter years, filibustered, foamed at the mouth, and insisted that natural gas prices could only be deregulated over their dead bodies, accepted the final stages of deregulation in the 1980s without so much as a roll call vote. Even in the short run, change is often the order of the day. Louisiana Senator Bennett Johnston's 1989 bill to open the coast of Alaska's wildlife refuge to oil drilling sank with the Exxon tanker that dumped millions of gallons of crude oil into Prince William Sound. Although Johnston had listed the bill as a top priority and pushed it through the Senate Energy Committee, the changed context of opinion engendered by the oil spill made it pointless even to bring the bill to the floor. Many other bills, or ideas for bills, are dead in the water before they are launched.

Participants in the legislative struggle can alter these strategic contexts. One of the problems with typologies of issue contexts is that they fail to account for the fungibility of their own categories: issues are crafted, not ordained. One can, for example, reduce water pollution by subsidizing control efforts, by regulating effluents, or by taxing them. One can meet the same basic objectives through what are known in the jargon of the discipline as distributive, regulatory, or redistributive policies.[3] A long-range strategic program— one that establishes general access, influence, and credibility; secures reputable sponsors; drafts a politically viable bill; and so on—is a prerequisite to success; but many a well-planned campaign has failed for lack of attention to the details of implementation, to what politicians sometimes call "spin." The playing field is not level in politics. But if the distribution of power is stable enough to define the general outlines of the legislative struggle in any given year, the issues that become viable in the legislative arena are precisely those whose outcomes are least predictable. Those who succeed are, as a rule, those who best know how to survey the shifting terrain. And the most important part of such a survey begins with an analysis of one's own major strengths and weaknesses.

Know Thyself

Most congressmen have neither the time nor patience for ambiguity and vagueness. Policy advocates should be able to provide information fluidly and well; they increase their effectiveness as they increase their knowledge resources. The point seems so obvious as to need no elaboration, yet it is not so simple to actually define the point at which one "knows" something well enough.[4] Unfortunately for politicians, most of the issues they must decide involve situations in which consequences run toward the less predictable end of this continuum. If we knew with certainty how to end poverty, cure cancer, or lower crime rates, we would probably do it; politics exists because we don't.

One way of dealing with this uncertainty is through a subtle shift of focus from the evaluation of outcomes to the weighing of preferences. Instead of asking who will be helped and hurt by a given decision, politicians have a tendency to redefine the question in terms of who *thinks* they will be helped and hurt. This shift of emphasis transfers the burden of policy evaluation to the affected parties, and, from the perspective of the policy advocate, puts a premium on unity. To the extent that politicians deal in preferences, the more clearly such preferences are conveyed, the more credible the source. The lack of internal democracy in most groups and the time devoted to internal communications that we discussed in Chapter 2 have their roots in the problem of effectiveness. Few things are more destructive of a lobbyist's credibility than dissension in the ranks.

Know Others

If the first commandment of legislative influence is to know thyself, the second is to know others. "There is," says Thomas Sowell, "no one named 'society' who decides anything."[5] Nor does "the Congress" make any decisions. Rather, bills and resolutions are passed by 435 representatives and 100 senators acting out of a rich and diverse mix of incentives, ideologies, perceptions, and motives. One lobbyist said the following of a bill that would have prohibited the FCC from banning cigarette advertisements:

> What you do is to try to figure out first what the congressmen's interests and problems are. Then you can make an appeal to those interests. In this case, they could start with a group of tobacco-district congressmen. For them tobacco is important, since actual jobs are at stake. They started with that core. Then there was a group who was worried by the usurpation of powers by the regulatory agencies. You could appeal to them on that basis. You gradually build your support by making these appeals according to what the congressman is interested in.[6]

Effective lobbying, like effective advertising, often involves the manipulation of perspectives and perceptions. One cannot, of course, be all things to all people; but the market for political intelligence, like the market for consumer products, can be classified and segmented. It should go without saying that the better you know the members, the better you are prepared to make the most effective approach. Although different MCs have different orientations to the job, there is no substitute, as one lobbyist put it, "for knowing a member's district like he knows it himself. Nothing, nothing, is more effective than convincing a member that a vote is not only right but that it will fly back home."

Good counting is important in another way. MCs want to know how to vote, with whom they will be voting, and what the margin of victory or defeat is likely to be. It is one thing to vote with your usual allies; it is quite another to be the only Pennsylvanian, the only conservative Republican, or the only woman to vote with the other side. A rough, overall head count is also useful. To call in the chips and say "Congressman, we really need you, it's going to be close," and then win by an overwhelming margin is not only embarrassing but destructive of credibility.

These rules are easier to state than to effectuate. Even the House whip organizations—experienced, organized, and sophisticated as they are in taking the body temperature of the House—confront significant obstacles. Some members are chronically indecisive or (recall Senator Muskie's "they haven't gotten to the M's yet") reluctant to reveal their voting intentions. Many more harbor genuine uncertainties. Sometimes, as one Democratic zone whip put it, a new issue comes "like a bolt out of the blue . . . and it's the first time I've ever seen it." It's hard to get accurate information from someone who "doesn't know how he's going to vote." And it's hard "asking him how he's going to vote if I don't even know how I'm going to vote."[7]

Lobbyists tend to be conservative in their counts and, if anything, to underestimate their own political influence. Most organizations use some system resembling a five-point scale arraying members from (1) definitely with us, and (2) probable supporter, to (5) definitely against. Major attention is generally directed toward the first two groups, and if their votes are needed, those classified as 3s (undecided). Those predefined as hostile are seldom contacted. In one classic case study, "The tactical basis of pressure group activities seemed to be to assist men already on their side to do the job of persuading fellow legislators. Direct persuasion of uncommitted or opposed congressmen and senators was a minor activity of the lobbies."[8] In their interviews, Bauer, Pool, and Dexter frequently heard complaints from members who felt they had been too easily written off—who wanted, in other words, to be "pressured" and never were.

All this makes sense in terms of our argument about the flow of legislative intelligence. MCs are most likely to be influenced by those with whom they already agree and with whom they have already established relationships of mutual credibility and trust. What it underscores here is the importance of knowing who you are dealing with about what. Lobbyists, it seems to us, are more sophisticated in their head counts than they were in the 1950s when Bauer, Pool, and Dexter conducted their interviews. At the same time, however, the process has become less predictable: with floor amendments being more common, it is harder to know in advance what the membership will, in the final analysis, be asked to vote up or down. For policy advocates, the process is different than it was in the days of the big mules. When the legislative struggle was dominated by the chairs of the standing committees, it wasn't necessarily easier to get things done—effective access was, in fact, sharply restricted by the conservative leanings of most committee chairs—but it was a whole lot easier than it is today to know where you stood. More and more, policy advocates must be able to ply their wares not just to a few key actors but to a wider audience.

The closer one gets to the actual point in time at which an idea for policy becomes an actual law, the more the focus of attention shifts to the 535 members of Congress. Bills are drafted in many offices, campaign strategies devised in countless settings; but key tactical decisions are member-focused. Only an MC can actually put a bill in the hopper, testify before the Rules Committee, or cast a vote. All the strategic planning that goes into gaining access, bill drafting, and so on can come to naught if you don't have MCs on your side to navigate the intricacies of the legislative stream.

Understanding the Process

"Most of us," says George Reedy, "live in a world where yea is yea and nay is nay. It is only in Congress that yea can be nay and nay can be yea."[9] Reedy goes on to relate the fascinating if convoluted story of a 1956 housing bill in which conservative Southern Democrats were able to give their party's liberal leaders a smashing victory without appearing to have voted liberally at all. Southern unity was part of the story, but in this case as in many others, knowledge of the intricacies of the rules was the key to success.

Party leaders, particularly in the House, are advantaged in their ability to shape the outcomes of the legislative struggle through their ability to affect timing, the order of business, and the rules under which bills are considered. Former Speaker Wright offered a naked display of his powers in this area in 1987 when he held open a vote for more than ten minutes while his aides lined up the last vote needed to secure passage of the so-called deficit reduction package. Although this was seen by his critics as a uniquely raw usurpation of power, we have already seen that procedural devices are becoming more significant in the process—particularly in the House, where the Rules Committee has re-emerged as a key actor.

In 1988, Representatives Henry Hyde (R-IL) and Richard Cheney (R-WY) offered an amendment to the Intelligence Authorization Bill that would have eliminated restrictions on covert aid to the Nicaraguan Contras. Even on C-SPAN, where crowd reactions are carefully kept off-screen, the surprise and anger of House Democrats was palpable. By not informing Committee Chairman Louis Stokes (D-OH) of their intent to offer the amendment, Hyde and Cheney had violated "one of the House's most widely accepted norms of comity."[10] The move failed by a vote of 190-214, but it both underscored and intensified growing tensions between the parties over the restrictive rules under which House business has increasingly been conducted. Had Hyde and Cheney "not offered their amendment by surprise, they would not have been able to offer it at all, or so they feared."[11] Increasingly, the House leadership has used suspension calendars, closed rules, and related procedural devices as methods of—depending on your perspective—"riding roughshod over minority rights" or "expediting the flow of House business." In a similar though less comprehensive vein, the Senate leadership's growing resort to complex consent agreements can be seen as an effort to manage uncertainty in the Upper Body.

The crafting of these restrictive rules and agreements for the consideration of legislation puts a premium on effective strategic planning. Especially at the Rules Committee stage, in most cases, decisions are being made before general House sentiments have jelled. Bill managers must attempt to conspire with the Rules Committee to figure out which amendments are likely to be most dangerous before anyone knows what those amendments are. They must also attempt, as best they can, to predict what kinds of compromises will be necessary for final passage. A device that is finding increasing favor in the House is a rule permitting only those amendments printed in advance in the *Congressional Record*. Bill managers are fond of these rules on amendments if only because they provide "time to dissuade members from offering them, to negotiate compromises when possible, or to prepare arguments, mobilize opposition, and draft second-degree amendments when necessary. If floor managers in the contemporary House tend to be less experienced on the floor and less expert about the bills they bring to the floor, these advantages of the advance notice requirement can be attractive indeed.[12]

Obviously it takes a wily opponent—or opponents willing to violate the norms of comity, as were the Republican leaders on the issue of Contra aid in 1988—to get around these restrictions. But it can also take some fancy foot-work on the part of bill sponsors to get around their own restrictions when miscalculations occur and coalitions begin to unravel. If you close a bill to unfriendly amendments, you may also close it to the last-minute concession that can save it from defeat. Even the Hyde-Cheney resolution on Contra aid, though it raised the partisan hackles of the majority, came close to passing.

Senate leaders have less control, because they must rely on unanimous consent and because the "leverage individual senators gain from threatened filibusters protects their floor amending opportunities."[13] In both houses, however, attempts to limit unpredictable floor activities have succeeded to the degree that "the strategic context of floor activity has been altered fundamentally by the shift to more restrictive rules. The possibility of protective rules has become a part of nearly everyone's calculations at the early stages of the legislative process for highly controversial measures."[14] Knowledge of the rules has always been important to policy advocates, but the relationship between substance and procedure has been increasingly blurred, and both the locus and timing of coalition-building have been altered.

The reforms of the 1970s made the floors of both houses strategic and tactical battlegrounds of importance. The resulting shift in power was as welcome to those who deplored the politics of cozy little triangles, centered in strong committees, as it was unwelcome to those who saw floor amendments as disruptive to the expert processing of policy. To a considerable extent, the growing reliance on special rules and suspensions has served to redress this balance and push the bargaining process back into the committee rooms. If the Big Mules who once dominated those little legislatures are not quite as domineering as they were thirty years ago, neither have they lost all their teeth.

------------------- ✳ -------------------

ISSUE COALITIONS

Logic suggests that rational actors, confronted by the necessity of gaining allies, will create "coalitions just as large as they believe will ensure winning and no larger."[15] Coalition theory is useful in analyzing voting behavior in the U.S. Congress as much for what it fails to predict as for what it does. For although the logic of building so-called minimal winning coalitions is clear, the fact that most bills pass with considerably better margins than 50 percent plus one is revealing.

What it tells us first is that the process of coalition-building in Congress takes place in a world of imperfect information. Unlike the world of the theoretical model, the real world of Congress is one of confusion and instability. There are patterns on which one can build: many issues recur in essentially the same form, and certain relatively stable blocs of votes can be identified from past behavior. Many of these blocs, however, are less stable than, say, the party groupings of parliamentary systems. A second problem that arises in studying coalition behavior in Congress is that the size of the necessary winning coalition is itself a variable. For example, one cannot line up 51 votes in the Senate and count on victory if the opponents are prepared to filibuster and it takes 60 votes to end debate. You can push a bill through the House without the possibility of amendments, but to do so you need the additional support of a majority of the Rules Committee, or the two-thirds vote needed to pass it under suspension of the rules. When we add the president as an actor, the possibility of a veto raises the threshold for winning to two-thirds in both houses.

A third problem in developing a theory of legislative coalitions is attributable to the complexity of the process that derives from the sheer number of actors who can, and often do, get into the game. Most game theory models work on the basis of considerably smaller "n's" than one finds in many real congressional games. Fourth, it is at least arguable that many issues in U.S. politics are not the kinds of "zero-sum" or winner-loser issues that game theory typically describes. The deeply ingrained spirit of reciprocity that characterizes consideration of these issues is to "softball" what coalition theory is to "hardball."[16] Finally, the strategic problems of legislative policy advocates in the United States are complicated by the differential weights given to various actors in the system by virtue of their formal roles, committee memberships in particular. Through their abilities to screen the proposals going to the membership, to draft the bills from which the members must work, and, through special rules and agreements, to set the bargaining rules, committee members in general and chairmen in particular have powers that simple models of winning coalitions cannot accommodate. And on most issues there are more than a few Rhett Butlers on the scene who "frankly, don't give a damn."

Despite these caveats, the legislative struggle in essence boils down to a series of struggles to put together coalitions sufficient in size to win. The value of game theory is in stressing the fact that "coalitions qua coalitions have no value themselves; it is only the outcomes they can bring about which have empirical significance."[17] To be sure, there are few participants in the legislative struggle who have so much as a passing knowledge of game theory. Yet the focus on outcomes, the ability to put together winning coalitions in the face of numerous uncertainties and quirks, is one that unites effective practitioners with academic theorists.

Campaign Leadership

"When we think we lead," Lord Byron wrote, "we most are led." The interactions between leaders and led take on particular significance in collegial bodies such as Congress where the ultimate test of leadership is measured almost entirely in terms of one's ability to motivate others. John Manley once noted that "Political scientists have shied away from individual or personality-centered studies of Congress." A preference for those aspects of the process that can be generalized explains much of our reluctance to emphasize personality data, data whose "extreme variability," as Manley puts it, "stands as a barrier to generalization." Of even greater importance, however, is the problem of analytically isolating the variable of leadership from its presumed effects. It is difficult, Manley says, "to say how much of the legislative process is due to individuals and how much is due to the situational factors that affect them."[18] Former Ways and Means Chairman Wilbur Mills (D-AR), generally acknowledged to be one of the biggest of the Big Mules, was once appropriately described as "an expert in followmanship."[19]

Most studies of congressional leadership have defined the term in its most narrow sense to include only those holding such formal titles as Speaker or Minority Leader.[20] Despite the formal powers conferred by House and Senate rules, the general conclusion of most such studies is that "institutional context rather than personal skill is the primary determinant of leadership power."[21] It is similarly agreed that the context of the contemporary Congress is far less conducive, in terms of formal powers and inclinations toward "followership," than in previous historical periods.

There is also a general consensus in the literature on congressional committees that the powers of committee leaders have attenuated in the postreform Congress. What this means, in essence, is that the kind of leadership that derives from formal roles, party or committee, is not what it used to be. Leadership based on the kinds of interpersonal skills, on knowledge, on "followership," on contexts and situations, is all the more important.

Informal leadership in a collegial body is subtly different from our everyday concept of leadership. Almost invariably it involves bargaining rather than command. Legislative leaders succeed only by reaching accommodations with other members of the legislative system with whom they have an ongoing collegial relationship. Whether we can actually call this role in bargaining "leadership" is not clear. In a study of Chicago politics, Edward Banfield described one mayor whose "idea of a beautiful world was to sit around a table and have the opposing parties come to an agreement for which he would then take the credit without ever having opened his mouth."[22] In this extreme case, the "leader" is clearly the dependent variable, the tool of outside groups and other forces. It is far from the charismatic model in which the leader makes things happen by making people do things that they would not otherwise do. Charismatic or revolutionary leadership of this kind, Andrew McFarland notes, is much "easier to understand than the role of leadership in settled societies in which politicians may seem to be limited to routine, unimportant decisions and to bargaining over incremental changes in governmental policies."[23] But it is precisely this latter kind of leadership that is best understood and appreciated on the Hill. As Manley wrote of Wilbur Mills:

> The leadership of the Chairman . . . is a subtle process in which Mills "leads but he does it by compromising." Committee members see Mills as

the legitimate leader of the Committee, as the central figure on the Committee, as the man who gives the Committee direction and who shapes the decisions of the Committee. But they also see him as a shaper of decisions, not a dictator. To them he is an extremely skillful leader who responds to them in such a way that his conclusions, drawn from their discussions, become their conclusions. . . . Leadership is part and parcel of the group process and the members think that Mills is a leader without parallel.[24]

"Power," Charles Merriam wrote many years ago, "is not strongest when it uses violence, but weakest. It is strongest when it employs the instruments of substitution and counter attraction, of allurement, of participation rather than of exclusion, of education rather than annihilation. Rape is not evidence of irresistible power in politics or sex."[25]

The Organization of Group Support

The fluidity of leadership power in the postmodern Congress puts a particular premium on bloc formation. Both within the House and Senate and among outside groups, coalition-building is crucial. In the absence of disciplined parties, few voting patterns in Congress ever duplicate themselves precisely (as they do, say, in Great Britain); but most close observers, most of the time, can predict in advance how most members will vote on most issues. Whether these divisions have a substantial partisan or ideological base, whether they differ according to the kinds of issues in question, or how much they are related to exogenous factors can, for now, remain a moot point. But E. W. Kelley's words on legislative coalitions most certainly apply to the Congress of the United States: "The past interactions of actors, particularly in coalition situations, can strongly affect subsequent coalition behavior. Trust and various negotiating norms can become established. Actors who have never successfully interacted may not be inclined to think the probability of doing so in the future to be high."[26]

Party and ideological labels provide crude but meaningful starting points. Right-wing Republicans like Jesse Helms (R-NC) and left-wing Democrats like Ted Kennedy (D-MA) are likely to question their own judgments if they wind up on the same side of many contested issues. Although the blurring of lines between these extremes is significant, the success of many a policy advocate depends on his or her ability to project major cleavages in advance. This is where "knowing others" really counts.

Friends and Allies.   The starting point for a policy advocate who has already established access on the Hill, decided to pursue a legislative course of action, drafted a bill, and decided who should introduce it how and when, is to find those members who are willing and able to carry the flag effectively. If they occupy positions of influence, such as subcommittee chairmanships, so much the better.

It might seem that the organization of support among those with interests in common is an easy task. It is indeed true that unfurling a banner and sounding clear bugle notes will usually summon a few loyal and eager souls to battle. But to build a solid phalanx around the banner is much harder. MCs and group leaders, particularly the more powerful ones, tend to be over-worked. The rank and file tend to be apathetic, even where their most immedi-ate interests are involved. As we have seen, lobbyists expend a great deal of their time and effort building vertical support within their own ranks to keep enthusiasm at a high level. So do legislative leaders.

At a tactical level, the problem of mobilizing friends is made more difficult by the tendency for the dynamics of the legislative power structure to put one in a position of competing with one's closest allies. To attempt to mobilize key liberals on the Judiciary Committees to devote their attention to an immigra-tion issue, for example, may be to divert their attention from civil rights. Farm groups must generally work most closely with the same relatively small number of key actors on the Agriculture Committees, and so on. The conventional view of the group struggle sees lobbyists of different ideologies competing to change the policy perspectives of MCs; the insider to the process sees all lobbyists—particularly those working in the same fields—as competing for the time and energy of key members. One union lobbyist, whose top priority during the Carter administration was a bill of rather narrow concern to the industry that employed most of his members, told us quite bluntly that his key problem was with the AFL-CIO: "The harder they push labor law reform, cargo preference, and common situs picketing—and don't even think I'm not with them on all those issues—the less chance I have of getting my foot in the door."

Game theory suggests another problem in dealing too effectively with one's allies. Overly large coalitions, it suggests, have a tendency to self-destruct.

> Every coalition has internal conflicts over the division of spoils. When pressure from an opposing coalition is great, so great in fact that the opposition may win and thereby deprive the coalition of any spoils to distribute, these internal conflicts are minimized. But when pressure from the outside diminishes, there is less urgency to settle internal conflicts amicably simply because they are not so dangerous to the oversized winner as to the minimal winner.[27]

It is the rare legislative tactician, however, who feels he or she has too few friends. And it is clear that large coalitions, when they cross normal lines of alliance, can be advantaged by the breadth of their contacts. With groups as diverse as the company itself, the United Auto Workers, the NAACP, and the Conference of Mayors supporting the Chrysler bailout in 1979, the coalition not only had access to virtually every member of Congress, but their "argu-ments could be carefully tailored to fit each congressman's vulnerability."[28]

Neutrals. A difficult dilemma is always faced by those who attempt to win friends among those who would otherwise be neutral. On the one hand, new allies may mean added strength against opponents. On the other hand, the broader one's support becomes, the less one can get depth of agreement and the more one must compromise. The recruitment of support from one group may create difficult tensions among other supporters and may even alienate them completely. As coalition theory predicts, a point is usually reached at which additional support is not worth either the additional effort needed or the repercussions that might result.

There is a marked tendency toward neutrality and inactivity on the part of groups that are not directly affected by a given issue. E. E. Schattschneider dealt with this tendency in his study of the tariff by distinguishing between primary interests and secondary interests. He describes "resolute minorities . . . surrounded by vast marginal aggregates whose impulses to action were almost never able to formulate themselves. The politics of the tariff are apparently predicated on the belief that slumbering and smoldering interests would remain passive while a few men who knew what they wanted acted with decision."[29] The extent to which secondary interests can be activated obviously depends largely upon the ability of primary interests to prod them out of their slumber. This prodding can be accomplished, generally, by one of three methods.

First is that of invoking previously established loyalties. For example, advocates of the Chrysler bailout appealed to members of the New York delegation by pointing to the almost unanimous support the Michigan delegation had given New York during its fiscal crisis a few years earlier. And of course they invoked party unity. This is a tactic that hardly needs illumination; what is worth noting is the crucial nexus between "strategic" and "tactical" maneuvers. The policy advocate who has chits to deal, who has built long-standing alliances, is in a position to mobilize secondary interests as few others can.

Second, side payments and deals can be a factor. Sometimes, more rarely than most lay persons probably believe, these deals are explicit. Usually they are tacit, founded not in direct quid pro quos but in long-standing logrolling patterns and general norms of reciprocity. As we shall argue in our discussion of bargaining, deals in Congress seldom take explicit form; yet they probably account for a large proportion of the institution's policy output. And the most frequently consummated kind of deal is that in which members who are essentially neutral are persuaded to go along for future, unspecified considerations.

A third, more risky, tactic for dealing with neutrals is to ignore them in the hopes that their votes will divide more or less randomly and allow an organized bloc to prevail. The risks of such a plan are obvious, but it does have the twin advantages of conserving resources and not mobilizing opponents. By pretending through inaction that the issue is "no big deal," it is sometimes possible to get people to believe you.

Neutralizing the Opposition.   In some cases, enemies can be treated as if they were neutrals. Since they too have time and resource constraints that limit the number of battles they can fight at any one time, the option of sneaking things through sometimes works. This is particularly the case at the end of the session when backlogs of unfinished business remain, or during consideration of other issues to which your opponents must devote their resources. Through a combination of fancy footwork in the drafting stage and shrewd tactics in committee and on the floor, Congress in 1976 very nearly enacted a technologically dubious requirement that all coal-burning plants be equipped with "scrubbers." Buried in the House Committee Report was legislative history defining the vague wording of the bill's Section 111 in such a way as to require scrubbers on all new plants.

Because the utility industry concentrated its assault on the very idea that Congress ought to give special protection to clean air areas, no significant lobby invested resources in documenting the shaky relationship between universal scrubbing and any of the aims that Congress was considering. After the new Section 111 left the House committee, nothing was said that suggested general congressional awareness of the unnecessary expense, and doubtful environmental benefit, generated by forced scrubbing.[30]

There are times when opponents, like neutrals, can be converted through bargaining. When the numbers are there, moreover, the temptation to simply ignore the opposition, to steamroll them into the ground, is strong. It is a temptation, most legislative tacticians would argue, to be avoided for strategic reasons. Tomorrow is another day, and the opponent you humiliate on Wednesday may be just the person whose vote you need on Thursday.

Divide and conquer is a time-honored maxim of social combat. For example, supporters of the original Full Employment Bill made a special point of trying to split business opposition to the legislation. "The qualified support of a small number of influential businessmen . . . made it possible for the sponsors to claim that ' . . . small businessmen want full employment. . . . Enlightened businessmen want full employment.' "[31] Government organization itself provides a splendid opportunity for the divide-and-conquer strategy. Any private organization opposing a legislative proposal originating in an executive agency inevitably tries to promote interagency or intra-agency squabbles or to create an executive-congressional conflict. The former provides a springboard for bewailing "executive confusion" (or making a joke of it), while the latter arouses indignation toward executive dictatorship and abuse.[32] Despite the best efforts of OMB to make sure the administration speaks with one voice, the frequency with which these divisions appear is testimony to the divergence of interests underlying government activities. The presidential task of organizing interagency support for a legislative program is as much a three-in-one job of organizing friends, winning neutrals, and splitting the opposition as any similar task among nongovernmental groups.

The greatest opportunities for divide-and-conquer strategies lie within the political parties. Here one deals with aggregations supported by interests even more divergent than those behind government agencies. Despite abstract talk about the two-party system and the importance of party responsibility, when it comes to specific issues the difference between success and failure often rests on the shoulders of those who can breach party unity most effectively. Reaganomics, the pattern of lower taxes and redirected spending priorities established in 1981, could not have been effected without the Democratic boll weevils who voted with the Republicans on the key issues.

Bargaining

The concept of bargaining does not seem, as a general proposition, to have a high moral connotation. Associated with such negative terms as *wheeling and dealing* and *selling out*, the idea of political compromise is generally regarded as somewhat less noble than "standing up for one's principles." Perhaps, as Thomas Schelling suggests, this is because "The word 'compromise' has . . . two different, meanings. Compromising a principle sounds wrong. Compromising between principles is all right."[33]

Whatever the reason for the low public esteem of the process, the latter of Schelling's two kinds of compromise is at the heart of the legislative process. Without it, the system simply could not work. There are some issues that involve virtually no bargaining; these arise from so universal a sense of public feeling that MCs respond almost as one in rushing a measure through. Although many members later came to feel that they had been manipulated into making a poor decision, this was quite clearly the case with the Gulf of Tonkin Resolution in 1964. No bargaining was called for because virtually everyone was responding to the same stimulus in the same way. But as long as there are issues about which people disagree, or about which they care with greater or lesser degrees of intensity, bargaining and compromise will continue to be central features of the legislative struggle.

One very important caveat should be entered here. Bargaining does not always take place, even on important and controversial issues. For bargaining to occur, the parties to the issue must be more interested in producing a policy than they are in reporting their positions. This is generally not the case on issues like school prayer, busing, and the death penalty; here the "electoral payment" for MCs is "purely for the positions taken. Of course," David Mayhew argues, "congressmen must at all times generate an impression that they are interested in winning victories, but there may not be much behind the impression. The simple fact that Congress records a roll call, whether close or one-sided, supplies no evidence that anyone has engaged in any mobilizing activity."[34]

Not all of the compromises worked out in the legislative struggle involve actual bargaining in the sense that Congressperson A explicitly works out a deal with Congressperson B. Charles Lindblom uses the term *partisan mutual adjustment* to define a category of coordinating devices that include but are not limited to actual bargains. For convention's sake, we will continue to use the generic term *bargaining,* but the importance of these other kinds of adjustment cannot be minimized in the legislative struggle, or even, perhaps, in life. There are many everyday cases in which people "bargain," or coordinate their behavior, without actually negotiating.[35] Politicians are masters of such techniques. Indeed, it is one of the most salient characteristics of bargaining in the U.S. Congress that it is almost never explicitly articulated. There are a number of important reasons for such silence.

First, a legislative system, unlike a market economy, has no universal measure of exchange. Is a vote for the Chrysler bailout worth one dam in a rural district or two? Trading in this kind of market, as Stanley Kelley has provocatively suggested, is more like that of primitive societies that lack universal measures of exchange.

It is a barter market, and the traders must deal in rough equivalences. They may equate an appointment at a given level with a vote on a bill, for example, in the same way that a person may equate two invitations to cocktails with one invitation to a soiree. . . . They also may have to do much trading speculatively and on credit. That is, they may have to perform a service now with the understanding, and on the chance that, a comparable service will be performed in return at some time in the future.[36]

Second, the previous existence of stable coalitions often obviates the need for specific deals. One lobbyist for the National Farmers Union described the steps taken by farm leaders to deal with a particularly sticky situation on the House floor. Although the parliamentary situation confronted by the chairman of the Agriculture Committee, Robert Poage (D-TX), was fairly complex, he made no special effort to contact those labor-oriented Democrats who were his normal coalition allies. In fact, "he apparently expected such behavior by labor to flow rather 'automatically' from the rural support for the minimum wage; there was little explicit communication linkage between Poage and the AFL-CIO in specific regard to the Findlay motion."[37] Poage simply assumed—correctly, as it turned out—that his old coalition partners would take their voting cues on the floor and go along as usual. No bargaining, no negotiation; but Findlay was defeated as the result of a "deal" that never actually had to be made.

A third problem in tracing legislative bargains is that our mores, as Kelley says, "will not permit a congressman to advertise publicly that his vote on an issue about which he cares little is negotiable and that he is willing to trade it for something he and his constituents want more."[38] Thus, those who have consummated a deal in the legislative market "have a mutual interest in hiding its existence." The language is elliptical at best.

> A congressman may simply plead to a prospective trading partner that a problem is keeping him so busy that he is not sure that he will have time to look into the matter that the other has put before him. Or ideas may be put together as if by chance. One legislator makes a request of another legislator who discusses the matter on its own terms and then apparently as an afterthought goes on, "Oh, by the way . . ." Trading in patronage, in short, normally proceeds only according to certain rules of etiquette.[39]

In the theoretical terms of game theory or of Lindblom's "partisan mutual adjustment," the range and variety of bargaining situations is enormous. We will confine ourselves to the articulation of a relatively general typology of seven distinct patterns.[40]

1. Probably the simplest and most common form of bargaining in Congress combines assertion and acquiescence. Except that it is almost never perceived as such, we might call it "command," the kinds of situations in which individuals or groups are allowed to get what they want simply because nobody wants to make the effort to oppose them. When MCs intervene with the bureaucracy, when bills slide through on the consent calendar, or when Congress by a virtually unanimous vote whoops through a resolution condemning the Supreme Court's decision on flag-burning, a form of tacit bargaining has occurred. Others may go along out of fear or respect for the policy advocate,

out of a spirit of reciprocity, or as a means of cultivating good will. In some cases they may be too lazy, indifferent, or intimidated to do anything but acquiesce.

2. The reverse of this coin is what Lewis Froman calls "anticipated reaction": it involves the policy advocate who, in effect, acquiesces without bargaining. Adjustments of this kind are most likely to take place at the drafting stage or even earlier in the process. "As in unilateral action this form of bargaining does not involve an actual interchange between two or more people, but unlike unilateral bargaining the possible reactions of other decision-makers are taken into account in the decision."[41]

3. The next category, the simple logroll, is perhaps the most familiar form of legislative bargaining. Founded in the norm of reciprocity, it tends most commonly to be found in so-called pork barrel bills. This "you scratch my back, I'll scratch yours" syndrome of project trading is either not as common or more subtly done than in previous years. Reaganomics has made the discretionary funds available to Congress so small that project trading can only take place on a limited basis; but the fact is that vote trading for rivers and harbors projects and for omnibus bills that similarly contain particularized benefits for particular kinds of interests are still very much a part of the legislative system.

4. The time logroll is more subtle. A classic example in 1964 involved the delicate timing of the votes on Food Stamps and the Wheat-Cotton Bill, which were juggled to be certain that the trade of Southern Democratic votes for the former and Northern Democratic votes for the latter did not come unglued. Such explicit connections are not the rule, as we have noted. Among individual members, it would indeed be a bit gauche to suggest a formal deal. As one member puts it,

> There isn't any definite exchange of favors. Like ——— may come up to me and say that this thing means a lot to him and his district and ask for my support, but when I need him, I'm not going to go back and remind him that I voted with him and now I want him to vote with me. And if I were to say something like, "Remember this when I need you," it would be like questioning his integrity. But I do think that if I ask him for something in the future, he might remember. And if I would have fought him on this, then he'd say, "Where was ——— when I needed him?"[42]

Time logrolls are, in many instances, institutionalized, particularly within the Democratic party. Labor support for farm programs has a long history. There are countless ideological, regional, and even personal alliances that persist over time. Thus, a fifth form of legislative bargaining—similar to a time logroll—involves the mobilization of coalition support.

5. No deals, tacit or even implied, need to be consummated as long as coalition leaders make it clear that the vote in question involves a coalition issue. This tactic works when members value group solidarity, which they quite frequently do. "Coalition research," Barbara Hinckley has pointed out, "suggests that . . . (1) partners in a stable alliance very seldom oppose each other,

choosing instead to remain inactive; (2) this constraint on opposition holds across issues, including issues outside the areas of traditional alliance."[43]

6. A sixth form of legislative bargaining is compromise, which, unlike most other forms, usually is explicit. It most commonly occurs with dollar amounts: you want $8 billion, I want $7 billion, let's compromise at $7.5 billion. It goes without need for elaboration that some kinds of issues are far more susceptible to this kind of compromise than others.

Imagine an MC who believed that the people of Nicaragua should be allowed to settle their own problems (there were quite a few such MCs in the 1980s). If the issue were simply one of giving aid to the Contras or not, his or her voting decision would quite simply be no. Throughout the 1980s, however, the issue never came up in such simple terms. Generally, there were three alternatives: full military and economic aid; "humanitarian" (nonmilitary) aid only; or no aid at all. The dilemma confronted by those favoring no aid at all was that they seldom had enough votes to prevail. If they were willing to compromise and work with a middle bloc of voters, they could often limit U.S. aid to nonmilitary items; but if they voted against humanitarian aid, the result would usually be a shifting of middle votes to the right and a vote for military as well as humanitarian aid. To prevent the worst evil, in other words, you had to be willing to vote for a lesser evil. You had to be willing, in a sense, to sell out.

7. There is one final form of bargaining that raises a different set of ethical problems. Side payments are extraneous inducements to act. They may be either punishments (such as threats to support someone else for reelection or a coveted position in Congress) or promises of reward (such as patronage, campaign contributions, even bribes). Party leaders, by their own testimony, are able to confer far fewer of these favors than were Rayburn, Johnson, and others; but presidents and private groups have substantial resources at their command, and individual members quite frequently trade favors of this kind, particularly during battles for leadership positions.

Many kinds of side payments—bribes, for example—are illegal. Other kinds may not get you put in jail, but you wouldn't want your mother to know about them. Side payments in this grey area are probably more common in novels than they are in the real world; but to the extent that they are a factor, they are probably hidden. Most side payments, we also expect, are more part of a process of time logrolling than of actual payoff. A lobbyist or fellow member curries favor with a key MC not as part of a specific deal, but to create an atmosphere for future negotiations that guarantees a friendly reception.

———————————— ✳ ————————————

CHANGING POLITICAL CONTEXTS

The conditions under which these various forms of bargaining occur vary according to the members involved, the kinds of issues, timing, and so on. The job of the legislative tactician is to recognize which of these contextual factors can and cannot be changed. Groups differ in the kinds of lobbying techniques they find most congenial and effective. Members, too, are not identical in personal and political resources. Although such variations make generalization risky, some patterns seem fairly clear.

Redefining Issues

Skilled lobbyists don't like to be surprised by what happens in committee or on the floor, but they sometimes are, and the balance of political power can change quite dramatically. Effective lobbying campaigns involve extensive advance planning, planning that, in an ironic sense, may actually limit the lobby's effectiveness at the tactical stage. Large groups, such as the AFL-CIO or major trade associations, are most effective when their members are most fully mobilized behind specific proposals for action. The better organized the campaign (in its early stages in particular), the more effective it is likely to be. But as Michael Hayes observes,

> Such cumbersome campaigns once initiated are quite difficult to maneuver with any precision. This reduces the flexibility available for tactical shifts and provides the congressional leadership with at least one important resource: its control over the timing of hearings, floor debates, and roll calls. This also helps to explain the efforts by lobbyists to obtain firm voting commitments from legislators, for such commitments once made are almost inviolate and thus represent limits on the tactical flexibility available to congressmen as circumstances change.[44]

It is such unpredictability that makes the legislative process itself important, that makes the outcome of the legislative struggle something more (or less) than the outcome of the group struggle, that puts a premium on tactical skills. Even within Congress, party and committee leaders are sometimes surprised by changing conditions.

One of the most effective tactics for altering an existing balance of political power is to change peoples' perceptions of the issues. Lyndon Johnson was a master of such perceptual sleights of hand, getting diverse wings of the Democratic party to agree on the bottom line even as they disagreed as to why. Omnibus bills, particularly when considered under closed rules, offer different choices than the same issues would present in disaggregated form. The Food Stamps program, for example, began as an explicit, negotiated logroll combining an urban-focused poverty program with more traditional programs of farm aid. "Later as the program expanded and as resentments grew over the failure of one side or the other to keep up its part of the bargain, committee members moved to merge the programs in an omnibus bill." The failure of the Reagan administration to break the alliance or significantly change the programs thus joined shows "how well the omnibus approach to farm and nutritional programs had become."[45]

The leadership is also in a strong position to manipulate perceptions by altering the form in which proposals are considered on the floor. An antibusing

amendment that might pass on its own, for example, can be defeated when presented as a procedural issue (i.e., in the form of a rule that bans such amendments).

Christopher Bosso's account of the life cycle of a single cluster of issues provides fascinating insights into the long-range dynamics of issue definition and politics. In a convincing case study of Schattschneider's nexus of scope and politics, Bosso shows how a broadening in the scope of conflict created a sea change in the politics of pesticide control:

> Each shift in the scope of conflict means exclusion or inclusion of actors. . . .Subgovernment politics involve "small" issues; pluralist styles concern "big" ones. But the pesticide case shows that the same issue can be "small" or "big" based entirely on the breadth of problem perception. Issues are not born big or small; they are made that way by actors seeking to keep out or bring in allies.[46]

How does one go about bringing in or keeping out allies? Obviously, as Bosso's and other studies have shown, some shifts in the scope of conflict follow broad historical patterns or paths of technological change. Even in the short run, a dramatic event such as the 1989 Alaska oil spill can dramatically alter the way in which an issue is perceived. But altering the scope of politics is also very much a part of the legislative struggle, a product of the deliberate tactical efforts of policy advocates to tip the scales in their direction. From the early stages of coalition-building and grass roots lobbying discussed in Chapter 2, through attempts to stem or augment the flow of legislative intelligence; in efforts to stack committees and structure jurisdictions; in the ways bills are drafted and timed, the legislative struggle almost always involves questions about the scope of conflict. The winners of these strategic battles go to committees and to the floor with enormous advantages.

The process does, however, offer opportunities to shift these balances, to change the scope of conflict, and in some cases to unbalance seemingly dominant coalitions. The "open" Congress of the 1970s gave interest groups numerous new points of access to the legislative struggle, but the same opening process gave competing interests, sometimes even individual members of the House and Senate, new resources to open new lines of communication that could seriously disrupt established policy subsystems.

Going Public

Almost any time that Congress and the president become embattled in a contest for the attention of the public at large, Congress loses. "Going public" has long been a major weapon of presidential power. It needs no elaboration here. Nor need we belabor the relative obscurity in which most members of the House play out their congressional careers. When they move beyond the confines of their own districts, the fact is that representatives find it generally difficult to command serious public attention and almost impossible to make waves without a "live" issue. In the normal run of events, the only sure way to make the national news is to get indicted.

Senators are in a somewhat better position vis-à-vis the media and the general public. Indeed, Nelson Polsby suggests that "the essence of the Senate is that it is a great forum, an echo chamber, a publicity machine" in which "passing bills . . . is peripheral" to its central functions of cultivating "national constituencies," formulating "questions for debate and discussion on a national scale," and incubating "new policy proposals."[47] When the target of publicity is a more specialized public of policy experts, the role of Congress, even the House, is not insignificant—especially for specialized markets of bureaucrats, lobbyists, outside experts, or even legislative staff persons. The media, moreover, likes a fight. Once an issue has been joined, once it is clear that there is a contest, notepads, cameras, and microphones are seldom far behind. MCs as individuals love it. Whether it actually helps them or not, most politicians tend to view a moment of exposure in the national media as worth its weight in political gold. More important for our purposes, the mutual interests of MCs and journalists in conflict-laden situations can serve as a device for changing the scope of conflict. There is, to be sure, a great deal of posturing and debate in Congress that has everything to do with electoral ambitions and nothing to do with legislation. Pushing this garbage aside, however, we can find some very real legislative meaning in the rhetoric.

--------------- ✳ ---------------

CONCLUSION: ESTABLISHING A BARGAINING POSITION

On almost any given day while Congress is in session, a small cabal of men and women are meeting to plot a campaign for passage of a bill. In the early stages of such campaigns, the composition of the group is likely to be largely extra-congressional, made up largely of lobbyists, bureaucrats, perhaps a few White House and legislative staff assistants. The more the policy moves from concept to bill, from bill to law, the larger the proportion of senators and representatives on the scene.

When we reach the legislative arena, moreover, there is a gradual widening in the number of members involved in the deliberative process. Many of the same considerations about scope and conflict that Schattschneider identified for the polity as a whole apply at the microcosmic level within the Congress. When you change the scope of conflict, when you move specifically from the subcommittee level to the full committee, from the committee level to the House or Senate as a whole, you change the nature of the game being played. *Subcommittee politics* is a term that accurately and appropriately describes the dynamics of some issues. Full committees continue to play an important role. Both the House and Senate floors, it is generally agreed, have become increasingly important forums for the definition of public policy. As you move from one of these levels to the next, the scope of conflict tends to expand.

9

---- ✳ ----

MANAGING
COMMITTEE
ACTION

W oodrow Wilson's description of government by the Standing Committees of Congress remained reasonably apt at least until the reforms of the 1970s. Since then, power has devolved away from full committees in two directions. On the one hand, we have seen the evolution of subcommittee government, a development that in theory should have enhanced the power of subgovernments and of interests that benefit from distributive politics. On the other hand, committees are under increasing challenge from the floor where even relatively junior members feel fewer constraints about attempting to amend committee bills.

If the legislative struggle is no longer government by the standing committees, the continuing importance of committees cannot be gainsaid. If only because the committees have the first real legislative crack at evolving laws and the edge of expert knowledge, most of the real crafting of bills continues to take place at the committee and subcommittee levels. Although decisions made on the floor are less likely to simply ratify those that the committees produce, the floor changes that do occur, mild or drastic, are usually the outgrowth of views formulated by a minority group of committee members. When the House and Senate disagree, as is often the case, the conference committees that craft the terms of compromise are almost invariably drawn from the committees of original jurisdiction.

———————— ✳ ————————

THE HEARINGS: STAGING AND PERFORMANCE

The first decision is whether to have a hearing at all. Action without hearings seems, by Wilson's account, to have been the rule in the nineteenth century, and the only witnesses called at those that were held tended to be MCs themselves.[1] In recent years, it has become an oddity for a committee to report an important bill without hearings. Indeed, the failure to schedule testimony is generally considered the equivalent of a bill's death sentence.

In court a man is presumed innocent until proven guilty; in Congress a bill is presumed dead until enough pressure is brought to gain a hearing. In the formal rules of most committees, the decision whether to have hearings is made by majority vote. In practice, on most committees, the actual decision is made by the committee or subcommittee chair and implemented by the staff. On some committees, especially in the Senate, wide latitude is accorded committee leaders to hold hearings on almost any subject that strikes their fancy. The shelves of federal depository libraries are filled with printed hearings on an unbelievably wide spectrum of topics, reflecting the efforts of groups and individuals to give their favorite topics sufficient publicity to attain agenda status.

The decision to hold hearings in no way implies subsequent action. A hearing has the virtue of giving direct satisfaction, of "blowing off steam," and can often serve as an alternative to legislative action. It is, as we shall see, a particularly useful device of administrative oversight, and it can also be staged to delay or prevent legislative or executive action.

Timing the Show

The most obvious problem of timing is one of when hearings should be held. The Budget committees begin their hearings almost as soon as the president's budget arrives from the printer. Appropriations subcommittees also work on fairly predictable schedules. On emergency measures, particularly those requested in special presidential messages, hearings usually are begun quite promptly, sometimes within twenty-four hours. On most measures, however, committee and subcommittee leaders have genuine discretion. In the case of the Versailles Treaty, Senator Henry Cabot Lodge, chairman of the Senate Foreign Relations Committee, planned a strategic delay before initiating hearings that seems designed to have let the general euphoria of the Armistice run its course. It rather neatly robbed the president of his usual advantage in the court of public opinion.

A second problem involves where hearings should begin. When two committees in the same house are engaged in a jurisdictional struggle, the tendency is for each to try to beat the other to the draw in hopes of putting its own particular spin on the issue. The same question also comes up with respect to choosing between House and Senate committees handling identical or similar measures. The preferred strategy is to have hearings started in whichever committee is most favorable to a particular viewpoint. Frequently, cooperation between the bill's primary sponsors and their staffs produces an agreement similar to that reported in a case study of the Environmental Education Act of 1970 in which the House Committee held thirteen days of hearings compared with the Senate's two.[2] The House Committee went first and bore the brunt of the action largely because it had more interested members and therefore a greater capacity to give the bill needed publicity. Senate hearings were perfunctory by prearrangement to speed the process. In contrast, when the House Judiciary Committee in 1978 held lengthy hearings on the Criminal Code Reform Act, the point was to increase the bill's chances of survival by waiting for action in the Senate, where sentiment for the bill was stronger. The hope, as the bill's Senate sponsor candidly admitted, was that "the lopsided Senate vote (72 to 15) would boost the bill's chances in the House."[3]

Sometimes a full committee will preempt one of its subcommittees by holding hearings before referring the bill. In part this is a matter of committee traditions. House Ways and Means, for example, reflecting the days when it had no subcommittees, continues to examine most major bills at the full committee level. The Senate has always been more full committee–oriented than the House, and the gap seems to be growing. While more than 90 percent of House hearings in the 96th Congress were held at the subcommittee level, the comparable figure for the Senate was only 65 percent.[4] Some chairmen have been accused of taking all the interesting work for themselves and giving subcommittees the crumbs. During his 1981–85 tenure as chairman of Senate Commerce, Bob Packwood (R-OR) "just took the major issues and preempted them."[5] Although such power grabs are often just that, there is usually a policy motive too, a desire to put a particular emphasis on the material brought out.

A third problem is one of how long the hearings should be. On minor bills or in an emergency atmosphere, committee time is of necessity rationed. The National Industrial Recovery Act, one of the most far-reaching statutes of the early New Deal, was the subject of only three days of public hearings in each house. Long, drawn out hearings are occasionally sought for the purpose of delaying or even derailing potential action. Opponents of school prayer, for example, have repeatedly welcomed the testimony of any and all who wish to offer their views, a tactic that offers three advantages at least. By not "screening" witnesses beforehand, the committee attracts sufficient fruits and nuts to the hearings that the more measured words of stronger proponents are obscured. Then, as the arguments repeat themselves and the more famous witnesses complete their acts, press attention disappears. Finally, when proponents of action complain about delay, one can point to the many hundreds of supporters still waiting to be heard.

Open or Closed Doors?

Although the Legislative Reorganization Act of 1946 contained a strong presumption in favor of open hearings, more and more committees found it convenient to keep the doors closed. By the 1960s, 43 percent of all committee meetings in the House and Senate were open only to members, or to members and staff only.[6] Most of the closed meetings were for markup sessions, but a strikingly high proportion, particularly for the Appropriations committees, were for the taking of testimony. It is doubtful, moreover, that these figures report the full story. There are many differences of degree between a door that is wide open and a door that is tightly closed. Many hearings that are nominally public are "quickie" operations called on short notice with no effort to inform all interested parties. As far as providing public information goes, they might just as well have been secret in the first place.

The sunshine laws adopted in the 1970s have been superficially effective. But although the proportion of closed sessions formally counted by *Congressional Quarterly* dropped to a low of 7 percent in 1975 and has been negligible since then, the goals of reformers have not been met. Closed hearings were opposed because of their presumed tendency to favor insiders and thus weigh the scale against the general public. It was the hope of reformers that sunshine laws would bring the public into the committee room and broaden the scope of conflict. Instead, it has been more the insiders themselves who have come through the opened doors. Although most Appropriations hearings are now open,

> While the lobbyists swarm to the meetings, the press is elsewhere. The explanation is that while the press reports the byplay of political battle, speculation on the outcome of a critical vote, and conflicts between personalities, it regularly fails to report the hard, grubby decisions on the budget. It is so intrigued by tactics that it misses the substance. . . . In general . . . the substance of the hearings of the appropriations committees is added to the great unread literature of the world.[7]

On important issues today, closed hearings are most likely to occur on foreign policy issues that the administration feels involve questions of national security. There are risks in this strategy, particularly when committee opinions are sharply divided. Not only can the administration be accused of covering up, but it may find itself unable to control the flow of information. At times, paradoxically, the best way to guarantee full news coverage for testimony is to have it presented at a closed hearing. What would be a fairly dull story as it transpired in open hearings can become exciting headline news if it represents an inside tip on what happened at a hush-hush meeting. When a story reaches the press through a leak rather than through official channels, it is the leaker rather than the official who sets the spin. This is why the executive officials dealing with national security issues are seldom terribly forthcoming even in closed hearings. The chief benefit for them in closing the doors is that their testimony is thereby surrounded with an aura of high significance.

There is no doubt, however, about the utility of closed hearings as a means of promoting a more intimate give and take between witnesses and committee members. Many witnesses will speak more freely, and committee members will behave differently, when the emphasis is more upon exploring the issues than upon offering opportunities for publicity. Before "sunshine" flowed into the hearing room, it was not uncommon for a committee to set the stage for its public hearings (if they were held) by holding a closed hearing first. On a less formal basis, much the same happens today as committees set up special task forces or working groups of legislative and executive personnel to consult with private groups (if necessary) and prebargain the exchanges to take place in open hearings.

The Dramatis Personae

"Anytime a bill is presented in Congress," a small businessman told a Senate committee in 1945, "I can close my eyes and visualize who will appear. They will be about the same people who usually testify for or against a bill. You never have any new blood."[8] Although the cast of characters is much larger today than it was in 1945, the usual suspects are just as likely to be rounded up.

One reason why the same people testify repeatedly is that top officials, by virtue of their positions and prominence, are almost obligated to appear at hearings on "their" issues. They do so to satisfy clients as well as constituents. A prominent lobbyist or bureaucrat who testifies before one committee on Tuesday can hardly send a subordinate to another committee the next day. During any given month, the secretary of commerce may appear before a dozen different committees on a dozen different bills. And the national director of the Chamber of Commerce may appear at something like half of those same meetings. The Cabinet member or chief lobbyist who sends a subordinate creates the impression, whether intended or not, that the issue in question is of less importance. The House Banking Committee in 1990 refused to move a thrift bailout bill on the stated grounds that the administration's failure to send top officials showed a lack of interest in the legislation.

Occasionally a private organization will bring in grass roots witnesses to add freshness and variety to a committee hearing. In 1947 a welder from Schenectady was brought before a Senate committee to defend postwar price controls. His brief and moving statement prompted one senator to remark on how "very healthy for the Committee" it was "for common people to bring these matters to Congress."[9] To bring common people to Congress, however, is not always easy or effective. It involves transportation and hotel costs, and time to familiarize a relatively unsophisticated citizen with the legislative situation. A committee may play along with the illusion that it is hearing an uncoached and unbiased sample of grass roots opinion, but everyone knows that the common people on the stand are typically brought to Congress by uncommon people or organizations. For such people to bring, say, a homeless person to Washington, put him up in a nice hotel, buy him a new suit, and then send him back to the streets with a fresh newspaper blanket can appear cynical indeed.

Sometimes a committee will itself go to the grass roots. In 1968 George McGovern (D-SD) lobbied successfully for the creation of a Select Senate Committee on Nutrition and Human Needs, which he used as the vehicle for a series of field investigations that attracted widespread media coverage. By combining statistical reports on the surprising extent of malnutrition in the United States with dramatic, grass roots depositions of persons suffering from extreme poverty, the McGovern Committee "not only stimulated the Nixon administration into tripling its food stamp budget and doubling its school lunch program, but gave McGovern the national platform he needed to become a serious contender for the Democratic presidential nomination in 1972."[10]

Celebrity witnesses are useful for attracting the attention of the press and maximizing the attendance of committee members. Movie actors and athletes are good copy, and it is a rare MC who doesn't recognize a good photo opportunity. A particularly effective witness is the expert who can make technical issues vivid and personally relevant. One congressman described how a prominent physician's testimony on cancer had him checking "for bumps and bruises" and dreaming of the worst. "And then more recently I lay awake listening to my heart after hearing the heart-trouble talk. . . . And here I am listening to this mental health talk . . . and I wonder what I am going to dream about tonight." As Aaron Wildavsky asks, "Who would vote against appropriations for medical research after being subjected to this treatment?"[11]

On important and highly controversial measures a committee may receive many more requests to testify than can possibly be honored. This may simply be the product of the large variety of interested groups or, in some cases, of deliberate campaigns to pack or protract the hearing. In either case the committee members are faced with a problem of rationing the available time. Although some witnesses can be persuaded to submit written statements, vanity or the political needs of the witnesses may make that difficult. For some lobbyists, their very jobs may hinge on their ability to tell supporters about how effectively they were able to convey the group's views. In most instances the responsibility for making these choices is in the hands of the committee or subcommittee chairmen and their staff assistants.

One way to ration is to set up a schedule that favors friends and supporters. A blatant case of such stacking was Senator John East's (R-NC) refusal in 1981 to invite prochoice witnesses to testify on a series of antiabortion bills. In this particular case, the witness list was so biased that the fairness issue came to overwhelm all others in the press and East's maneuver rather badly backfired. There are, of course, more subtle ways of stacking the deck. A witness who is scheduled at the same time as a major event is unlikely to make the evening news. The later a witness is scheduled, the less likely he or she is to have the full attention of committee or subcommittee members.

The wise chair, unlike the late Senator East, is careful not to play these games too blatantly. Not only can it create bad feelings, but it can also be seen as a confession of weakness. Moreover, the potential witness who is denied one forum can usually find another. Multiple referrals in the House, the rivalries between House and Senate committees, overlaps between substantive committees and appropriations, and the very loose House and Senate rules about who can hold hearings about what, combine to make it almost certain for a witness who wants to be heard to find a forum.

Most House committees have formal rules that grant the minority the right

to at least one day of testimony, but there is seldom any real need to invoke such formal requirements. More often than not, in both the House and Senate, the general outline of who will testify when is resolved at the staff level. Since no one has an abstract right to testify, questions sometimes arise as to whom to exclude, but conflict of this sort is rare. While some people would like to see their opponents' more bizarre supporters on the stand, it would be unseemly to push it. While no one wants to offend their own kooky friends, neither do they want to see them on the evening news. Scheduling problems are also relatively rare. Although there are some ambiguities of protocol, the Washington pecking order has evolved a series of rather well-defined rules: MCs are listed in order of seniority, Cabinet members go before their subordinates, and so on. What to do with a private-sector witness like Ralph Nader, who has been known to insist on going first or not at all, is sticky; but such situations arise infrequently. The more difficult problems arise with those who do not want to appear at all.

Sound strategy often calls for withholding testimony entirely or for delaying until the last possible moment. In the development of the Clayton Antitrust Act, long hearings were held before the House Judiciary Committee from December 1913 to April 1914, but one can leaf through a thousand pages of oral testimony without finding a word from a single government witness. From the perspective of President Woodrow Wilson,

> the decision to keep the Administration position unrecorded during the formative stage was a deliberate one dictated by the strategic needs of the occasion. . . . When it became apparent that the stringency of regulation envisioned in the proposed bill was impossible of realization, Wilson was able to disclaim responsibility for it and demand sweeping changes in the direction of moderation.[12]

Since the time when President Washington refused to convey information to the House with regard to the Jay Treaty, presidents have invoked the doctrines of national security and executive privilege to justify the withholding of information from Congress; and Congress's use of its investigatory powers has also produced its share of private citizens who have been forced to testify against their will.

We shall see in our discussion of formal investigations that citizens do have a certain limited right to silence. The basic rule, however, is quite clear. In the terms of the statute: "Every person who, having been summoned as a witness by the authority of either house . . . willfully makes default or who, having appeared, refuses to answer any question pertinent to the matter under inquiry shall be deemed guilty of a misdemeanor."[13] In laymen's terms, if you don't testify, you can go to jail.

There are many reasons why contestants in the legislative struggle would try to force reluctant dragons into the hearing room. The purpose may be merely to elicit support from timid witnesses who would like to stay on the fence instead of taking a position. Or the purpose may be to bring opponents out in the open— and subject them to antagonistic questioning by committee members—rather than allow them to carry on their opposition behind the scenes. It can also give a case greater credibility to have it put in the record by its opponents. Senator Kefauver (D-TN) and his staff had substantial documentation for their charge that the major pharmaceutical companies were overcharging for many prescription drugs. They chose instead to elicit the information from the companies themselves, a source that was hardly open to question.[14]

Rarely must a committee resort to its subpoena powers. In most cases, the method used is to extend a written invitation backed by the implied threat of adverse publicity. Sometimes, when subpoenas are issued in connection with legislative testimony, it is at the instigation of the witnesses themselves. During World War II, for example, many government officials found that by having a committee subpoena them as witnesses they could achieve a dual objective of making their case in public and also maintain a record of being opposed to the washing of dirty linen in public.

Representing the President

There is one important contestant in the legislative struggle whose name never appears on the list of dramatis personae—the president of the United States. It is not merely that presidential testimony before a congressional committee would be a task too time-consuming for a busy person; it would also be beneath the dignity of the office to submit to committee interrogation. Not until the hearings in 1973 that preceded the vote to impeach President Nixon had any committee of Congress seriously proposed that a president come before it as a witness.[15] If there are compelling reasons for a meeting—and in the area of foreign policy in particular there sometimes are—then it is Mohammed who goes to the mountain. Whole committees, House and Senate leaders, committee chairs, and ranking minority members are not infrequent visitors to the best-known occupant of 1600 Pennsylvania Avenue.

The question often arises as to who should appear to explain the president's position. In a sense, all agency heads are representatives of the president and must have their testimony cleared by the Office of Management and Budget to see that it is in accord with the president's program. Yet in an equally important sense, every agency representative is on his or her own because presidents need the freedom to shift their own positions at subsequent stages of the legislative process. Department and agency heads are sometimes sent to hearings to float trial balloons and (mixing metaphors) test the political waters before the administration's official line is defined. In "we" versus "they" situations, however, most presidents are reluctant to rely on their department heads. "The Cabinet departments," one former White House aide (quoting another) suggests, "cowed by their congressional oversight bodies, tend to cave in to such requests, willing to sacrifice a little bit of their president's executive privilege to save themselves a large measure of grief. 'We had to watch them like hawks,' observed Lloyd Cutler, 'We, more than they, were the protectors of the presidential office.' "[16]

More delicate questions arise in connection with the president's closest associates in the White House and Executive Office. Various parts of the extended White House often come before congressional committees to expound the president's program. They have also been known to refuse to appear or to provide documents requested by Congress. What is usually cited here is the doctrine known broadly as "executive privilege."

During Senator Joseph McCarthy's (R-WI) investigation of alleged communist infiltration of the army, President Eisenhower wrote a letter to Defense Department employees urging them not to cooperate. Effective administration, Eisenhower argued, requires "that employees of the executive branch be in a position to be completely candid in advising with each other on official matters, and . . . that any of their conversations or communications, or any documents or reproductions, concerning such advice [not] be disclosed."[17]

A similar case had been made by President Truman's first chairman of the Council of Economic Advisors, who feared that Council members might be asked to testify on matters on which the president had taken a position contrary to their advice. Although the other two members of the Council took the opposite position and ultimately prevailed, the problem is one that won't go away. Even the Kennedy and Johnson administrations, both of which formally pledged themselves to more open policies, came not only to justify the withholding of information but, in certain cases of national security, to asserting a "right to lie."

Executive Reports and Documents

The need for secrecy in the conduct of foreign affairs has long been accepted as a justification for the withholding of information from Congress. There are numerous statutes in this and other areas in which Congress has prohibited the release of information not just to the public but to itself. Congress, for example, is virtually prohibited from examining the returns of individual taxpayers or the replies of individual citizens to the decennial census. Such statutory exceptions aside, the criteria for denying information to Congress seem fairly simple: "there should be full disclosure for domestic and nonsecurity affairs, but the President should have authority to withhold information from Congress on foreign and national security matters."[18]

This criterion, simple as it sounds, is unsatisfactory for two reasons, as Arthur Maass points out. First is the impossibility, in practice, of drawing a meaningful line between foreign and domestic issues. Second, "for those aspects of foreign and security affairs that require secrecy—presumably from the enemy—should there be no information available to the legislature? Of course there should be. Congress needs secret information to perform its role."[19] The first of these problems is manifested in the tendency of some presidents to cast the net of "national security" so widely as to make the foreign/domestic policy dichotomy a joke. Perhaps the most extreme assertion of executive privilege came in the early days of the Senate's investigation of the so-called Watergate scandal when the Nixon administration's attorney general Richard Kleindienst claimed a blanket exemption: "if the President directs anybody who has a document or information or directs anyone not to appear, that person would have the power not to comply with the congressional request."[20] Although it is true, as Kleindienst pointed out, that cooperation is the norm in 99.9 percent of the cases, the Nixon administration's broad assertion of executive privilege would have virtually eliminated whatever leverage Congress might have had in negotiating for controversial facts. The courts have proven extraordinarily reluctant to intervene. In the case of the Nixon tapes, for example, the Senate Watergate Committee, stymied in its efforts to obtain information from the White House, sought judicial remedy only to be told by a federal district court that the court lacked jurisdiction. Even after an act was passed conferring such jurisdiction, relief was refused on technical grounds.

Even though, as James Hamilton puts it, "Congress's chances of success in a court battle with a President are less than sanguine,"[21] it is noteworthy that when the House or Senate as a whole is able to present an overwhelming majority against executive privilege, it almost invariably prevails. Congress and its committees have a variety of tactics at their command to force production of executive evidence. An administration bill may be shelved in committee until information is forthcoming or defeated on the floor. Appropriations sought by a president may be denied or reduced. An ambassadorial or Cabinet appointment may be rejected. Additional investigations of the executive branch may be initiated. Prominent congressmen may use their national forums to castigate a president for guile, lack of cooperation, or worse.

Such approaches may work.[22]

In fact, they usually do. And if they work against the administration, despite the deference of the courts, it seems reasonable to expect that the ability of Congress to extract information from private citizens is substantial. It is.

The Power to Probe

Generally, the difference between a formal investigation and an ordinary hearing is between a situation in which testimony can and cannot be compelled. In actual practice, the blurring between hearings and investigations is too complex to sustain; what is important is that Congress and its committees have long enjoyed powers to probe private actions that may or may not pertain to specific items of legislation.

When Major General Arthur St. Clair lost 630 men in an encounter with the Shawnee Indians in 1791, the House voted to launch an investigation. From the St. Clair investigation through the last session of the 69th Congress (1926), the country witnessed a total of 330 investigations.[23] More than twice as many investigations were conducted between 1933 and 1958 than in the entire preceding history of Congress,[24] and in the first session of the 82nd Congress alone, more than 130 investigations were authorized.[25] No one, to our knowledge, has been counting in more recent years, but it seems safe to estimate that more than two thousand investigations have been conducted by congressional committees since St. Clair met his match in the forests of Ohio, most of them in the past fifty years.

Paralleling the acceleration of investigative activity has been a marked change in the scope and function of legislative inquiries. For more than a century, congressional investigations were concerned almost exclusively with internal governmental problems such as problems of membership and procedure in the houses of Congress and corruption in government. This tradition continues to attract public attention in such investigations of the executive branch as the Iran-Contra hearings, or in the House Ethics Committee's investigation of former speaker Jim Wright. Such uses of the investigative power have not gone uncriticized. Congressional investigations of the scandals of the Harding administration prompted one distinguished jurist to characterize the investigators as "professional searchers of the municipal dunghills."[26] Oliver North and his defenders seem to have felt much the same way about the Iran-Contra investigation some sixty-odd years later.

Even more controversial was the New Deal Congress's use of investigations—less a "check on administration" and more a means of exerting "social leverage." Investigations increasingly were designed to rally public sentiment behind administration measures.[27] Thus, the Pecora Committee cleared the way for the Securities and Exchange Acts, the findings of the LaFollette-Thomas Committee gave impetus to labor legislation, the utilities investigations of the Black Committee led to legislation regulating public-utility holding companies. The press delighted in reporting the forced testimony of the nation's normally reclusive business elite, and "the leaders of the Roosevelt administration rightly concluded that investigations were unsurpassed as a means of formulating and awakening popular support for the governmental measures they had in mind."[28]

In an ironic twist the technique of exerting social leverage through investigations came to be used for quite different ends. So profound was the change that many of the strongest supporters of investigative omnipotence began urging restraints, while some of the most vocal critics of the New Deal probes became staunch defenders. Hugo Black, who as a senator from Alabama had led an extraordinarily revealing probe of the utilities industry, became, as an associate justice of the Supreme Court, one of the severest critics of the House Committee on Un-American Activities and its Senate counterparts. Many of those business leaders who had most deplored the New Deal probes became staunch supporters of Wisconsin Senator Joseph McCarthy's investigations of supposedly subversive activities.

Ideology and partisanship were factors in these reversals, but there was more at stake here than a question of whose ox was being gored. There are significant differences between the New Deal inquiries and those of Senator McCarthy and his cohorts. In the first place, the New Deal inquiries were clearly aimed at broad economic problems that were felt to be susceptible to legislative relief. Individuals were questioned more about their activities than their opinions or organizational affiliations. Exposures of individual wrongs, if they occurred, were clearly incidental to the main purposes of the inquiry. Later investigations, and not just those involving subversive activities, frequently focused more on the individuals being investigated than on the problems under investigation. Critical questions in the Kefauver crime probes, as in the hearings of the Committee on Un-American Activities, were more likely to be phrased in terms of "who," "when," and "where" rather than "what," "why," and "how." Second, although the New Deal inquiries sought to pave the way for legislative alleviation of social evils, the postwar investigations—whether into crime, un-American activities, or labor racketeering—sought to do through investigation and systematic exposure that which basically could not be done by legislation. The publicity-conscious New Dealers paved the way for this kind of inquiry, but the changing focus of the process lends consistency to, for example, Senator-then-Justice Black's seeming reversal.[29]

What the New Deal and McCarthy era investigations had in common was their use of subpoena power to dramatize issues and influence public opinion. What was different in the latter period was the use of "exposure for exposure's sake," in the words of Chief Justice Warren.[30] To suggest that such investigations were designed simply as trials in disguise, however, is to miss a major point. As with the New Deal investigations, there was an important message. Especially when televised, or in traveling from one community to another, the exposure function of investigations blends into a propaganda role, contributing, as the House Committee on Un-American Activities put it, "to the awakening of the too complacent to the reality that the danger is here."[31] By personalizing the alleged threat of domestic communism, the committees played an important combatant role in what Telford Taylor aptly dubbed the "Cold Civil War." Better, by constraining so many former communists to invoke the Fifth Amendment, the investigators conveyed the impression that there were many more *present* members of the Communist party than was actually the case. What better way to convey the impression of a clear and present danger of domestic subversion than "the turning of the spotlight on the squirming creatures you have seen on the stand here."[32]

PERFORMANCE AT THE HEARINGS

Colonel "Ollie" North leaves the civilian clothes he wore to the White House at home and testifies before the Iran-Contra Committee in full Marine dress. . . . A frustrated senator lectures him (and the TV cameras) on the "real" meaning of patriotism. . . . An ex-communist gives essentially the same testimony in fourteen different cities (and gets front page attention in each). . . . A masked "mystery witness" admits to having dumped toxic wastes in a local stream. . . . A press agent puts a midget in J. P. Morgan's lap and the front pages of virtually every paper in the country feature the picture of a financial "giant" being called on the carpet in Washington.

Incidents like these, confined largely but not exclusively to congressional investigations, illustrate the degree to which contrivance and showmanship—"hype," if you will—are part and parcel of the hearings process. That a healthy dose of showmanship is involved should not, however, obscure the very important functions that hearings and investigations play in the legislative struggle. If the performances run the gamut from high intelligence to common buffoonery, to those interested in politics the sum total of public hearings is "an indispensable key to the puzzles of that vast sweep of legislation in the full arena of the House. Here he sees the headsprings of law."[33] To the policy advocate, it is a crucial point of direct contact with members of Congress. And for the member of the House or Senate, it is one of the principal means of learning the bases of conflict and compromise.

Congressional Attendance

Most members of Congress have the feeling that they are cut into little pieces by competing demands for their time. As important as each committee issue may seem, it often takes second place to constituency problems, office crises, or other demands. Multiple subcommittee assignments and workloads that come in spurts tend to further prevent full committee attendance at public hearings. Most committees try to coordinate subcommittee meeting times to avoid overlap, but coordination between full committees cannot be achieved, and even some overlap in the same committee is unavoidable. With an average of more than five hundred House committee meetings a month, the administrative complexity of the scheduling process is enormous. As Thomas O'Donnell says,

> Committee scheduling is perhaps the most complicated aspect of legislative operations in the House. The shortage of appropriate rooms, the unevenness in committee workloads, the overlapping of substantive jurisdictions, and the multiplicity of individual assignments make coordination of committee scheduling a Herculean task. In their efforts to effectively plan and manage their time, all committees operate under enormous and persistent handicaps.[34]

It is unusual to have full committee attendance at public hearings. Often a member will rush in for a cameo role, thumb through staff notes, ask a question or two, and then, murmuring regrets to the chairman, hastily depart. Not infrequently, there are more staff persons than members in the hearing room; and although they very, very rarely are allowed to open their mouths, it is the staff persons' notes that usually form the basis for the questions thrown out by MCs on the run.

Particularly since the demise of Senator McCarthy and the formal abolition of the House Committee on Un-American Activities, small committee attendance has almost never been an important legal problem. In practical, everyday terms, its effect is to detract from a hearing's significance as a means of getting ideas across to members or of obtaining general publicity. As members wander in and out and follow their own prestructured agendas of questioning, it can also prove difficult to pursue a coherent line of attack or develop an effective case. Such individualistic, "lone wolf" patterns of questioning are, it seems, increasingly common.[35]

The various contestants in the legislative struggle have an obvious interest in rounding up committee members, particularly friends and supporters. One device that is often employed by local groups is to have their own MC lead off the testimony in hopes that the norms of collegial reciprocity will increase attendance. As a matter of courtesy, most committees not only welcome testimony from other representatives and senators but allow non-committee members to participate in hearings on issues in which they have strong district interests.

The Testimony

The Legislative Reorganization Act of 1946 requires witnesses to submit written statements in advance of appearance, and the rules of most committees require it (typically, by seven days). The hope was that "tedious oral repetition of testimony could be avoided, much valuable time would be saved, and the conduct of committee hearings could be greatly expedited."[36] It usually is. Most experienced policy advocates understand the flow of communications involved in the system of legislative intelligence and are content to have their statistics and main points circulated in written form.

There are exceptions: the occasional witness who glues his or her eyes to the text and doggedly plods ahead despite the snores of everyone else in the room; the perennially disorganized, who submit perfunctory remarks to meet the formal rules but only finish their "real" testimony the night before the hearing; and those who leave deliberate blanks so as to leave a surprise or two for their opponents. But unless one has worked things out with a committee member in advance, it is usually wise to make the main points in writing. A subcommittee chair with no more than one or two colleagues in attendance may wield so fast a gavel that little more than the written record appears. Because most committees adhere fairly strictly to the "five-minute rule" (giving each member five minutes of questioning), even a friend on the committee may not be able to give you all the time you need to salvage your case.

In oral testimony, informality and apparent spontaneity is the rule, even if it has to be carefully rehearsed. There is a large element of performance. A Cabinet member may be flanked by literally dozens of expert advisers, but it is bad form to turn to them too often. It is even worse form to be uninformed or, worse, wrong. Quite frequently, a major witness will be carefully rehearsed with staff aides who attempt to think of every nasty question a hostile committee member might ask. In many cases, moreover, the process is staged in advance: the staff of Representative X works with the Witness Y to develop a series of expert questions and answers they can both put in the record. Years ago, when ventriloquist Edgar Bergen and his dummy, Charlie McCarthy, were popular comic personalities, such hearings were known as "Charlie McCarthies." Unlike wooden dolls, however, the performances of real-life "dummies" do not always come off without a hitch. "One official reported some embarrassment when he not only answered the first question he had planted but, inadvertently, the next one as well."[37]

"There is no substitute for knowing what you are talking about."[38] At the other extreme, there is probably nothing more dangerous than a bluff. Not only are the senior members of most subcommittees pretty well informed in their areas of specialization, but there is usually someone in the environment who will eventually come forth to destroy a bluffer's credibility. Whether one should argue or defer, stick to one's guns or display a willingness to compromise, there are no universal answers. Some highly successful policy advocates could be extraordinarily pugnacious—Roosevelt's secretary of the interior Harold Ickes and Richard Nixon's attorney general John Mitchell come immediately to mind. Other witnesses maintain attitudes of deference bordering on the obsequious. When asked stupid questions, they will answer with respect rather than impatience. When asked difficult or embarrassing questions, they will emphasize their willingness to cooperate and act in accordance with the "doctrine of apparent candor" (a term coined by a high government official during World War II to describe his agency's attitude when dealing with congressional committees). When slapped in public, they will turn the other cheek. Behind their backs, such witnesses are likely to be described as "true gentlemen," a form of high praise. They are also referred to as wimps, a less flattering label to be sure, but one that at least is better than those reserved for liars, blusterers, and fools.

The Interrogation

Seated together in a group facing the witness, committee members make an impressive appearance. They enjoy something of the same institutional dignity that surrounds a group of judges in a courtroom. They feel important, too, as can be corroborated by anyone who has sat as a committee member at a public hearing.

And they are important! The behavior of a committee member can make one witness's testimony an outstanding success. He or she can confound the well-laid plans of another witness and convert his or her presentation into a dismal failure. Committee interrogation, like cross-examination in a courtroom, is an art in itself. An effective interrogation must be based upon a clear understanding of the objectives to be achieved, the background and character of the witnesses, and a grasp of the basic facts involved in the matter at hand.

A friendly interrogation will often start by questions that build up the character and competence of the witness. It will allow the witness to put his or her strongest arguments out front and to anticipate the opposition's strongest rebuttals. The five-minute rule is ignored and witnesses are invited to expound at length. If the witness lacks specific information, he or she is invited to submit later research and clarifications for publication in the official hearing record. Questions are often rhetorical: "Isn't it true that . . ." or "In your vast experience . . ." are the frequent lead-ins to the interrogatories' recitals of their own favorite arguments. "He was," as Earl Latham describes the chairman of one such hearing, "his own best witness and he spoke to the record through many voices."[39]

An unfriendly interrogation is quite different. It may very well begin with questions that demonstrate the incompetence or unreliability of the witness or the organization he or she represents. Few investigating committees have ever matched the House Un-American Activities Committee's knack for making an unfriendly witness look bad. When it was clear that a witness would take the Fifth Amendment, he or she was likely to be asked not simply about membership in the Communist party but whether he or she was "an international Communist agent with the mission of training the hard core revolutionaries in the process and techniques and strategies of that conspiracy to overthrow this government by force and violence."[40] During the Korean War, a point was frequently made of connecting the witnesses' alleged communism with those forces killing our boys in Asia. Despite the fact that most of the unfriendly witnesses had dropped their party activities decades before the war in Korea, the rules regarding the Fifth Amendment required them to refuse to answer such questions no matter how they were phrased. Even an unfriendly witness's seeming acts of patriotism could be used against him, as in the case of a World War II hero who was asked if he wasn't motivated by the fact that "we were a co-belligerent with Russia."[41]

The Record

Although such tricks are not at all uncommon, it is worth reiterating our earlier point on the intelligence value of hearings. While much of what happens at this stage in the legislative struggle appears as pure blue smoke and mirrors, the published records of legislative hearings provide a valuable source of both information and propaganda. The publication of a statement in a committee report gives it a certain amount of dignity and status. The record is also used as a means of publishing various supplementary memoranda and reports that could not otherwise be readily available. Furthermore, committee members can usually have sufficient copies printed to allow widespread distribution among members of a key policy subsystem. Although the utility of some hearings is diminished by poor organization, rambling testimony, and numbingly boring prose, others successfully bring together the best and most current ideas in a field. Whole articles and speeches (and even college term papers) can be constructed largely from the materials compiled in these printed hearing reports.

The published record is not always an accurate reflection of what went on at a committee hearing. Both witnesses and committee members are usually given an opportunity to correct their remarks. Theoretically, they are supposed to catch only errors made by the transcribers and improve upon the grammar of an extemporaneous discussion. In practice, this opportunity is habitually used to change the meaning of what was actually said and even to add entirely new material. In addition, the chairman of the committee often makes, and allows others to make, many off-the-record statements. When this happens, the official reporter rests for a moment. On these occasions some of the juiciest bits of testimony (and funniest jokes) are recorded only in the memory of those in the room.

Nor is the transcribed record of a committee hearing always published. The House Rules Committee, for example, never publishes transcripts of its hearings on special rules, even though it meets in open session. Moreover, although they are available in the committee office, many transcripts are not actually printed prior to floor action and are thus virtually useless to all but the most assiduous researchers.

MARKUP

Although the House and Senate floors have become increasingly important arenas of amendment and legislative bargaining, most of the major and minor changes in the original drafts of legislation continue to be made at the committee and subcommittee sessions known as markups or marks. The mark is the guts of the legislative struggle.

The move from the hearing stage to markup is to move, as Charles Tiefer puts it, from "being a little investigatory commission to a little legislature."[42] As in the decision whether or not to have hearings, the powers of the committee or subcommittee chair in deciding to go to mark are formidable. In 1983, after the House had adopted a resolution favoring a mutual U.S.-U.S.S.R. nuclear weapons freeze, a majority vote of the Senate Foreign Relations Committee forced its reluctant chair to go to mark; but this was and is an exceptional circumstance. Committee (or subcommittee) chairs are normally allowed to decide not only what legislative issues will be debated in scheduled meetings but which bill (in the case of competing bills on the same subject) will serve as the starting point for debate.

When and How

As with hearings, the decision whether to hold the original markup sessions at the full or subcommittee level can be significant. Subcommittee sessions tend to be considerably less formal, with staff persons playing more prominent roles. And because they tend to be less publicly visible (i.e., less interesting to the press), they are likely to be considerably more accessible to the influence of interest groups. Senate committees—perhaps because of quorum problems—are far less likely to conduct markups at the subcommittee level; some House committees—most notably Ways and Means—are equally disinclined.

On those committees that delegate substantial powers to their subcommittees, MCs who fail to influence subcommittee deliberations have the option of appealing to the full committee, and those who lose their amendments in subcommittee can usually get a second chance in the full committee mark. It is generally considered bad form, however, for a subcommittee member to raise issues in the full committee that he or she had not brought up (or reserved the option of reconsidering) in the smaller group.

Markup starts with a draft chosen by the chair or, in the rare case of disagreement, by majority vote. Although this decision is usually routine, it can have strategic significance. In 1982, for example, the chair of the Senate Environment and Public Works Committee, Robert Stafford (R-VT), ignored a variety of bills extending the Clean Air Act and began the markup with the original act itself. As noted by *Congressional Quarterly*, "the panel plowed through the existing law section by section, a procedure that forced members who favored changes to muster a majority each time they wanted to propose a modification."[43]

"Reading the bill" is a common procedure. Once individual MCs have had the opportunity to make general comments, the chair will usually start with the first section and read the measure line by line. Prompted by spur-of-the-moment ideas, or carefully briefed by staffers or lobbyists, members suggest the striking of several lines, the change of key words, or the substitution of an entirely new section for the old. On controversial bills, lobbyists crowd the committee room and adjacent corridors to offer last-minute hand signals and winks, or to pass suggested drafts to friendly members. Senator Robert Dole (R-KS) coined the phrase *Gucci gulch* to describe the path members are sometimes forced to tread through the expensive shoes and last-minute pleadings of these denizens of the corridors. Each change agreed to in a bill is carefully noted by the staff and appears in the next day's "committee print," which shows deleted material with a line through it ~~like this~~ and new material in *italics*. When more than one bill is involved, the markup process is sometimes facilitated by a "comparative print" in which sections of the two bills are printed in side-by-side columns.

The reading of a bill in markup is a valuable intellectual discipline. Even for those who faithfully attend preliminary hearings, line-by-line analysis and argument is likely to bring out hidden meanings that would otherwise lie undiscovered. Forced to defend the use of a particular word or phrase, even the sponsor of a bill may discover new nuances of interpretation. It can also be a grueling operation. The finest points may take up a whole day's discussion, as when a Senate subcommittee in the early 1960s spent three hours deciding whether its goal was pollution "abatement" or "control." The nine months Senator Stafford's committee devoted to markup of the 1982 Clean Air Amendments was unusual but not unique.

The Committee Reports

The most decisive form of action that a committee can take on a bill is inaction. This negative form of action almost invariably means the death of a measure. Nor is the corpse assigned elsewhere for burial. When committee members kill a bill by inaction, they do not discharge themselves of the measure and report it to the floor. Nor do they even prepare a written report stating why and wherefore.

Occasionally, committee members will merely report a measure to the floor with no recommendation for either favorable or adverse action. This is something less than a burial but also less than a genuine endorsement. Or the members of a committee may report a bill to the floor but very specifically reserve the right of committee members to propose amendments when the measure comes up on the floor. The purpose of such strategies, as a rule, is to force floor confrontations between, for example, the administration's position and that of the committee majority.

An entirely favorable report may be less than meets the eye. In 1949 the House Commerce Committee's reporting of a bill to curb the powers of the Federal Trade Commission was intended simply as a sort of shot across the Commission's bow. Both the bill's advocates and opponents had agreed that no attempt would be made to call the measure off the calendar and have it considered on the House floor.

Regardless of a committee's true motives, the point at which a bill is "ordered reported" becomes a vital benchmark in its progress toward passage. At this point, the scope of conflict shifts dramatically from a relatively small group of focused specialists to a very different set of actors: first to the party leaders and members of the House Rules Committee responsible for scheduling, then to the House or Senate as a whole. Committee control is no longer guaranteed at these stages, but it remains strong. Committee leaders are the first and, usually, the only witnesses before the House Rules Committee, the only pleaders before Senate party leaders, and thus the primary forces in scheduling decisions. As floor managers, committee leaders tend similarly to dominate questions of timing and tactics. The floor manager, for example, may simply accept an amendment, a maneuver that—in the absence of strong opposition—is akin to the committee having reported the amendment on its own. The fact that a committee has reported a measure does not mean that it has abandoned its fate.

When subcommittees report to the full committee, they usually present the bill itself and any proposed amendments. Sometimes a written report will be prepared more as a proposed draft for the full committee's final report than as a direct public statement.

The reports of full committees, in contrast, invariably consist not only of the bill and amendments but also of a written report, which is given the same number as the reported bill. Abner Mikva and Patti Saris suggest that such reports have little direct significance, serving at best "to educate the legislative assistants of non–committee members." At the same time, as the former congressman and his co-author concede, the "public relations value is considerable."[44] By serving as campaign documents in floor debate and by developing group support, they sometimes play an important role in focusing the direction of subsequent struggles. Together with the minority report, if one is filed, the committee report sets the parameters of debate; for non–committee members and time-pressed legislative assistants, moreover, these documents are a treasured source of "quick-fix" bill summaries. They are particularly useful in the House, where the so-called Ramsayer Rule (named for a former member of that name) requires that all changes in existing law be explicitly noted, along with committee estimates of the costs likely to be incurred in carrying out the purposes of the bill. (The Senate's Comden Rule is less explicit.)

The quality of committee reports varies, and the reader who takes their arguments at face value runs certain risks. Generally the product of considerable staff attention with inputs from members, executive branch officials and lobbyists alike, the growing tendency has been for reports to contain reasonably full explanations of whatever action is recommended. From time to time, to be sure, there are committee reports that completely gloss over important points. This usually develops in situations in which there is no dissension within the committee and no clearly organized opposition is likely. Whatever their intramural utility may be, committee reports can have significant long-run policy implications. In seeking extrinsic guides to the meaning of a statute, the courts are likely to rank committee reports first in importance. Administrators also rely heavily on committee reports if only because they tend to be the documents of legislative history that are most readily available. There are those who feel that "to draft a statute in broad or ambiguous terms and then to insert a statement in a committee report which . . . , if clearly expressed in the statute, might not have been accepted by the Congress . . . [is] morally indefensible."[45] But there is little doubt that the effect of many committee reports is to substantially expand the terms of the bills they accompany.

Committee Voting

The strategic importance of the decision whether to order a bill reported makes the final vote in committee one of interest to a particularly wide audience. A bill not reported is all but dead; one reported by a narrow margin is likely to face much tougher sledding on the floor than one that slides through with little resistance. Not surprisingly, the rules regarding these final committee votes are considerably more strict than at other stages in the committee process. In most committees, a quorum of actual bodies (not proxies) must be present to report a bill.

There are devices for evading these quorum rules. In the Senate and, on rare occasions, in the House, "legislation is 'polled out,' reported by written ballot or telephone. Another approach is the 'rolling quorum,' which permits legislation to be reported out as long as a quorum appeared at some time during a mark-up."[46] When the bill is essentially unopposed, it may even be reported in flagrant violation of quorum rules; but this makes it subject to a point of order that will almost certainly be sustained.[47] If failure to achieve a quorum indicates the existence of controversy, as it often does, such points of order will almost invariably be raised.

Obviously, a tactic of those who are opposed to a bill but outnumbered, is to boycott the final mark. Worse, from the standpoint of a bill's proponents, is when they become inadvertent victims of secondary boycotts, as almost happened with a 1970 health bill. The problem here was not the health service bill itself but a totally separate issue of occupational safety, which happened to be in line for final action in the same Senate subcommittee. The health bill was in effect being held hostage.[48] Even more common are bills held hostage not to any particular piece of legislation but to the whole decision environment of the committee. There are some committees—House Education and Labor, and House Foreign Affairs being the most notorious—that sometimes seem all but incapable of reaching consensus about anything.

For students of Congress, one of the most important reforms of the 1970s was that which required committees to keep records of important votes. Formal votes do not, of course, tell us everything we would like to know about the forces effecting legislative outcomes, but they have proven a useful tool for the analysis of floor decisions. Even more than votes on the House and Senate floors, however, committee roll calls must be analyzed with unusual care. Except on final votes to report, for example, many of the votes recorded in committee are actually cast by proxies. Richard Hall's sample of figures on three House committees, for example, showed between 34 and 45 percent of the members either voting by proxy or not at all.[49] In most committees—particularly in the House—the rules governing proxies are quite strict,[50] but there is no doubt that a considerable amount of fudging occurs. Tiefer reports a case, for example, in which two senators both claimed to have the proxies—one for a yea vote, the other a nay—of the same absent member.[51] "Well, he must have changed his mind after we talked," one of the disputants blandly claimed. And even where the rules are strict, there is no denying that proxy votes cannot reflect the *informed* judgment of absent members. As one reform report put it, "You cannot argue with a proxy; a proxy cannot consider an offered amendment; a proxy cannot compromise."[52] In practice, as Hall suggests, "proxy voting tends to augment the power of the active, not preserve the authority of the absent."[53]

Formal roles are important factors here: chairs and ranking minority members are most likely to be present at most meetings. The attendance of other members varies according to the prominence of the issue, the number of cameras, personal interests, and the salience of the issue for an individual member. Politically, this is likely to increase the impact of subgovernments: those with the strongest constituency or ideological interests in legislation are the MCs most likely to show up. Committee votes have a tendency, then, to amplify the patterns impressed on committees by recruitment patterns. Just as committees are not mirror images of their parent bodies, "For any given issue, the membership of a committee is typically more diverse than the subset of self-selected members who dominate committee deliberations."[54]

Not surprisingly, committees that tend to attract ideologically polarized subsets of the membership tend to be highly polarized in their voting behavior. However, generalization in this area is difficult. With little change in the issues confronting them, some committees have "developed entirely new factional alignments" in relatively short periods of time: even from one Congress to another, there are "substantial variations."[55] Some committees, it seems, have "personalities" that transcend both recruitment patterns and issues. Most commonly, this is a function of leadership: the House Committee on Ways and Means, for example, has always attracted a highly partisan membership and dealt with some of the system's most polarizing issues; when Wilbur Mills was chairman, however, it was one of the House's best-integrated committees. There are also important differences between the House and Senate. Regardless of subject matter, it seems that "partisan acrimony" is generally "stronger on House committees."[56]

It doesn't take long, during the typical markup session, to get a feel for the committee or subcommittee's operative dynamic. In a partisan, highly polarized committee, the bargaining table is a barricade: minority members fire a series of amendments across the table that are consistently rejected. Only when backroom negotiations have failed and a majority party member brings his or her amendment to the committee table is there unpredictable controversy. In a bipartisan mark, the lines between Republicans and Democrats or liberals and conservatives remain fairly strong, but real effort is made to secure agreement on a bill that will eventually become law. Richard Fenno has suggested that there are essentially two types of House committees:

> One type is identified by the House orientation of its decision rules, the autonomy of its decision-making processes, its emphasis on committee expertise, its success on the House floor, its members' sense of group identity, and the relatively higher ratio of member to nonmember satisfaction with its performance. The other type is identified by its extra–House-oriented decision rules, the permeability of its decision-making process, the de-emphasis on committee expertise, its lack of success on the House floor, the absence of any feeling of group identification, and the relatively higher ratio of non-member to member satisfaction with its performance.[57]

Although Fenno himself admits that these are "over-simplifications" and others have expressed doubts that "so broadly conceived a typology can serve the purpose of comparison,"[58] the general categories continue to have considerable utility. And committee integration, particularly integration that crosses party lines, is closely related to success on the floor.[59]

———————— ✳ ————————

CONCLUSION: TAKING IT TO THE FLOOR

Despite the importance of committee unity, even the most sharply divided committees get most of their bills passed in some form or another. As Gerald Strom puts it,

> about 90 percent of reported bills are eventually passed by the full chamber, and many of those that do not pass die not from outright rejection but from lack of time, as they are pending action at the time Congress adjourns. Moreover, the floor seldom makes any major change in reported bills. Amendments to bills in the full chamber are generally minor ones that do not substantially alter the main provisions of the bill as reported from committee.[60]

Whether this high rate of success confirms the continuing validity of Woodrow Wilson's generalization about government by the standing committees is not as clear. The "appearance of committee dominance," John Kingdon says, comes about "in part *because* committee members generally anticipate House reaction well enough that confrontations between House and committee are rare."[61]

There is little doubt that committees wield enormous influence at the margins of legislation in their domains. Committee membership brings with it the ability to shape the fine points of the law: to insert a technical amendment to the tax code, in the case of Senate Finance or House Ways and Means; to fix the location of a research facility or military base, in the case of Agriculture or Armed Services. In the broad outlines of policy, however, the standing committees are constrained by their anticipation of what will happen on the floor. As Kingdon has shown, if "the whole House membership had a well-formed attitude on a given measure, the committee position could not prevail against it."[62]

10

※

THE WAR ON
THE FLOOR

O nce a bill has been favorably reported, its chances of becoming law increase dramatically: compared with the roughly nine out of ten bills that die in committee, fewer than one in ten are killed on the floor, in conference, or at 1600 Pennsylvania Avenue. Many of those that do suffer such a fate, moreover, will have been sent knowingly to their death for symbolic or strategic reasons. Bill managers are sometimes beaten on the floor, but they are rarely surprised.

If action in the full House or Senate floor is seldom dramatic, anticipation of what might happen on the floor permeates the calculations of those who work behind the scenes. When the performance on stage flows smoothly, it is seldom by chance. The more uneventful the performance, the more likely it is that a bill's managers have done their job of anticipation well. The floor vote, like a final exam, is far more reflective of a semester of study than of last-minute cramming.

※

SETTING THE STAGE

Performances on the floor, like those on stage, are sometimes appreciated only by those with knowledge of the art. Like an East Indian dance in which the flick of an eyebrow has profound meaning, a harmless-looking motion may have tremendous implications. A dramatic clash between opposing members may be a ritual of stereotyped routines. A bill may go unamended, uncriticized, and undefeated less because it is noncontroversial than because the important compromises have already been made. Not all outcomes are predictable: Yogi Berra's famous statement about baseball—"the game ain't over until it's over"—applies to the legislative struggle as well. There are moments of surprise when even the most savvy observers are caught off guard by hidden opponents or last-minute changes of sentiment; as in baseball, however, weak teams are more likely than the strong to be beaten in the late innings.

Getting There Is Half the Fun

In the heyday of the congressional establishment, few bills were amended on the floor. The 1970s saw a dramatic increase in floor activity and significance. In the 1950s, fewer than 10 percent of the measures brought to the House floor were subject to one or more amendments, compared with almost 30 percent in the 93rd Congress (1973–74).[1] The 1970s, however, represented the high tide of floor action; the percentage of measures subject to amendment has declined steadily to fewer than one in seven.[2] In purely numeric terms, the number of House floor amendments rose slowly in the 1950s and 1960s (from just under 400 in 1955–56 to fewer than 800 in 1971–72); leapt to almost 1,600 in 1979–80; then dropped back down to about 1,000 in 1985–86.[3]

It is not by accident or simple coincidence that the decrease in House floor amendments coincides with an increase in closed and restrictive rules. In 1975–76, when floor activity was high, almost 85 percent of the bills brought to the House floor came under "open" rules; by 1985–86, that percentage had declined to 55.[4] What has happened here is simple to describe, profound in tactical implications. The hegemony that the standing committees enjoyed in the middle decades of this century began to erode in the 1970s. It has been partially restored in the House of the 1980s not so much as the product of powerful norms as by resort to formal rules. In the contemporary House, in other words, coalition-building strategies have re-emerged in importance. The need to put out fires, to cope with last-minute surprises on the House floor, which was common in the 1970s, is less acute.

Although a similar function can be performed by more elaborate unanimous consent agreements in the Senate, the need for unanimity frustrates central control. The length and complexity of such agreements in the 1980s has apparently "had no straightforward effect on the degree of 'restrictiveness' of agreements."[5] At first glance, in fact, more complex agreements seem in many ways to have dispersed agenda control. On some major bills—the 1990 Clean Air Bill was a case in point—virtually the entire Senate gets into the act, behaving almost like a giant markup session. In most cases, however, we suspect that the reality of agenda control in both the Senate and the House points in the same direction. Regardless of who crafts them, increasingly elaborate decision-making structures probably favor those who are best positioned to anticipate the direction of debate, that is, committee members working with and through the leadership. Those House members who testify before the Rules Committee, and those Senators most likely to take an interest in a bill as it comes off the calendar, are most likely to be those who have already been closely identified with the issue at hand. By structuring the terms of floor debate and amendment they can further prefigure outcomes.

Because there is no Rules committee, the scheduling powers of Senate party leaders are enormous—as long as nobody objects. The ability of a single senator to block a consent agreement or to hold a bill—thus blocking consideration entirely—makes these powers largely irrelevant on issues of broad concern. It is quite a different story in the House.

Closed and restrictive rules are the most obvious procedural devices for influencing substantive outcomes, but they are by no means the only ones. Bills brought to the House floor under suspension of the rules, for example, are not amendable; and use of the suspension calendar, like the use of restrictive rules, is on the rise. That it tends to be an instrument of the majority party was clearly exemplified in the case of a 1983 farm bill. Here, although the committee vote was unanimous, the minority was not informed of the chair's intent to follow the suspension route (the ranking minority member claimed that he had been "stuck in an elevator"). Once the bill came up on the suspension calendar, his only procedural option was to try to defeat the bill. It could not be amended or challenged on a point of order. In fact, it was vetoed, thus giving the minority a second crack at negotiating its amendments.[6] Committees can also restrict the range of possible floor amendments by reporting all the changes made in committee in the form of one comprehensive committee amendment. Such an amendment, offered in the nature of a substitute for the original bill, has the effect of "locking out" other changes. "It is not in order to amend an amendment previously agreed to."[7] A committee can also seek a special order from the Rules Committee restricting amendments.

Although restrictive rules must be approved by a House majority, in many cases it is easier to get members to deny themselves a vote than it is to get them to vote no. As Barbara Sinclair suggests, MCs sometimes prefer to have their choices constrained. Members may, for instance, be willing to vote for a rule barring amendments requiring a balanced budget or prohibiting school busing, even though, were the amendments offered, they would vote for them.[8] It also works the other way. One of the most facile tactics available to the opponents of a popular proposal is to kill the rule rather than the bill itself. "Oh, I didn't vote against that," you can tell the folks, "my objection was to the procedure."

Dealing with Amendments

Within the context provided by the Rules Committee in the House and consent agreements in the Senate, most of the tactical decisions regarding floor amendments are in the hands of the bill's floor manager. Typically, the committee or subcommittee chair that reported the bill acts as floor manager. His or her efforts are usually supplemented by the majority party leaders and, increasingly in the House, by special leadership task forces assigned the tactical responsibility for a particular bill. The floor manager has the authority to decide whether to fight a proposed amendment or accept it as "friendly." In the latter case, the floor manager—sometimes by prearrangement, sometimes by fast thinking—

can simply decide to compromise or accommodate a potential ally by incorporating amendments into the committee bill. The floor manager is also, as a rule, in control of debate time, and he or she may have considerable influence in deciding the order in which amendments are considered.

Typically, bills are considered section by section. Under the formal rules of the House, each section is read aloud by the clerk before being opened to amendments; in practice the actual reading is dispensed with by unanimous consent. Those who wish to offer amendments must be particularly alert at this stage. As Charles Tiefer explains,

> The "window" for offering the amendment is narrow. An amendment cannot be offered before the Clerk reads the portion to which it applies, but if Members miss that reading, they also cannot offer the amendment after the Clerk moves on to reading subsequent sections. Many is the time when a Member patiently waits to offer his amendment or point of order to a particular section, becomes distracted by conversation just when that section goes by, and misses his "window."[9]

For purposes of offering amendments, an MC must be recognized by the chair, who in theory has considerable discretion, but who in practice turns first to committee members in order of seniority. The advantage in timing that this gives the committee chair is not insignificant and is reinforced by his or her right to offer the first amendment to an amendment. Thus, a clever bill manager can sometimes diffuse the impact of a proposed amendment by watering it down or substituting a less destructive alternative. Either way, committee leaders are usually in a strong position to decide the order of voting on amendments.

Almost two thousand years ago, Pliny the Younger provided an example of a situation in the Roman Senate in which the order of voting was crucial to the outcome. In this case, a group of freedmen had been accused of murdering the consul Afranius Dexter. The Senate was divided into three groups of roughly equal size: the acquitters (A), who believed that Dexter was a suicide and that his accused murderers should be released; the banishers (B), who favored banishing the alleged murderers to an island; and the convictors (C), who favored condemning the freedmen to death. What Pliny discovered is that whichever alternative was voted first would lose. If Pliny's motion to acquit (A), for example, was first on the agenda, it would lose to a coalition of the supporters of B and C. Banishment (B) would lose to the supporters of A and C, and C would lose to A and B. If the order of voting does not determine who wins, it does decide who loses.[10]

The House Rules Committee has used a procedure, known as "King of the Hill," that modifies this dilemma. Devised by former chairman Richard Bolling (D-MO) to handle a complicated series of budget proposals in 1982, a King-of-the-Hill rule permits the House to cast consecutive votes on a series of substitutes. The winner is the last plan to pass. Although this procedure still disadvantages the proposal voted on first, it does not doom it; and it enables MCs to choose a backup position unavailable under traditional procedures. More important, it provides members with a means of putting their real policy preferences on record. On the 1982 budget bill, "The procedure provided political cover to legislators who could cast votes on seven budgetary plans and explain their actions to constituents in any manner they chose."[11] The gloomy fact remains, however, that it is impossible to devise a voting procedure that is truly neutral in its effects.

Subtle questions of moods can play a role on the floor. Party lines tend to remain tight in the wake of highly charged battles. MCs are likely to be less generous toward "trivial" amendments late at night, or when time is scarce. When numerous amendments are offered to a single bill, certain rhythms of surge and decline seem to develop: "If it hits a couple of votes going left, the boys are then looking to tack back and go to the right. The rhythm of the place is important. You want to structure a debate so you catch the wave."[12]

There are three basic forms of agenda manipulation. (1) By not reporting certain bills, committees dominate the most basic form, which is the exclusion of certain options. A closed rule can perform this same function in the House, as in some cases can a hold or objection to a consent agreement in the Senate. (2) Order manipulation, as we have noted, is sometimes crucial. (3) Most subtle of all is the manipulation of perceptions. Committees affect perceptions by deciding what gets combined with what: tax reform succeeded in 1986 because it was perceived on the Senate floor as a package so delicately crafted that the Finance Committee's "no-amendment" strategy was the only viable alternative to no bill at all. Leaders sometimes manipulate the meaning of a vote by juxtaposing it with another. All of these maneuvers, however, depend upon a shrewd and calculated understanding of the mood of the Congress. Good tactics, like good strategies, are founded in good counting.

Counting Heads

The most elaborate and (with a significant caveat) most accurate systems of counting are the House whip organizations. The caveat is that the effectiveness of the whip organizations is confined to one side of the aisle, Republican or Democratic. A whip count, as one Democrat told Sinclair, is "a process, not an event."[13] It begins, on important bills, virtually at the moment a bill emerges from committee. It continues, typically, to the moment of final passage. "Because of an improved whip system and because members will respond more candidly to leadership polls than to lobbyist or White House polls, [party leaders] have perhaps the most important information in a legislative struggle— information on where the votes are and (sometimes) what it will take to win certain people over."[14]

Although lobbyists, party leaders, and other policy advocates can usually make shrewd guesses in advance as to where the House or Senate will go on a particular bill, they are only guesses. One close study of the 93rd Congress, for example, found only about two-thirds of House Democrats ready to state a clear opinion on the first whip count.[15] Even then, there are many questions to ask before tactical planning begins: Where are the soft spots? What are the patterns of uneasiness? Is there, for example, a particular region or faction most opposed to the bill? What substantive objections, perhaps curable by amendment, are being raised? Is there a pattern of responses that suggests particular interest group activity?

Sometimes at this point the leadership will seek outside help. Representatives of organized labor frequently cooperate in the whip planning of House Democrats, even on issues remote from their immediate interests. The lobbying group may in turn activate its supporters in the home districts of wavering members; a House member "may never realize that constituent calls and letters . . . are initiated by Washington-based lobbyists who are themselves responding to requests from the party leadership and whip staff for assistance in vote gathering."[16] A lobbyist may also be able to provide information on potential supporters in the other party. On complicated bills, the leadership core expands as attempts are made to sample opinions on a widening range of potential amendments and political pressures. White House and agency liaison offices are likely to work closely with members of the administration's party leadership on the Hill.

———————— ✳ ————————

THE TALKING

It is customary among journalists and political scientists to lampoon talking on the floor of Congress as useless babble. At the other extreme are those like Woodrow Wilson who have glorified congressional debate as an ideal method of informing the nation and clarifying issues. Neither the skeptic nor the idealist approaches the variety and complexity of the real uses of the talk immortalized in the *Congressional Record*.

Its Purpose

During the early nineteenth-century debate on the Missouri Compromise, a representative from Buncombe County, North Carolina, was pleading for a chance to talk, despite the impatient pleading of other members for an immediate vote. He explained that he wanted merely to "make a speech for Buncombe." His frank admission of purpose gave American speech two new words: *buncombe* and its shortened form, *bunk*.

In a very real sense, most floor speeches on pending legislation are buncombe.[17] But if the purpose of most floor speeches is simply to build a record for the consumption of specific supporters, such motives do not imply lack of sincerity or meaning. In fact, the most effective buncombe is both sincere and informative, and a careful reading of an MC's floor talk is sometimes a useful way of telling to whom he wishes to appeal.

Does floor talk play a part in legislative campaigns? Certainly it is not the decisive weapon it seems to those who equate oratorical ability with influence. Speech making, no matter how eloquent, cannot by itself organize group support or supplant other forms of propaganda. By the time a bill comes to the floor, opposing lines are generally drawn tightly enough to resist the major changes that may be attempted through speech making alone. The Kennedy brothers, John and Ted in particular, have been capable of some of the most eloquent oratory heard on the Hill. Yet JFK's rhetoric on the Senate floor (and even his later role as president) never brought him into a position of genuine institutional leadership. Brother Ted's influence has waxed and waned less according to his eloquence than to the relative strength or weakness of the political forces behind him.

Nevertheless, it would be a mistake to universalize the sweeping generalization of one former legislator who remarked, "In the twenty-eight years that I have been a member of one or the other branches of Congress, I have never known a speech to change a vote."[18] There are four distinct purposes (other than that of a filibuster) that speech making may serve in a legislative campaign.

The first is to provide a medium of communication between those who are lined up on the same side of a question. Despite the vaunted efficiency of the whip organizations, floor statements are often the quickest and most effective methods of passing the word among members of Congress. Shifts in strategy, last-minute switches in the White House position or in that of a key lobbyist, new facts, these can sometimes be effectively conveyed only on the floor.

The second purpose is to strengthen the cohesiveness of a group, fan the enthusiasm of supporters, and provide umbrellas of rationalization for the insecure. Richard Fenno suggests that the ways in which MCs present their positions can sometimes be more important back home than the positions themselves.[19] More important, it "is wrong to assume that the only legitimate use of analysis is to assist the policymaker in discovering a solution to a problem. Policymakers need retrospective (postdecision) analysis at least as much as they need prospective (or predecision) analysis, and probably more."[20]

Debate provides nonexperts with rhetorical justifications to use in the district. Since there is always uncertainty as to which votes will have to be explained, members have a tendency to "stockpile" good arguments, many of which are culled from floor debate and the *Congressional Record*. It stands to reason that the most effective speech is likely to be one that sets forth an appealing and defensible line of argument that can be taken over by a listener (or reader) and adapted to his or her own uses. When backed by a possible exchange of favors among MCs and vigorous campaigning by noncongressional forces, speech making can provide the post hoc rationalizations sufficient to keep potential waverers in line.

By the same logic, the third purpose of debate is to win additional votes. On most issues there are a number of MCs who go to the floor undecided, especially on amendments. Cue-taking is common; when successful floor amendments raise puzzling new questions and cut members free from previous commitments, patterns of communication change and the number of members seeking unusual sources of guidance can be quite large. Speech can also play a role in the process of persuasion by changing the tempo of a campaign. A Roosevelt administration bill for compulsory control of the civilian labor force passed the House early in 1945 and seemed certain of passage in the Senate. But a vehement and lengthy attack on the bill led by Senators Joseph O'Mahoney (D-WY) and Wayne Morse (R-OR) gave business organizations and organized labor the time to mount a vigorous counterattack on the administration's position. Within a week's time so many senators had switched into the opposition camp that the administration's leaders dropped the bill rather than risk a resounding public defeat.

The fourth purpose of speeches in Congress is to help lay the basis for future campaigns. Some of the best floor talks are made by those who are on the losing side and have no immediate hope of winning. Speeches help keep the colors flying. For the winning side, they help the task of keeping the campaign alive until victory is won in the other house, in the conference committee, or at the stage of presidential signature. For either side, when a bill is due to become law, they help prepare the ground for carrying on the contest in the administrative and judicial arenas.

Also worth noting is the latent function of debate in forcing members more fully to inform themselves about the issues under consideration. The fear of looking foolish can be an effective goad to good study habits, and study sometimes changes minds. Donald Matthews quotes a Senate staff assistant whose boss was floor managing a bill that "he really didn't feel strongly about at first. Only as the fight progressed and he had to argue for the bill and defend it from attacks, did he become convinced it should pass."[21] The contribution of floor speeches to the building of personal reputations in Buncombe or to the conduct of legislative campaigns is not always needed. In fact, too much talking can have the effect of attracting too much attention from latent sources of opposition. Many of the most influential MCs are people of few words. This lesson was learned by Speaker Joseph Cannon during his early days in the House. His maiden speech, an elaborate defense of a bill to amend the postal code, stirred the opposition of many older House members and the press. "More legislation," he later reflected, "is delayed and embarrassed by too much speaking by the defenders than by the opponents.[22]

Who Talks?

The importance of cue-giving sometimes makes it more important to decide who talks than what is said. A routine task of campaign leadership is to line up a roster of influential members long in advance. Although this sometimes proves difficult, more serious problems arise when there are too many potential speakers than too few. To prevent chaos, methods have evolved in both houses for deciding who can speak and in what order. Not surprisingly, the rules governing debate in the larger House of Representatives are considerably more restrictive than those of the Senate. In the House, "The order of recognition to offer amendments is within the discretion of the Chair, but practice indicates that he should recognize members of the committee handling the bill in order of their seniority on the committee."[23] Essentially the same is true in the Senate, and the rules on debate follow from those on amendments. In both houses, the rise of subcommittee government has blurred the lines. Typically, it is the bill manager (frequently, in the postreform House, the subcommittee chair of the reporting committee) who manages the bill on the floor and thereby controls debate. In effect, recognition goes first to the bill manager, then to his or her chief antagonist, who—it is usually assumed—is the ranking minority member. These members, in turn, subcontract their time by yielding the floor to others so many minutes at a time.

The Control of Debate in the House

The intentional prolongation of talk is a useful weapon of obstruction. Its early use in the United States was so frequent that the colorful word *filibuster,* which originally referred to a small swift vessel and then to a lawless piratical venture, was taken over to describe it. Although the first filibusters occurred in the House, it soon became evident that the body was too large to rely on the rather crude device of moving the previous question to end debate. As a result, an extremely intricate system of additional time controls has been developed. To begin with, there are some thirty kinds of motions that are, by rule or by precedent, nondebatable. These include motions dealing with the previous question itself, adjournment, laying on the table, and certain appeals from the decision of the chair.

Another is a set of limitations on the time that may be devoted to various kinds of business. In the Committee of the Whole, where most House business is conducted, consideration of a bill begins with one hour of "general debate" in which the bill is considered without amendments or motions of any kind. Upon expiration of this first hour, amendments are considered under the five-minute rule, which allows an amendment's sponsor and its opponents a total of five minutes to make their case.

Finally, various limits are set upon the total time that may be used in debate. By unanimous consent or, more commonly, under special orders adopted from the Rules Committee, general debate may be curtailed. When the offering of amendments is prohibited or restricted, debate under the five-minute rule will be limited as well. The cumulative effect of these devices is to give the majority substantial protection against too much talk. MCs may not be free to say all that each would like, but at least they can comment, most of the time, on germane issues and are free from indefinitely prolonged discussion.

Filibustering in the Senate

Even as floor talk in the House came under increasingly rigid control, in the Senate it became a more frequently used and effective legislative weapon. For decades, senators from the South were better known than any others for their filibustering activities; and the modification or abolition of the rule allowing unlimited debate was a major goal of Senate liberals. This is no longer the case. Even those who, in principle, regard the filibuster as undemocratic are not above using it as the situation demands.

Ignoring technical distinctions, there are, in essence, two kinds of filibusters. One is the individualistic effort of a lonely soul or two who hopes by his or her efforts either to galvanize Senate and/or public opinion to the cause or, more simply, to get good press. There is a folkloric quality to these acts of singular bravado: Strom Thurmond (then a Democrat from South Carolina) holds the record, twenty-four hours and seventeen minutes in a vain attempt to kill a 1957 civil rights bill. But there are those who would question Thurmond's record on the grounds that he had help: friends who would use quorum calls and other dilatory tactics to give the senator time for the bathroom. By these standards, the true champion of extended debate is Wayne Morse (D-OR), who singlehandedly, without relief, held the floor for almost twenty-three hours.

Morse lost. So did Thurmond. The truly effective filibuster is one that has enough members to sustain it and insufficient opponents to stop it. Timing may also count. Extended debate, or the threat of the same, increases in effectiveness as adjournment nears. Short of this, the best time for a filibuster is when the calendar is crowded with many other bills that are being pressed by groups or agencies that cannot be ignored. In the classic filibuster, such considerations are academic. Given a sufficient number of like-minded colleagues, debate responsibilities can be rotated in such a way as to put the burden on the other side. In the best organized filibusters against civil rights, for example, Southerners divided the day into four-hour shifts. Refusing to yield (except to one another), the Southerners were well rested while their colleagues slept on cots in the cloakroom to answer the quorum calls of each Southerner looking for a moment of respite.

There are a number of Senate rules designed to restrain floor talk. As in the House, many questions are nondebatable. These include motions to adjourn, to take a recess, to lay a matter on the table, and nineteen other motions.[24] When the calendar is being called and a bill is allowed to come up for consideration, no senator may speak more than once or for more than five minutes. On all other bills no senator is allowed to speak more than once on the same day. Although these restrictions are often suspended, they help to expedite part of the Senate's business, particularly on routine matters. Quite frequently, the Senate limits itself to a specific number of hours of talking or sets a specific hour at which a vote will be taken. Unlike the House, where this is accomplished by a majority vote on resolutions from the Rules Committee, the Senate does this by unanimous consent. Once such an agreement has been reached, it is almost ironclad, for it may later be amended only by another unanimous consent agreement. Quite frequently, in the years since one-time majority leader Mike Mansfield developed the scheme in the 1970s, the Senate has run its filibusters on one track and other business on another. Although the bill being debated is still in trouble under this two-track system, the force of the filibuster is somewhat weakened by this procedure since it cannot be used to stop *all* Senate business.

The most celebrated Senate rule is Rule XXII, the oft-revised cloture procedure used to end debate. "Simply stated, cloture is the Senate's way of telling verbose senators to shut up."[25] The Senate has shown an increasing willingness to do just that. From the inception of the rule in 1919 through 1970, cloture was successfully invoked only 10 times. Between 1971 and 1980 there were 41 successful cloture votes, and from 1981 through 1988 another 40.[26]

The filibuster, however, remains a potent fact of Senate life: it is more important in explaining the dynamic of the institution than statistics can show. Former Senate Parliamentarian Floyd A. Riddick, who began his career in the House, once described the rule on unlimited debate as the "biggest contrast" between the House and Senate.[27] In the words of one senator,

> The rules of the Senate give tremendous power to the individual member if he feels strongly about something. He can literally stop the Senate. For example, in my two years in the Senate, we have never had a debate stopped. If an individual wanted to debate and wanted to prevent a vote from occurring, we have never in my experience taken action that stopped him. We had cloture motions adopted, but after cloture you've got 100 hours of debate. So that if one member really is opposed to something and willing to stand up on the issue, it is very, very difficult to do anything.[28]

---------------- ✳ ----------------

THE VOTING

During any given two years, a member's floor vote may be recorded upward of a thousand times, and he or she may participate in a comparable number of unrecorded votes. The questions on which MCs express themselves run the broadest conceivable gamut of public policy issues. To some extent, the voting process is much the same in committee; but despite the sunshine laws that have opened most committee votes to public scrutiny, floor voting remains far more public. It is floor votes that get published in the *Congressional Quarterly* and the daily press, that are used to compile "presidential support scores" and similar indices, and that form the bases of interest group ratings. Like the score in a game, it may not fully indicate how well you played, but it is what goes down in the books.

The Number of Votes Needed

In committee, disputed questions are decided by majority vote. On the floor, mathematical requirements are more complex. Unanimous consent is required for the approval of bills taken from the Consent and Private Calendars in the House and, in both houses, for many questions of procedure.

Many questions call for a two-thirds vote of approval. Perhaps the best known of these is the constitutional requirement for a two-thirds vote in the Senate to ratify a treaty. Executive frustration with the ability of a recalcitrant third of the Senate to undo years of international diplomacy has led to increasing reliance on executive agreements and other evasions of Senate advice and consent. In fact, senators have used the need for extraordinary majorities as a lever for extracting concessions from the White House. Of the 1,046 treaties

submitted for ratification up to 1944, 104 were rejected or shelved. More interesting, perhaps, 167—almost one of every six—were amended.[29] There is bargaining leverage here as well. Former South Dakota Democrat James Abourezk was a vigorous and persistent opponent of legislation to deregulate the price of natural gas. Although his 1977 filibuster failed, the bill died in Conference and came back for a second round in 1978 with the support of President Carter and his energy secretary, James Schlesinger. It was then, as Abourezk describes it, that he

> discovered another lever I could pull—my vote on the Panama Canal Treaty. Getting the treaty ratified by the Senate was a major centerpiece of Carter's foreign policy. Although I had previously announced my support for the treaty, I decided to use my vote, which at that point happened to be the crucial 67th, as a bargaining chip to stop Carter and Schlesinger from completing their effort to deregulate natural gas.[30]

In the end, Abourezk backed down and voted for the treaty as originally intended. Gas was deregulated; but the stroking from the White House that Abourezk received in the meantime rather tellingly points up the strong position of an individual senator that derives from the two-thirds vote requirement.

Beyond the constitutionally mandated two-thirds vote on treaties, the two-thirds voting requirement is quite common. In addition to treaties, the Constitution mandates two-thirds majorities in both the House and Senate to approve a resolution proposing a constitutional amendment, to expel a member, or, in the House, to impeach. A two-thirds vote in both houses is required to override a presidential veto (i.e., all a president needs to sustain his or her position is one-third plus one in either house).

There are also certain special instances, though less celebrated, in which the House of Representatives requires a two-thirds vote. Perhaps the most important of these is on a motion to suspend the rules and pass a bill, a fast-tracking procedure that has found increasing favor with the House leadership. A two-thirds vote is also required to pass more esoteric motions such as dispensing with Calendar Wednesday or the private Calendar, or for considering a report from the Rules Committee instead of waiting until the following legislative day. In all other cases a simple majority vote is sufficient. This does not mean that a majority of either house—or anything approaching it—must actually take positive action. With a bare quorum of 218 present and voting, a motion on a bill or an amendment may theoretically be carried by as few as 110 representatives. On unrecorded votes, even a bare quorum is often not present. Moreover, in the Committee of the Whole, where one hundred members constitute a House quorum, major amendments can be approved when supported by as few as fifty-one votes, less than one-eighth of the total membership.

One very special kind of vote deserves repetition: the power of a single senator to prevent action on a bill by entering a "hold." A hold is, in effect, a notice that a senator would refuse to grant a unanimous consent agreement to consider a particular bill or amendment. It can have the effect of killing a bill, although the more frequent outcome is a negotiated settlement. Party leaders have generally honored most holds, but excessive use of the device, particularly by Senators Howard Metzenbaum (D-OH) and Jesse Helms (R-NC) in the 1980s, has made the issue more delicate.

The Recording of Votes

Voting attendance in the House has increased dramatically in recent years, especially since the Legislative Reorganization Act of 1970 made it more difficult to keep votes off the record. There is widespread agreement among students of Congress that when the House abandoned its system of quasi-anonymous "teller" votes, there were substantial political implications.

Not including unanimous consent, there are technically four methods of voting in the House and three in the Senate. The first and fastest is a simple voice vote in which the presiding officer asks "those in favor to signify by saying 'Aye' " and, after a brief pause, "those opposed, 'No.' " The result of such a vote is typically announced in tentative terms, at least in the Senate. In the words of one majority leader, "it is always, I think, the understanding here that the Chair, in announcing the vote, will say 'the ayes appear to have it; the ayes have it.' That gives any Senator, who may be distracted by thinking about something else for the moment, an opportunity to ask for the yeas and nays."[31]

Such courtesies are not always observed in the House, where the vote is often conducted and counted in a single phrase: "All in favor 'aye,' opposed 'no,' the 'nos' clearly have it and the amendment is rejected." Unless someone objects, that is the way it will stand. In both houses, of course, the outcome of such votes typically has nothing whatsoever to do with the volume of sound recorded on either side of the issue. Those whose previous political soundings indicate that they can win will ask for a more precise count.

In the House, this frequently means a standing division in which those favoring a bill rise and are counted, followed by those opposed. Only vote totals are announced; there is no public record of how individual members voted. "Few issues are decided at this stage because division votes do not allow enough time for many absent members to reach the floor."[32] Standing divisions, though allowed by the rules, are seldom seen in the Senate.

When the outcome is in doubt, or when members wish to publicize their stands (and those of their opponents), there is usually a call for a recorded vote. In the Senate and, until the adoption of electronic voting in 1972, in the House, this means a roll call. By the terms of Article I, Section 5 of the Constitution, "the Yeas and Nays of the Members of either House on any question shall, at the desire of one-fifth of those present, be entered upon the Journal." Twenty senators, in other words, or eighty-seven members of the House have a constitutional right to a recorded vote. In the Senate, a roll call vote remains a literal calling of the roll. With sometimes excruciatingly long pauses between names, the clerk calls the list of senators in alphabetical order. "Mr. Akaka . . . Mr. Baucus . . . Mr. Bennett . . . Mr. Bentsen . . . ." Although the clerk peers expectantly around the chamber as if he expected Senator Akaka suddenly to emerge from the cloakroom, it is not usually until late in the alphabet or on second reading of the names that most senators respond to the ringing bells and arrive on the floor. Seldom is a Senate roll call completed in fewer than twenty minutes.

With 435 names to call, taking votes could be very time-consuming in the House. Calling for a recorded vote on every possible question had indeed become a significant tactic of obstruction that was a factor in the 1972 decision to install a system for recording votes electronically. In the modern House, when the yeas and nays are ordered, the wall behind the speaker lights up with the names of each member. At selected points in the House chamber, there are slots that accept individually coded cards and allow each MC to vote "yes," "no," or "present." When he or she pushes the appropriate button, a light appears next to his or her name, and a computer records the vote for publication. MCs have, as a rule, fifteen minutes to the end of voting time.

In the Senate, a motion for a roll call must be seconded by one-fifth of those present. Technically, this means a total of eleven senators given a presumed quorum of fifty-one members. But what if only ten senators are present and no one raises the quorum question? Are two votes sufficient to order a roll call? How long shall the Senate wait during a quorum call for sufficient seconds to appear? Although technically the requirement remains a minimum of eleven, actual practice has become quite permissive. Today, as Tiefer concludes, it is generally "understood that as a courtesy, the leadership almost invariably helps Senators to obtain a roll call."[33]

Some Consequences of Reform

These changes in the formal rules of the House and informal norms of the Senate have had consequences beyond a simple increase in quantity. Publicized votes shift the locus and focus of attention. An unrecorded vote never was an anonymous vote, hidden from the general public as it was. To committee and party leaders, to those lobbyists concerned enough to go to the galleries, the question of who voted how was never much of a mystery. What the increase in recorded voting did was to expand the scope of conflict. In the 1960s, when you voted against the position of a committee chair, or the party leadership, or the most intensely involved group leaders, they were the audience for your vote. Now that audience is considerably larger; floor actions have increasingly become "platforms for members to reach outside audiences, in order to impress their constituents or develop statewide or national reputations. Posturing and grandstanding are replacing serious discussion and argument."[34]

Barbara Sinclair suggests that this expansion in the scope of conflict has posed particularly difficult problems for the House Democratic leadership in its struggle to build majority coalitions.[35] From the perspective of Democratic party leaders this has clearly been the case; but the problem is truly a generic one for all who seek brokered majorities. Public votes are, almost by definition, votes that weaken the forces of brokerage and compromise.

Carefully crafted legislation is not the only, or the highest priority of the House. During the floor debate and amendment process, making ideological points, . . . protecting the interests of particular groups, asserting an individual prerogative, or altering a broader policy direction . . . are all competing priorities of significant rank.[36]

It is precisely these latter priorities that are advantaged by publicity.

The trend toward recorded votes also affects questions of timing, as does electronic voting. Although the speaker can hold the vote open for a few extra minutes, electronic voting not only gives less time but makes it more difficult to locate wavering members. The speed at which the clerk calls the roll remains an artifact in the Senate, and if that won't suffice, there are countless methods for holding a vote open.

Although electronic voting makes strategic delays more difficult, it has opened new tactical possibilities. One is the "fast vote," in which a bill's supporters all vote early in the hopes of creating a "lurch effect." "We've gotten 120 votes on the board in the first minute and a half," one House member explained. "Then when members who intended to oppose it came in, they'd see the overwhelming vote and decide to go along."[37]

The Range of Alternatives

In most cases, most members vote a clear yea or nay. Yet these are by no means the only alternatives available.

Delays and Switches. There are a number of variations in the way a member votes yes or no. During a roll call, a member can withhold his or her vote until the last minute. In this way, the member can see which way the wind is blowing and either jump on the bandwagon or satisfy the folks back home without alienating party leaders. On closely contested issues, the leadership likes to have a few such late deciders in reserve. For example, it was the senators waiting in the cloakroom who gave the Senate Democratic leadership its one-vote margin in the original passage of Medicare. As relatively conservative Democrats, they were, on the one hand, skeptical of the policy and leery of the political implications of a "yes" vote in their home states. On the other hand, they recognized the importance of the issue to the Democratic party in general and to its presidential candidate, John F. Kennedy, in particular. An important source of Sam Rayburn's power as speaker was his ability to get a significant part of the normally conservative Texas delegation to withhold its votes on key party issues.

A member can also vote one way when his or her name is first called (or lighted on the board), and then, before the outcome is announced, switch to the other side. Electronic voting seems to have made switching almost as common as holding back votes. In either case it is a game that can be played by both sides, and it usually is. Rarely does either party go into a close vote without holding a few votes in reserve.

Absence. A member may dodge an issue by being absent. Absenteeism may be purposeful even when a member goes to the trouble of stating how he or she would have voted. Through this in-between method of recording one's views a member can express an opinion for or against a bill and at the same time go along with those who would rather have no vote at all than one on the wrong side. One lobbyist unashamedly boasts of having gotten a notoriously heavy drinker so drunk at lunch that he slept through a key vote: "I couldn't convince him on the merits, so I kept him off the floor. And the best part is that he thanked me the next day for a good lunch." Many absences, of course, are occasioned by sickness or important business. On hotly contested measures intense pressure is put on absentees to return. There are many recorded instances of members making dramatic, last-minute airplane flights back to Washington, tottering onto the floor against doctor's orders, or even being brought in on a stretcher. In one extreme case in 1988, the majority leader ordered the sergeant-at-arms to arrest absent senators and forcibly bring them to the floor.

Not Voting. A member may refrain from voting even when present. On this matter one finds a fascinating tangle of conflicting rules and precedents. The rules, for example, indicate that every member must vote unless excused. Attempts during the nineteenth century to compel members proved futile; the silence of Senator du Bois in 1893—despite a large vote refusing to excuse him—seems to have established an unwritten right to silence. Although the rules permit deductions from the paychecks of those failing to attend to their legislative duties, it doesn't happen.

Another long-standing, seldom-invoked parliamentary tradition is that, to use the words of Section XVII of Jefferson's Manual, "where the private interests of a member are concerned in a bill or question, he is to withdraw." On rare occasions in both houses members have asked to be excused because of their financial interests in a pending measure. The two representatives who abstained from voting on a 1962 bill to increase disability benefits for veterans were not the only disabled veterans in the House. The controlling precedent, as stated in Deschler, is that "Observance of the requirement . . . is the responsibility of the individual Member. And the Speaker has indicated that he would not rule on a point of order challenging the personal or pecuniary interests of Members . . . , but would defer to the judgment of each Member as to the directness of their interest."[38]

Pairs. A member may enter into a "pair" with another MC. The avowed purpose of a pair is to redress the imbalance that is created when one member is unavoidably absent for a vote. One member, who would have voted on the other side, presumably enters into an agreement that neither will vote but that one will be listed as "paired for" and the other as "paired against." Some absent members have "indefinite" or "general" pairs with others. When one party to this two-person agreement is absent, the other is obliged not to vote unless "released." In actual practice, pairing is usually a fiction sustained by party clerks. Since poor attendance has often been used as a negative campaign issue, absent members seek pairs as a means of showing the flag. "I won't be here on Tuesday," a member may tell his or her party clerk, "See if you can pair me up." Frequently, the majority and minority clerks will simply compare their lists of known absentees to see what kinds of pairs they can arrange for the *Record.* Pairs of this kind are largely cosmetic. Where it becomes important is in the case of what is known as a "live" pair. A live pair occurs when a present member withholds a vote by consenting to pair with an absent member on the opposite side of the question. When the leadership cannot persuade a wavering member to go along, it can sometimes get a live pair as the next best thing.

A classic case study in the effective use of live pairs occurred in 1964 during the consideration of an antipoverty bill strongly supported by the Senate's Democratic leadership. The key senator involved was Herbert "Hub" Walters, a party stalwart who was filling the seat of Tennessee's recently deceased Estes Kefauver. At issue was an amendment that would have allowed some states to opt out of certain antipoverty plans. Walters supported the amendment. Among the absent Democrats were both supporters and opponents of the amendment, but the leadership persuaded Walters to take a live pair with Edward Kennedy (D-MA), an opponent of the amendment. Had Walters voted, the tally would have been 46 to 45; by taking the pair, Walters created a 45-45 tie and the amendment failed. The actual voting situation was more complicated, involving four roll calls on both substance and procedure.[39] While Walters appeared to be simply honoring his "agreement" with Senator Kennedy, in reality he was giving the leadership a vote.

In view of such variations, a simple listing of the vote fails to convey a full picture of voting decisions. By listing pairs and by polling members to ask how they would have voted if present or paired, *Congressional Quarterly* provides as full a compilation of the formal record as one can get. Most students of legislative voting behavior have tended nonetheless to focus only on the yeas and nays actually cast. These votes represent the ones that actually count in making policy; they avoid the ambiguities of pairs and announced positions.

The Pain of Decision

Most members of Congress would probably join with former representative Jerry Voorhis in his rueful comment on the pain of voting: "It would be a great deal easier if only one could answer 'Fifty-five percent aye,' or 'seventy percent no,' or 'I vote aye but with the reservation that I do not like Section 3 of the bill,' or, 'I vote no, but God have mercy on my soul if I am wrong, as I very well may be.' "[40]

It is difficult to disaggregate and weigh the forces that produce particular outcomes, and the final vote is only a small part of an ongoing struggle. However, despite important conceptual problems, the many aggregate and interview studies of legislative voting together can help us to infer quite a bit about how congressmen vote, what pressures they respond to, and how they decide.

Party Voting. Legislators display a high degree of consistency over time in making choices on recurring issues. There are also patterns of consistency that cut across a variety of issues and suggest that they are responding to common cues. "Because the legislator's decision is made publicly, he tries to anticipate how his decision will be viewed by relevant groups. If he acts on this knowledge, and if other legislators look to the same groups as well, then they will be deciding in terms of a common frame of reference."[41] In some systems, these frames of reference are easy to find. In Britain's House of Commons, one source of pressure dominates all others: 999 times out of 1,000, members divide their legislative votes strictly along party lines. Other forces may indeed play a role in British politics, but they play that role through the parties and not, as in the United States, alongside them.

Although party is the best predictor of roll call voting behavior in the U.S. Congress, it is clear that the parties have many rivals for influence. The increasing ability of incumbent congressmen to earn reelection without party help could be expected to have had some reflection in a lowered sense of party loyalty in Congress. Until the 1980s the oft-described "dealignment" of parties in the electorate appears indeed to have had more than a faint echo on Capitol Hill. The lower party unity scores of Democrats as opposed to Republicans in earlier years, founded in a sharp regional division between the generally liberal Northern wing of the party and its more conservative Southern counterpart, was once a dominant feature of congressional politics. In the 1950s in particular, the so-called Senate establishment was almost synonymous with the conservative coalition of Republicans and Southern Democrats. Its reputation was so powerful that the influential *Congressional Quarterly* has continuously compiled records of "coalition votes"—those in which majorities of both Republicans and Southern Democrats oppose the stand taken by a majority of Northern Democrats. At its statistical peak in 1961, the coalition appeared on 30 percent of all contested House votes and 32 percent in the Senate.

As important as these regional splits have been, it is testimony to the strength of party loyalties on the Hill that the coalition appeared on a relatively limited set of issues and was never quite as dominant as it sometimes appeared.

Still, the North-South split in the Democratic party has, by all odds, proven the most enduring and significant of all demographic predictors of congressional voting. More than ethnicity, urban-rural cleavages, per capita income, and the like, regionalism ranks second only to party as a predictor of House and Senate voting patterns. Even among Republicans, there are discernable differences between the generally more liberal Northeasterner and the rest of the party.

Party and Constituency in the Contemporary Congress. The worst chapter in E. E. Schattschneider's 1960 classic, *The Semisovereign People,* was that in which he predicted "the nationalization" of American politics. Or maybe it was the best. Schattschneider was either terribly wrong or terribly prescient. It was only in the 1980s that his vision of a politically competitive South effectively emerged below the level of the presidential vote.[42] It is this development of a genuine two-party system in the South that best explains the recent rise in legislative partisanship. A very sharp rise in Democratic party unity coincides with a dramatic drop in the appearance of the conservative coalition. The party unity scores of Southern Democrats in the House went from an average of 53 in the 1970s to 71 in the 1980s, and in the Senate from an average of 51 to 68. And the trend has continued in 1990–91. To be sure, most (though by no means all) of the boll weevils who supported the Reagan program in 1981 were

Southerners. Not a few of them, however, have become Republicans, as have most of the newly elected Southern conservatives. Moreover, there are a growing number of Southern Democrats—generally from urban areas or those with large minority populations—whose voting records are virtually indistinguishable from those of their Northern Democratic colleagues. Even in the Senate, the geographic locus of conservative coalition scores is fading: in 1988, North Carolina Democrat Terry Sanford's coalition score was identical (at 26 percent) to that of Ohio Democrat Howard Metzenbaum. That Metzenbaum is often considered the left-wing equivalent of North Carolina's senior senator, right-wing leader Jesse Helms, adds special irony to this statistic, though it may also have been a factor in Sanford's 1992 defeat.

It also suggests something important about the relationship between party and constituency variables in association with roll call votes. Though they shared a geographic constituency, Sanford and Helms had radically different effective constituencies. Charles Bullock and David Brady made this point in more general terms in 1983. After studying the records of split-party state delegations in the Senate of the 93rd Congress, they concluded as follows:

> Our research . . . runs contrary to the simple constituency model. The party variable, while itself being influenced by constituency characteristics, is a stronger direct predictor than constituency operating alone. . . . And there is a significant relationship between different reelection constituencies and split party control. Thus constituency and party are both related to differences in voting behavior between senators from the same state.[43]

There are, to be sure, important differences in the strength of party and constituency variables according to policy dimensions. For example, Julius Turner and Edward Schneier found that procedural issues had a higher partisan loading than substantive questions, and that those issues involving the interests of the parties as organizations—patronage issues, for example—generated sharp party cleavages. They also found a tendency for each party to be "oriented toward certain interest groups: the Democrats toward organized labor and farmers, for example, and the Republicans toward business." Finally, there were certain issues on which the parties had apparently staked out long-term ideological positions, most notably health, welfare, civil liberties, and foreign trade. "Only on issues which failed to ignite significant ideological controversies, which promised little reward to the party faithful, or which did not mobilize significant economic interest groups did the parties fail to present clearly differentiated records to the voter."[44]

More statistically elegant methods have been used by subsequent researchers to refine the categories of voting blocs. For example, Aage Clausen found relatively stable policy coalitions associated with five policy areas: government management, social welfare, international involvement, civil liberties, and agricultural assistance. "Different alignments form," he argued, "as the policy content changes."[45] The thrust of such policy-focused studies has been frequently replicated;[46] but its validity has come under increasing scrutiny with the suggestion that there are important ideological strands of consistency that cut across all policy areas in the increasingly polarized atmosphere of the 1980s.[47] On the one hand, the issue coalitions of earlier years have, in Melissa Collie's words, "been far more ephemeral than was suggested in the earlier applications."[48] To take just one example, *the* dominant party issue of the 1890s through the 1950s, the one that most consistently set Republicans against Democrats, was the tariff. Yet in the 1980s it was Democrats, always the party of free trade, who led the fight for protectionism. The increasing internal unity of the Democratic party, on the other hand, has created new patterns of consistency across issue dimensions that lend growing credibility to Schneider's ideological approach.

Growing party unity in the 1980s, particularly among the traditionally strife-torn Democrats, undercuts the policy coalition approach. Yet despite the greater "willingness of party members to vote on the basis of their party affiliation, it is also true that such inclinations do not arise out of thin air."[49] In one sense, it can be argued that this growing polarization across issue domains reflects the rise of more polarizing issues and the concomitant decline of the subsidy politics of more affluent times. There is little doubt that it also reflects the long-awaited nationalization of American politics that was prematurely predicted by Schattschneider. In a very subtle sense, recent roll call records suggest that the long-anticipated realignment of parties actually has taken place. Historically, as David Brady has pointed out, "each time there has been a realignment of voters the percentage of party votes in the House has risen during the realignment period."[50] Although Brady does not suggest the converse—that a rise in party voting might signal the arrival of a realignment—the data are highly suggestive.

Roll call votes are so accessible, so dramatic, so definitive in their impact on public policy that it is tempting to overgeneralize from the patterns they portray. The Hill *is* a more polarized, more partisan place in the 1990s. The war on the floor, however, is the kind of noisy, sharp battle that sometimes hides the subtle maneuvers and negotiations taking place offstage.

11

✳

THE ROAD TO LAW

R oll call votes define neither the sum nor the finale of the legislative struggle. A bill cannot be sent to the President until it is passed in identical form by both House and Senate. Should one house change a single comma of the other's bill, some process of adjustment must take place. Nor can a bill become law without some form of presidential assent.

✳

RESOLVING DIFFERENCES BETWEEN THE HOUSE AND SENATE

The simplest form of bicameral adjustment is outright acquiescence or denial. It is quite common for one house or the other simply to accept an amended bill from the other body and re-pass it in amended form as a clean bill. An elaborate technical vocabulary describes the variety of ways in which this may be done. The House, for example, may simply accept a motion to "agree to a House bill with Senate amendments" (or vice versa); it may "concur" in the Senate (or House) amendments; or, if it was the body amending the original bill, "recede" in its own amendments.[1] At the other extreme, one house may simply refuse to consider the amended bill. This is a relatively rare occurrence and is normally a tactical stance taken to force a process of accommodation.

The process of accommodation takes one of two forms: amendments between houses or the use of conference committees. As bills have become longer and more complex, it is not surprising that resort to such mechanisms of conflict resolution have become more common. Since the 1950s, the proportion of bills passed in identical form has steadily and significantly declined, as has the number of bills on which no agreement between the houses has been reached. On important issues in the 1980s, about three-quarters involved some mechanism of bicameral accommodation.[2]

Amendments between Houses

The process of reciprocal amending can be elaborate. In an extreme case, the Federal Oil and Gas Royalty Management Act of 1982 went back and forth seven times before the two houses could agree. Although this was exceptional, some ping-ponging of bills is not uncommon. Sixteen percent of the laws enacted in 1981–82 went back and forth three times; almost 7 percent, four times.[3] Because the rules technically permit no more than two rounds of perfecting amendments in each house, there are limits as to how far this process can be extended: the Oil and Gas Act of 1982 was highly unusual. There is nothing, however, to prevent one house or the other from creating more than one vehicle. In the closing days of the 95th Congress, the House passed three nearly identical bills creating new parks to "accommodate Senators and to speed passage of the measure"[4] by allowing the Senate to choose the version it liked best. Generally informal negotiations accompany such maneuvers. Bill sponsors, senior committee members and their staff aides, or party leaders will seek to work out informal lines of agreement to guide the amending process. Still, it remains a striking aspect of the legislative struggle how often these kinds of accommodations fail. The relative autonomy of the two chambers is a fact of continuing political significance.

One impediment to cooperation is scheduling. Party leaders do consult each other about major priorities, and some deadlines and timetables are built into the budget process; but there are virtually no formal bicameral mechanisms to coordinate the timing of bills. The wise strategist tries to coordinate his or her lobbying efforts to bring matters to a common head, but a passed bill in one house may be long forgotten by most members before it re-emerges in amended form from the other body. The differing rules of the two bodies, in particular the Senate's lack of an effective rule of germaneness, can add a significant technical dimension to the problem of bicameral accommodation,[5] and the bargaining situation gets especially tricky as the end of the session approaches. One house may simply adjourn, leaving the other with a take-it-or-leave-it choice on outstanding bills; and the threat of a last-minute filibuster in the Senate can kill a controversial bill even after a House-Senate consensus has been achieved.[6]

Conference Politics

Although only about 20 percent of all bills actually go to a formal conference, the more important and controversial the issue, the more likely it is that conferees will be appointed.[7] Conference committees are among the least conspicuous and most potent actors in the system, occupying, in Fenno's phrase, a "penultimate position in the legislative process."[8] Former Senator Bennet Champ Clark (D-MO) once offered a motion that "All bills and resolutions shall be read twice and, without debate, referred to conference." Jesting though he was, his proposal highlights the regard that members of the House and Senate have for this critical institution: "the conference committee," in the words of one, "is the central core of the power."[9]

To Have or Not to Have a Conference. So important can the conference committee become that there are times when almost everything that takes place before seems like rehearsal and preliminary maneuvering. In Clem Miller's words, "the conference report is far more than a compromise between the houses. Very frequently it is a goal, a haven for legislative policy. It is a rare House chairman who pilots his bill through the House without keeping at least one eye on the conference which will almost certainly result."[10]

It is not uncommon for members of Congress to accede to amendments that they really oppose on the theory that they can more easily be killed in conference. "I am in complete disagreement with the theory of the Senator," one bill manager candidly admitted in debate, but in order to move the bill along "I am willing to accept the proviso in the hope that the conference will eliminate the amendment."[11] It did. This is not mere posturing. Because the conference committee is the legislative arena in which pure barter is most likely to occur, the most obvious strategy is one of loading a bill with bargaining chips. By including sufficient "conference bait," the felicitous phrase used by the *Wall Street Journal* for material to be traded away, it is possible for committee leaders simultaneously to satisfy the political needs of their House or Senate colleagues while also increasing their conference leverage. Russell Long (D-LA) was reportedly a master of such "corn shucking": "He would sit quietly while the Senate passed dozens of amendments. Then, in conference with the House, he would throw the amendments away, like the husk on an ear of corn, until he reached the legislative kernels he wanted to retain."[12]

The obverse strategy is that of excluding items you know are wanted in the other body. Lawrence Longley and Walter Oleszek report a case in 1980 in which a House subcommittee deliberately deleted a program for Louisiana sheriffs that had been in effect since 1976. "It's pretty simple," one House strategist told the Washington *Post*, "The subcommittee knew Russell Long would hit the roof when he got wind of this. Now they'll have something to trade with him when the bill goes to conference."[13] Bills involving dollar amounts, or numbers in general, are particularly predisposed to maneuvers of this kind. "Maybe we can live with 10 percent," former House Ways and Means Chairman Wilbur Mills once said of a tax proposal, "but if we send it over there they'll make it 15 and we'll have to live with 12. So let's make it 8."[14]

There is some risk in these approaches to conference, particularly in the Senate. Because of its weak rules of germaneness, "Senate bills can become so cluttered with unrelated amendments that they prevent the legislation from ever reaching conference."[15] The addition of nongermane amendments, moreover, may dramatically alter the political balance of the conference committee by giving members of those committees affected by the amendment the right to sit as conferees. If the two houses are too far apart, one or the other may simply refuse to appoint conferees. This can happen in the Senate, theoretically at least, by the refusal of even a single senator to agree to a unanimous consent request; and a motion to appoint conferees is susceptible to a filibuster. In the House, until 1965, the Rules Committee had the power to effectively prevent compromises through conference, and although the new Rule XX took that power away, "There remain theoretical possibilities for how the House could still kill a bill on the way to conference even though it had majority support."[16] In 1982 the threat of a conference filibuster did, indirectly at least, kill the Department of Justice's authorization and its antibusing amendment, but this appears to have been the exception that tests the rule. In both the House and Senate, "the more likely reasons for a bill to die on the way to conference are lack of time at the end of a session, or one chamber's belief that the gap between the versions is too big to bridge in conference."[17]

Most senators and representatives understand that "Loyalty to the chamber's position can . . . be strained by committee ties."[18] Since conferees are drawn almost exclusively from the committees of original jurisdiction, the theory of pluralistic subgovernment suggests that the conference committee would typically be an arena in which the special interests represented on the committees would get a final chance to undo the damage done on the floor. Two students of committee politics have gone so far as to suggest that it is this "ex post veto power" inherent in committee domination of the conference stage that gives the standing committees their extraordinary power in the U.S. Congress: "The conference may be less an arena for bicameral conflict than one in which kindred spirits from the two chambers get together to hammer out a mutually acceptable deal."[19] Although there is no denying the insight of this argument, it oversimplifies the very complex sources of committee power, one of the most important of which is the committee's ability to anticipate what will happen on the floor.

Although there is a presumption (once both houses have agreed "in principle") that conferees will be appointed, the conference process is likely to be opposed by those who have reason to believe that a conference will be dominated by members with an objectionable point of view. In 1972, for example, the House took the unusual step of refusing to appoint conferees on a minimum wage bill. At issue was an amendment to a House bill sponsored by John Erlenborn (R-IL) that made the House figure considerably lower than that originally reported by the Education and Labor Committee or adopted by the Senate. "All too often," Erlenborn argued, "the House speaks its will by amending legislation. . . . All too often the other body passes a bill similar to that rejected by the House. And almost without exception the conference committee members appointed by the House accede more to the provisions of the other body than they try to protect the provisions which the House had adopted."[20]

The Selection of Conferees. Nominally, conferees are chosen by the respective presiding officers of each house. In actual practice, these officials almost invariably accept the recommendations of the chairs of the committees of original jurisdiction. There is a subtle difference between the House and

Senate in that the Senate's requirement for unanimous consent approval gives the leadership almost no room to bargain with committee leaders. The speaker has, at once, more and less wiggle room. On the one hand (although the situation has rarely arisen), he or she "may choose conferees in addition to those the chairman has proposed, or even veto some who offend his personal or political sensibilities."[21] Both the speaker and the standing committee chairs, on the other hand, are increasingly constrained by the need to consult with subcommittee leaders. Many House committees have formal rules or long-standing norms that automatically include members of the subcommittee that handled the original bill. Particularly in the Senate, the "right" to serve as a conferee is one in which seniority still counts. In 1992 Speaker Foley put the House on notice that service on conference committees would no longer be treated as a matter of right for certain key members, though in practice he continued, by and large, to honor the traditional privileges of senior subcommittee members.

Party ratios almost invariably are mathematical replicas of prevailing committee ratios, and the presiding officer will follow the recommendation of the minority leadership in naming names. On a small conference, this can put a dissident member of the majority party in a particularly strategic position. Close party divisions in the Senate during the 1980s, for example, typically resulted in Senate conference delegations that were divided 5-4 or 3-2 between majority and minority. By joining with the opposition, one dissident member could swing the balance.

Once the small inner sanctum of concentrated power, conference committees have grown. Omnibus bills, multiply referred, have increased the number of legitimate aspirants to a conference role. The extreme case was the budget reconciliation conference of 1981 in which 256 members of the House and Senate—just short of half the total Congress—held 58 meetings to reconcile nearly 300 differences between the House and Senate bills.[22] Generally the meeting is more intimate. "Conferences typically involve roughly between nine and about fifteen House members and somewhere between six and about thirteen senators."[23] Since the conferees of each house vote as a unit, size is not a factor except as it affects the atmosphere for bargaining. Far more important than their numbers are the political orientations of conferees. "Committee chairs," Charles Tiefer notes, "balance many factors relating to the particular bill in making appointments—which subcommittee handled the bill, which Members were most active on the bill, or will be able to win support of a necessary voting bloc when the conference committee reports back, or will represent the interests at stake in the bill."[24]

There are longer range considerations as well: committee chairs can and do use conference appointments to reward past loyalties or court new ones; to satisfy outside groups; or to strike a balance between competing committee factions. Seniority, though far less important in the postreform Congress, is important in the sense that it is difficult to pass over without reason. These considerations sometimes produce a roster of conferees who are less than zealous in their support of the bill approved by the house they represent. In fact, if one wanted to stretch the point, one might whimsically claim that any similarity between the views of the House or the Senate and those of the conferees representing them is purely coincidental. Although the rules technically require individual conferees to support the bill as it passed their chamber, this is not always a realistic expectation. As Longley and Oleszek convincingly suggest, conferees can frequently "confront great uncertainties in trying to determine chamber interests and wishes from . . . a tangled legislative history."[25]

The so-called runaway conference, one that adds or deletes material from the bills of both houses, is not unknown. But Gilbert Steiner's classic finding in 1951, that it "has not been a consistently irresponsible 'third house' of Congress," is sustained in more recent research.[26] Theoretically, either house may change its conferees if they fail to defend adequately the measure passed by the house. Actually this is almost never done, for the fact is that the conference itself is but a stage in the struggle: if it comes up with a compromise that one house or the other considers a "bad" bill, it will not pass.

Powers of Conferees. The rules of Congress have almost always contained provisions limiting conferees to the disagreements between the two houses. The methods of sidestepping these provisions are numerous. It is not always easy, to begin with, to discern exactly what is new and what isn't. A committee may, for example, strike both Senate and House language to produce a compromise that combines the spirit if not the language of both. Or it may devise language that is additive, rather than balancing, in its effects. The most frequent parliamentary device of conference power, however, is the amendment in the nature of a substitute. When this happens, everything is technically under disagreement and the conferees are thereby free to start from scratch and write an entirely new measure.

An attempt was made in the Legislative Reorganization Act of 1946 to strengthen the prohibition against conference inclusion of "matter not committed to them by either House," and subsequent reform bills have contained similar language. The distinction has proven almost impossible to sustain. In 1938 a Civil Service Retirement bill came from the House with provisions for annuities averaging $1,155. The Senate bill provided for annuities averaging $1,090. The conference bill provided for an average annuity of $1,402. In defense of the conference report, Senator Taft (R-OH) said, "This does not seem to me to make the report subject to a point of order. One may question the wisdom of the conferees in doing that, but it seems to me that there may be circumstances which would lead the Senate to say, 'Well, if you are going to change it, we think this is a fair way to change it.' "[27]

The Senate is somewhat more liberal than the House in the latitude it allows its conferees, particularly since 1970 when the House modified its rules. The real constraints on conference action have always been, and continue to be, political. What has happened in more recent sessions of Congress is a rising incidence of challenges to the final reports of conferees. Steven Smith relates this to the corresponding upswing in amending activity with which "more members, particularly those who sponsored amendments, would see a personal stake in the conference outcome."[28] It remains relatively unusual, nonetheless, for a conference report to be rejected.

Conference Action. Until 1975, the activities of conference committees were shrouded in secrecy, even more than executive sessions of standing committees. Staff members were only grudgingly admitted, and employees of the executive branch remained suspect well into the 1960s. As for lobbyists, journalists, and the general public . . . forget about it. Whether the sunshine laws of the 1970s have been effective remains a subject of continuing debate. They are, for one thing, frequently bypassed. In the 1986 conference on tax reform, "After the first two days of meetings, the conferees secluded themselves behind closed doors and did not meet again in public until the final night of the conference, three weeks later. Packwood and Rostenkowski both believed that they had to shield the conference from lobbyists, the press, and the public in order to make progress.[29]

It is not at all uncommon to hold semisecret conferences that are only nominally open to the public. A clever article in the Capitol Hill newspaper *Roll Call* outlined a variety of such ploys from the squeeze play, where the conference is held in a room too small for anyone but the conferees themselves, to the committee caucus, in which the real work is done before or after the formal meeting. One of the neater gambits described was the football huddle, in which the tough bargaining is done in full view of the public but in inaudible tones.[30] "A conference committee," said one member, when Carl Vinson (D-GA) and Richard Russell (D-GA) sat respectively as chairs of the House and Senate Armed Services Committee, "is two gentlemen from Georgia talking, arguing, laughing, and whispering in each other's ears."[31]

Partly through resort to devices such as these, the essential character of the conference committee has not been substantially changed. "Rather than being the catalyst for sweeping transformation of conference committee politics and processes, the opening of conference committees has had far more subtle and modest consequences than either its proponents or opponents expected."[32] It does seem as if "the presence of lobbyists in the conference room may cause subtle changes in the context of conference decision making."[33] As one labor lobbyist noted, "I can find out who rolled me and let them know that we weren't pleased."[34] And there is more time-consuming posturing, particularly in the early meetings. But whether the doors are open or closed, the conference committee remains the site of some of the hardest direct bargaining to be found in the legislative arena.

We have had access to the transcripts of some "pre-sunshine" conferences. The language of bargaining is sometimes less elliptical than in postreform meetings, but the substance is the same. A senator might be less likely to say, "We just gave you two; you owe us this one"; but the same sentiment can be conveyed by a sigh. Whether in public or private, participants in a conference know that the final language of any law that may be passed is now being written, and they are eager to both press any minor advantage and make final settlements on issues that can no longer be postponed. Their basic weapon is their ability to obtain the support or acquiescence of a majority of their own house.

Oceans of ink have been spilt over the question of which house most frequently wins in conference. The answers are less interesting than the theories that explain them. The key advantage of the House lies in its technical competence. Despite the growing importance of staff and noncongressional information sources, House conferees are, quite simply, better informed than their Senate colleagues. Given this obvious advantage, the most striking finding on conference success is the frequency with which the Senate "wins." In his exhaustive examination of appropriations, Richard Fenno suggested that Senate success was best explained by the upper body's greater ability to play interchamber hardball: "The Senate is stronger in conference because the Senate Committee and its conferees draw more directly and completely on the support of their parent chamber than do the House committees and its conferees."[35] Numerous refinements of this central thesis have tended to support its central thrust.[36]

Senate committees, as we have seen, tend to be more "representative" of the body as a whole, and the force of intense minorities is considerably less. The threat of a filibuster is a major weapon of Senate conferees. Everything else being equal, senators in conference are in a better bargaining position. Of course, everything else is seldom equal. Congressional insiders continue to believe that it is the House that usually prevails.[37] The problem is partly one of definition. The real "victors" in conference are not senators or representatives but those people who gain or lose from the decisions made. Some have more influence on one house or the other and on some individual conferees. Moreover, in the unfolding of any legislative battle, they often change their strategy and objectives as a measure moves from one house to another and then to a conference committee. When the House "yields" to the Senate—especially, it seems, when it involves spending more money—it is almost by prearrangement. We say "almost" because "arrangement" is too strong a word for a ritual that goes something like this: the House authorizes a big program, which the Senate accepts. The House then cuts the actual appropriation, enabling representatives to cast recorded votes in favor of both big programs and small expenditures. Many of the cuts are restored in the Senate, which then "wins" in conference. The savvy policy advocate will sometimes accept apparent defeat in the House while working all the time for restoration in conference.

The Politics of Anticipation

As much as it makes sense academically to trace through the legislative process step by step, and as much as participants must move through a fairly consistent series of obstacles—from committee to the floor, from the floor to conference, and so on—the successful strategist can never fully disaggregate his or her tactics. What happens in a subcommittee is often as much a product of what is anticipated in the full committee, on the floor, or even in conference, as it is of the subcommittee's own political dynamic. What happens in conference happens in anticipation of reactions not just in the House and Senate but in the White House as well.

When conferees emerge from a session on major legislation, they know they have been through a tense experience. "When I first came to Congress," one member said many years ago, "I was told that all major legislation was a matter of compromise. . . . I did not fully realize what it meant until a conference on this bill when, after spending eleven and a half hours yesterday giving and taking, adding and subtracting, sparring for advantage back and forth, we finally succeeded in coming to an agreement."[38]

Conferees habitually report back to their respective bodies in tones of despair and fatigue. "It was this bill or nothing," is a refrain echoed again and again in the personal explanations of conferees: "We had a gun barrel at our heads," said one. "It was either this compromise or nothing. . . . We did not raise any white flag—had it not been for the time element and immediate adjournment slapping us in the face, I would have hung the jury until Gabriel blows his trumpet."[39] Sometimes this is pure rhetoric, but there are times when agreement really does prove impossible. Here the conferees have the option of simply reporting their failure back to their respective houses or of filing partial conference reports. Partial reports are most common on appropriation bills for which the few outstanding problems are either voted on separately or left for later consideration.

Once conferees have agreed, the bill is reported back to the House and Senate. Timing can be important here, as the body that moves first has the option of recommitting the bill for further changes. The second house can cast only a simple up-or-down vote. Conference reports are seldom rejected—"no more perhaps than once or twice a session"[40]—which is a reflection either of the care usually taken by conferees to craft compromises that will pass both houses, or of careful strategic planning. In 1981, in a case nicely illustrative of a triumph of tactics over substantive preferences, the House rejected a sugar subsidy program by deleting it from the farm bill. The vote was 213 to 190. House and Senate conferees, drawn from the Agriculture Committees, restored the program and secured passage in the Senate, which promptly adjourned. Too late for a new conference, the House had the choice of rejecting the entire farm bill or swallowing the bitter sugar pill: it chose the latter by 205 to 203.[41]

Bargaining in conference is often made still more complicated by the need to anticipate the reaction sixteen blocks away in the Oval Office of the president. This is seldom a matter of guesswork, as executive branch officials have become a routine presence at many conference committee meetings. On a technical matter such as tax reform, the Treasury's computers and general knowledge of the tax code make it one of the most effective lobbies working the Hill. And the president's ability to bargain with individual conferees gives the White House added leverage. Lurking in the corner, like grandpa's shotgun, is the further possibility of a veto. On major issues, conferees must craft their reports with an eye not just toward acceptance by the House and Senate but toward the White House as well. Woodrow Wilson argued that by use of the veto power, the president "acts not as the executive but as a third branch of the legislature."[42] It is to this third house that we now turn.

------------------------------ ✳ ------------------------------

THE PRESIDENT VOTES

If you visit the office of an influential congressman, there are likely to be a few White House pens, those used for signing bills into laws, decorating the walls. They are to legislators as deer heads are to hunters: trophies of the sport. Although final passage into law marks a dramatic stage in the legislative struggle, enrollment—the formal printing of a bill passed by both houses—is as much a beginning as an end. Just as graduation ceremonies are celebrated as commencement, enrollment often serves to celebrate a time of transition from the end of one phase of the legislative struggle to the commencement of another. When the roll call is over and the bill manager accepts the congratulations of his or her colleagues, it may be tempting to believe that there is prophecy in the Latin words inscribed over the Senate's double doors: *Novus Ordo Seclorum*—a New Order of the Ages. Perhaps there should be another set of doors beyond that with a legend that reads something like "Not So Fast, Champ."

The Veto Power

The great bulk of measures jointly acted upon by Congress has always been presented to the president. But there are two interesting exceptions to (or evasions of) this provision: constitutional amendments and concurrent resolutions. Only twice has a president signed a proposed constitutional amendment: Buchanan in 1861 and Lincoln in 1865. It is interesting to note that in the latter case, after Lincoln notified Congress that he had signed the proposed thirteenth amendment ending slavery, the Senate immediately adopted a resolution declaring Lincoln's signature unnecessary.

Concurrent resolutions represent a more frequent type of evasion of the requirement for both congressional and presidential participation in lawmaking, especially in the days before the Supreme Court's negative ruling on the legislative veto in the *Chadha* case. Although an impressive argument can be made that the legislative veto, when confined to powers already delegated by regular statutes, does not deny the president any of the privilege given him by the Constitution, a court majority has ruled otherwise, upholding (as it has refused to do for constitutional amendments) the seemingly clear intent of the Founding Fathers in Section 7.

Except for constitutional amendments and matters relating largely to the internal affairs of the House and Senate, virtually all legislative enactments must cross the president's desk.

The President's Approval

By the time a bill has surmounted all the obstacles it has faced from the time of introduction to approval by both houses of Congress, the odds are in its favor. In the great majority of cases, the president's decision is to interpose no additional obstacles. The Constitution provides two methods by which a president can transpose a bill into a law. In the most familiar, there is a formal signing ceremony in which the aforementioned pens are distributed among appropriate MCs. The president also has the option of reluctant acquiescence: the Constitution provides that if the president neither signs nor vetoes a bill within ten days, "the same shall be a Law, in like Manner as if he had signed it."

When the president wishes to underscore a legislative victory, bill signing can be developed into a full-fledged ceremony in which elaborate attention is given to every detail of the guest list, timing, and so on. If all goes well, the media will feature Very Important People (VIPs) crowding around the president as he signs his name, using one pen per letter so that the most important of the VIPs can take pens home as trophies of their endeavors.

From time to time, presidents have used the occasion of bill signings as opportunities to impart their own spin on subsequent interpretations. When the Hobbs Anti-Racketeering Act was passed in 1946, President Truman sent a message to Congress that put a special interpretation of his own upon certain ambiguous provisions. Although many of the Act's sponsors intended it to modify various aspects of the Wagner Act and other important labor bills, for tactical reasons the bill was drafted in such a way as to leave the matter open to interpretation. Truman's statement on signing included a strong defense of the right to strike.[43]

The statement aroused a storm of protest from those who favored an antilabor interpretation of the measure. The distinguished columnist Arthur Krock attacked the president's message on the grounds that it would now become an essential part of the legislative record and enter into judicial consideration of the meaning of the Act.[44] Edward Corwin, perhaps that decade's leading scholar of the Constitution, was considerably less alarmed. For the Court to consider the president's views on matters of this type, he wrote, "would be to attribute to the [president] the power to foist upon the houses intentions which they never entertained."[45] Presidents have continued to use the vehicle of bill signings to lobby future Congresses, the public, and state governments; but attempts, such as Truman's, to alter the legal interpretation of a bill through a signing statement fell into disuse until they were resurrected by the Reagan White House in the 1980s. Only a small flurry of editorial and congressional indignation greeted the president's crude attempt to rewrite legislative history.[46] Although no one of Corwin's stature has emerged to offer similar reassurances, you can take it from us: the president's statements in signing a bill have no more weight in the proper compilation of its legislative history than those of any garden-variety lobbyist.

The President's Disapproval

From a purely statistical viewpoint, presidential disapproval of bills that have been approved by Congress is of little consequence. The total number of bills actually vetoed has averaged considerably less than one half of 1 percent of those sent to the White House. From a broader view, these statistics are somewhat misleading. Presidential disapproval often comes on issues of major importance and can provide the most dramatic examples of conflict between president and Congress. The threat value of the veto power is also of incalculable importance even when it is seldom actually used.

The Role of the Veto. The original intent seems to have been that the president's veto would be used very rarely, mainly as a shield "against invasion by the legislature: (1) of the right of the Executive, (2) of the judiciary, (3) of the states and the state legislatures."[47] Rarely was the president expected to veto a bill merely because he felt that his judgment was better than that of the Congress.

Well into the twentieth century, private bills were the target of about 40 percent of all vetoes.[48] The significance of what was happening, however, had less to do with the subject matter of vetoed bills than with the political message conveyed. There is perhaps nothing more expressive of the nature of the veto in the modern Congress than the sentiment attributed to Franklin Roosevelt who, we are told, "was known to say to his aides 'Give me a bill that I can veto' to remind legislators that they had the President to reckon with."[49]

Reforms in the handling of private member bills have helped cut back on the number of vetoes exercised by modern presidents, especially since Eisenhower; but the rather striking rise and fall in the incidence of vetoes from an average of 5 per year in the Johnson years to more than 26 for Gerald Ford and 11 for George Bush has other roots as well. So low was the incidence of significant veto activity in the Kennedy, Johnson, and Nixon years that an early draft of our chapter outlines for this book included a section on the decline of the veto power. Gerald Ford proved us wrong when he made the use of the veto power an essential weapon of his presidency, but our reasoning on the issue from 1974 continues to make some sense.

The combination of a weakened White House, high inflation rates, and a Democratic Congress almost forced Ford to adopt a veto strategy.[50] Divided party control of the White House and one or both branches of the Congress would seem to be a major factor here. Indeed, it has traditionally ranked among the best statistical predictors of high veto rates.[51] Yet it is more than a little interesting to note that Richard Nixon, facing an overwhelmingly Democratic Congress, used the veto power with about the same frequency as Jimmy Carter. The old saw, that weak presidents are more likely than strong ones to resort to vetoes, may also be operating here. For example, lame ducks— presidents in their last years of office— are considerably less formidable. Presidents from Truman through Reagan were 51 and 0 in their first years, 57 and 13 in their last: that is, of the 51 formal vetoes cast by presidents in their first year in office, not a single one was overridden by Congress; almost 20 percent of those cast by lame ducks went down to defeat. Our reasoning from the 1970s, however, was a bit more subtle. What occurred to us was the changing strategic meaning of the veto that developed with the institutionalization of the legislative presidency. Because his aides and representatives are on the Hill every day, even in the previously closed inner sanctums of markups and conference committees, the president no longer needs the veto power to send a message. What the modern veto represents is a breakdown in such communications, an appeal, from one side or the other, to public opinion.

What we have seen is the ritualization of the veto in which, typically, both sides know it is coming, know why it is coming, and—for one reason or another—want it. This analysis cannot be pushed too far. There are certain constants in the use of the veto that cannot be gainsaid: foreign policy issues, for example, have seldom invoked vetoes, while issues involving executive prerogatives rank high on the list.[52] There seems little doubt, moreover, that the growing use of omnibus bills in Congress has made the strategic calculus far more complex and open to the kinds of communications failures and miscalculations that necessitate recourse to formal vetoes. The "all or none" character of the president's veto power has come to be one of its most significant strategic attributes. This, together with questions of time and context, means that even the best-staffed White House will always use the veto power from time to time, even if only as a threat.

All or None.   Unlike the governors of most states who have an "item-veto" power, the president cannot approve part of a bill and reject another part. In his 1984 State of the Union message, President Reagan said that "It works in 43 states. Let's put it to work in Washington for all the people." Every recent president has made a similar plea, and every recent Congress has turned it down.[53] In practice, presidents are not quite as constrained by this limitation on the veto power as their rhetoric would suggest. There are three ways in which this procedural fact can be circumvented and in which the president may obtain a wider area of choice.

First, the president may veto an entire bill on the grounds that it contains a few items of which he disapproves. In the case of appropriation bills, where delayed action might impede the normal operations of the government, such a course is not an easy one. These bills have become favored carriers of legislative riders, but despite the disruptions that delay can sometimes cause, vetoes do occur. In 1982, for example, President Reagan vetoed an emergency supplemental appropriation bill twice in one month, forcing Congress to grudgingly delete the objectionable items lest the entire government be forced to close shop. The public, Reagan showed, is no less inclined to blame Congress for the government's paralysis than it is the president.

Second, the effect of an item veto can be obtained by administrative policies. The Constitution requires the president to "take care that the Laws be faithfully executed." Although the word *execute* in this context no doubt means "to implement or put into effect," there is a double entendre in the phrase. When a rider providing for a loan to fascist Spain was added to the

Omnibus Appropriation Act for fiscal year 1951, President Truman "executed" it by simply announcing that he would not proceed with the loan. The Budget and Impoundment Control Act of 1974 makes this authority somewhat less lethal than it once was, yet the Reagan administration was quite successful in securing "cuts in already appropriated funds, particularly in education, housing and urban development, and interior."[54] These amount to what one former counsel to the clerk of the House called "de facto vetoes," which can be "more effective than any veto you could write into a statute."[55] In the decade from 1976 through 1985 there were an average of 105 deferrals a year reported by the administration, of which an average of fewer than 11 were disapproved by Congress.[56]

The mores of government life are somewhat different with respect to regulatory acts and laws other than appropriations. Here the execution must be more subtle. For better or worse, Richard Nixon blazed new trails in this area with the discovery, particularly in his last few years in office, that the apparatus of the bureaucracy built for the pursuit of liberal objectives could also be used to subvert those objectives and bypass a hostile (and essentially liberal) Congress.[57] It was in the Reagan years, however, that conservatives most fully embraced the notion that "the modern presidency could be characterized as a doubled-edged sword, which would cut in a conservative as well as a liberal direction." The Reagan presidency, one scholar has argued, "eschewed efforts to modify the statutory basis of liberal reform, seeking instead to bring about fundamental policy departures through acts of administrative discretion."[58]

When persons were appointed who were philosophically opposed to the missions of the agencies they headed, the political environments of many key agencies were radically altered. In some cases, inaction became a force of administrative leadership. When the executive branch refused to appoint replacements for retiring members of the Consumer Product Safety Commission, for example, the agency reached a point at which it could no longer convene the legal quorum needed to put staff recommendations into effect. Executive orders were issued requiring all kinds of new reviews for proposed regulations, and those in charge of such reviews, particularly in the OMB, proved capable of long delays. By freeing the Reagan presidency from the need to gain congressional concurrence for some of these organizational shifts, the Supreme Court's *Chadha* decision was an important addition to the rise of the activist, conservative presidency. Although such acts of sabotage may not be quite as effective as an item veto in marking particular programs for execution, they can also be more difficult to override.

The third way in which presidents may exercise powers similar to those granted by the item veto is by securing grants of such power from Congress itself. Beyond the technically complex provisions governing impoundments and other budgetary controls, Congress rather frequently grants the White House large areas of discretion in the actual enforcement of the laws. The foreign aid bill, for example, almost always includes some funds for countries that are strategically important but politically unpopular. Congress might prefer not to give military assistance to, say, Turkey, but members know that the president will veto a bill containing an outright ban. So they pass a bill banning aid to Turkey unless the president determines it is "in the national interest" to do so. The effect is to give the White House a veto power with regard to this section of the bill.

The Pocket Veto. The pocket veto provision puts the president in an unusually strong position at the end of a session. Any bill sent to the Congress during the ten days before adjournment can be prevented from becoming law by presidential decision with no possibility of overriding action by Congress. This can have an important bearing on the legislative tactics of policy advocates, who, particularly if they are strong in the Senate, can use the Upper Body's opportunities for delay to push a bill under the shade of the ten-day umbrella. At the same time, a postponement of adjournment can be used as a device to prevent the exercise of the president's pocket veto power. This was one of the major strategies used by President Andrew Johnson's opponents during the embattled Reconstruction days.

Although the ten-day rule seems straightforward, it has been the subject of considerable controversy. For many years, it was commonly believed that the president could not sign a bill after Congress had adjourned. The idea that a pocket veto was more or less automatic after adjournment was formally laid to rest by the Supreme Court in 1932;[59] but like a bad penny, the issue keeps turning up. On December 14, 1970 (note the date and start counting to ten), the Family Practice of Medicine bill was enrolled and sent to President Nixon. Both the House and Senate adjourned on December 22 for the Christmas holidays—the Senate for four days, the House for five. Not counting Sunday, December 20, the magic day ten arrived on Christmas Day. Bright and early the next day, despite the fact that the clerk of the Senate was in his office and the Senate was reconvening the next non-Sunday, Nixon pocket vetoed the bill. This was too much for a federal district court, which ruled unanimously (in a case that the White House did not even bother to appeal) that the bill was law since so short an intersession adjournment could no longer produce the kind of "public uncertainty" that might have prevailed in the days before modern communications. The possible uncertainty remaining about the issue, the court suggested, was "whether an intersession adjournment 'prevents' the return of a vetoed bill. Hopefully," the decision continued, "our present opinion eliminates that ambiguity."[60] It didn't.

The issue arose again in 1983 when President Reagan pocket vetoed a bill to require certification of human rights in El Salvador as a precondition of aid. This too has been ruled unconstitutional. "[U]pholding Reagan's pocket veto," Louis Fisher effectively argues, "would give the President an absolute veto that the framers had deliberately withheld."[61] It would seem as if the pocket veto is now likely to prove a factor only in the case of final adjournment. At the same time, the pocket veto is so powerful an instrument of raw presidential power that there are almost sure to be ways in which future presidents will seek to circumvent the seeming clarity of the issue.

The Politics of Presidential Choice

The extensive growth of formal liaison has made the veto itself less a discrete event in the legislative struggle than once it was. In a very major sense, the process of presidential (or, at least, executive branch) decision has always been under way long before a bill arrives at the White House. The president is committed to specific legislative enactments by the programs he presents to Congress, by proposals presented by agency officials, and even by campaign platforms.[62] No matter how strong the general commitment, however, a presidential recommendation for a maternity leave program does not commit a president to signing any bill that may set up a mandated program for maternity leaves. Thus, bills requiring large corporations to guarantee new parents the right to re-employment following leave time was vetoed by President Bush in 1990 and again in 1992, despite the president's ringing call for maternity leaves during his 1988 campaign.

No matter how close the liaison between Congress and the White House may be, moreover, some mystery will still surround the question of whether the president will sign a bill. At the end of the 79th Congress in 1946, one of the most important measures was the bill to extend price controls. Before action on the conference committee compromise, reporters at one of his press conferences asked Harry Truman if he would veto the bill. Tristram Coffin has recorded his answer: "The President replied primly, 'I never discuss legislation.' "[63] In this particular case Democratic leaders in Congress thought the president would sign the bill and were shocked when his veto message was delivered.

It is not at all uncommon for presidents to refuse to predict, even privately to their supporters on the Hill, what they will or will not sign. In part this reflects the natural caution of a person facing a situation of uncertainty: as often as not, it is not until the final stages of conference committee deliberations that anyone can know what the words in a bill are really to be. As for the president and his immediate advisors, moreover, there is often a lot of technical study that must be completed to understand a proposed law's full implications.

Agency Clearance. From the time of George Washington to the present, presidents have requested the views of agency heads on whether they should approve or disapprove of enrolled bills. Where more than one agency is involved, more than one opinion will be sought. The process of soliciting and compiling these reports has been increasingly centralized through the Office of Management and Budget, which offers its opinions as well. On the great majority of measures, this puts the OMB in a position of tremendous influence.[64] Yet a president cannot always depend entirely upon agency advice or the assistance of the OMB in pulling agency views together completely. Agency recommendations tend to be specialized and to see problems from personal and agency perspectives rather than from those of the White House. OMB officials often seem inclined to use technical criteria, which are politically unreliable. In the words of one former White House aide,

The departments were inclined to recommend approval of borderline legislation. That made life easier with the congressional committee which oversaw their affairs and had most likely written the bill in question. It also pleased their constituencies. . . . Budget, on the other hand, was almost primly righteous. If a bill did not square with the President's program, was too expensive, or set a bad precedent, Budget was for a veto.[65]

Usually there is a member of the White House staff who serves as a final filter to the president, drawing upon the OMB and agency reports, the pleadings of concerned legislators, and analysis of the political stakes involved.

Campaigning. There is one important difference between campaigns at earlier stages in the legislative struggle and those after a bill has been sent to the White House. In the latter instance, the campaign centers more than ever upon the thoughts and actions of one man. At this stage any road that can lead to that one man is usually deemed a worthwhile road to travel. MCs and leaders of private organizations will often call upon a president or write him beseeching letters in an effort to obtain the decision they prefer. Heavy contributors to the president's election campaign may be brought into the picture. In fact, any person who knows a person who knows a person who knows how to get the president's ear fits into this phase of the legislative struggle. All the established techniques involved in the organization of group support, the application of pressure, and the dissemination of propaganda may again be called into use. Behind the formalities of the clearance process, executive agency officials often enter vigorously into the conflict. A Cabinet member who feels strongly about a measure may try to circumvent a contrary report from the Budget Office by going directly to the president. More discretely, budget aides and even members of the White House staff may try their hand at internal lobbying.

Even if the campaign for a veto fails, there are different ways to give up. For example, a pocket veto while Congress is in session is not effective, and the bill becomes law; but it does so automatically and relieves the president from having to put his or her signature on a lousy law. Or he can hold his nose and sign, as was recommended in the memo Harry McPherson sent to Lyndon Johnson on the Safe Streets Act of 1968:

(I recognize that you must sign this bill.)
But it is the worst bill you will have signed since you took office. . . . If you choose to veto the bill and take half an hour of TV time to explain why, I will work around the clock to produce a statement. If—as I think you must—you sign it, I hope the signing statement will blast those provisions of the bill (and there are many) which are obnoxious, and resolve to seek their repeal—treating them as continuing questions of public policy.[69]

Should the president decide to issue a formal veto, the battle is not over. Courtesy dictates that the bill's sponsors be notified. "Wake him up," Lyndon Johnson ordered Harry McPherson, after a late-night decision to veto a pet project of Arizona Senator Carl Hayden. "I don't want to do this to him without warning."[67] A special clerk, the only White House staff person allowed on the House or Senate floor, must formally present the bad news to

Congress, where, as one clerk recalls, they "have on occasion been literally hissed and booed—usually goodnaturedly—off the floor of both houses."[68]

Postveto Battles. One reason for such negative reactions is the general effectiveness of the veto power. Technically, the term *veto* is misleading. In Latin it means "I forbid," a meaning that accurately applies to the ability of a permanent member of the Security Council of the United Nations to prevent many kinds of action by a single vote. It is inaccurate when applied to the president's disapproval of a measure, for the simple reason that the president cannot forbid; his disapproval can be overruled by a two-thirds majority in both houses.

In fact, this seldom happens.

Statistically, the veto override power can accurately be described as follows: "From 1969 to 1984 congress enacted 5,957 measures; the President vetoed 184; and Congress overrode 24 of these vetoes. On the average, there were 1.5 overrides per year, but fully half of the overrides came during the brief post-Watergate Ford presidency. In any event, the override procedure accounted for only .4% of all measures that became law during the fifteen-year period."[69]

Despite the statistical unlikelihood of an override, some of the most dramatic debates in Congress have taken place upon the consideration of such a resolution. Here the conflicting voices reach the last ostensible stage in the legislative struggle. If only because the Constitution requires a recorded vote, participation on veto votes is unusually high, and the conflict at this particular point is on an all-or-none basis. No amendments are allowed.

Predictably, party lines tighten around a veto vote. To vote against a president of your party on a substantive issue is one thing; to vote against his position when the publicity level is high is something else again. The three most likely scenarios for veto overrides are (1) when the president underestimates the sentiments within his own party in favor of a bill; (2) when he knows the veto will lose but wishes to dramatize the bill; or (3) when both the president and the Congress know what will happen but choose, for various reasons, to publicly underscore their differences.

Congress need not act upon a bill. Even if one house votes to override, if party leaders feel they lack the two-thirds vote needed, the other body may do nothing.

------- ✳ -------

CONCLUSION: THE VETO WALTZ

The growing sophistication of White House and agency liaison officials should have obviated the need for formal vetoes long ago. That it is seldom now a factor at minor levels—in terms, for example, of private member bills—tells us something about the contemporary veto. In essence the veto has become a symbolic act, a special event in which the White House and Congress have agreed, perhaps for reasons of their own, to go their separate ways in dramatic form. The veto is a symbol of failed liaison. Not only are vetoes seldom defeated, but when they are, it is seldom a surprise.

To imply that such charades are demagogic, however, is not to denigrate their importance in our system. Veto fights, more often than not, occur over issues that sharply divide the public. They are likely to be what campaign strategists call "leverage" issues, those that so sharply define party or other groupings that they can be used in campaigns. The old veto—one based in late-discerned policy differences—is virtually a dead letter; the new veto—a deliberate shot across the White House or congressional bow designed to appeal to a wider public—defines the current state of the art.

Like many state-of-the-art technologies, the new veto is not always what it seems. With each player playing its institutional role, veto politics becomes a game of chicken, a question of who will be first to swerve from true confrontation. On the public works issue, Carter in 1977 swerved first, a position he later came to regret. Whether the confrontation in 1978 helped him more is problematic. It was, without question, a classic, a veto that was almost retrograde in its directness and simplicity, serving as a challenge not just to Congress as an institution but particularly to members and leaders of his own party in both the House and Senate. It stands, however, as an exception to the rule. The veto itself has become essentially a media event, an orchestrated attempt by both Congress and the White House to expand the scope of conflict and appeal to a wider public.

During his four years in the White House, George Bush had but one veto overridden. With rare exceptions, moreover, he was almost never expected to lose. Over and over the Democratic Congress passed bills mandating maternity leave, liberalized voter registration laws, and campaign finance reforms that they knew would not become law. Sometimes, as in the 1990–92 struggle for civil rights legislation, the battle took on the classic strategic character of traditional veto fights. Here, as in the prebargaining that sets the stage for conference committee deliberations, congressional Democrats kept adjusting the level of the bill's sanctions to meet the president's demands; and the president, after securing a few concessions in each new draft, finally signed the bill.

The major significance of the veto, as perhaps it always has been, is its transformation of congressional mathematics: the essence of presidential leverage on the Hill, the force that sets the White House apart from all other policy advocates, lies in its ability to require a two-thirds vote to win. These mathematics give the president a resource unavailable to any other actor in the system. Nor does his power end there. The president has many ways to execute a law. These, no less than the formal veto, loom over all stages of the legislative process on Capitol Hill.

12

---✳---

EXECUTING THE LAW

"Administration of a statute," as David Truman has argued, "is, properly speaking, an extension of the legislative process."[1] Many statutes, he points out, are the products of unstable, often tenuous alliances that are held together, in part, by leaving the details vague. Others are produced by coalitions that are temporary at best. Many regulatory laws, especially, are passed by unstable majorities coalescing around a particular scandal or outrage. When the law is passed, the coalition dissolves and the "regulated" groups become the administrators' only audience. "It takes majorities to pass legislation, but . . . a minority under our system may have sufficient nuisance value to affect executive policy."[2]

Perhaps the most dramatic override of an act of Congress is a decision of the Supreme Court ruling the law unconstitutional. There are, however, less spectacular but equally effective means by which courts can subvert if not veto legislative acts. One need not even be a judge or a bureaucrat to veto a bill. Those who drank during Prohibition, who drove over 55 miles per hour in the 1980s, or who discriminated against minorities in the 1970s, 1980s, or 1990s were effectively casting their own social vetoes on acts of Congress.

Although convention, formal structures, and convenience combine to suggest the separate treatment of the legislative, executive, and judicial processes, policy-making power refuses to follow such clear paths. Paul Appleby argued years ago that

> courts can be judged and their decision-making understood only in the
> light of what is done by Congress and by administrators; that administra-
> tion can be judged and its policy-making understood only in the light of
> what is done by courts and Congress and the administrative hierarchy
> itself; that Congressional policy-making similarly can be understood only
> in the light of what is done by courts and by administrators; that the

three branches can be understood only in the light of popular political activities.[3]

He is still right.

———————— ✳ ————————

BUREAUCRATIC SABOTAGE

"It would be an alarming doctrine," the Supreme Court argued in 1838, "that Congress cannot impose upon any executive officer any duty they may think proper." Despite the president's constitutional authority for the faithful execution of the laws, the Court argued that "the duty and responsibility" of executive branch employees "grow out of and are subject to the control of law and not the direction of the President."[4] Although this may still be sound legal doctrine, political realities are considerably more complex. From time to time, there are major instances of renegade bureaucratic behavior. Oliver North's use of a rich variety of financial gimmicks to provide financial aid to the Nicaraguan Contras, despite the Boland Amendment's clear prohibition of such aid, was unusual but not unique. Although the principals in the case have conveniently lost their memories, it is unlikely that North could have gone as far as he did without the tacit if not overt support of the White House.

What we are suggesting here is that major evasions of statutory mandates are unlikely to take place in political vacuums. Indeed, it seems quite clear—particularly in light of Congress's rather cursory investigation of the Iran-Contra scandal and Colonel North's later emergence as a minor hero—that Contra aid enjoyed the support of significant legislative, White House, and public constituencies. What might appear to be a quasi-autonomous bureaucratic usurpation of power often turns out, on closer examination, to have the support of at least a significant part of the agency's clientele.

Bureaucrats and Politicians

Career bureaucrats, like Colonel North, tend to harbor a certain contempt for politicians. As experts and (in some cases) believers, they "know" that "There are correct ways of solving problems and doing things. Politics is seen as being engaged in the fuzzy areas of negotiation, elections, votes, compromises—all carried on by subject matter amateurs. Politics is to the professions as ambiguity is to truth, expedience to rightness, heresy to true belief."[5]

Members of Congress and the appointed bureau chiefs, Cabinet secretaries, and even presidents are sometimes regarded as annoying distractions from the real job at hand. Nonetheless, once a legislative-executive agreement has been codified in the form of a statute, it carries considerable weight. "The law," one astute observer remarked, "matters a great deal to bureaucrats. It sets the goals toward which agencies are expected to work and provides some indication, however vague, of the means to be used to get there. The law also puts limits on bureaucrats. Any agency that engages in actions for which it lacks statutory authority is a better than even money bet to find itself in court explaining why."[6]

The law is also likely to provide a considerable range of "wiggle room," areas for bureaucratic discretion more or less intentionally provided by Congress. It is in these murky corners of the law that bureaucrats who wish to exercise a form of veto power are most likely to succeed. Indeed, there are some areas of public policy in which Congress seems to have intended to give the bureaucracy a free hand. As Clark Clifford has said of the covert, often illegal activities of the Central Intelligence Agency (CIA) during the period 1947–74, "Congress chose not to be involved and preferred to be uninformed." If that statement seems overblown, consider the argument of the then chairman of the Senate Armed Services Committee on the issue: "It is difficult for me to foresee that increased staff scrutiny of CIA operations would result in either substantial savings or a significant increase in available intelligence information. . . . If there is one agency of the government in which we must take some matters on faith, without a constant examination of its methods and sources, I believe this agency is the CIA."[7]

Few agencies have the political clout to sustain such sacred cow status. The Federal Bureau of Investigation under J. Edgar Hoover enjoyed similar congressional indulgence, it is sometimes suggested, because Hoover had such extensive files on the foibles and failings of so many legislators. More frequently, it is subsystem support that provides an agency with the congressional leverage to get away with the undermining of a seemingly clear statutory commandment. The possibility that the law will say one thing and an agency's key congressional clients something else is strong enough to make the term *legislative intent* something of a joke. It must be remembered too that statutes are more permanent than legislative or political leaders. Rather than going through the tedious process of completely rewriting an agency's statutory authority, Congress and the administration may acquiesce in a long-term series of administrative modifications of the law that eventually amount to a complete overhaul.

For the bureaucrat who is bent on evading the law, the one strategy that dominates all others is that of making key allies. None of these are of greater importance for most agencies than the members and staffs of the relevant House and Senate subcommittees. Close seconds in importance are client groups, appointed officials, and, of course, the White House. When all of these ducks are in line, the possibilities for evading the letter of the law are broad; when none of them support you, the chances are nil. It would be nice if we could set forth a neat typology of the more typical instances that fall between these extremes—if we could show, for example, that having the White House on your side is more important than a key subcommittee; or that a firmly entrenched and united subgovernment will always put a White House appointee in his or her place. The available studies yield no such broad generalizations.

At the same time, we can draw upon the literature to suggest the kinds of bargaining contexts that either enhance or detract from the possibility of bureaucratic sabotage. The most basic weapon of the bureaucracy is its capacity for inaction and delay. It is more porcupine than tiger, most dangerous when it is least active. In his discussion of the bureaucracy and the president, Dennis Riley suggests that when an agency has the statutory authority to act "and just isn't using it . . . there is probably a reason why it isn't using that piece of its legal mandate in that way."[8] Whatever the real reason for inaction, moreover, some excuse can almost always be found: "Oh, I guess we misunderstood." "Well, we've been so busy with X that we haven't even been able to think about Y." "It can't be done." "We're doing the best we can." In both the public and private sectors, these are familiar bureaucratic lines.

Speaking specifically of the White House, Riley argues that

> If the President's problem with an agency centers on something he wants it to start doing, keep your money on the bureaucrats.
>
> If, on the other hand, the President wants to stop something, it is time to give some careful thought to switching sides. Now the Chief is pretty much an even bet.[9]

Riley's argument can usefully be extended to cover almost any outside advocate—legislative, executive, judicial, or private. Getting bureaucrats to act is always more difficult than stopping them. To put it another way, bureaucratic nonfeasance is more common than malfeasance. It is, moreover, the single most effective weapon against congressional control.

A second broad generalization we can venture is that the more technical the issue, the less the likelihood of outside oversight—particularly, it would seem, from the administration. Although MCs as individuals and Congress as an institution are not supposed to be experts on anything, the cumulative experience of subcommittee members and their staffs can be considerable, particularly in the long-tenured, highly specialized postreform Congress. Legislative staffs tend to be younger and to stay in office for far shorter terms than their bureaucratic counterparts, but the evidence is strong that "these young, relatively inexperienced, more liberally educated (i.e., generalist) congressional committee staffers have an impressive record of experience in the specialized areas (fields) of the agencies their committees oversee."[10] Through long periods of fruitful interaction, moreover, the members themselves are usually in an excellent position to draw upon the invisible colleges of policy experts in the private sector.

The president with his White House staff is, by way of contrast, a novice. Cabinet members and other appointed officials are often even less technically competent. Appointed as much for his or her political skills and previous service, the typical member of the Senior Executive Service lacks both Washington experience and technical expertise. His or her average tenure in office, moreover, is likely to be about two years.[11] The time demands from constituent groups, MCs, interagency and advisory committees are also significant. As one veteran puts it, "Minimal time is left for managing the department, even if a secretary is one of the rare political executives with a taste for administration."[12] There is a tendency, as Hugh Heclo puts it, for the "important characteristics that appointees share—impatience, short-term tenures, inexperience as a group— [to be] at war with what they most need, a patient fashioning of relationships of trust and confidence."[13] It would be misleading to conclude that the White House and its political appointees are without resources. Far from it.

> Bureaucratic sabotage does occur (and should at times be expected), but political executives are not without means of defense. . . .
> Washington offers more opportunities to search for allies than is suggested by any simple image of political executives on one side and bureaucratic opponents on the other.[14]

Help (or further obstruction) can also be found in the Congress. Partly because they are political, appointed officials sometimes bring with them, sometimes develop, their own communications networks on the Hill; and there are ways in which bureaucrats can force the hands of legislators. By working with interest groups, going public on controversial issues, or doing a bad job of administering a law, bureaucrats and their supervisors can force legislative re-evaluations of key statutes.

Legislative Oversight

A natural corollary to legislative oversight of administration is "that the need for such oversight increases with executive initiative in policy and the delegation of discretion under the broad terms of statutes."[15] The clearer the statutory guidelines, it would seem to follow, the less the need for further scrutiny. Yet the equation is never that simple. Although a vaguely worded statute may seem to indicate ambiguity of purpose in Congress as a whole, it may very nicely suit the precise political agenda of a key pair of subcommittees and the policy subsystems they represent. A finely detailed statute, conversely, may indicate a congressional lack of confidence in other methods of oversight. What are those other methods?

Probably the most effective are those associated with the power of the purse. If agencies, as one Senate committee has said "are able to bend the more ambiguous language of authorizing legislation to their own purposes, the dollar figures in appropriations bills represent commands which cannot be bent or ignored except at extreme penalty to agency officials."[16] The House rule prohibiting legislation in appropriation bills puts important limits on the scope of such sanctions, making it easier to restrain bureaucratic action than to promote it. But the line between positive and negative sanctions is written in sand, and the waves that wash the boundaries between authorizing and appropriating committees, particularly in the area of oversight, are rewritten with every tide. For both kinds of committees, the most common tools are nonstatutory. Formal hearings and investigations, informal contacts, and public debates all serve as instruments of legislative oversight. The importance of such devices is growing. Ardith Maney uses the term *policy shaping* to describe the "system of small changes" that seems presently to "characterize the policy process."[17] A dramatic increase in the oversight activities of both House and Senate committees in the Nixon years more than held its own through the 1980s and shows no sign of abating in the 1990s.[18] The nature of this policy-shaping activity seems to be changing as well.

In the Reagan and Bush years, Congress often found itself trying to collaborate with agency officials instead of controlling them. Except in the areas of national security and defense, fiscal oversight has come so strongly from the White House and OMB that even the House Appropriations Committee, once dominated by a budget-cutting norm, joined the ranks of the "spenders." In this kind of divided government, policy shaping makes sense as a collaborative enterprise used by subgovernment leaders to escape the more hostile controls likely to come out of the White House and OMB. A Congress confronted with a hostile administration may be far tougher than one dealing with its political friends in forging subgovernmental links.

Another aspect of the oversight process that has come to the fore in the years of divided government is that which invokes the Senate's powers of advice and consent in the area of presidential appointments. For both the bureaucracy and the courts, the Congress has become increasingly assertive in the use of its Senate power to confirm major appointments. Statistics in this area are virtually worthless, since presidents seldom push appointments they know will fail. Despite the highly charged rejection of President Bush's nomination of former senator John Tower as secretary of defense in 1989, the proportion of rejected high-level appointments has been relatively constant. Indeed, the Tower rejection was rather unique. Typically, as the leading scholar in the field has written, "the President is accorded wide latitude in the selection of members of his Cabinet, but nominations to other offices are scrutinized with varying degrees of care."[19] Outright rejection is very rare, but the White House generally consults key senators in advance.

As might be expected, the various modes of oversight overlap. A senator might push the approval for a member of one regulatory commission in exchange for the right to promote his or her candidate for a vacancy on another. A nominee might be cleared for approval provided he or she commits to a particular line of policy. A nomination stalled in one Senate committee may suddenly be reported to the floor when the White House "coincidentally" announces a change in its policy on a seemingly unrelated issue.

Oversight and Political Decentralization

Oversight particularizes. It is not something in which Congress as a whole normally participates. For a variety of reasons, both historical and institutional, the United States is virtually unique in its legislature's capacity and inclination for intervention in the day-to-day workings of the government. It is the only country studied "in which members of Congress and senior civil servants report more frequent contacts with one another than with department heads."[20] "End runs" around senior administrators are almost routine.

The pattern of administrative decentralization that this encourages runs in two directions. To whatever extent they do or do not develop in practice, the opportunity created for the development of subgovernments is unparalleled.

Subgovernments in the United States are nurtured in the recurring contacts between the policy specialists of congressional subcommittees and their public and private sector clients. It would not be exaggerating by much to use the terms *clientelism* and *oversight* interchangeably.

There is a second way in which the effectiveness of oversight particularizes politics. Through the constituency concern of individual members, administrative decisions are decentralized in regional terms as well, that is, they are localized. Formal oversight hearings are larded with questions and comments seemingly designed to display members of Congress at their most parochial. As Christopher Foreman says, "One good way to attract the attention of a member of Congress is by putting something into his or her district that provides jobs, prestige for the member or district, or some valued service. But an even *better* way to attract it is by threatening to take that something out."[21] And if you *really* want vigorous oversight activity, you can propose to put something nasty, like toxic or nuclear wastes, into local areas.

Constituent services are even more local and particularistic. Casework enhances the advantages of incumbency. No less important is its impact on governance and the character of the Washington community. The day-to-day interactions between agencies and the Hill can both displace and facilitate formal oversight. Casework is itself a form of oversight that provides a sort of early warning system for the identification of emerging problems. Frequent complaints about a particular law or agency are not unlikely to produce more comprehensive oversight efforts. It was a series of nearly identical complaints to his district office in 1990 that alerted West Virginia Democrat Bob Wise to a change in food stamps regulations that was affecting his constituents. Using his position on the Government Operations Committee as a bully pulpit, Wise held a hearing on the subject that prompted the Department of Health and Human Services to rescind its regulation.[22]

There is a sociological dimension to this activity that also deserves attention. Lewis A. Dexter's proposal that members of Congress and their staff assistants be prohibited from cohabiting with their counterparts in the executive branch still ranks as one of the loonier reform proposals ever seriously proposed, but the concern it reflects is dead serious and the argument interesting.[23] Dexter's suggestion that we have separate institutions sharing both powers and dwellings serves as a useful metaphor for the day-to-day interactions that characterize the American system. Although constituency casework is becoming more common in Britain, it is hard to imagine backbenchers in Parliament ever forming the kinds of working (and social) relations with their counterparts in Whitehall that the denizens of Capitol Hill have with the folks downtown.

--- ✳ ---

CONGRESS AND THE COURTS

Members of the judicial branch are not as much a part of these social and political networks. An almost Puritanical abstraction from the day-to-day business of policy-making is part of the court system's cultivated image. It should not, however, obscure the judiciary's very real part in the legislative struggle, or its involvement in the politics of executing the laws.

More often than not, the judiciary is in the business of administering statutes. Although their structures and procedures are somewhat different, courts and bureaucracies often have analogous roles vis-à-vis the enforcement of statute law. The Federal Horse Protection Act, for example, prohibits the transportation or sale of sore horses. The Act provides certain key definitions and exceptions but leaves it to the courts, not to an existing agency or newly created Bureau of Sore Horses, to enforce its provisions. One estimate puts the number of subjects that similarly vest direct enforcement powers in the federal judiciary at more than three hundred.[24]

A far larger number of statutes depend for their administration on some form of interaction between courts and administrators, or between courts and private litigants. In the typical case, the statute regulates or prohibits certain activities, empowers an agency to police said acts, and provides guidelines to the courts for enforcing the law and punishing violators. For most citizens, most of the time, the "law" is not the statute, not the piece of parchment churned out by Congress and signed by the president. Thus, for example:

> In the course of producing the Sherman Act . . . the Iowa farmer who felt that it cost too much to ship his corn to Chicago lent his sovereign power to a statute; but the statute did not command the Burlington railroad to lower its freight charges; instead it prohibited "contracts in restraint of trade" and other equally abstract actions. . . .
>
>   A statute will accomplish very little, of course, so long as it remains words in a book. It must now be put into action; that is, from being a compact verbal formula, it must now be spread until it alters the behavior of many citizens. But the process of enforcement, like the process of enactment, does much to guarantee that the law's results will differ from those that any citizen would have chosen.[25]

It is in this process of enforcement, in turning verbal formulae into actions that alter behavior, that bureaucrats and judges serve their primary roles.

The Overrated Importance of Judicial Review

Nothing has fascinated students of the U.S. court system more than the Supreme Court's power, known as judicial review, to rule acts of Congress unconstitutional. In fact, this aspect of judicial power is relatively minor. "I do not think," Justice Holmes once said, "the United States would come to an end if we lost our power to declare an act of Congress unconstitutional."[26] The total number of cases is quite small, averaging fewer than one a year since the founding of the Republic; many involve trivial issues. The ability of Congress and the president to "overrule" the Court is also substantial. "By itself," Robert Dahl concluded in 1957, "the Court is almost powerless to affect the course of national policy."[27]

In the years since Dahl wrote his landmark essay on the role of the Court, activist justices have shown a considerably greater willingness to declare federal laws void. Almost as many cases (51) involving judicial review were handed down between 1957 and 1987 as during the entire pre-1957 period (Dahl had counted a total of 78 between 1789 and 1957).[28] The pace of judicial activism, moreover, appears to be accelerating; the supposedly conservative Burger and Rehnquist Courts are using the power of judicial review at about one-and-a-half times the rate of the supposedly activist Warren Court.

Even when the Court rules an act of Congress and/or the president unconstitutional, the result is not necessarily a reversal of policy. What is sometimes overlooked in examining Justice Marshall's celebrated decision establishing the power of judicial review (*Marbury v. Madison*) is that Marbury did not get his judgeship: Madison, though opposing the doctrine on which the decision was based, won the case. Even more important, as Dahl noted, Congress quite frequently finds some way or another of overturning the Court's original ruling. This, too, is happening less frequently than in the past. In a sharp challenge to the pattern delineated by Dahl, Jonathan Casper found only one legislative override of a court decision in the 1957–74 period he examined, and Susan Lawrence's figures point in the same general direction for more recent cases.[29]

Interestingly, however, this rising level of judicial "activism" does not seem to have produced anything like the storm of controversy that engulfed the Court in the New Deal years or even in another period of anti-Court sentiment in the 1950s. Many of the laws overturned by the Warren Court in particular were older statutes, laws in which the current Congress might be presumed to have less stake. All of the Warren Court's resorts to judicial review, moreover, were in cases involving questions of individual civil rights and liberties, areas of policy in which the concept of judicial review is often considered compatible with democratic theory.[30] Even in the case of the more activist Burger Court, nearly two-thirds of the cases involved issues of basic rights, and about 62 percent "old" laws.[31] What is perhaps most interesting about the vast majority of these cases is how little notoriety they achieved. According to Lawrence, 65 percent of the Warren and Burger Court cases are not so much as mentioned in the index to the *Congressional Record*. Fully 25 percent escaped the notice of the *New York Times*.[32]

Although an entire cottage industry has revolved around the philosophical question of whether the exercise of judicial review is compatible with democratic theory, it has generally taken an extraordinary combination of personalities and events to elevate (or lower) this dialogue to the level of actual policy. The main function of the Supreme Court, and of the court system in general, is that of resolving cases and controversies in the light of existing law (including, of course, the law laid out in the Constitution).[33]

The Underrated Power of Judicial Enforcement

If the power of the courts to overrule acts of Congress has often been exaggerated, its role in the legislative struggle has not. As much as the literature of law and political science has focused on the concept of delegated powers as applied to the bureaucracy, it is curious how little attention has been given those powers similarly delegated to the courts. The "sore horse" act, mentioned previously, is one of many in which the Congress has explicitly granted the courts the authority to "fill in the details" of a vaguely phrased statute. "Congress frequently passes the buck to the courts to avoid controversial choices and then blames judges for issuing decisions that it in fact required."[34] Even where authority has not been explicitly delegated, moreover, the role of the courts is far from trivial. The considerable leeway and power granted to U.S. courts in the interpretation of individual statutes is reinforced by their ability to pick and choose among them. Like the common law, statute law in the United States is cumulative: when Congress passes a statute, it supplements rather than supplants existing law (unless specifically saying otherwise). Just as lawyers and judges often shop for common law precedents to bolster their particular points of view, so does the area of overlap in statutory precedents encourage the legal system to decide which law it wants to enforce.

Vaguely worded statutes invite litigation, even when they apparently vest the primary power of interpretation in an administrative agency. It is up to the Justice Department to decide whether a particular business merger represents a combination "in restraint of trade" under Section I of the Sherman Anti-Trust Act. But even an administration dedicated to strict enforcement of the anti-monopoly laws is constrained by the virtual certainty that its decision will be taken to the courts (whose decisions in the area of antitrust laws are almost as ambiguous as the statute in which they are grounded). The Congress, as we shall argue, has a variety of mechanisms by which it can redirect the courts' interpretations of ambiguous statutes. The point is that it is power seldom used. One analyst has suggested that there is

> an implicit expectation in Congress's willingness to pawn off onto the courts the important business of giving content to our national laws. To put it bluntly, Congress expects the courts will construe its meaning broadly, resolving ambiguities in favor of the left. . . . The expectation . . . is that the courts will ratchet out the scope of the rights that Congress lacked the nerve to create explicitly.[35]

The basic point, that Congress frequently passes the buck to the courts on controversial issues, is beyond serious question. It also seems clear that federal courts in the 1960s and 1970s, in particular, showed a willingness to ratchet out the scope of law, especially in cases involving civil rights and liberties. Sometimes this was done, even by defying rather clear statutory guidelines.

In the school busing cases, to give one clear illustration, the intent of Congress as embodied in the Civil Rights Act of 1964 seems unambiguous enough. The Act's Section 2003 specifically prohibited any "official or court" from issuing "any order seeking to achieve a racial balance in any school by requiring the transportation of pupils or students from one school to another." Beginning with the 1971 case of *Swann v. Charlotte-Mecklenberg* (the original school busing case), the courts have simply ignored this language. But while it has, "in fact, ignored the manifest intent of Congress by permitting and sometimes requiring mandatory busing . . . the Court has never declared section 2003 unconstitutional."[36] Judicial review, it would seem, can take place even when it isn't called judicial review.

In recent years the ratchet has turned in a quite different direction. To an extent with the Burger Court, frequently since Rehnquist, there has been a narrowing rather than a broadening of rights so clearly in defiance of statutory guidelines that Congress has moved vigorously to re-emphasize its mandates. Once again the best illustration is in the area of civil rights, where the flagship case is almost certainly *Grove City College v. Bell*. In this 1984 decision a divided Court—again without ruling the law unconstitutional—gave a unique twist to what had heretofore seemed a relatively lucid legislative mandate. At issue was Title IX of the 1972 Education Act Amendments. The object of this legislation was to use the carrot of federal aid as a stick against discrimination. Title IX specifically required the Office of Education to withhold federal funds from institutions that discriminated on the basis of gender. The Supreme Court's ruling was that funds could be withheld only from the specific program or activity found guilty of discrimination. In the case of Grove City, its sports program (which relied not at all on federal funds) could thus continue to virtually exclude women while the College continued to receive its government checks for everything else.

Legislative Oversight of the Courts

Grove City appears to be part of a series of civil rights decisions sharply narrowing the scope of the law, particularly in the area of employment discrimination. In virtually all of these cases, Congress has moved swiftly, as the chair of the Senate Judiciary Committee put it, "to repair the damage."[37] *Grove City* was dispatched by a 1988 law that simply said that when one part of an institution is receiving federal aid, the entire institution is barred from discriminating. Congress succeeded in overriding a Reagan veto to, in effect, overrule the Court. For three years it was unable to overcome Bush vetoes of a series of other antidiscrimination bills, but the negotiations between the White House and Congress on how best to curb the Court provide a classic case study of the separation of powers in action. "The successful reversal of an important Supreme Court decision or line of decisions is no easy task," one scholar has argued.[38] This is almost certainly true when Congress and the president are divided. Yet a determined majority can be effective, as Congress showed in overruling *Grove City*. When the political climate is favorable, moreover, even a reluctant president can be moved, as George Bush apparently was in 1991 when he signed a bill into law that included sections he had earlier described as unacceptable.

Direct reversal of the Court has not often been necessary. All three branches have at times worked together—for example, to restrict the powers of the states. Indeed, a strong case can be made that Congress and the Court have been coconspirators in expanding the powers of the federal government. Throughout its history, moreover, the courts have shown extraordinary restraint in intruding upon the most sacred powers of the coordinate branches, most notably the foreign policy prerogatives of the White House and the spending powers of the Congress. Whether the judiciary's caution in this area has been a continuing exercise in self-restraint or a recognition of political realities is moot. "Because self-restraint is a compound of policy and power, separation of these two elements is possible only in the realm of logical analysis."[39]

This is not the place for a review of the extensive literature on the concept of judicial self-restraint. It is worth noting, however, that the Congress is not limited to statutory remedies in its attempts to check activist courts. Just as legislative oversight of administration can be accomplished by means other than passing laws, so are there other methods in which the legislative and judicial branches interact. Perhaps the crudest weapons of legislative oversight are those aimed at the functioning of the courts themselves. The judiciary's budget, like that of any agency, must be appropriated by the Congress and approved by the White House. Despite frequent threats, the Congress has seldom invoked this power in a punitive manner, though it seems more than likely that failures to increase judges' salaries have sometimes reflected congressional pique at a particular line of decisions. Congress also has the power to revise the structure of the federal court system; and the Senate's power to proffer its advice and consent to major appointments has frequently been used to influence the ideological balance of the courts. The rejection of the hard-nosed conservative Robert Bork in 1987 marked the twenty-sixth time that a nominee to the Supreme Court failed to receive Senate confirmation. That's about one out of every five, with many of the rejections having been made on ideological grounds.[40] What Joseph Harris says about presidential nominations in general applies to Supreme Court nominees in particular: "Most contests over the President's nominations have been grounded on political questions rather than the qualifications of the nominees."[41] This is clear in the hearings on important nominations, such as that of Clarence Thomas in 1991, in which the questions were so sharply focused on court issues that "a neutral observer might mistakenly have thought that an oversight hearing was in progress."[42]

The Senate's power of advice and consent is even greater at the district court level, where the practice of "senatorial courtesy" usually applies. Here, a senator of the president's party is usually given an effective veto over nominations in his or her state, a practice that "virtually transfers the nominating function for these offices from the President to the individual senators of his party."[43]

The cannon in Congress's arsenal of court control devices is its seemingly clear power under Article V of the Constitution to fix the courts' jurisdictions. This power has been manifestly employed only once. During the early stages of Reconstruction, just as impeachment proceedings against President Andrew Johnson were getting under way, the Supreme Court accepted a case on appeal that "directly raised the question of the constitutionality of the Military Reconstruction Act, a question which the Republicans were quite anxious to avoid. . . . An adverse decision," William Lasser says, "could easily impact not only on Reconstruction generally but on the impeachment as well."[44] Acting hastily, the House and Senate, despite a presidential veto, removed the Court's jurisdiction.

A case can be made that this act was itself unconstitutional. Early in the history of the Republic, Justice Story articulated an interpretation of Article V that continues to have many adherents. In Story's reading of the Constitution,

> The judicial power of the United States *shall* be vested (not *may* be vested) in one supreme court and such inferior courts as congress may, from time to time ordain and establish. . . .
>
> If, then, it is a duty of congress to vest the judicial power of the United States, it is a duty to vest the whole judicial power.[45]

But in 1869 the Court refused to be drawn into the showdown with Congress that such a ruling might have produced. Writing for the Court in *Ex Parte McCardle*, Justice Chase refused to inquire as to "the motives of the legislature. We can only examine into its power under the Constitution; and the power to make exceptions to the appellate jurisdiction of this court is given by express words."[46]

Scholarly opinion is far from unanimous in upholding the validity of the *McCardle* rule,[47] and it has never again been put to a formal test. But the threat of a challenge to the courts may accomplish the same virtual ends. The most famous such threat was, of course, Franklin Roosevelt's "court packing" proposal in 1937. The proposal to change the composition of the court to give it a Roosevelt-appointed majority failed in Congress and has often been viewed as "one of Roosevelt's most serious political blunders."[48] Yet it can also be said that although the president lost the battle, he won the war. In the famous "switch-in-time that saved nine," the Court's record in supporting the constitutionality of the New Deal was far more positive in its 1937 term than it had been in 1936.

In the 1950s, the Supreme Court confronted similar threats to its jurisdiction, this time from the Congress. Interestingly, the result was much the same:

> the course of the Warren Court's conflict with Congress followed a well-worn pattern. First came decisions on important aspects of public policy. Historically these issues have varied . . . but the next step has been one of severe criticisms of the Court coupled with threats of remedial and/or retaliatory legislative action.
>
> The third step has usually been a judicial retreat.[49]

It is possible to force some sort of logical rationale to many of these shifts, and to suggest that the Court's retreat was founded in something other than fear. As Lasser puts it, "Scholars have marveled at the Court's ability to survive the fiercest of battles. What they have failed to realize is the Court's enemies, for the most part, were shooting blanks."[50] Whatever the Court's enemies have been shooting, it is at least equally plausible to follow the logic of Peter Finley Dunne's "Mr. Dooley" in his insistence that the Supreme Court follows the election returns. The Court's retreat from the economic sphere in 1937 has become a rout, and its continuing refusal to meddle even on the margins of foreign policy suggests that it is at least sensitive to political realities. It may be, as Murphy puts it, that "Because self-restraint is a combination of policy and power, separation of those two elements is possible only in the realm of logical analysis."[51] In the real world of politics, however, the logic of judicial self-restraint seems fairly clear: the states, which have almost no weapons of retaliation, have been consistent losers at the federal bar; Congress and the presidency have not.

Justice Douglas wrote in a widely quoted 1964 opinion affirming a right to privacy that "We do not sit as a super-legislature to determine the wisdom, need, and propriety of laws that touch economic problems, business affairs or social conditions. This law, however, operates directly on an intimate relation of husband and wife and their physician's role in one aspect of that relation."[52] Nor, clearly, does the Court sit as an arbiter of the propriety of undeclared wars, covert activities, or foreign policy operations in general. But the reasonable inference from Douglas's argument is that the Court does sit in a super-legislative role vis-à-vis the states and particularly in the defense of individual rights. And it sits in that position largely because Congress and the president have allowed it.

——————— ✳ ———————

SOCIAL VETOES

Bertram Gross has used the term *contained deviation* to describe the kind of social regulation that anticipates a certain range of evasion.[53] The most familiar cases are probably state and local traffic codes for which a certain amount of evasion is commonplace: typically, no one gets arrested for going 60 miles an hour where the formal law says 55. Motorists and police officers, over time, develop an implied contract to set the "real" speed limit, which is usually (in our own respective New York and California experiences) somewhere between 65 and 70.[54] Similarly, the Internal Revenue Service expects a certain amount of tax evasion and programs its audits to catch only the larger deviations from formal law.

Americans are among the world's most law-abiding people. Foreign visitors are often surprised when their American hosts stop at traffic lights on deserted streets. We evade relatively few taxes. But a study of legislative strategy would be incomplete if it failed to acknowledge the limitations of the Congress and of the government in general in its ability to really make public policy. A law, even in some cases a law that is conscientiously administered and enforced by the courts, is not necessarily a policy. People, it seems, drank nearly as much during Prohibition as they did before and after the Constitution was amended to outlaw the sale of alcoholic beverages.

Prohibition is a classic case of a purely social veto: a law that was supposed to be enforced was indeed enforced, and still it failed. Legislatures do, from time to time, pass laws like the Prohibition Amendment that prove essentially unenforceable. In most cases—and Prohibition is not an exception—non-enforcement is to some degree a matter of choice. The United States could have been an alcohol-free society in the 1920s, as it could be a drug-free society today, were the legislative, executive, and judicial authorities willing and able to pay the price of true enforcement. That it probably would have meant the abolition of many cherished rights—from habeas corpus to search and seizure restraints—seems fairly obvious. We might no longer have a constitutional democracy, but we could be alcohol and drug free. The history of authoritarian governments shows that few laws are truly unenforceable.

The line between laws that are unenforceable and those for which the price of enforcement is too high is not easily drawn. Indeed, a favorite argument of those opposed to legislation is to suggest that though the goals be laudable, enforcement is problematic. Opponents of civil rights legislation frequently rationalized their views in the 1950s and 1960s by suggesting that "you can't legislate social relations."

Although such arguments frequently serve as smokescreens for substantive objections, it is true that some laws are considerably more likely to produce compliance than others. The more a law disrupts existing social or economic relations, the less likely it is to be widely accepted. Although logic would suggest that such a law would be unlikely to pass, there are numerous exceptions to this logic.

First, in some cases of more or less blatant hypocrisy (especially involving issues of morality) it is not unusual for people to express their higher aspirations in laws that they may not feel personally constrained to obey. Years ago, Ernst Freund observed how the void left by the decline of ecclesiastical authority in areas as diverse as marriage, gambling, and even fraud and defamation came gradually to be filled by the state. In both England and the United States, it was "with the advance of democracy [that] the legislative policy toward these evils becomes gradually more aggressive."[55] They have also been notoriously unsuccessful in part for the same reasons that the ecclesiastical authorities failed to abolish sin. Just as the worst sinners are often found among the loudest voices in the Sunday choir, so were some of the Congress's biggest lushes among the loudest public champions of Prohibition.[56]

A second kind of popular yet unenforceable law is one that targets passionate minorities. The true believer who takes pride in his or her deviance from popular norms may even take pride in publicly flaunting the laws targeted at his or her behavior. Behavior that can essentially be kept private is another area in which social vetoes are frequently invoked. Although laws against sodomy, narcotics, and spouse abuse come immediately to mind, there are a host of common activities that more subtly defy statutory control. Small businesses regularly defy environmental laws, safety codes, and affirmative action principles that their larger counterparts cannot. Moreover, the law and its enforcement tend to encourage such defiance by (logically) targeting punitive action against the big guys. An understaffed regulatory agency would quite properly be seen as wasting its resources if it targeted its enforcement activities at the small fry while letting the whales swim free. There are many, many statutes that recognize this by exempting various small firms from a wide variety of regulations, taxes, and other laws.

Finally, the process of legislative bargaining often produces laws that invite defiance. In a characteristic scenario, liberals—eager to establish a new statutory principle—attempt to win the support of more moderate colleagues by weakening the law's enforcement provisions. Or a clever industrial lobbyist suggests a few "technical" amendments to a pending bill that will ensure protracted litigation when and if the law is ever enforced. Businessmen and women sometimes violate the law by inadvertence, sometimes in the hope that they will not be caught. "But a goodly number of violations are probably the result of conscious deliberation on the part of corporate executives who believe the benefits to be obtained from violating the law outweigh the costs that might accrue to themselves and the corporation."[57] One study of violations of the law by Fortune 500 companies found 477 of them subject to some sort of penalty in one two-year period. Almost half were warnings or product recalls, and in some cases they involved small fines that in effect become part of the cost of doing business.[58]

---- ❋ ----

CONCLUSION: LAW AND SOCIAL COMBAT

Late in 1990, George Bush vetoed a bill amending the Civil Rights Act of 1964 and other laws on employment discrimination. The Civil Rights Act of 1990, as the bill was called, was explicitly designed to overrule a series of Supreme Court decisions in its 1988 and 1989 terms that—from the perspective of the Leadership Conference on Civil Rights and other representatives of minority groups—seriously crippled their ability to enforce the antidiscrimination sections of the earlier statutes. Both before and after the veto, representatives of the White House met with key legislators and with Ralph Neas, executive director of the Leadership Conference, in attempts to work out compromise language. According to at least one published account, both the president's advisors and the bill's congressional supporters were divided as to both substance and strategy.[59] Among the many issues in dispute was the administration's insistence on severely limiting the ability of women and members of religious minorities from collecting punitive damages for past acts of discrimination. This, as one civil rights attorney told us, "is a virtual license to discriminate." Absent significant penalties, in other words, many corporations would simply defy the law.

It is not our purpose here to elaborate this case: after many complex maneuvers, the president eventually signed a bill. We describe it to underscore the mixing of legislative, executive, and judicial; of public and private that characterizes the process of making public policy; but there is still one step left in the continuing process of combat on the legislative terrain—that of changing the terrain itself.

13

---✳---

REFORMING THE
SYSTEM

T he mid-1990s seem destined, like the 1970s, to produce one of the periodic tides in the history of Congress that subsequent scholars will identify with "reform." If the changes of the 1970s gave us a "postreform Congress," it will be amusing if not instructive to see what label will be affixed to the rereformed Congress of the late 1990s.

Certain landmark legislative acts define key turning points in the history of Congress. The revolt against Speaker Cannon in 1911, the Legislative Reorganization Act of 1946, and the various acts of the House, the Senate, and the House Democratic caucuses in the "post-Watergate" session of 1975–76 were watersheds of this kind that may well be replicated in 1993 and 1994. Such dramatic flashes of change often blind observers to the fact that change in the electoral system, congressional organization, and formal and informal rules is a continuing process. The legislative process is altered almost daily by state laws, courts, executive decisions, and acts of the Congress itself. Many of these changes are pushed by people who would recoil in horror from the prospect of being known as reformers. Yet, if they are really serious about legislative strategy, they know that efforts to change the system are used by all major participants in the legislative process.

Change has many sources. Some proposed reforms are little more than grandstand plays designed to impress constituents or a wider public. Others are founded in deep thinking about long- or short-term ideals for a more orderly society, better relationships among the branches of government, or how decisions are made about particular policy issues. Some people effect changes in the system without knowing it: in working to shape policy through legislation they do something that actually has the effect of institutional reform. Many other changes derive from the sometimes acknowledged self-interest of their proponents in making it easier to pursue a legislative agenda. All have consequences. An entire book could be written (and some have) exploring the pros and cons of a single major proposal.

It is not our purpose here to provide a laundry list of proposals that may or should appear on an agenda of legislative reform for the 1990s. In using a few illustrations, we seek to underscore the connections between power and reform that experienced legislative strategists almost intuitively understand. Just as Clausewitz described war as an extension of diplomacy, so is reform an aspect of legislative strategy.

------------------ ✳ ------------------

THE CONGRESSIONAL CONTESTANTS

If a theme can be abstracted from the many diverse campaigns for the House and Senate in 1992, it clearly revolves around the word *change*. In many cases, the kinds of changes proposed involved the functioning of the political system itself, in particular with the ways in which we choose our elected officials. Few issues cut more closely to the bones of our system of government.

Were it not a strategic issue, nonvoting would be a major scandal. The citizens of the United States are considerably less likely to vote than those of any other functioning democracy in the world. The problem, moreover, could be substantially addressed by a few simple changes in the rules. Easier registration, longer election days (perhaps even a move to Sunday, as in many European countries), and more publicly funded information on campaigns would certainly contribute to a marked expansion of the suffrage. In a society of highly sophisticated personal identification systems, the argument that making voting easier would increase the likelihood of fraud is essentially a decoy for those who feel most threatened by an expanded electorate. Nonvoters are not a random sample of the population. They are considerably more mobile, younger, less educated, and less affluent than those who do vote. Although the public debate on the so-called motor voter idea has been framed in terms of fraud and democratic values, the real issues are strategic. When congressional Democrats overwhelmingly supported, and President Bush vetoed, bills that would have linked renewals of driving licenses with voter registration, the real issue—more or less openly acknowledged by both sides—was a sense that nonvoters, if registered, would be more likely to vote Democratic. Laws that make it easier to vote are generally likely to be supported by Democrats and the groups that benefit from having more Democrats in office, and opposed by Republicans and their allies. As one Republican strategist admitted, "I don't want everyone to vote. Our leverage in the election quite candidly goes up as the voting population goes down."[1]

There is another level of calculation that lurks at a deeper, seldom-acknowledged level of this issue, a level that accounts for the fact that many states controlled by Democrats have done little to make voting a less costly activity. Here we confront the fact that election laws are made by elected

officials, those who have succeeded under the existing rules of the game. Whatever their party allegiances or political ideologies may be, each of them is likely
to feel at least slightly threatened by changes in the rules that worked for them
before. Even if an expanded electorate was more Democratic, an elected Democratic official has no guarantee that the new voters would support him or her in
a primary race.

The electoral advantages provided by incumbency are enormous, particularly for members of the House. To the extent that these advantages are built
upon policy responses—that is, to the extent that incumbents are getting re-
elected because they are doing what their constituents want them to do—there
is no real incumbency problem. To the extent that it is built upon unfair
advantage—gerrymandered districts, disproportionate access to campaign finances, and the use of staff resources to perform constituent services and gain
name recognition—it is quite plausible to argue that increased incumbency
produces increased isolation of the governing community. This latter feeling
underlies much of the sentiment in favor of various proposals to set fixed term
limits such as the twelve-year restriction adopted in Colorado in 1990 and by
fourteen other states in 1992.

Such term limitations are of dubious constitutionality. They are also bad
law, as are most laws that restrict the options available to the electorate. To lose
the knowledge that comes with legislative experience is to relinquish influence to
those who have subject-matter expertise.[2] A case can be made for periodic
infusions of new blood, but the idea of limiting MCs to twelve or fewer years in
office seems rather clearly to have more to do with weakening the Congress vis-
à-vis other actors in the system. "In a capital city in which expertise is power, the
frequent circulation of amateur legislators would only increase the relative influence of the permanent congressional staff, the federal bureaucracy, and the
entrenched Washington establishment of lobbyists and insiders."[3] Whatever the
merits of the particular case, for example, it is highly unlikely that the American
people ever would have known about their government's aid to the Iraqi government in the period leading up to its invasion of Kuwait. Only the long experience
and extensive contacts of Representative Henry Gonzalez (D-TX) could begin to
counter the administration's efforts to hide its embarassing prewar embrace of
Saddam Hussein.

Rather than deny voters the chance to reelect those who really are doing
good jobs; rather than restrict the capacity of the Congress to oversee the
bureaucracy and provide needed constituent services, the more logical direction of reform is toward a leveling of the campaign playing field. Devices such
as public financing of campaigns, free media, and postal privileges for challengers offer one rather obvious avenue. Restrictions on gerrymandering, though
less likely to have significant effects on competition, may provide another
avenue of possible reform.[4] Perhaps the most important method of increasing
electoral competition is that of increasing the ability of party organizations to
effectively recruit candidates and compete for votes.

If there is one thing on this list that unites virtually all contemporary
politicians and lobbyists (privately, at least), it is a profound distaste for the

current system of campaign finance. Lobbyists and PAC directors resent being "shaken down" by politicians almost as much as politicians resent having to devote so much of their time and energy to shaking the money tree. Yet the chances of significant reform in this area are slim, again because strategic calculations dictate markedly different directions for change. "In this and other electoral reforms, currently successful officeholders are not likely to become advocates of change, preferring, instead, to drag their feet and throw up smokescreens of scary rhetoric."[5] Although the unusually large number of nonincumbents arriving in Washington offers an almost unique opportunity for electoral reform, the chance of deadlock in this area is high. Absent an aroused public, elected politicians can be trusted with electoral reforms as foxes can be counted upon to guard chicken coops.

---------------- ✳ ----------------

REFORMING CONGRESSIONAL STRUCTURE

Reducing the number of subcommittees, reducing the number of committees on which a member can serve, eliminating organizational redundancies and jurisdictional overlaps—all these reforms and more seem subject to the principle of perpetual reorganization, which in itself is probably a good thing. The notion that there is some rational, "best" way of arranging committee jurisdictions is not. With appropriate irony, Harold Seidman has noted that,

> In ancient times alchemists believed implicitly in the existence of a philosopher's stone which would provide the key to the universe and, in effect, solve all of the problems of mankind. The quest for coordination is in many respects the twentieth-century equivalent of the medieval search for the philosopher's stone. If we can only find the right formula for coordination, we can reconcile the irreconcilable, harmonize competing and wholly divergent interests, overcome irrationalities in our government structures, and make hard policy choices to which no one will dissent.[6]

No reorganization can escape or overcome the enormous complexity of substantive interrelationships that inhere in modern society. Any effort to simplify aspects of formal structure will create new complexities in other parts.

But just as the search for the philosopher's stone sometimes led the ancient alchemists to inadvertent discoveries, it can be a useful exercise for the Congress to periodically reexamine and redefine its committee system. Change for the sake of change is not silly, except for those people who have a vested interest in existing power relationships. The sweeping reforms proposed by the Bolling Committee in 1975 were largely rejected by the House. "The Select Committee's jurisdictional package threatened too many careers and political relationships to gain passage."[7] But it did open many of these relationships to public scrutiny and move the Congress to a whole series of "major renovations" that made the institution "more democratic, more responsive, more accountable, and more open to public view."[8]

There is little doubt that the Congresses of the 1990s will continue to redefine the boundaries of power between the party and committee systems. Caucus control over subcommittee chairmanships seems likely to be strengthened in the House; and despite the enormous resistance of the Senate to restraints on the prerogatives of individual senators, attacks on gridlock are high on most observers' lists of needed reforms. Even in divided government, the annual inability of Congress and the president to pass their annual appropriation bills by the October 1 deadline is a disgrace.

Reform does not necessarily mean the strengthening of an institution's capacity to act. Indeed, many of the reform proposals of the 1990s, whether by inadvertence or design, will more than likely weaken the Congress as an institution. Even a seemingly innocuous set of "ethical" reforms has implications for the distribution of power. Take, for example, the 1992 scandal surrounding the so-called House bank.[9] A few MCs (or their secretaries) will be inconvenienced by the closing of the service, and there may be some rather trivial saving of money. Despite the media attention the so-called scandal of the House bank received, it has no serious strategic or tactical significance. What makes the case of the House bank interesting is its connection with a long list of coeval attacks on congressional perquisites in general. Although it will probably make little difference in the big picture if MCs lose their free gymnasiums and cheap car washes, "reforms" that eliminate legislative perks while leaving those of executive agencies and private groups untouched can make a difference. In the short run, they diminish the time and ability of MCs to focus on questions of public policy. In the long run, they impact on the kinds of people willing to serve: how many top-flight businesspersons, lawyers, or professors are likely to give up *their* free gymnasiums and parking spaces for a job that pays less? Reductions in staff allowances are targeted even more directly to weaken the power of the legislative as opposed to the executive branch. They emanate from predictable sources.

An even more naked grab for power is the presidency's perennial quest for a line-item veto. Although the president's powers of recision and deferral are already quite substantial, there is merit to the notion that many unnecessary local projects could be stricken from omnibus spending bills by a president armed with this new power, perhaps with some real savings to the taxpayer. But there is far more to this proposed reform than meets the eye, for its real purpose is to change the overall balance of power between the branches. One doubts, on the one hand, that a president would use his or her line-item veto to eliminate the pet projects of his or her most powerful legislative allies. Can one imagine President Bush, for example, crossing Minority Leader Robert Dole (R-KS) by striking a project in Kansas? On the other hand, a president armed with the line-item veto would be able to employ its threatened use as a powerful instrument for pushing his own pet projects. Think of the leverage, for example, that a line-item veto would have given George Bush in his fight to fully fund his Star Wars program in 1992. Those key MCs trying to trim spending could be warned quite simply: "You vote for full funding or every project you propose for your district— whatever its merits—gets lined out of every bill that comes across my desk."

Such battles between the branches of the federal government (or, to put it more precisely, battles between policy advocates allied with different branches of the government) are perennial sources of "reform" proposals. So are fights for turf within the House and Senate themselves.

--- ✳ ---

CHANGING RULES AND PROCEDURES

Every two years, each newly elected class of representatives must adopt a set of rules. The Senate considers itself a continuing body whose rules carry over from one session to the next. In theory this makes it easier to change the rules of the House than those of the Senate, and it is the Senate, most observers agree, that has become most bogged down in its own procedures. The major barriers to changes in the rules of the Senate stem from its tradition of individualism and the rules on debate that give the tradition teeth. The last serious attempt to streamline Senate procedures—essentially by making it easier for the leadership to impose germaneness and time restrictions—was blocked by a filibuster in 1986.

> Lacking the authority to set the Senate agenda by the vote of simple majorities, the majority party leader must rely on minority support and, on a day-to-day basis, on unanimous consent to bring legislation to the floor. Lacking a general germaneness rule, the Senate leader cannot keep issues off the Senate floor for long. Consequently, agenda setting in the Senate is a process of negotiation, compromise, and mediation to a degree that would seem exotic in the House.[10]

Because the Senate was never meant to be efficient, such exotic rules have many fans. And for most of the Senate's history, some degree of functional efficiency was achieved through the strength of the institution's informal norms, reciprocity in particular. The Senate was saved from ossification by the fact that it has long been the world's quintessentially collegiate body.

As party lines have tightened in the 1980s and 1990s, however, and as the spirit of comity has declined, the dilemma of the Senate has become almost a metaphor for the dilemma of democracy in the United States. Absent a system of party discipline, is it possible for the Congress to represent its diverse constituents and still get things done?

Gerald Ford, when he was the House minority leader, once observed that " 'Reform' is a tricky word; change per se is not necessarily the same as progress. Each and every proposal for reform of Congress must be weighed against other suggested reforms, and all must be weighed in the balance of power between the branches of government."[11] They must also be weighed in terms of their impact on policy advocates of every stripe. Reforms are seldom neutral in intent (as Ford no doubt knew but did not say), never neutral in their effects. As Roger Davidson and Walter Oleszek concluded their study of the reforms of the 1970s,

Institutional reforms cannot insure the continued vitality of Congress. As George Mahon, chairman of the House Appropriations Committee once said, "We need more reform not of procedures and methods, we need more reform of the will." And as seasoned observers of American politics will agree, this can only arise when citizens hold their elected officials strictly accountable not only for policy initiatives but for the institutional forms through which these policies can be processed. In this as in so many other ways, we get just about the kind of government we deserve.[12]

In periods of reform, when the tides of general public opinion run strong, the scope of conflict changes and the chances that broad segments of the public will indeed give their attention to "institutional forms" increase. If the 1990s, like the 1970s, provide a flow of such heightened awareness, the possibilities for major change are strong. In the long run, however, issues of reform—like issues of policy—are decided as much by the skills of policy advocates in making their case as by the strength of their armies or the righteousness of their causes.

NOTES

Preface

1. For more than thirty years, the American Political Science Association has sponsored an annual Congressional Fellowship Program that provides a one-year residency on Capitol Hill divided between offices in the House and Senate. It is our guess that as many as half of those currently listed as legislative scholars in the discipline have worked as congressional fellows. Many others, like the authors of this book, have worked independently for members of the House or Senate.
2. Two major exceptions are the classic study of reciprocal trade by Raymond A. Bauer, Ithiel de Sola Pool, and Lewis Anthony Dexter, *American Business and Public Policy* (New York: Atherton Press, 1964) and the more timely study of the bill creating the Department of Veteran's Affairs by Paul C. Light, *Forging Legislation* (New York: W. W. Norton, 1992).
3. Bertram M. Gross, *Organizations and Their Managing* (New York: The Free Press, 1964), p. 11.
4. Edward V. Schneier and Bertram M. Gross, *The Congress Today* (New York: St. Martin's Press, 1993).
5. Thomas C. Schelling, *Choice and Consequence* (Cambridge, MA: Harvard University Press, 1984), pp. 198–99.
6. *Ibid.*, p. 199.
7. *Ibid.*, p. 202.

1 Constructing a Legislative Campaign

1. Thomas C. Schelling, *The Strategy of Conflict* (Cambridge, MA: Harvard University Press, 1960), pp. 4–5.

2. Harold Lasswell, *Politics: Who Gets What, When, How*, 3d ed. (New York: World Publishing, 1958), p. 100.
3. Bertram M. Gross, *Organizations and Their Managing* (New York: The Free Press, 1964), p. 263.
4. Schelling, *Strategy*, p. 1.
5. Karl von Clausewitz, *On War*, rev. ed. (London: K. Paul Trench, Trubner and Co., 1911), book 2, chapter 1. Admiral Mahon simplified this distinction with the suggestion that tactics begin at the point of actual contact with the enemy.
6. Calvin J. Muow and Michael B. MacKuen, "The Strategic Agenda in Legislative Politics," *American Political Science Review* 86 (March 1992): 87. This major contribution to the study of legislative politics came to our attention just as we were completing our final draft of this book. Its implications go far beyond the authors' limited claim to have shown that "agendas" are strategic.
7. Morton Grodzins, "The Federal System," in *Goals For Americans: The Report of the President's Commission on National Goals* (Englewood Cliffs, NJ: Prentice-Hall, 1960), p. 275.
8. E. E. Schattschneider, *The Semisovereign People* (New York: Holt, Rinehart and Winston, 1960), p. 48.
9. Lief Carter, *Administrative Law and Politics* (Boston: Little, Brown and Co., 1983), p. 15.
10. For a general history of the issue, see Edward G. Carmines and James A. Stimson, *Issue Evolution: Race and the Transformation of American Politics* (Princeton: Princeton University Press, 1989).
11. Daniel M. Berman, *It Is So Ordered* (New York: W. W. Norton, 1966), p. 31.
12. Gary Orfield, *The Reconstruction of Southern Education* (New York: John Wiley and Sons, 1969), p. 360.
13. Senator Edward M. Kennedy (D-MA) quoted in the Congressional Quarterly's *Weekly Report*, 25 March 1972, p. 641.
14. President Richard M. Nixon in *ibid.*, p. 647.
15. A number of instances in which Congress "reversed" the Court are described in the classic unsigned note, "Congressional Review of Supreme Court Decisions: 1945–1957," *Harvard Law Review* 71 (1958):1324.
16. Stephen K. Bailey and Edith K. Mosher, *ESEA: The Office of Education Administers a Law* (Syracuse, NY: Syracuse University Press, 1968), p. 185.
17. Herbert Kaufman, *Red Tape* (Washington, DC: The Brookings Institution, 1977), pp. 15–16.
18. Martha Derthick and Paul J. Quirk, *The Politics of Deregulation* (Washington, DC: The Brookings Institution, 1985), p. 26.
19. Murray Weidenbaum, *The Modern Public Sector* (New York: Basic Books, 1969), p. 11.
20. American Federation of State, County, and Municipal Employees, *Passing the Bucks* (Washington, DC: AFSCME, 1983), p. 9.
21. Michael Lipsky, "Protest as a Political Resource," *American Political Science Review* 62 (December 1968): 1154.
22. Quoted in Charles Clapp, *The Congressman* (Washington, DC: The Brookings Institution, 1963; Garden City, NY: Doubleday Anchor, 1964), p. 158. It is possible for this strategy to backfire, as other members of the Brookings roundtable pointed out. Since few of the bills introduced in any given session are likely to pass, opposing candidates may be able to make political capital of the poor "batting average" of the ambitious sponsor.

23. Lewis Anthony Dexter, *How Organizations Are Represented in Washington* (Indianapolis: Bobbs-Merrill, 1969), p. 59.
24. Paul Light, *Artful Work: The Politics of Social Security Reform* (New York: Random House, 1985), chap. 16.
25. John W. Kingdon, *Agendas, Alternatives, and Public Policies* (Boston: Little, Brown and Co., 1984), p. 170.
26. Hugh Heclo, *A Government of Strangers* (Washington, DC: The Brookings Institution, 1977), p. 226.
27. William P. Browne, *Private Interests, Public Policy, and American Agriculture* (Lawrence: University Press of Kansas, 1988), p. 101.
28. Representative Barney Frank (D-MA), quoted in Hedrick Smith, *The Power Game* (New York: Random House, 1988), p. 666.
29. Senator William Armstrong (R-CO), quoted in the *New York Times*, 25 September 1987, p. 22.
30. Richard E. Neustadt, *Presidential Clearance of Legislation* (unpublished doctoral dissertation, Harvard University, 1950), p. 172.
31. *Grove City College v. Bell*, 464 U.S. 555 (1984).
32. Morris S. Ogul, *Congress Oversees the Bureaucracy* (Pittsburgh: University of Pittsburgh Press, 1976), p. 161.
33. Aaron Wildavsky, *The Politics of the Budgetary Process*, 4th ed. (Boston: Little, Brown and Co., 1984), p. 101.
34. Clifford J. Durr, "The Defense Plant Corporation," in Harold Stein, ed., *Public Administration and Policy Development* (New York: Harcourt, Brace and Co., 1952), p. 294.
35. Elizabeth Brenner Drew, "The Quiet Victory of the Cigarette Lobby," *Atlantic Monthly*, September 1965, p. 76.
36. V. O. Key, Jr., "Legislative Control," in Fritz Morstein Marx, ed., *Elements of Public Administration* (New York: Prentice-Hall, 1946), p. 351.
37. Harold Seidman, *Politics, Position, and Power*, 2nd ed. (New York: Oxford, 1975), pp. 65–66.
38. Arthur F. Bentley, *The Process of Government* (Bloomington: Principia Press, reissue, 1949), p. 353.
39. George E. Reedy, *The U.S. Senate* (New York: New American Library, 1986), pp. 202, 203.
40. Quoted in Norman John Powell, *Responsible Public Bureaucracy in the United States* (Boston: Allyn and Bacon, 1967), p. 12.
41. *Ibid.*

---- ✳ ----

2 Contestants for Power

1. Sun Tzu (trans. Thomas Cleary), *The Art of War* (Boston: Shambhala Publications, 1988), p. 56.
2. E. E. Schattschneider, *The Semisovereign People* (New York: Holt, Rinehart and Winston, 1960), p. 4.
3. Lawrence F. O'Brien, *No Final Victories* (New York: Ballantine Books, 1974), p. 249.
4. The most comprehensive listing, compiled largely from official registrations with the Clerk of the House of Representatives and updated annually, is Arthur C. Close,

John P. Greff, and Regina Germain, eds., *Washington Representatives* (Washington, DC: Columbia Books, various years).

5. Of the six thousand individuals and groups who actually filed official reports in 1989, about 62 percent filed late and more than 90 percent submitted incomplete forms. Milton Socolar, *Federal Lobbying: Federal Regulation of Lobbying Act of 1946 Is Ineffective,* testimony before the Subcommittee of Government Management, Senate Subcommittee on Governmental Affairs, reprinted as General Accounting Office Document T-GGD-91-56, July 16, 1991.

6. Paul W. Cherington and Ralph L. Gillen, *The Business Representative in Washington* (Washington, DC: The Brookings Institution, 1962), p. 7.

7. James Q. Wilson, *Political Organizations* (New York: Basic Books, 1973), p. 152.

8. Graham K. Wilson, *Interest Groups in the United States* (New York: Oxford University Press, 1981), p. 78.

9. J. David Greenstone, *Labor in American Politics* (New York: Alfred A. Knopf, 1969), pp. 321–22.

10. Paul Edward Johnson, "Organized Labor in an Era of Blue-Collar Decline," in Allan J. Cigler and Burdett A. Loomis, eds., *Interest Group Politics*, 3d ed. (Washington, DC: Congressional Quarterly Press, 1991), p. 39.

11. Andrew S. McFarland, *Common Cause: Lobbying in the Public Interest* (Chatham, NJ: Chatham House, 1984), p. 43. For a more restrictive definition, one that insists that a public interest lobby is one whose goals do not materially advance its members' interests, see Jeffrey M. Berry, *Lobbying for the People* (Princeton: Princeton University Press, 1977), pp. 6–10.

12. *Ibid.*, p. 3.

13. Harold Wilensky, *Organizational Intelligence* (New York: Basic Books, 1967), p. 48.

14. Louis Fisher, *President and Congress* (New York: The Free Press, 1972), pp. 85–100.

15. Abraham Holtzman, *Legislative Liaison: Executive Leadership in Congress* (Chicago: Rand-McNally and Co., 1970), p. 2.

16. Douglass Cater, *Power in Washington* (New York: Vintage Books, 1964) popularized and Ernest S. Griffith, *The Impasse of Democracy* (New York: Harrison-Hilton Books, 1939) introduced these terms and the important concepts underlying them.

17. R. Douglas Arnold, *Congress and the Bureaucracy* (New Haven: Yale University Press, 1979), pp. 50–51.

18. See, for example, the case studies in Alan F. Westin, ed., *Whistle-Blowing!* (New York: McGraw-Hill, 1981).

19. David H. Haider, *When Governments Come to Washington* (New York: The Free Press, 1974), p. 55.

20. Karl von Clausewitz, *Principles of War* (Harrisburg, PA: Military Service Publishing Co., 1942), p. 19.

21. Quoted in Norman J. Ornstein and Shirley Elder, *Interest Groups, Lobbying and Policymaking* (Washington, DC: Congressional Quarterly Press, 1978), p. 72.

22. We refer, of course, to the survivors and not the guest of honor, who—in most earthly jurisdictions—has lost his or her right to vote.

23. Corinne Lathrop Gilb, *Hidden Hierarchies* (New York: Harper and Row, 1966), p. 217.

24. John T. Tierney, "Organized Interests and the Nation's Capitol," in Mark P. Petracca, ed., *The Politics of Interests: Interest Groups Transformed* (Boulder, CO: Westview Press, 1992), p. 211.

25. Robert J. Massie, Jr., "Giving America the Business," *The Nation* 234 (May 8, 1982): 551.

26. Robert H. Salisbury, "An Exchange Theory of Interest Groups," *Midwest Journal of Political Science* 8 (January 1969): 1–32.
27. *Ibid.*
28. David B. Truman, *The Governmental Process* (New York: Alfred A. Knopf, 1951), p. 167.
29. *Ibid.*, pp. 161–62.
30. *Ibid.*, p. 337.
31. Richard E. Neustadt, *Presidential Power*, 2d ed. (New York: John Wiley and Sons, 1976), pp. 132–33.
32. *Ibid.*, p. 135.
33. *Ibid.*, p. 148.
34. Michael J. Malbin, "Rhetoric and Leadership: A Look Backward at the Carter National Energy Plan," in Anthony King, ed., *Both Ends of the Avenue* (Washington, DC: American Enterprise Institute, 1983), p. 231.
35. Jeffrey M. Berry, *The Interest Group Society* (Boston: Little, Brown and Co., 1984), p. 97.
36. Michael T. Hayes, *Lobbyists and Legislators* (New Brunswick, NJ: Rutgers University Press, 1981), p. 62.
37. For an extreme case to the contrary, see James Boyd, *Above the Law* (New York: New American Library, 1968). Boyd was the administrative assistant to Senator Thomas J. Dodd (D-CT), whose leaks to the press led to Dodd's Senate censure and ultimate defeat.
38. John W. Kingdon, *Congressmen's Voting Decisions*, 2d ed. (New York: Harper and Row, 1981), chap. 10.
39. Thomas Sowell, *Knowledge and Decisions* (New York: Basic Books, 1985), p. 9.
40. Tierney, "Organized Interests," p. 216.
41. Lester W. Milbrath, *The Washington Lobbyists* (Chicago: Rand-McNally, 1963), p. 68.
42. Quoted in Joseph C. Goulden, *The Superlawyers* (New York: Weybright and Talley, 1971), pp. 142–43.
43. Edward O. Laumann and John P. Heinz with Robert L. Nelson and Robert H. Salisbury, "Washington Lawyers and Others: The Structure of Washington Representation," *Stanford Law Review* 37 (January 1985): 490–91.
44. Milbrath, *Washington Lobbyists*, pp. 140–41.
45. *Ibid.*, pp. 141–42.
46. Quoted in Ornstein and Elder, *Interest Groups*, p. 79.
47. Charles S. Mack, *Lobbying and Government Relations* (New York: Quorum Books, 1989), pp. 58–59.
48. *Ibid.*
49. Kay Lehman Schlozman and John T. Tierney, "More of the Same: Washington Pressure Group Activity in a Decade of Change," *Journal of Politics* 45 (May 1983): 365.
50. See, for example, the case cited in Charles Clapp, *The Congressman: His Work As He Sees It* (Garden City, NY: Doubleday Anchor, 1964), pp. 194–95.
51. Quoted in Roger H. Davidson and Walter J. Oleszek, *Congress and Its Members* (Washington, DC: Congressional Quarterly Press, 1981), p. 358.
52. Cherington and Gillen, *Business Representative*, p. 59.
53. Clapp, *The Congressman*, p. 190.
54. Michael T. Hayes, *Incrementalism and Public Policy* (New York: Longman, 1992), p. 49.

55. Elizabeth Drew, "Charlie," in Cigler and Loomis, eds., *Interest Group Politics,* p. 230. Originally published in the *New Yorker,* 9 January 1978.
56. Bruce C. Wolpe, *Lobbying Congress* (Washington, DC: Congressional Quarterly Press, 1990), p. 37.
57. Hayes, *Incrementalism,* p. 52.
58. Kay Lehman Schlozman and John T. Tierney, *Organized Interests and American Democracy* (New York: Harper and Row, 1986), p. 398. These variables are to some extent manipulable. A key lobbying skill, as we shall argue in subsequent chapters, is the ability to change the visibility or perceived character of an issue.
59. For an extended and interesting discussion of the different patterns of power manifest on different kinds of issues, see David C. Kozak, *Contexts of Congressional Decision Behavior* (Lanham, NY: University Press of America, 1984).
60. Schattschneider, *The Semisovereign People,* pp. 34–35.
61. *Ibid.,* p. 2.

3   *The Legislative Terrain*

1. Donald R. Matthews, *The Social Background of Political Decision-Makers* (New York: Random House, 1954), p. 41.
2. *The Federalist,* no. 57 (New York: Modern Library, n.d.), p. 372.
3. Richard F. Fenno, Jr., *Home Style: House Members in Their Districts* (Boston: Little, Brown and Co., 1978), p. 24.
4. *Ibid.,* p. 18.
5. John Kingdon, *Candidates for Office: Beliefs and Strategies* (New York: Random House, 1966), p. 45.
6. Fenno, *Home Style,* p. 234.
7. *Ibid.,* p. 35.
8. *Ibid.,* p. 192.
9. Bruce Cain, John Ferejohn, and Morris Fiorina, *The Personal Vote* (Cambridge, MA: Harvard University Press, 1987), p. 228.
10. John L. Jackley, *Hill Rat* (Washington, DC: Regnery Gateway, 1992), p. 104.
11. Glenn R. Parker, *Homeward Bound: Explaining Changes in Congressional Behavior* (Pittsburgh: University of Pittsburgh Press, 1986), p. 153.
12. Fenno, *Home Style,* p. 185.
13. John F. Bibby, *Congress Off the Record* (Washington, DC: American Enterprise Institute, 1983), p. 49.
14. Much of the data on contributions in this chapter are taken from various reports of the Federal Election Commission. These are available from the commission and in most depository libraries. According to these reports, the peak year for PACs was 1988: 4,268 filed reports. Of the 4,172 filing in 1990, 1,795 were corporate; 1,062 were independent organizations; 774 were trade and related associations; and 346 were labor-affiliated.
15. For discovering this lovely contradiction we are indebted to Larry Sabato, "Parties, PACs, and Independent Groups," in Thomas E. Mann and Norman J. Ornstein, eds., *The American Elections of 1982* (Washington, DC: American Enterprise Institute, 1983), pp. 72, 87.
16. Quoted in Mark Green, *Who Runs Congress?* (New York: Bantam Books, 1979), p. 14.

17. Steven F. Stockmayer, executive vice president of the National Association of Business PACs, quoted in Charles R. Babcock and Richard Morin, "Following the Path of Self-Interest," *Washington Post* (National Weekly Edition), 25 June–1 July 1990, p. 14.
18. Janet M. Grenzke, "PACs and the Congressional Suppliant: The Currency is Complex," *American Journal of Political Science* 33 (February 1989): 9.
19. Quoted in The Center for Responsive Politics, *PACs on PACs: The View from the Inside* (Washington, DC: Center for Responsive Politics, 1988), p. 32.
20. Alexander Heard, *The Costs of Democracy* (Garden City, NY: Doubleday, 1962), p. 96.
21. Edward M. Epstein, "Business and Labor under the Federal Election Campaign Act of 1971," in Michael J. Malbin, ed., *Parties, Interest Groups, and Campaign Finance Laws* (Washington, DC: American Enterprise Institute, 1980), p. 140.
22. Heard, *Costs of Democracy*, p. 104.
23. Gary C. Jacobson, *The Politics of Congressional Elections*, 2d ed. (Boston: Little, Brown and Co., 1987), p. 65.
24. R. Kenneth Godwin, *One Billion Dollars of Influence* (Chatham, NJ: Chatham House, 1988), p. 132.
25. *Ibid.*, p. 133. The study cited by Godwin is Kirk Brown, "Campaign Contributions and Congressional Voting," unpublished paper delivered at the 1983 Annual Meeting of the American Political Science Association.
26. Justin Dart, quoted in Larry Sabato, *PAC Power* (New York: W. W. Norton, 1984), p. 122.
27. David Jessup, "Can Political Influence Be Democratized? A Labor Perspective," in Malbin, ed., *Parties*, p. 27.
28. Norman J. Ornstein, Thomas E. Mann, and Michael J. Malbin, *Vital Statistics on Congress 1991–1992* (Washington, DC: Congressional Quarterly Press, 1992), p. 125.
29. David W. Brady, "Personnel Management in the House," in Joseph Cooper and G. Calvin MacKenzie, eds., *The House at Work* (Austin: University of Texas Press, 1981), p. 152.
30. Joel D. Aberbach, *Keeping a Watchful Eye* (Washington, DC: The Brookings Institution, 1990), p. 81.
31. Harrison W. Fox, Jr., and Susan W. Hammond, *Congressional Staffs: The Invisible Force in American Lawmaking* (New York: The Free Press, 1977), p. 66.
32. The congressional pay raises of the 1990s lifted the ceiling for staff salaries as well, so that by mid-1992 there were some eighty-eight Senate staffers with six-figure incomes. Twenty of those making over $100,000 were on the staffs of individual senators. Jeffrey Berman and Shawn Westfall, "88 Staffers in Senate Now Make $100,000+" *Roll Call*, 11 June 1992, p. 13. For individual offices, the clerk hire allowance is a lump sum. Thus, the MC who has one highly paid aide probably has a number of poor peons as well. Many lobbyists have expense accounts (not to mention salaries) that exceed the salaries of those legislative aides they seek to influence.
33. These figures are calculated from the clerk hire reports for the fourth quarter of 1990 in the *Report of the Clerk of the House*, 102d Congress, 1st session (1991).
34. The term, which describes professional staffers who move from office to office, is from John Jackley's generally poor but occasionally insightful "insider" account of life on the Hill. See note 10 of this chapter.
35. Commission on Administrative Review, United States House of Representatives,

Final Report, vol. 1, (Washington, DC: Government Printing Office, 1977), pp. 672–73.

36. Fox and Hammond, *Congressional Staffs,* p. 27.
37. See Robert H. Salisbury and Kenneth Shepsle, "Congressional Staff Turnover and the Ties-That-Bind," *American Political Science Review* 75 (June 1981): 381–96.
38. Arthur Maass, *Congress and the Common Good* (New York: Basic Books, 1983), p. 115.
39. Former Senator William Hathaway (D-ME), quoted in Maurice B. Tobin (ed. Joan Shaffer), *Hidden Power* (Westport, CT: Greenwood Press, 1986), p. 90.
40. Frank Church (D-ID), quoted in *ibid.,* p. 91.
41. Michael J. Malbin, *Unelected Representatives: Congressional Staff and the Future of Representative Government* (New York: Basic Books, 1980), p. 239.
42. Brady, "Personnel Management," p. 154.
43. Malbin, *Unelected Representatives,* chap. 10, *passim.*
44. The distinction between line and staff is not always clear and can be misleading if it is assumed that staff officers do not control programs. A budget bureau—or for that matter, a congressional appropriations committee—is strictly speaking a staff agency. But by determining the amount that can be spent on each agency's policy it has a lot of effective programmatic power. For an elaboration of this point, see Gerald G. Fisch, "Line-Staff Is Obsolete," *Harvard Business Review* 39 (September–October 1961): 67–79.
45. Roger H. Davidson and Walter J. Oleszek, *Congress against Itself* (Bloomington: Indiana University Press, 1977), p. 264.
46. *Ibid.,* p. 219.
47. Walter J. Oleszek, *Congressional Procedures and the Policy Process* (Washington, DC: Congressional Quarterly Press, 1978), p. 55.
48. Abner J. Mikva and Patti B. Saris, *The American Congress* (New York: Franklin Watts, 1983), p. 148.
49. Steven S. Smith and Christopher J. Deering, *Committees in Congress* (Congressional Quarterly Press, 1984), p. 135.
50. *Ibid.,* p. 149.
51. Heinz Eulau, "The Committees in a Revitalized Congress," in Alfred de Grazia, ed., *Congress: The First Branch of Government* (Garden City, NY: Doubleday, 1967), p. 210.
52. Richard F. Fenno, Jr., *Congressmen in Committees* (Boston: Little, Brown and Co., 1973).
53. *Ibid.,* p. 108.
54. Smith and Deering, *Committees,* pp. 139–40.
55. *Ibid.,* p. 143.
56. Roger H. Davidson, "Congressional Leaders As Agents of Change," in Frank H. Mackaman, ed., *Understanding Congressional Leadership* (Washington, DC: Congressional Quarterly Press, 1981), p. 136.
57. The president pro tempore is usually the most senior member of the majority party. Although he or she is fourth in line of succession to the presidency and receives such perquisites as a private limousine, the office is largely ceremonial.
58. Steven S. Smith, "The Senate in the Postreform Era," in Roger H. Davidson, ed., *The Postreform Congress* (New York: St. Martin's Press, 1991), p. 182.
59. Steven S. Smith, *Call to Order: Floor Politics in the House and Senate* (Washington, DC: The Brookings Institution, 1989), p. 44.
60. We use this rather vague term because variations in the kinds of rules "are now so

numerous and complicated that the most conventional labels—modified open and modified closed rules—no longer do justice to their richness." Stanley S. Bach and Steven S. Smith, *Managing Uncertainty in the House of Representatives* (Washington, DC: The Brookings Institution, 1988), p. 55.

61. *Ibid.*, pp. 56–57.
62. Kiewiet and McCubbins make an interesting case that House Appropriations never was as strong an independent force as Fenno describes it, but rather that its members are "agents of their respective parties." D. Roderick Kiewiet and Matthew D. McCubbins, *The Logic of Delegation* (Chicago: University of Chicago Press, 1991), p. 63.
63. Robert Bendiner, *Obstacle Course on Capitol Hill* (New York: McGraw-Hill, 1964), p. 16.
64. Lewis A. Froman, Jr., *The Congressional Process* (Boston: Little, Brown and Co., 1967), p. 17.
65. Wendell Johnson, "The Fateful Process of Mr. A Talking to Mr. B," *Harvard Business Review* 31 (January–February 1953): 49–56.

---

4 Establishing Influence

1. Joseph M. Bessette, "Is Congress a Deliberative Body?" in Dennis Hale, ed., *The United States Congress* (Chestnut Hill, MA: Boston College, 1982), p. 10.
2. *Ibid.*, p. 9.
3. Bernard Asbell, *The Senate Nobody Knows* (Baltimore: Johns Hopkins University Press, 1978), p. 114.
4. Ross K. Baker, *Friend and Foe in the U.S. Senate* (New York: The Free Press, 1980), p. 40.
5. Quoted in John R. Hibbing, *Choosing to Leave* (Washington, DC: University Press of America, 1982), p. 90.
6. Norman J. Ornstein, "Can Congress Be Led?" in John J. Kornacki, ed., *Leading Congress: New Styles, New Strategies* (Washington, DC: Congressional Quarterly Press, 1990), p. 14.
7. *Ibid.*
8. *Ibid.*, p. 38.
9. David R. Mayhew, *Congress: The Electoral Connection* (New Haven: Yale University Press, 1974).
10. Walter F. Murphy, *Elements of Judicial Strategy* (Chicago: University of Chicago Press, 1964), p. 49.
11. Baker, *Friend and Foe*, p. 147.
12. Hubert Humphrey (D-MN), quoted in Merle Miller, *Lyndon: An Oral Biography* (New York: G. P. Putnam's Sons, 1980), p. 149.
13. Clem Miller (ed. John W. Baker), *Member of the House* (New York: Scribners, 1962), pp. 105–6.
14. Baker, *Friend and Foe,* p. 137.
15. *Ibid.*, p. 46.
16. Miller, *Member,* p. 106.
17. *Ibid.*, pp. 39–41.
18. Baker, *Friend and Foe,* p. 45.
19. Murphy, *Elements,* p. 54.

20. Quoted in James A. Miller, *Running in Place* (New York: Simon and Schuster, 1986), p. 83.

21. Quoted in Samuel C. Patterson, "Party Leadership in the U.S. Senate," in John Hibbing, ed., *The Changing World of the U.S. Senate* (Berkeley, CA: IGS Press, 1990), p. 90.

22. Randall B. Ripley, *Party Leaders in the House of Representatives* (Washington, DC: The Brookings Institution, 1967), p. 159.

23. Edmund Muskie (D-ME), quoted in Asbell, *The Senate Nobody Knows*, p. 210.

24. An MC, quoted in Donald R. Matthews and James A. Stimson, *Yeas and Nays* (New York: John Wiley and Sons, 1975), p. 86.

25. Quoted in Baker, *Friend and Foe*, p. 43.

26. Matthews and Stimson, *Yeas and Nays*, p. 61.

27. Neil MacNeil, *Dirksen: Portrait of a Public Man* (New York: World Publishing, 1970), p. 137.

28. Niccolo Machiavelli, *The Prince* (New York: Modern Library, 1950), pp. 64, 63.

29. Asbell, *The Senate Nobody Knows*, pp. 120–21.

30. John F. Bibby, *Congress Off the Record* (Washington, DC: American Enterprise Institute, 1983), p. 26.

31. Doris Kearns, *Lyndon Johnson and the American Dream* (New York: Harper and Row, 1976), p. 117.

32. Randall B. Ripley, *Power in the Senate* (New York: St. Martin's Press, 1969), p. 112.

33. Baker, *Friend and Foe*, p. 248.

34. *Ibid.*, p. 228.

35. John M. Barry, *The Ambition and the Power* (New York: Penguin Books, 1990), pp. 529–30.

36. Murphy, *Elements*, p. 82.

37. John E. Jackson, *Constituencies and Leaders in Congress* (Cambridge, MA: Harvard University Press, 1974), p. 135.

38. It can be argued that there is an optimal limit to a coalition's size, a point between being too small to be effective and too large to be cohesive. The literature on this question is extensive. Usually cited as the standard source is William H. Riker, *The Theory of Political Coalitions* (New Haven: Yale University Press, 1962).

39. John F. Manley, *The Politics of Finance* (Boston: Little, Brown and Co., 1970), p. 124.

40. John W. Kingdon, *Congressmen's Voting Decisions*, 2d ed. (New York: Harper and Row, 1981), p. 87.

41. Donald R. Matthews, *U.S. Senators and Their World* (New York: Vintage Books, 1960), pp. 216–17.

42. Bibby, *Congress*, pp. 24–25.

43. "The Helms Network," Congressional Quarterly *Weekly Report*, 6 March 1982, p. 500.

44. Michael Foley, *The New Senate* (New Haven: Yale University Press, 1980), pp. 168–69.

---- ✳ ----

5 Legislative Intelligence

1. Richard Cyert and James March, *A Behavioral Theory of the Firm* (Englewood Cliffs, NJ: Prentice-Hall, 1963), p. 86.

2. Quoted in Charles Clapp, *The Congressman: His Work As He Sees It* (Garden City, NY: Doubleday Anchor, 1964), p. 165.
3. Anthony Downs, *An Economic Theory of Democracy* (New York: Harper and Row, 1957), p. 215.
4. Stimson Bullitt, *To Be a Politician* (Garden City, NY: Doubleday, 1959), p. 54.
5. Downs, *Economic Theory*, p. 215.
6. John W. Kingdon, *Congressmen's Voting Decisions*, 3d ed. (Ann Arbor: The University of Michigan Press, 1989), p. 245.
7. *Ibid.*, p. 240.
8. Aaron Wildavsky, *The Politics of the Budgetary Process*, 4th ed. (Boston: Little, Brown and Co., 1984), p. 15.
9. Charles A. Lindblom, "The Science of 'Muddling Through,' " *Public Administration Review* 19 (Spring 1959): 79–88.
10. House of Representatives, Commission on Administrative Review, *Final Report*, 95th Cong., 1st sess., 1977, vol. 1, pp. 670–71; and David C. Kozak, "Decision Settings in Congress," in David C. Kozak and John D. Macartney, eds., *Congress and Public Policy*, 2d ed. (Chicago: Dorsey Press, 1987), p 307.
11. Quoted in Harrison W. Fox, Jr., and Susan Webb Hammond, *Congressional Staffs* (New York: The Free Press, 1977), p. 126.
12. Quoted in Louis Sandy Maisel, "Congressional Information Sources," in Joseph Cooper and G. Calvin Mackenzie, eds., *The House at Work* (Austin: University of Texas Press, 1981), p. 259.
13. Kingdon, *Congressmen's Voting Decisions*, p. 205.
14. *Ibid.*, p. 206.
15. *Ibid.*, pp. 207–8.
16. Donald R. Matthews and James A. Stimson, *Yeas and Nays: Normal Decision-Making in the U.S. House of Representatives* (New York: John Wiley and Sons, 1975), p. 32.
17. Charles A. Vanik, "Congress Is Deliberative: Compared to What?" in Dennis Hale, ed., *The United States Congress* (Chestnut Hill, MA: Boston College, 1982), pp. 18–19.
18. Matthews and Stimson, *Yeas and Nays*, p. 45.
19. On the general concept of the two-step flow of communications, see Elihu Katz and Paul F. Lazarsfeld, *Personal Influence* (Glencoe, IL: The Free Press, 1955). The concept was first applied to the legislative process in Edward Schneier, "The Intelligence of Congress: Information and Public Policy Patterns," *Annals of the American Academy of Political and Social Science* 388 (March 1970): 14–24 and a paper on the same subject delivered at the 1969 meeting of the American Political Science Association. Parts of this chapter are based on those essays. Although the concept of the two-step flow has gained widespread acceptance among students of Congress, it has lost much of its explanatory power among students of the media.
20. Alexander Hamilton, John Jay, and James Madison, *The Federalist*, no. 56 (New York: Modern Library, n.d.), p. 366.
21. *Ibid.*, no. 53, p. 351.
22. *Ibid.*, p. 352.
23. Clapp, *The Congressman*, p. 124.
24. Jack L. Walker, "The Origins and Maintenance of Interest Groups in America," *American Political Science Review* 77 (June 1983): 390–406; and Chapter 5 (with David C. King) of Walker, *Mobilizing Interest Groups in America* (Ann Arbor: University of Michigan Press, 1991).

25. Mark A. Peterson, *Legislating Together: The White House and Capitol Hill from Eisenhower to Reagan* (Cambridge, MA: Harvard University Press, 1990), p. 117.
26. Harold L. Wilensky, *Organizational Intelligence* (New York: Basic Books, 1967), p. 57.
27. Representative Thomas B. Curtis (R-MO), quoted in John S. Saloma III, *Congress and the New Politics* (Boston: Little, Brown and Co., 1969), p. 213.
28. Wilensky, *Organizational Intelligence*, p. 57.
29. The official handbook of procedure of the House once read that "generally speaking, and in the absence of convictions to the contrary, members are justified in voting with the committee." *Rules and Manual of the House of Representatives* (Washington, DC: Government Printing Office, 1963), p. 213.
30. Peterson, *Legislating Together*, p. 116.
31. David B. Truman, *The Governmental Process* (New York: Alfred A. Knopf, 1951), p. 372.
32. Clem Miller (ed. John W. Baker), *Member of the House* (New York: Charles Scribners' Sons, 1962), p. 14.
33. Commission on Administrative Review, *Final Report*, pp. 632–33.
34. For a strong argument on presidential weakness—particularly in the areas of national security and economic policy—see William F. Grover, *The President as Prisoner: A Structural Critique of the Carter and Reagan Years* (Albany: State University of New York Press, 1989).
35. Quoted in Christopher J. Bosso, *Pesticides and Politics: The Life Cycle of a Public Issue* (Pittsburgh: University of Pittsburgh Press, 1987), p. 8. Bosso's book can be read as a fine example of the way in which information systems change.
36. J. McIver Weatherford, *Tribes on the Hill* (New York: Rawson, Wade Publishers, 1981), p. 124.
37. For the extreme case, see Richard W. Boyd and David J. Hadley, "Presidential and Congressional Response to Political Crisis: Nixon, Congress and Watergate," *Congress and the Presidency* 10 (Autumn 1983): 214.
38. Quoted in Anthony King, "A Mile and a Half is a Long Way," in Anthony King, ed., *Both Ends of the Avenue* (Washington, DC: American Enterprise Institute, 1983), p. 254.
39. Eric L. Davis, "Congressional Liaison: The People and the Institutions," in King, ed., *Both Ends*, p. 81.
40. William Greider, "The Education of David Stockman," *The Atlantic* 248 (December 1981): 44–45.
41. Richard F. Fenno, Jr., *The President's Cabinet* (New York: Vintage Books, 1959), p. 198.
42. *Ibid.*, p. 199.
43. Dean Acheson, quoted in *ibid.*, p. 208.
44. Diana M. Evans, "Lobbying the Committee: Interest Groups and the House Public Works and Transportation Committee," in Allan J. Cigler and Burdett A. Loomis, eds., *Interest Group Politics* (Washington, DC: Congressional Quarterly Press, 1991), p. 259.
45. Hugh Heclo, "Issue Networks and the Executive Establishment," in King, ed., *Both Ends*, p. 103.
46. Bosso, *Pesticides and Politics*.
47. *Ibid.*, p. 12.
48. William P. Browne, "Interest Niches and the Limits of Interest Group Influence," in Cigler and Loomis, eds., *Interest Group Politics*, p. 347.

49. *Ibid.*, p. 346.
50. Jack H. Knott and Gary J. Miller, *Reforming Bureaucracy* (Englewood Cliffs, NJ: Prentice-Hall, 1987), p. 143.

———————— ✳ ————————

6 *Legislative Parenthood*

1. George F. Hoar, *Autobiography of Seventy Years*, vol. 2, (New York: Scribners, 1903), p. 363.
2. This rule has its origins in a curious incident in 1972 when "six bills separately sponsored by six different Members dealing with four aspects of the subject of fire research and safety were placed in the hopper without the knowledge of those Members. Neither the chief sponsor nor the other Members were able to explain the source of the introduction of those bills." William Holmes Brown and Lewis Deschler, *Procedure in the U.S. House of Representatives*, 4th ed. (Washington, DC: Government Printing Office, 1982), p. 175.
3. Richard Harris, *The Fear of Crime* (New York: Frederick A. Praeger, 1969), p. 21.
4. The late Senator Thomas Dodd apparently engaged in activities that very closely resemble a strike bill. According to one of his former aides, the senator in 1964 "announced an investigation of the motion-picture industry by the Juvenile Delinquency Subcommittee . . . to concern a particular kind of salacious film . . . primarily for teenage 'drive-in' audiences."

    The motion picture industry responded by preparing "a fancy brochure . . . on the evils of censorship" allegedly written by Dodd and widely circulated with his permission.

> Next, movie people showed up for a fund-raising reception for Dodd held in, of all places, Hollywood. . . . In June of 1964 [a representative of the industry, Edward] Cooper approached [Subcommittee Counsel] Carl Perian with a $500 check for Dodd's campaign. . . .
> "I can't have anything to do with money from you Ed," Carl said. "In view of our investigation, it would be improper." Cooper, unabashed, then went directly to Dodd, who accepted the check personally. . . .
> Nothing more was ever heard of the investigation.

    James Boyd, *Above the Law* (New York: New American Library, 1968), p. 184.
5. Charles Clapp, *The Congressman* (Garden City, NY: Doubleday, 1964), p. 122.
6. See, for example, Richard Fenno, *The Making of a Senator: Dan Quayle* (Washington, DC: Congressional Quarterly Press, 1989).
7. Clapp, *The Congressman*, p. 120.
8. Randall B. Ripley, *Power in the Senate* (New York: St. Martin's Press, 1969), p. 175.
9. Clapp, *The Congressman*, p. 123.
10. Quoted in Joseph A. Califano, Jr., *Governing America* (New York: Simon and Schuster, 1981), p. 93.
11. Quoted in Donald G. Tacheron and Morris K. Udall, *The Job of the Congressman* (Indianapolis: Bobbs-Merrill, 1966), p. 183.
12. Earl Latham, *The Group Basis of Politics* (Ithaca, NY: Cornell University Press, 1952), p. 190.
13. Hedrick Smith, *The Power Game* (New York: Random House, 1988), p. 54.
14. See, for example, the letter from Russ Hemminway of the National Committee for

an Effective Congress requesting cosponsorship of Representative McDonald's campaign finance bill, reprinted in Robert L. Peabody, Jeffrey M. Berry, William G. Frasure, and Jerry Goldman, *To Enact a Law* (New York: Praeger, 1972), p. 40.

15. John M. Barry, *The Ambition and the Power* (New York: Viking Books, 1989; Penguin Books, 1991), p. 93.

16. James Madison, Alexander Hamilton, and John Jay, *The Federalist,* no. 53 (New York: Modern Library, n. d.), p. 351.

17. Charles Lindblom, "The Science of 'Muddling Through,' " *Public Administration Review* 19 (Spring 1959): 79–88.

18. Frank E. Horack, Jr., "The Common Law of Legislation," *Iowa Law Review* 23 (Spring 1951): 43.

19. This examination of the Elementary and Secondary Schools Act is based on the first-rate account of Eugene Eidenberg and Roy D. Morey, *An Act of Congress* (New York: W. W. Norton, 1969), pp. 75–95.

20. Eric Redman, *The Dance of Legislation* (New York: Simon and Schuster, 1973), p. 43.

21. *Ibid., passim.*

22. In Stephen K. Bailey's *Congress Makes a Law* (New York: Vintage, 1954), Professor Gross is given some credit for his role in drafting the bill. Actually, Bailey—at Gross's request—underplayed the staff role in order to save Gross from embarrassment.

23. Carter Glass, *Adventures in Constructive Finance* (Garden City, NY: Doubleday, 1927).

24. This dialogue, along with a fascinating case study of coalition politics, is found in Congressional Quarterly, *The Washington Lobby* (Washington, DC: Congressional Quarterly, 1971), p. 75.

25. Harry Jones, "Some Reflections on a Draftsman's Time Sheet," reprinted in Frank C. Newman and Stanley S. Surrey, eds., *Legislation: Cases and Materials* (Englewood Cliffs, NJ: Prentice-Hall, 1965), p. 555.

26. *Ibid.*

27. Paul Light, *Artful Work: The Politics of Social Security Reform* (New York: Random House, 1985), p. 205.

28. Quoted in C. Lawrence Evans, "Participation and Policy Making in Senate Committees," *Political Science Quarterly* 106 (Fall 1991): 481.

29. Richard E. Neustadt, *Presidential Power* (New York: New American Library, 1964), p. 102.

30. Hugh Heclo, "Introduction: The Presidential Illusion," in Hugh Heclo and Lester M. Salamon, *The Illusion of Presidential Government* (Boulder, CO: Westview Press, 1981), p. 3.

31. William P. Browne, *Private Interests, Public Policy, and American Agriculture* (Lawrence: University Press of Kansas, 1988), pp. 218–19.

32. *Ibid.,* p. 219.

33. Edmund M. Muskie (D-ME), quoted in Bruce I. Oppenheimer, "Changing Time Constraints on Congress: Historical Perspectives on the Use of Cloture," in Lawrence C. Dodd and Bruce I. Oppenheimer, eds., *Congress Reconsidered,* 3d ed. (Washington, DC: Congressional Quarterly Press, 1985), p. 397.

34. Paul Weisberg and Phillip B. Waldrop, "Fixed-Interval Work Habits of the Congress," *Journal of Applied Behavioral Analysis* 5 (Spring 1972): 96.

35. Senator Sanford's (D-NC) 1990 bill to designate a wilderness area in western North Carolina suffered such a death. Since Senate holds can be placed anonymously through the party leadership, there is no way to know who actually blocked this

seemingly noncontroversial act. A good guess would be Sanford's conservative colleague, Jesse Helms (R-NC), whose antipathy to environmental issues is well known.

36. Allen Schick, *Congress and Money* (Washington, DC: The Urban Institute, 1980), p. 545.

37. See, for example, the conversation among members reported in Charles O. Jones, *Every Second Year* (Washington, DC: The Brookings Institution, 1967), p. 28.

38. *Ibid.*, p. 80.

39. Gary King and Lyn Ragsdale, *The Elusive Executive* (Washington, DC: Congressional Quarterly Press, 1988), p. 43.

40. Quoted in Jack Valenti, *A Very Human President* (New York: W. W. Norton, 1975), p. 144.

41. The literature on this phenomenon is astutely summarized and examined in Samuel Kernell, "The Presidency and the People: The Modern Paradox," in Michael Nelson, ed., *The Presidency and the Political System* (Washington, DC: Congressional Quarterly Press, 1984), pp. 233–63.

42. See the figures compiled by Paul C. Light in *The President's Agenda* (Baltimore: The Johns Hopkins University Press, 1982), pp. 42, 45.

43. "One-house bills" are fairly common in state legislatures with divided party control. With a Republican Senate and a Democratic House, for example, wildly irresponsible bills can go sailing through one house while its members are secure in the knowledge that their fine-sounding prose will die in the other body and never become law.

44. Many key bills in 1981 were given political momentum by early and often decisive votes in the Senate. These votes carried a symbolic message as well, since it was Republican victories in the 1980 Senate elections that gave credibility to the notion that the Republican "mandate" was something more than a rejection of Jimmy Carter. Norman J. Ornstein, "Assessing Reagan's First Year," in Norman Ornstein, ed., *President and Congress: Assessing Reagan's First Year* (Washington, DC: American Enterprise Institute, 1982), p. 91.

45. Katherine E. Rudder, "Tax Policy: Structure and Choice," in Allen Schick, ed., *Making Economic Policy in Congress* (Washington, DC: American Enterprise Institute, 1983), p. 211.

46. Eidenberg and Morey, *An Act of Congress*, p. 163.

47. Light, *Artful Work*, p. 194.

48. Dennis. S. Ippolito, *Congressional Spending* (Ithaca, NY: Cornell University Press, 1981), p. 222.

49. Lance T. LeLoup, *Budgetary Politics*, 3d ed. (Brunswick, OH: King's Court, 1986), p. iv.

50. Theodore Sorensen, *Kennedy* (New York: Harper and Row), p. 476.

51. Arthur Schlesinger, Jr., quoted in James L. Sundquist, *Politics and Policy* (Washington, DC: The Brookings Institution, 1968), p. 256.

52. Abraham Holtzman, *Legislative Liaison* (Chicago: Rand-McNally, 1970), p. 150.

53. Richard E. Neustadt, *Presidential Power: The Politics of Leadership with Reflections on Johnson and Nixon* (New York: John Wiley and Sons, 1976), p. 5.

54. Light, *President's Agenda*, p. 163.

55. *Ibid.*, pp. 156, 157.

56. Neil MacNeil, *Forge of Democracy* (New York: David McKay, 1963), p. 331.

57. Anthony King, "A Mile and a Half Is a Long Way," in Anthony King, ed., *Both Ends of the Avenue* (Washington, DC: American Enterprise Institute, 1983), p. 261.

58. Fred I. Greenstein, ed., *The Reagan Presidency: An Early Assessment* (Baltimore: Johns Hopkins University Press, 1983), p. 184.
59. King, "A Mile and a Half," p. 258.
60. Jeff Fishel, *Presidents and Promises* (Washington, DC: Congressional Quarterly Press, 1985), p. 170.
61. M. Kent Jennings, "Legislative Politics and Water Pollution Control, 1956–61," in Frederic N. Cleaveland et al., eds., *Congress and Urban Problems* (Washington, DC: The Brookings Institution, 1969), p. 87.
62. Wilbur Cohen, "Discussion," in William S. Livingston, Lawrence C. Dodd, and Richard L. Schott, eds., *The Presidency and the Congress* (Austin: University of Texas, 1979), p. 204.
63. Quoted in John E. Moore, "Controlling Delinquency: Executive, Congressional and Judicial," in Cleaveland et al., eds., *Congress*, p. 118.
64. Randall B. Ripley, *Party Leaders in the House of Representatives* (Washington, DC: The Brookings Institution, 1967), p. 122.
65. Rowland Evans and Robert Novak, *Lyndon B. Johnson: The Exercise of Power* (Cleveland, OH: World Publishing Co., 1966), pp. 115, 117.
66. Ripley, *Party Leaders*, pp. 117–18.
67. Ripley, "Legislative Bargaining and the Food Stamp Act, 1964," in Cleaveland et al., eds., *Congress*, pp. 303–5.
68. Raymond A. Bauer, Ithiel de Sola Pool, and Lewis Anthony Dexter, *American Business and Public Policy* (New York: Atherton Press, 1963), p. 426.

---- ❋ ----

7 The Art of Drafting

1. Aaron Wildavsky, *The Politics of the Budgetary Process* (Boston: Little, Brown, 1974), p. 22.
2. *Ibid.*, pp. 21–22.
3. Quoted in Jeff Fishel, *Presidents and Promises* (Washington, DC: Congressional Quarterly Press, 1985), p. 170.
4. Felix Frankfurter, "Some Reflections on the Reading of Statutes," *Columbia Law Review* 47 (1947): 528.
5. Jack Davies, *Legislative Law and Process* (St. Paul, MN: West Publishing, 1975), p. 143.
6. *Federal Trade Commission v. The Sperry and Hutchinson Company*, 405 U.S. 233 (1972), 238.
7. An understandable summary of the complex issues involved in establishing these allocation formulae can be found in Norman C. Thomas, *Education in National Politics* (New York: David McKay Co., 1975).
8. Allen Schick, *Congress and Money* (Washington, DC: Urban Institute Press, 1980).
9. A useful, if somewhat legalistic, analysis of legislative-executive conflict in this area can be found in R. Shep Melnick, "The Politics of Partnership," *Public Administration Review* 45 (September/October 1985): 653.
10. Daniel Patrick Moynihan, *Maximum Feasible Misunderstanding* (New York: The Free Press, 1965), offers a lively perspective on the origins and interpretations of this provocative statutory phrase.
11. A detailed examination of the different judicial treatments accorded various kinds of entitlement programs is found in an unsigned commentary, "Congressional Pre-

clusion of Judicial Review of Federal Benefit Dispersement: Reasserting the Separation of Powers," *Harvard Law Review* 97 (Fall 1984): 778. On the fight to change the rules of the Veterans' Administration see Paul C. Light, *Forging Legislation* (New York: Norton, 1992), Chapter 1.

12. Gwendolyn B. Folsom, *Legislative History: Research for the Interpretation of Laws* (Charlottesville: University Press of Virginia, 1972), p. 7.

13. *Hirschey v. FERC*, 777 F. 2d 1 (D.C. Cir., 1985), 8.

14. Some of these declarations, on the other hand, have had important ramifications. For example, many of those dealing with human rights put the burden of proof on the Reagan and Bush administrations and forced them to publicly justify assistance to various repressive regimes.

15. William N. Eskridge, Jr., and Philip P. Frickey, *Cases and Materials on Legislation: Statutes and the Creation of Public Policy* (St. Paul, MN: West Publishing, 1988), p. 840.

16. National Conference of Commissioners on Uniform State Laws, "Drafting Rules for Writing Uniform or Model Acts," reprinted in Horace E. Read, John W. Mac-Donald, Jefferson B. Fordham, and William J. Pierce, *Materials on Legislation*, 4th ed. (Mineola, NY: Foundation Press, 1982), p. 254.

17. R. M. Gibson, "Congressional Concurrent Resolutions: An Aid to Statutory Interpretation," *Journal of the American Bar Association* 37 (1951): 422.

18. In most parliamentary systems, "private member bills" are those introduced by individual members; the usually more important "government bills" are presented by the party in power. In the United States, all bills—whether drafted by the administration or not—must be introduced by MCs. "Private member bills" are "private" to those affected by them.

19. Barbara Hinkson Clark, *The Legislative Veto: Congressional Control of Regulation* (Boulder, CO: Westview Press, 1983), p. 1.

20. *Immigration and Naturalization Service v. Chadha*, 103 S. Ct. 2764 (1983), 2789. For a thorough history and analysis of the case, see Barbara Hinson Craig, *Chadha: The Story of an Epic Constitutional Struggle* (New York: Oxford University Press, 1988).

21. For a list of post-*Chadha* legislation in seeming violation of the rule, see the essay by L. Howard Levinson, "Congressional Oversight of Agency Rulemaking: Options Available after Chadha" in "Constitutional Amendment to Restore the Legislative Veto," *Hearings,* United States Senate, Committee on the Judiciary, Subcommittee on the Constitution (98th Cong., 2d sess., 1984), p. 207.

22. As quoted in Dennis DeConcini and Robert Faucher, "The Legislative Veto: A Constitutional Amendment," *Harvard Journal on Legislation* 21 (1984): 55. Use of joint resolutions—to either affirm or overrule administrative action—seems to have become the preferred form for post-*Chadha* legislative vetoes, although various reallocations of funds must still be cleared through the Appropriations Committees. An insightful discussion of these alternatives can be found in Joseph Cooper, "The Legislative Veto in the 1980s," in Lawrence C. Dodd and Bruce L. Oppenheimer, eds., *Congress Reconsidered* (Washington, DC: Congressional Quarterly Press, 1985), pp. 364–89.

23. Rudolph G. Penner and Alan J. Abramson, *Broken Purse Strings: Congressional Budgeting, 1974–88* (Washington, DC: Urban Institute Press, 1988), p. 95.

24. Lewis A. Deschler and William Holmes Brown, *Procedure in the U.S. House of Representatives*, 4th ed. (Washington, DC: Government Printing Office, 1982), p. 373.

25. David Halberstam, *The Best and the Brightest* (New York: Random House, 1969), p. 419.
26. Connie Mack III, "Federal Deficits: Source and Solution," in "Budget Reforms," *Hearing*, United States Senate, Committee on Governmental Affairs (100th Cong., 2d sess., 1988), p. 404.
27. See, for example, the arguments in "Treaty Ratification Process and Separation of Powers," *Hearing*, United States Senate, Committee on the Judiciary, Subcommittee on Separation of Powers (97th Cong., 2d sess., 1982).
28. Richard Haass, "The Role of Congress in American Security Policy," in John F. Reichart and Steven R. Sturm, eds., *American Defense Policy*, 5th ed. (Baltimore: Johns Hopkins Press, 1982), p. 557.
29. *Chicago and Southern Airlines v. Waterman Steamship Corp.*, 333 U.S. 103 (1948), 111.
30. Paul C. Light, *Artful Work: The Politics of Social Security Reform* (New York: Random House, 1985), p. 235.
31. Mark A. Peterson, *Legislating Together* (Cambridge, MA: Harvard University Press, 1990), p. 63.
32. Howard E. Shuman, *Politics and the Budget: The Struggle between the President and the Congress*, 2d ed. (Englewood Cliffs, NJ: Prentice-Hall, 1988), p. 75.
33. Davies, *Legislative Law and Process*, p. 142.
34. For a full history, see T. R. Reid, *Congressional Odyssey: The Saga of Senate Bill* (San Francisco: W. H. Freeman and Co., 1980).
35. Davies, *Legislative Law and Process*, p. 59.
36. *Ibid.*, pp. 59–60.
37. Henry Thring, *Practical Legislation*, 2d ed. (Boston: Little, Brown and Co., 1902), p. 9.
38. U. M. Rose, "Title of Statutes," in Read et al., *Materials on Legislation*, pp. 150, 151.
39. Walter J. Oleszek, *Congressional Procedures and the Policy Process* (Washington, DC: Congressional Quarterly Press, 1978), p. 55.
40. Reid, *Congressional Odyssey*, pp. 17–21.
41. Francis J. McCaffrey, *Statutory Construction* (Brooklyn, NY: Central Book Co., 1953), pp. 58–59.
42. Sir Courtney Ilbert, *The Mechanics of Law Making* (New York: Columbia University Press, 1914), p. 110.
43. Thring, *Practical Legislation*, pp. 53–54.
44. Deschler and Brown, *Procedure*, Sections 28.1–31.14, pp. 606–15. See especially Section 28.13.
45. Elias Lieberman, *Unions before the Bar* (New York: Harper, 1950), p. 323.
46. Maury Maverick, "Gobbledygook," *Public Administration Review* 4 (Summer 1944): 151.
47. The chicken-thief metaphor and much of the argument here is taken from the enduringly rich article by Alfred F. Conrad in the 1947 *Yale Law Journal*, "New Ways to Write Laws," reprinted in Read et al., *Materials on Legislation*, pp. 237–49.
48. *Ibid.*, p. 244.
49. *Ibid.*, pp. 239–40.
50. Arthur Maass, *Congress and the Common Good* (New York: Basic Books, 1983), p. 139.
51. Jeffrey H. Birnbaum and Alan S. Murray, *Showdown at Gucci Gulch* (New York: Random House, 1987), pp. 240–43.

52. Maass, *Congress and the Common Good*, p. 141.
53. See Section 27 of Deschler and Brown, *Procedure*, pp. 485–625.
54. The essence of this strategy was frankly outlined by Senator Lodge in his book *The Senate and the League of Nations* (New York: Scribners, 1925).
55. Daniel M. Berman, *A Bill Becomes a Law*, 2d ed. (New York: Macmillan, 1966), p. 114.
56. Jerry Voorhis, *Confessions of a Congressman* (Garden City, NY: Doubleday, 1947), p. 98.
57. Neil MacNeil, *Forge of Democracy* (New York: David McKay, 1963), p. 365.
58. Quoted in Oleszek, *Congressional Procedures*, p. 71.
59. Christopher J. Bosso, *Pesticides and Politics: The Life Cycle of a Public Issue* (Pittsburgh: University of Pittsburgh Press, 1987), p. 171.
60. Oleszek, *Congressional Procedures*, p. 161.
61. Davies, *Legislative Law and Process*, pp. 57–58. The allusion to the bridge refers to a movie in which a group of Allied prisoners in World War II help the Japanese build a strategic bridge over the River Kwai. Although the prisoners are conscious of the bridge's strategic value—and ultimately destroy their own work—they do a good job of building the bridge itself.
62. *Ibid.*, p. 58.
63. Alan Murray, "House Funding Bill Riders Become Potent Policy Force," *Congressional Quarterly Weekly Report* 38 (1 November 1980): 3252.
64. *Ibid.*, p. 3251.
65. L. White Busbey, *Uncle Joe Cannon* (New York: Holt, 1927), p. 271.
66. Charles Tiefer, *Congressional Practice and Procedure* (New York: Greenwood Press, 1989), p. 421.
67. *Ibid.*, p. 429.
68. Ross K. Baker, *House and Senate* (New York: W. W. Norton and Co., 1989), p. 71.
69. Phil Gramm (R-TX), quoted in *ibid.*, pp. 71–72.
70. Stephen Kemp Bailey, *Congress Makes a Law* (New York: Vintage Books, 1950), p. 224.

---- ❈ ----

8 Organizing Support

1. David C. Kozak, *Contexts of Congressional Decision Behavior* (Lanham, MD: University Press of America, 1984).
2. Amitai Etzioni, *The Active Society* (New York: The Free Press, 1968), p. 293.
3. This typology was created by Theodore Lowi in an influential book review and a variety of subsequent essays. The terms are more or less self-explanatory: *distributive politics* are those perceived as benefiting one particular group at no one's particular expense; *redistributive* as taking from one and giving to another. In political terms, *regulatory policies* are those that burden or encumber one identifiable group while providing dispersed benefits.
4 Thomas Sowell, *Knowledge and Decisions* (New York: Basic Books, 1984), p. 9.
5. *Ibid.*, p. 97.
6. John W. Kingdon, *Congressmen's Voting Decisions*, 2d ed. (New York: Harper and Row, 1981), pp. 165–66.
7. Quoted in Barbara Sinclair, *Majority Leadership in the U.S. House* (Baltimore: Johns Hopkins University Press, 1983), pp. 133–34.

8. Raymond A. Bauer, Ithiel de Sola Pool, and Lewis Anthony Dexter, *American Business and Public Policy* (New York: Atherton Press, 1963), p. 442.
9. George E. Reedy, *The U.S. Senate* (New York: New American Library, 1986), p. 115.
10. Stanley Bach and Steven S. Smith, *Managing Uncertainty in the House of Representatives* (Washington, DC: The Brookings Institution, 1988), p. 3.
11. *Ibid.*
12. *Ibid.*, p. 47.
13. Steven S. Smith, "Taking It to the Floor," in Lawrence C. Dodd and Bruce I. Oppenheimer, eds., *Congress Reconsidered*, 4th ed. (Washington, DC: Congressional Quarterly Press, 1989), p. 342.
14. Bach and Smith, *Managing Uncertainty*, p. 110.
15. William H. Riker, *The Theory of Political Coalitions* (New Haven: Yale University Press, 1962), p. 47.
16. John B. Gilmour, "Hardball and Softball Politics: A Theory of Coalition Size in Congress," paper presented at the 84th Annual Meeting of the American Political Science Association, Washington, DC, 1–4 September 1988.
17. Steven J. Brams, *Game Theory and Politics* (New York: The Free Press, 1975), p. 214.
18. John F. Manley, *The Politics of Finance: The House Committee on Ways and Means* (Boston: Little, Brown and Co., 1970), p. 99.
19. *Ibid.*, p. 100.
20. See, for example, the essays in Frank H. Mackamen, *Understanding Congressional Leadership* (Washington, DC: Congressional Quarterly Press, 1981).
21. Joseph Cooper and David W. Brady, "Institutional Context and Leadership Style," in *ibid.*, p. 44.
22. Edward C. Banfield, *Political Influence* (New York: The Free Press, 1961), p. 270.
23. Andrew S. McFarland, *Power and Leadership in Pluralist Systems* (Palo Alto, CA: Stanford University Press, 1969), p. 175.
24. Manley, *Politics of Finance*, p. 109.
25. Charles Merriam, *Political Power* (New York: McGraw-Hill, 1934), p. 233.
26. E. W. Kelley, "Theory and the Study of Coalition Behavior," in Sven Groennings, E. W. Kelley, and Michael Leiserson, eds., *The Study of Coalition Behavior* (New York: Holt, Rinehart and Winston, 1970), pp. 483–84.
27. Riker, *Theory of Political Coalitions*, p. 66.
28. Sinclair, *Majority Leadership*, p. 155.
29. E. E. Schattschneider, *Politics, Pressure and the Tariff* (New York: Prentice Hall, 1935), p. 112.
30. Bruce A. Ackerman and William T. Hassler, *Clean Coal/Dirty Air* (New Haven: Yale University Press, 1981), p. 39.
31. Stephen K. Bailey, *Congress Makes a Law* (New York: Columbia University Press, 1949), p. 77.
32. See, for example, "Availability and Reliability of Agency Information," *Hearings*, United States Senate, Committee on the Judiciary, Subcommittee on Administrative Practice and Procedure (98th Cong., 2d sess., 1985).
33. Thomas C. Schelling, *Choices and Consequence* (Cambridge, MA: Harvard University Press, 1984), p. 9.
34. David R. Mayhew, *Congress: The Electoral Connection* (New Haven: Yale University Press, 1974), p. 115.
35. Charles E. Lindblom, *The Intelligence of Democracy* (New York: The Free Press, 1965). For a highly readable introduction to the game-theoretical approach see

Thomas C. Schelling, *The Strategy of Conflict* (Cambridge, MA: Harvard University Press, 1960).

36. Stanley Kelley, Jr., "Patronage and Presidential Legislative Leadership," in Aaron Wildavsky, ed., *The Presidency* (Boston: Little, Brown, 1969), p. 271.

37. Weldon V. Barton, "Coalition-Building in the U.S. House of Representatives: Agriculture Legislation in 1973," paper delivered at the Annual Meeting of the American Political Science Association, Chicago, IL: August 29–September 2, 1974, p. 11.

38. Kelley, "Patronage," p. 271.

39. *Ibid.*, p. 272.

40. A similar, useful topology is developed in Lewis A. Froman, Jr., *The Congressional Process* (Boston: Little, Brown, 1967), p. 23.

41. *Ibid.*, p. 24.

42. Quoted in Kingdon, *Congressmen's Voting Decisions*, p. 101.

43. Barbara Hinckley, " 'Stylized' Opposition in the U. S. House of Representatives: The Effect of Coalition Behavior," *Legislative Studies Quarterly* 2 (February 1977): 5.

44. Michael T. Hayes, *Lobbyists and Legislators* (New Brunswick, NJ: Rutgers University Press, 1981), p. 67.

45. John Ferejohn, "Logrolling in an Institutional Context," in Gerald C. Wright, Jr., Leroy N. Rieselbach, and Lawrence C. Dodd, eds., *Congress and Policy Change* (New York: Agathon Press, 1986), p. 251.

46. Christopher J. Bosso, *Pesticides and Politics: The Life Cycle of a Public Issue* (Pittsburgh: University of Pittsburgh Press, 1987), p. 258.

47. Nelson W. Polsby, "Congress, Publicity and Public Policy," *Public Policy* 18 (Spring 1969): 11.

---------------- ✳ ----------------

9 *Managing Committee Action*

1. Woodrow Wilson, *Congressional Government* (New York: Meridian Books, 1956, originally published in 1885), pp. 71–73.

2. Dennis W. Brezina and Allen Overmyer, *Congress in Action: The Environmental Education Act* (New York: The Free Press, 1974), pp. 39–65.

3. Walter J. Oleszek, *Congressional Procedures and the Policy Process* (Washington, DC: Congressional Quarterly Press, 1978), p. 69.

4. Steven S. Smith and Christopher J. Deering, *Committees in Congress* (Washington, DC: Congressional Quarterly Press, 1984), p. 133.

5. Patrick O'Donnell, quoted in Maurice B. Tobin, *Hidden Power* (New York: Greenwood Press, 1986), p. 82.

6. Joint Committee on the Organization of Congress, *Final Report*, 89th Cong., 2d Sess. (1966), p. 66.

7. Howard E. Shuman, *Politics and the Budget: The Struggle between the President and the Congress*, 2d ed. (Englewood Cliffs, NJ: Prentice-Hall, 1988), p. 71.

8. Testimony of Harry Golden, *Hearings,* Subcommittee on Housing, Committee on Banking and Currency, United States Senate, 79th Cong., 1st sess. (August 23, 1945), p. 381.

9. Tristram Coffin, *Missouri Compromise* (Boston: Little, Brown and Co., 1947), pp. 161–62.

10. Michael Foley, *The New Senate* (New Haven: Yale University Press, 1980), pp. 195–96.
11. Aaron Wildavsky, *The Politics of the Budgetary Process*, 4th ed. (Boston: Little, Brown and Co., 1984), p. 120.
12. Lawrence H. Chamberlain, *The President, Congress and Legislation* (New York: Columbia University Press, 1946), p. 39.
13. 52 Stat. 942, 2 U.S.C.A. 192, quoted in Horace E. Read, John W. MacDonald, Jefferson B. Fordham, and William J. Pierce, *Materials on Legislation* (Mineola, NY: The Foundation Press, 1982), p. 394.
14. Richard Harris, *The Real Voice* (New York: Macmillan, 1964), p. 70.
15. The House Committee on Un-American Activities once attempted to subpoena President Truman. Truman's indignant refusal was widely applauded on the Hill and in the press, and the matter was quietly dropped.
16. Bradley H. Patterson, Jr., *The Ring of Power* (New York: Basic Books, 1988), p. 144.
17. Quoted in Arthur Maass, *Congress and the Common Good* (New York: Basic Books, 1983), p. 247.
18. *Ibid.*, p. 240.
19. *Ibid.*, p. 241.
20. From the April 1973 hearings of the Senate Subcommittee on Intergovernmental Relations, quoted in James Hamilton, *The Power to Probe* (New York: Random House, 1976), pp. 159–60.
21. *Ibid.*, p. 199.
22. *Ibid.*, p. 197.
23. Marshall E. Dimmock, *Congressional Investigating Committees* (Baltimore: Johns Hopkins Press, 1929), pp. 57–58.
24. James Burnham, *Congress and the American Tradition* (Chicago: Henry Regnery Co., 1959), p. 223.
25. George Galloway, *The Legislative Process in Congress* (New York: Thomas Y. Crowell Co., 1953), p. 305.
26. J. H. Wigmore, "Legislative Power to Compel Testimonial Disclosure," *Illinois Law Review* 19 (June 1925): 453.
27. Martin Nelson McGeary, "Congressional Investigations during Franklin D. Roosevelt's First Term," *American Political Science Review* 21 (September 1937): 680 and *passim*.
28. Telford Taylor, *Grand Inquest* (New York: Simon and Schuster, 1955), p. 85.
29. Compare his dissent in *Barenblatt v. United States*, 360 U.S. 109 (1958), with his article "Inside a Senate Investigation," *Harpers Magazine* 172 (April 1936): 275.
30. *Watkins v. United States*, 354 U.S. 178 (1957), 181.
31. United States House of Representatives, Committee on Un-American Activities, *Annual Report for the Year 1961* (Washington, DC: Government Printing Office, 1962), p. 134.
32. Representative Kit Clardy, House Committee on Un-American Activities, *Investigation of Communist Activities in the Los Angeles Area* (March-April 1953), Part III, p. 637.
33. Lauros G. McConachie, *Congressional Committees* (New York: Thomas Y. Crowell, 1898), p. 63.
34. Thomas J. O'Donnell, "Controlling Legislative Time," in Joseph Cooper and G. Calvin Mackenzie, eds., *The House at Work* (Austin: University of Texas Press, 1981), pp. 141–42.

35. James L. Payne, "The Rise of Lone Wolf Questioning in House Committee Hearings," *Polity* 14 (Summer 1982): 626–40.
36. Joint Committee on the Organization of Congress, *Organization of Congress*, S. Rept. 1011 (79th Cong., 2d sess., 1945), p. 11.
37. Wildavsky, *Politics of the Budgetary Process*, p. 86.
38. *Ibid.*, p. 87.
39. Earl Latham, *The Group Basis of Politics* (Ithaca, NY: Cornell University Press, 1952), p. 106.
40. *Communist Training Operations*, Hearings before the House Committee on Un-American Activities, 86th Cong., 1st sess., (1959), Part 1, p. 1045.
41. *Investigation of Communist Activities in the State of Michigan*, Hearings before the House Committee on Un-American Activities, 83rd Cong., 2d sess. (1954), Part 12, p. 7200.
42. Charles Tiefer, *Congressional Practice and Procedure* (New York: Greenwood Press, 1989), p. 164.
43. Quoted in *ibid.*, p. 168.
44. Abner J. Mikva and Patti B. Saris, *The American Congress*, (New York: Franklin Watts, 1983), p. 216.
45. Charles B. Nutting, quoted in Read et al, *Materials on Legislation*, p. 366. See also the contrary view of Justice Frankfurter in the Steel Seizure Case quoted in *ibid.*
46. Mikva and Saris, *The American Congress*, p. 212.
47. That is, unless the bill is presented under suspension of the rules or with a special waiver from the House Rules Committee. For a full recital of these technicalities see Chap. 17, Sect. 14 of Lewis A. Deschler and William Holmes Brown, *Procedure in the U.S. House of Representatives*, 4th ed. (Washington, DC: Government Printing Office, 1982), pp. 210–212.
48. Eric Redman, *The Dance of Legislation* (New York: Simon and Schuster, 1973), p. 137.
49. Richard L. Hall, "Committee Decision Making in the Post Reform Congress," in Lawrence C. Dodd and Bruce I. Oppenheimer, eds., *Congress Reconsidered*, 4th ed. (Washington, DC: Congressional Quarterly Press, 1989), p. 204.
50. A typical committee rule allows proxy voting "if the authorization is in writing . . . , designates the person who is to exercise the proxy authorization, and is limited to a specific measure or matter or any amendments or motions pertaining thereto." Rule IV, House Committee on the Judiciary, in U.S. House of Representatives, Committee on Rules, "Rules Adopted by the Committees of the House of Representatives," 100th Cong., 1st sess. (1987), pp. 164–65.
51. Tiefer, *Congressional Practice*, p. 174.
52. This is from the final report of the 1966 Joint Committee on the Organization of Congress, quoted in Tiefer, *Congressional Practice*, p. 172.
53. Hall, "Committee Decision Making," p. 204.
54. *Ibid.*, p. 217.
55. Joseph K. Unekis and Leroy N. Rieselbach, *Congressional Committee Politics: Continuity and Change* (New York: Praeger, 1984), p. 162.
56. Ross K. Baker, *House and Senate* (New York: W. W. Norton and Co., 1989), p. 86.
57. Richard F. Fenno, Jr., *Congressmen in Committees* (Boston: Little, Brown and Co., 1973), pp. 278–79.
58. Heinz Eulau and Vera McCluggage, "Standing Committees in Legislatures," in Gerhard Loewenberg, Samuel C. Patterson, and Malcolm E. Jewell, eds., *Handbook of Legislative Research* (Cambridge, MA: Harvard University Press, 1985), p. 422.

59. James W. Dyson and John W. Soule, "Congressional Committee Behavior on Roll Call Votes: The U.S. House of Representatives," *Midwest Journal of Political Science* 14 (Fall 1970): 645.

60. Gerald S. Strom, *The Logic of Lawmaking* (Baltimore: Johns Hopkins University Press, 1990), p. 85.

61. John W. Kingdon, *Congressmen's Voting Decisions* (New York: Harper and Row, 1973), p. 129.

62. *Ibid.*, p. 127.

10   *The War on the Floor*

1. Steven S. Smith, *Call to Order* (Washington, DC: The Brookings Institution, 1989), p. 18.

2. *Ibid.*

3. *Ibid.*, p. 17.

4. Stanley Bach and Steven S. Smith, *Managing Uncertainty in the House of Representatives* (Washington, DC: The Brookings Institution, 1988), p. 57.

5. Steven C. Smith and Marcus Flathman, "Managing the Senate Floor: Complex Unanimous Consent Agreements since the 1950s," *Legislative Studies Quarterly* 14 (August 1989): 365.

6. See Charles Tiefer, *Congressional Practice and Procedure* (New York: Greenwood Press, 1989), pp. 296–98 for a fuller discussion.

7. William Holmes Brown, *Deschler's Procedure in the U.S. House of Representatives* (Washington, DC: Government Printing Office, 1979), p. 522.

8. Barbara Sinclair, "Party Leadership and Policy Change," in Gerald C. Wright, Leroy N. Rieselbach, and Lawrence C. Dodd, eds., *Congress and Policy Change* (New York: Agathon Press, 1986), p. 187.

9. Tiefer, *Congressional Practice and Procedure*, p. 392.

10. Extensive discussions of this problem may be found in Kenneth Arrow, *Social Choice and Individual Values* (New York: Wiley, 1951), and Robin Farquharson, *Theory of Voting* (New Haven: Yale University Press, 1969).

11. Walter J. Oleszek, "Legislative Procedures and Congressional Policymaking: A Bicameral Perspective," in Christopher J. Deering, ed., *Congressional Politics* (Chicago: The Dorsey Press, 1989), p. 183.

12. Representative Les Aspin (D-WI), quoted in the *New York Times*, 13 May 1987, p. 21.

13. Barbara Sinclair, *Majority Leadership in the House* (Baltimore: Johns Hopkins University Press, 1983), p. 60.

14. Sidney Waldman, "Majority Leadership in the House of Representatives," *Political Science Quarterly* 95 (Fall 1980): 377.

15. Lawrence C. Dodd and Terry Sullivan, "Majority Party Leadership and Partisan Vote Gathering: The House Democratic Whip System," in Frank H. Mackaman, ed., *Understanding Congressional Leadership* (Washington, DC: Congressional Quarterly Press, 1981), p. 229.

16. Dodd and Sullivan, "Majority Party Leadership," p. 246.

17. This section was inspired in part by the classic approach on public debate of Thurman Arnold, *The Folklore of Capitalism* (New York: New York University Press, 1937). Arnold's essential argument is that public debate has little to do with

"the actual practical analysis of facts," much to do with ceremony, morale, and attempts "to create enthusiasm, to increase faith, and quiet doubt. . . . All prolonged public discussion of any measure can do is to reconcile conflicts and get people used to the general idea which the measure represents. . . . Public argument never convinces the other side, any more than in a war the enemy can ever be convinced. Its effectiveness consists in binding together the side on which the arguments are used." Pp. 379–81.

18. Carter Glass, quoted in George H. Hayes, *The Senate of the United States*, vol. 1 (Boston: Houghton Mifflin, 1938), p. 382.
19. Richard F. Fenno, Jr., *Home Style: House Members in Their Districts* (Boston: Little, Brown, 1978).
20. Giandomenico Majone, *Evidence, Argument, and Persuasion in the Policy Process* (New Haven: Yale University Press, 1989), p. 33.
21. Donald R. Matthews, *U.S. Senators and Their World* (New York: Vintage Books, 1960), p. 248.
22. L. White Busbey, *Uncle Joe Cannon* (New York: Holt, 1927), pp. 134–35.
23. Lewis A. Deschler and William Holmes Brown, *Procedure in the U.S. House of Representatives*, 4th ed., (Washington, DC: Government Printing Office, 1982), Section 29, paragraph 5.1.
24. A full list may be found in Floyd M. Riddick, *The United States Congress: Organization and Procedure* (Washington, DC: National Capitol Publishers, 1949), p. 375.
25. James G. Abourezk, *Advice and Dissent*, (Chicago: Lawrence Hill Books, 1989), p. 134.
26. Compiled from figures presented in Norman J. Ornstein, Thomas E. Mann, and Michael J. Malbin, *Vital Statistics on Congress 1989–1990* (Washington, DC: Congressional Quarterly Press, 1990), p. 163.
27. Quoted from a Senate oral history interview conducted in 1979 by Donald A. Ritchie and cited in Ross K. Baker, *House and Senate* (New York: W. W. Norton and Co., 1989), p. 68.
28. Phil Gramm (R-TX), quoted in Ross K. Baker, *ibid.*, p. 70.
29. Thomas M. Franck and Edward Weisband, *Foreign Policy by Congress* (New York: Oxford University Press, 1979), p. 137.
30. Abourezk, *Advice and Dissent*, p. 143.
31. Senator Robert Byrd (D-WV), quoted in Tiefer, *Congressional Practice and Procedure*, p. 527.
32. Congressional Quarterly, *How Congress Works* (Washington, DC: Congressional Quarterly Press, 1983), p. 50.
33. Tiefer, *Congressional Practice and Procedure*, p. 533.
34. Joseph M. Bessette, "Is Congress a Deliberative Body?" in Joseph Bessette, ed., *The United States Congress* (Chestnut Hill, MA: Boston College, 1982), p. 9.
35. Her position is most forcefully argued in Barbara Sinclair, "Coping with Uncertainty: Building Coalitions in the House and the Senate," in Thomas E. Mann and Norman J. Ornstein, eds., *The New Congress* (Washington, DC: American Enterprise Institute for Public Policy Research, 1981), pp. 178–220.
36. Norman J. Ornstein, "The House and Senate in a New Congress," in *ibid.*, pp. 368–69.
37. Sinclair, "Coping with Uncertainty," p. 165.
38. Deschler and Brown, *Procedure*, Chap. 30, Section 5.4, p. 685.
39. A fuller analysis may be found in Lewis A. Froman, Jr., *The Congressional Process* (Boston: Little, Brown, 1967), pp. 126–27.

40. Jerry Voorhis, *Confessions of a Congressman* (Garden City, NY: Doubleday, 1947), p. 233.

41. Duncan MacRae, Jr., *Dimensions of Congressional Voting* (Berkeley and Los Angeles: University of California Press, 1958), p. 209.

42. As recently as 1980, it could be argued that the overall level of Southern Democratic disloyalty had not faded. See Allan I. Abromowitz, "Is the Revolt Fading: A Note on Party Loyalty among Southern Democratic Congressmen," *Journal of Politics* 42 (August 1980): 568–72.

43. Charles S. Bullock III and David W. Brady, "Party, Constituency, and Roll-Call Voting in the U.S. Senate," *Legislative Studies Quarterly* 8 (February 1983): 42.

44. Julius C. Turner and Edward V. Schneier, Jr., *Party and Constituency: Pressures on Congress* (Baltimore, MD: Johns Hopkins University Press, 1970), p. 106.

45. Aage Clausen, *How Congressmen Decide* (New York: St. Martin's Press, 1973), p. 3.

46. A useful summary of the literature can be found in Melissa P. Collie, "Voting Behavior in Legislatures," in Gerhard Loewenberg, Samuel C. Patterson, and Malcolm E. Jewell, eds., *Handbook of Legislative Research* (Cambridge, MA: Harvard University Press, 1985), pp. 471–518.

47. Jerrold E. Schneider, *Ideological Coalitions in Congress* (Westport, CT: Greenwood Press, 1979).

48. Collie, "Voting Behavior," p. 483.

49. David W. Brady, Joseph Cooper, and Patricia Hurley, "The Decline of Party in the U.S. House of Representatives," *Legislative Studies Quarterly* 4 (August 1979): 395.

50. David W. Brady, *Congressional Voting in a Partisan Era* (Lawrence: University Press of Kansas, 1973), p. 182.

---- ❋ ----

11   The Road to Law

1. Charles Tiefer, *Congressional Practice and Procedure* (New York: Greenwood Press, 1989), pp. 771–80, has a full description.

2. Steven S. Smith, *Call to Order* (Washington, DC: The Brookings Institution, 1989), p. 206.

3. *Ibid.*

4. Congressional Quarterly *Weekly Report*, 28 October 1978, p. 3147.

5. Stanley Bach, "Germaneness Rules and Bicameral Relations in the U.S. Congress," *Legislative Studies Quarterly* 7 (August 1982): 341–57.

6. This was the fate of a key clean air bill in 1976. Bernard Asbell, *The Senate Nobody Knows* (Garden City, NY: Doubleday, 1978), p. 445.

7. Smith, *Call to Order*, p. 206.

8. Richard F. Fenno, Jr., "Foreword" to Lawrence D. Longley and Walter J. Oleszek, *Bicameral Politics* (New Haven: Yale University Press, 1989), p. viii.

9. Clem Miller (ed. John W. Baker), *Member of the House* (New York: Scribners, 1962), p. 114.

10. *Ibid.*, p. 113.

11. *Congressional Record*, 79th Cong., 2d sess., p. 6093.

12. This quotation from the *New York Times*, as well as the phrase from the *Wall Street*

Journal, are taken from Longley and Oleszek (*Bicameral Politics,* p. 162), who have written what is not only the definitive work on conference committees, but a fine book on the legislative process in general.

13. Quoted in Longley and Oleszek, *Bicameral Politics,* p. 158.

14. A member of the Committee quoted in John Manley, *The Politics of Finance: The House Committee on Ways and Means* (Boston: Little, Bown and Co., 1970), p. 264.

15. Longley and Oleszek, *Bicameral Politics,* p. 163.

16. Tiefer, *Congressional Practice and Procedure,* p. 789.

17. *Ibid.,* p. 790.

18. Longley and Oleszek, *Bicameral Politics,* p. 123.

19. Kenneth A. Shepsle and Barry R. Weingast, "The Institutional Foundations of Committee Power," *American Political Science Review* 81 (March 1987): 101. See also Keith Kreibiel's reply in the September 1987 issue (81: 929–35) and an article by Steven S. Smith, "An Essay on Sequence, Position, Goals and Committee Power," *Legislative Studies Quarterly* 13 (May 1988): 151–76.

20. Quoted in Smith, *Call to Order,* p. 224.

21. Longley and Oleszek, *Bicameral Politics,* p. 179.

22. *Ibid.,* p. 10.

23. *Ibid.,* p. 125.

24. Tiefer, *Congressional Practice and Procedure,* p. 797.

25. Longley and Oleszek, *Bicameral Politics,* p. 122.

26. Gilbert Y. Steiner, *The Congressional Conference Committee* (Urbana: University of Illinois Press, 1951), p. 173.

27. *Congressional Record,* 80th Cong., 2d sess., p. 1740.

28. Smith, *Call to Order,* pp. 225–26.

29. Jeffrey H. Birnbaum and Alan S. Murray, *Showdown at Gucci Gulch* (New York: Random House, 1987), p. 260.

30. Barbara Rosewiez, "The Sunshine Slowly Fades," *Roll Call,* 20 October 1983, p. 4.

31. Otis Pike (D-NY), quoted in Todd Siff and Alan Weil, *Ruling Congress* (New York: Grossman, 1975), p. 181.

32. Longley and Oleszek, *Bicameral Politics,* p. 61.

33. *Ibid.,* p. 59.

34. *Ibid.,* p. 60.

35. Richard F. Fenno, Jr., *The Power of the Purse: Appropriations Politics in Congress* (Boston: Little, Brown and Co., 1966), p. 667.

36. Longley and Oleszek, *Bicameral Politics,* p. 83.

37. See, for example, the persuasive arguments of Howard E. Shuman, *Politics and the Budget* (Englewood Cliffs, NJ: Prentice-Hall, 1988), pp. 79–80.

38. Representative Wolcott (R-MI), *Congressional Record,* 75th Cong., 3d sess., 10 June 1938, p. 8738.

39. Representative Frank Chelf (D-KY), *Congressional Record,* 80th Cong., 2d sess., 18 June 1948, p. 8859.

40. Longley and Oleszek, *Bicameral Politics,* p. 217.

41. For a full description, see R. Douglas Arnold, *The Logic of Congressional Action* (New Haven: Yale University Press, 1990), p. 125, and the works cited there.

42. Woodrow Wilson, *Congressional Government* (Boston: Houghton Mifflin Co., 1885), p. 52.

43. White House press release, 3 July 1946.

44. *New York Times,* 16 May 1947, p. A32.

45. Edward S. Corwin, *The President: Office and Powers* (New York: New York University Press, 1948), p. 344.

46. For the most thorough treatment of the issue, see Marc N. Garber and Kurt A. Wimmer, "Presidential Signing Statements as Interpretations of Legislative Intent: An Executive Aggrandizement of Power," *Harvard Journal on Legislation* 24 (Summer 1987): 363–96.

47. Paul L. Ford, ed., *The Works of Thomas Jefferson*, vol. 5 (New York: G. P. Putnam's Sons, 1905), p. 289.

48. Clarence A. Berdahl, "The President's Veto of Private Bills," *Political Science Quarterly* 52 (Fall 1937): 598.

49. Louis W. Koenig, *The Chief Executive*, rev. ed. (New York: Harcourt, Brace, Jovanovich, 1968), p. 137.

50. Paul C. Light, *The President's Agenda* (Baltimore: Johns Hopkins University Press, 1982), pp. 111–15.

51. See, for example, Gary W. Copeland, "When Congress and the President Collide: Why Presidents Veto Legislation," *Journal of Politics* 45 (August 1983): 696–710.

52. For a useful analysis of such patterns in recent years, see Albert C. Ringelstein, "Presidential Vetoes: Motivations and Classification," *Congress and the Presidency* 12 (Spring 1985): 43–55.

53. For a nice summary of the arguments against the analogy with state practices, see Louis Fisher, *Constitutional Conflicts between Congress and the President* (Princeton, NJ: Princeton University Press, 1985), pp. 159–62.

54. Gary King and Lyn Ragsdale, *The Elusive Executive* (Washington, DC: Congressional Quarterly Press, 1988), p. 127.

55. Stanley M. Brand, testimony before the House Committee on Rules, "The Deferral Process after Chadha," *Hearings*, 99th Cong., 2d sess. (1986), pp. 99–100.

56. From figures supplied by the General Accounting Office and cited in *ibid.*, p. 144.

57. Richard P. Nathan, *The Plot That Failed: Richard Nixon and Administrative Presidency* (New York: Wiley, 1975).

58. Sidney M. Milkis, "The Presidency, Policy Reform, and the Rise of Administrative Politics," in Richard A. Harris and Sidney M. Milkis, eds., *Remaking American Politics* (Boulder, CO: Westview Press, 1989), pp. 173, 177.

59. *Edwards v. United States*, 286 U.S. 482.

60. *Kennedy v. Sampson*, United States Court of Appeals, D.C. Circuit, 511 F. 2d 430 (1974), 441.

61. Fisher, *Constitutional Conflicts*, p. 154.

62. Contrary to popular prejudice, campaign platforms and rhetoric have proven a highly reliable guide to what presidents actually do in office. See Jeff Fishel, *Presidents and Promises* (Washington, DC: Congressional Quarterly Press, 1983).

63. Tristram Coffin, *Missouri Compromise* (Boston: Little, Brown, 1947), p. 170.

64. Stephen J. Wayne, Richard C. Cole, and James F. C. Hyde, "Advising the President on Enrolled Legislation," *Political Science Quarterly* 54 (Summer 1979): 303–18.

65. Harry McPherson, *A Political Education* (Boston: Houghton Mifflin, 1988), pp. 273–74.

66. *Ibid.*, p. 280.

67. *Ibid.*, p. 281.

68. Bradley H. Patterson, Jr., *The Ring of Power* (New York: Basic Books, 1988), p. 310.

69. Alan J. Field, "Separation of Powers: Boundaries or Balance," *Georgia Law Review* 21 (1986): 185.

✳
---

12 Executing the Law

1. David B. Truman, *The Governmental Process* (New York: Alfred A. Knopf, 1955), p. 439.
2. *Ibid.*, p. 442.
3. Paul Appleby, *Policy and Administration* (University: University of Alabama Press, 1949), p. 11.
4. *Kendall v. United States*, 12 Peters 524 (1838), 526.
5. Frederick C. Mosher, *Democracy and Public Service*, 2d ed. (New York: Oxford University Press, 1982), pp. 118–19.
6. Dennis D. Riley, *Controlling the Federal Bureaucracy* (Philadelphia: Temple University Press, 1987), p. 34.
7. Clifford is quoted from a personal interview, and Russell from a letter to the chairman of the Foreign Relations Committee cited in Frank J. Smist, Jr., *Congress Oversees the United States Intelligence Community, 1947–1989* (Knoxville: University of Tennessee Press, 1990), pp. 5, 6.
8. Riley, *Controlling the Federal Bureaucracy*, p. 53.
9. *Ibid.*
10. Joel D. Aberbach, "The Congressional Committee Intelligence System: Information, Oversight, and Change," *Congress and the Presidency* 14 (Spring 1987): 55.
11. G. Calvin MacKenzie, *The Politics of Presidential Appointments* (New York: The Free Press, 1981), pp. 7–8.
12. Harold Seidman, *Politics, Position and Power*, 3d ed. (New York: Oxford University Press, 1980), p. 171.
13. Hugh Heclo, *A Government of Strangers* (Washington, DC: The Brookings Institution, 1977), p. 170.
14. *Ibid.*, pp. 171, 228.
15. Arthur W. Macmahon, "Congressional Oversight of Administration: The Power of the Purse," *Political Science Quarterly* 58 (Summer 1943): 161.
16. Quoted in Lawrence C. Dodd and Richard L. Schott, *Congress and the Administrative State* (New York: John Wiley and Sons, 1979), p. 161.
17. Ardith Maney, "Influencing Policy without Passing New Laws: A Congressional Strategy for the 1980s," paper presented at the Annual Meeting of the American Political Science Association, San Francisco, CA, August 30–September 2, 1990, p. 19.
18. Joel D. Aberbach, *Keeping a Watchful Eye* (Washington, DC: The Brookings Institution, 1990), Chap. 2.
19 Joseph P. Harris, *The Advice and Consent of the Senate* (Berkeley: University of California Press, 1953), p. 2.
20. Aberbach, *Keeping a Watchful Eye*, p. 7.
21. Christopher H. Foreman, Jr., *Signals from the Hill* (New Haven: Yale University Press, 1988), p. 174.
22. "Guide to Congress," *Roll Call*, 10 September 1990, p. 17.
23. Lewis A. Dexter, " 'Check and Balance' Today: What Does It Mean for Congress and Congressmen?" in Alfred de Grazia, ed., *Congress: The First Branch of Government* (Washington, DC: American Enterprise Institute, 1966), p. 103.
24. Robert A. Katzman, *Judges and Legislators: Toward Institutional Comity* (Washington, DC: The Brookings Institution, 1988), p. 6.

25. William Letwin, *Law and Economic Policy in America: The Evolution of the Sherman Antitrust Act* (Chicago: University of Chicago Press, 1965), pp. 12–13.
26. Oliver Wendell Holmes, quoted in C. Herman Pritchett, *The American Constitution*, 3d ed. (New York: McGraw-Hill, 1977), p. 123.
27. Robert A. Dahl, "Decision-Making in a Democracy: The Supreme Court as a National Policy-Maker," *Journal of Public Law* 6 (Spring 1957): 284.
28. Susan E. Lawrence, "Exercising Judicial Review: An Empirical Examination of Supreme Court Decisions Declaring Federal Statutes Unconstitutional," paper delivered at the Annual Meeting of the American Political Science Association, San Francisco, CA, August 30–September 2, 1990, p. 6.
29. Jonathan D. Casper, "The Supreme Court and National Policy Making," *American Political Science Review* 70 (March 1976): 63.
30. Lawrence, "Exercising Judicial Review," p. 11. This would put these cases under what has become known as *Carolene* doctrine, after a footnote by Justice Stone in a case of that name. The essence of Stone's argument is that the courts should exercise extraordinary restraint in conducting judicial review, except in cases involving fundamental rights. For a fuller exposition, see Louis Lusky, "Footnote Redux: A *Carolene Products* Reminiscence," *Columbia Law Review* 82 (Fall 1982): 1093–1109.
31. Lawrence, "Exercising Judicial Review," pp. 10–11.
32. *Ibid.*, p. 23.
33. Herbert Wechsler, "The Courts and the Constitution," *Columbia Law Review* 65 (1965): 1006.
34. Katzman, *Judges and Legislators*, p. 11.
35. Gary L. McDowell, "Congress and the Courts," *The Public Interest* (Summer 1990): 96–97.
36. Edward Keynes, with Randall K. Miller, *The Court vs. Congress: Prayer, Busing, and Abortion* (Durham, NC: Duke University Press, 1989), p. 96.
37. Senator Edward Kennedy, quoted in the 1989 Congressional Quarterly *Almanac*, p. 316. Congressional Quarterly has an excellent summary of the key cases on this and the following pages.
38. William Lasser, *The Limits of Judicial Power* (Chapel Hill: University of North Carolina Press, 1988), p. 254.
39. Walter F. Murphy, *Congress and the Court* (Chicago: University of Chicago Press, 1962), p. 267.
40. A good summary may be found in Lawrence J. Tribe, *God Save This Honorable Court* (Cambridge, MA: Harvard University Press, 1985).
41. Joseph P. Harris, *The Advice and Consent of the Senate* (Berkeley: University of California Press, 1953), p. 377.
42. Robert W. Kastenmeier and Michael J. Remington, "A Judicious Legislator's Lexicon to the Federal Judiciary," in Katzman, *Judges and Legislators*, p. 72.
43. Joseph P. Harris, *The Advice and Consent of the Senate* (Berkeley: University of California Press, 1953), p. 377.
44. Lasser, *Limits of Judicial Power*, pp. 99, 101.
45. *Martin v. Hunter's Lessee*, 14 U.S. 304 (1816).
46. 74 U.S. 506 (1869), 514.
47. See, for example, Lasser, *Limits of Judicial Power*.
48. *Ibid.*, pp. 156–57.
49. Murphy, *Congress and the Court*, p. 247.
50. Lasser, *Limits of Judicial Power*, p. 262.
51. Murphy, *Congress and the Court*, p. 267.

52. *Griswold v. Connecticut*, 382 U.S. 479 (1964), 482.
53. Bertram M. Gross, *Organizations and Their Managing* (New York: The Free Press, 1964), pp. 540–41.
54. The state of Montana has legislated a form of "uncontained" deviation from the federally imposed 55/65 mile-per-hour limit. Knowing that they would lose federal highway funds if they attempted to abolish speeding regulations on rural highways, the state simply made the law inoperative by putting a maximum fine of $5 on speeding.
55. Ernst Freund, *Standards of American Legislation* (Chicago: University of Chicago Press, 1917, 1965), p. 19.
56. The more recent case of former congressman Robert Bauman (R-MD) is sad but fascinating. As a darling of the Moral Majority, Bauman publicly crusaded against a variety of perceived "sins" even as his own aggressive homosexuality threatened and, ultimately, destroyed his public career. His tortured but interesting autobiography never quite acknowledges the seeming hypocrisy of this behavior. Robert Bauman, *The Gentleman from Maryland* (New York: Arbor House, 1986).
57. Mike H. Ryan, Carl L. Swanson, and Rogene A. Buchholz, *Corporate Strategy, Public Policy and the Fortune 500* (New York: Basil Blackwell, 1987), pp. 167–68.
58. Marshall B. Clinard and Peter C. Yeager, *Corporate Crime* (New York: The Free Press, 1980), pp. 122–27.
59. Andrew Rosenthal, "Civil Rights Bill Gives Look at White House Split," *New York Times*, 22 October 1990, p. A15.

✻

13 Reforming the System

1. Paul Weyrich in Thomas Ferguson and Joel Rogers, "The Reagan Victory: Corporate Coalitions in the 1980 Campaign," in Thomas Ferguson and Joel Rogers, eds., *The Hidden Election: Politics and Economics in the 1980 Campaign* (New York: Pantheon, 1981), p. 4.
2. Strong evidence for this position, from the career patterns of contemporary MCs, is found in John R. Hibbing, *Congressional Careers: Contours of Life in the U.S. House of Representatives* (Chapel Hill: University of North Carolina Press, 1991).
3. Michael Lind, "A Radical Plan to Change American Politics," *Atlantic Monthly* (August 1992): 73–74.
4. As we saw in Chapter 2, it is impossible to imagine a system of districting that is "fair and equitable" in all the ways we would like it to be. Nor is it likely that we can (or should) remove politics from the process. The idea that some "neutral" source can magically design a political map better than that designed by people who understand politics doesn't make much sense. The direction of reform, as David Wells has argued with the authors, is more profitably focused on questions of "how," not "who." For example, a Colorado law that sets certain minimal standards of compactness and contiguity makes a good deal of sense.
5. W. Lance Bennett, *The Governing Crisis: Media, Money and Marketing in American Elections* (New York: St. Martin's Press, 1992), p. 209.
6. Harold Seidman, *Politics, Position and Power*, 2d ed. (New York: Oxford University Press, 1975), p. 190.
7. Roger H. Davidson and Walter J. Oleszek, *Congress against Itself* (Bloomington: Indiana University Press, 1977), p. 264. This book should be required reading for all members of the 1993 Joint Committee.

8. *Ibid.*, p. 271.

9. For those who missed it, the crisis surrounding the House bank derived from a report by the General Accounting Office that criticized certain procedures of a "Members Only" checking system supported by the House of Representatives. What the press seized upon was the evidence that MCs had been allowed to write checks against funds that had not yet been deposited. Although the bank never lost any money and few if any MCs profited from these practices, there was a widespread sense of outrage and the service was discontinued.

10. Steven S. Smith, "The Senate in the Postreform Era," in Roger H. Davidson, ed., *The Postreform Congress* (New York: St. Martin's Press, 1992), p. 185.

11. Quoted in Mary McInnis, ed., *We Propose: A Modern Congress* (New York: McGraw-Hill, 1966), p. xii.

12. Davidson and Oleszek, *Congress against Itself,* p. 274.

AUTHOR INDEX

SUBJECT INDEX